THE WORLD'S AIR FORCES

An illustrated review of the air forces of the world

THE WORLD'S AIR FORCES

An illustrated review of the air forces of the world

Published by Salamander Books Limited
LONDON

A Salamander Book

Published by Salamander Books Ltd.
129-137 York Way,
London N7 9LG,
United Kingdom.

ISBN 0 86101 563 0

Distributed in the United Kingdom by:
Hodder and Stoughton Services,
PO Box 6, Mill Road,
Dunton Green,
Sevenoaks,
Kent TN13 2XX

Editor: Bob Munro

Filmset by The Old Mill, London

Designed by Phil Gorton, Richard Hawke and Oxprint Ltd.

Colour Reproduction by Scantrans PTE Ltd, Singapore

Printed and bound in Italy

Contents

INTRODUCTION

Figures released by the renowned Stockholm International Peace Research Institute on the subject of military spending in 1990 make interesting reading. It is surely no surprise that global defence spending fell by 4 per cent, with the dramatic political upheavals in Eastern Europe, the soaring costs of defence systems, and the steady progress in superpower arms control talks cited as major influences.

And yet, the wars go on: no less than 31 major armed conflicts were waged in 1990, the majority of which have continued into 1991. And no-one can doubt that, for all the cuts in defence spending, the role of air power remains crucial and formidable. Over 150 nations around the world possess some form of air power, ranging from the modest transport fleet that can be counted on one hand to the tens of thousands of bombers, fighters, missiles, tankers etc. of the superpowers.

Whatever the size, whatever the military capabilities of the world's air forces, those charged with the responsibility of acquiring, operating and maintaining the world's air forces know that air power is here to stay. In its most overt form, it is a weapon of destruction; an awesome, brutal settler of conflicts, ruling from on high. Yet it can be — and often is — so much more. For the starving peoples' of Africa, it is a life-line dropping the proverbial manna from heaven; for those in distress on a mountain face or at sea, it is a life-saver coming to the rescue; and for those threatened by the forces of nature, it is a valued ally in the fight against the ravages of fire, earthquakes and floods.

So often such capabilities go unnoticed and unheralded, yet air forces around the world are conducting just such operations as you read these very words. The world perceives air power first and foremost by virtue of its fighting prowess, and its use in conflict as a multi-faceted weapon of destruction. And nowhere has the sheer versatility and importance of air power been better illustrated of late than in the Gulf War.

That the Gulf War was a relatively short conflict was due in no small part to the formidable array of aircraft deployed by the coalition of nations intent on halting the advances of the Iraqi war machine. In both quality and quantity, the coalition, led from the front by the US Air Force, ruled the skies from the outset. From the mass destruction wrought by mighty B-52 Stratofortress bombers to the unglamorous yet vital logistical support flights of "haulers" such as the C-130 Hercules, the Gulf War was proof positive that air power, however high-tech or humble, remains an asset of inestimable influence at a time when many of the checks and balances that pervade modern history are being challenged.

Does the spectacular success of air power during the Gulf War undermine the implicit message offered by the figures presented by the Stockholm Institute? Or could it be that the conflict represented the swan song of the world's air forces; one final fight before they fall victim to the blow torch in the name of world peace. The answer is somewhere in the middle, heralding a new sense of realism as the world moves closer to the 21st Century.

Conflicts around the world, be they major or minor, will continue, of that there can be no doubt. It is equally certain that the air forces of nations caught up in conflict will play their part, be it offensive or defensive, or both. Yet it is equally true that the latest technology is prohibitively expensive, keeping it out of the reach of many Third World forces. At the other end of the scale, the pressure remains intense for the superpowers to continue cutting back on both military spending and current force levels. The "less is more" philosophy is gaining ground, increasing the pressure on the aerospace industry to produce ever more versatile, operationally capable aircraft, that can be deployed in smaller numbers without compromising, let alone degrading, the overall effectiveness of the operator.

How such varying demands and requirements are met will clearly influence air forces around the world. But the future begins today, and a thorough understanding and appreciation of the diversity, complexity and importance of the world's air forces is an essential prerequisite if the serious student of military aviation is to be able to appreciate the significance of changes, both military and political, that will occur during this decade. The World's Air Forces provides the information you need in a highly comprehensive and heavily illustrated single volume.

NORTH AMERICA

Fighters
Bombers
Transports
Helicopters

CANADA

ONE of the few nations in the world with air, ground and sea elements unified into a single military entity, the Canadian Armed Forces (CAF) possesses a sizeable air component. Home-based echelons are organized into Groups according to function and all are administratively controlled by Air Command, even though some are operationally responsible to other CAF elements. Air Command headquarters are located at Winnipeg, Manitoba. Major contributions are made to the North American Aerospace Defense Command (NORAD) and to the North Atlantic Treaty Organization (NATO), with Canada's air power commitment to the latter being vested in the 1st Canadian Air Divsion (1 CAD), based in Germany.

Front-line elements are spearheaded by Fighter Group with headquarters at North Bay, Ontario. This has four fully-operational McDonnell-Douglas CF-18 squadrons which are mainly concerned with the air defence mission, although they are just as capable of being employed in tactical roles. Two of the four squadrons constitute a rapid reinforcement element and these could be hurriedly deployed to Europe to augment NATO, should the need arise. In the event of being called upon, they would operate from Lahr, Germany, as the 3rd (Fighter) Wing under the overall command of the 1st CAD, and periodic deployment exercises do allow them to train in Europe. In addition, there is a single home-based CF-18 squadron which provides on-type training for conversion and graduate pilots.

Other Fighter Group assets include some examples of the Canadair CF-5, but these are primarily utilized in the training role. There is also a single squadron which offers electronic warfare (EW) training with a few Canadair CC-144 Challengers and Lockheed CT-133 Silver Stars.

Although technically part of the Air Command, the Maritime Air Group reports to Maritime Command for purposes of operational control. Available forces consist of a mixture of fixed and rotary-wing craft, with the Lockheed CP-140 Aurora satisfying long-range anti-submarine warfare (ASW) and maritime reconnaissance requirements. In use with four squadrons, including a training unit, the Auroras are to be joined by three examples of the CP-140A Arcturus, which are being obtained as replacements for the few remaining Grumman CP-121 Trackers used on inshore patrol tasks. Helicopter ASW capability is vested in the Sikorsky CH-124A Sea King which routinely deploys aboard surface combatants, but this type is due to be replaced by locally assembled EH-101s. Other Maritime Air Group elements comprise a pair of utility squadrons which operate a mix of CT-133 Silver Stars and Bell CH-135 Twin Hueys.

Airlift capability is directed by the Transport Group with a diverse fleet of aircraft and helicopters. Almost inevitably, this has at its core a sizeable force of Lockheed CC-130 Hercules, other types on hand including the CC-137 (Boeing 707) tanker/transport, the Convair CC-109 Cosmopolitan, Boeing Canada CC-115 Buffalo and Boeing-Vertol CH-113 Labrador.

Support of ground forces is the principal task of No. 10 Tactical Air Group (TAG) which comes under the operational control of the Mobile Command, apart from one squadron that is stationed at Lahr with Canadian Forces Europe. Equipped entirely with helicopters, No. 10 TAG's few squadrons use CH-135 Twin Hueys, Bell CH-136 Kiowas and Boeing-Vertol CH-147 Chinooks on tactical and transport missions.

Training of aircrew is entrusted to No. 14 Training Group, an organization that has contracted in size in recent years but one that still depends on the Beech CT-134A Musketeer II and Canadair CT-114 Tutor to produce jet pilots for Fighter Group and 1st CAD. Helicopter pilots also learn basic flying skills on the CT-134A, before progressing to the Bell CH-139 JetRanger.

These regular force elements are augmented by a small second-line component known as the Air Reserve Group which has about half-a-dozen squadrons under its control. For the most part, they are equipped with CH-136A Kiowas, although one has Boeing Canada CC-138 Twin Otters for transport and rescue tasks and another uses CT-142 Dash 8s for navigator training.

Below: Conversion of this CC-137 transport to allow it to act as an aerial tanker has greatly enhanced the range and deployment capabilities of the CAF's CF-18s, two of which are seen here as they replenish their fuel tanks. Note the distinctive "shadow" canopies painted on their underfuselages.

CAF air elements are rounded out by the three CF-18 squadrons (Nos. 409, 421 and 439) that presently make up No. 4 (Fighter) Wing at Baden-Sollingen, Germany. Assigned to the 1st CAD and committed to NATO's 4th Allied Tactical Air Force (4 ATAF), No. 4 (Fighter) Wing has about 54 examples of the CF-18 which perform strike and attack duties. The 1st CAD also has a CT-133 Silver Star as a "hack" aircraft, and one CC-109 Cosmopolitan is usually detached to Europe by No. 412 Squadron for transport duties, although its days in service are surely numbered.

EQUIPMENT

Air Defence:
McDonnell Douglas CF-18A
Strike:
McDonnell Douglas CF-18A
Attack:
McDonnell Douglas CF-18A
Canadair CF-5A
Maritime Reconnaissance/ASW:
Lockheed CP-140 Aurora
Lockheed CP-140A Arcturus
Sikorsky CH-124A Sea King
Transport:
Boeing CC-137
Lockheed CC-130E/H Hercules
Boeing Canada CC-115 Buffalo
Boeing Canada CC-142 Dash 8
Convair CC-109 Cosmopolitan
Canadair CC-144 Challenger
Boeing Canada CC-138 Twin Otter
Boeing-Vertol CH-147 Chinook
Bell CH-135 Twin Huey
Tanking:
Boeing CC-137
SAR:
Boeing Canada CC-115 Buffalo
Lockheed CC-130E/H Hercules
Boeing Canada CC-138 Twin Otter
Boeing-Vertol CH-113/A Labrador/Voyageur
Bell CH-118 Iroquois
Bell CH-135 Twin Huey
Bell CH-136A Kiowa
EW Training:
Canadair CC-144 Challenger
Observation:
Bell CH-136 Kiowa
Utility:
SikorskyCH-124U Sea King
Training:
Canadair CT-114 Tutor
Lockheed CT-133 Silver Star
Beech CT-134A Musketeer II
Boeing Canada CT-142 Dash 8
Canadair CC-144 Challenger
Canadair CF-5A/D
Lockheed CC-130E/H Hercules
Bell CH-139 JetRanger
Liaison:
Lockheed CT-133 Silver Star
Bell CH-136A Kiowa

Above: The smart red, white and blue colour scheme previously applied to the CAF's CP-140A Auroras has given way to a rather sombre set of greys. A force of 18 such aircraft now provide Canada with a highly versatile means with which to patrol vast tracts of territorial waters.

Below: The essential and serious business of SAR helps explain the garish colours worn by the CH-113A Voyageur, just one of several aircraft types operated by the CAF in this role. Of note is the powerful undernose searchlight, which is used to help locate those in need of assistance during marginal weather.

Right: With a massive territory to cover, as well as overseas-based units to resupply, the CAF's transport fleet really has its work cut out. Leading the way is the CC-130E/H Hercules, whose work includes logistical support of far-flung outposts. Here, one such location gets a low-level "delivery".

Above: A controversial bomber both before and during its service life, Rockwell's B-1B Lancer equips a total of four Bomb Wings assigned to Strategic Air Command (SAC).

USA

THE FREE World's largest and most potent air force is that of the United States, elements of this air arm being permanently resident within Europe and the Pacific theatres as well as at home in the Continental US (ConUS). Regular force personnel levels handsomely exceed the 500,000 mark and the USAF is able to call upon the services of close to 250,000 "weekend warriors", plus a substantial number of combat-ready aircraft from the Air Force Reserve (AFRes) and the Air National Guard (ANG) should wide-scale mobilization be deemed necessary.

Overall command of this massive agency is entrusted to the President of the United States in his capacity as Commander-in-Chief of all the armed forces. In reality, of course, responsibility for management is devolved via a fairly complex chain of command and it is possible for the President's wishes to be achieved via different channels according to circumstances.

One channel progresses via the Department of Defense and the Secretary of Defense, through the Department of the Air Force and Headquarters US Air Force to the Air Staff and on to the major Air Force commands such as Tactical Air Command (TAC) and Military Airlift Command (MAC). The other goes via the Secretary and Department of Defense and then progresses to the Joint Chiefs of Staff, through the Joint Staff and on to the Specified Commands like Readiness Command (RedCom) and European Command (EuCom). It should be noted that the latter are usually composed of elements drawn from more than one of the United States' military services.

At the operational level, forces are assigned to a number of major commands, each of which specializes in a particular type of mission or has responsibility for a specific geographical area. Thus, Strategic Air Command (SAC) is tasked with training for and being prepared to undertake strategic warfare (i.e. nuclear war), whereas the United States Air Forces in Europe (USAFE) exercises control over tactical forces that are stationed within this overseas theatre of operations.

However, such is the complexity of the organization that these seemingly clear-cut lines of definition and areas of responsibility inevitably become ill-defined. A classic example of this is provided by SAC which has a sizeable presence within the continent of Europe — although this may be called upon to support SAC activities (such as intelligence gathering by RC-135 "ferret" aircraft), its principal task is to assist USAFE so that the latter can accomplish its missions and objectives. In much the same way, MAC has a permanent European presence.

To facilitate reference, each major command will be dealt with individually, starting with SAC which is the most powerful of the USAF's components when it comes to destructive potential.

The power stems from the fact that SAC is responsible for managing two of the three elements which comprise the US nuclear arsenal, namely manned bomber and intercontinental ballistic missile (ICBM) forces. Some modernization has occurred in recent years, most notably through deployment of the Rockwell B-1B Lancer and the LGM-118A Peacekeeper ICBM, but future plans seem certain to fall foul of the USA's massive budget deficit, with the Northrop B-2A stealth bomber and the rail-mobile Peacekeeper being amongst the victims of deep cuts in defence spending.

SAC has its headquarters at Offutt AFB, Nebraska, and it is from here that command activities are directed via two subordinate "numbered" Air Force organizations, specifically the 8th Air Force at Barksdale AFB, Louisiana, and the 15th Air Force at March AFB, California. Operational forces are assigned to these Air Force organizations largely on geographical lines, with 8th AF controlling assets in the east including the 7th Air Division at Ramstein AB, West Germany, which directs the activities of UK-based tanker and reconnaissance echelons at Mildenhall and Alconbury. In similar fashion, 15th AF is responsible for forces in the west, including the 3rd Air Division at Hickam AFB, Hawaii. Until recently, 3rd AD resources included B-52G bombers at Andersen AFB, Guam, but these have now been withdrawn, leaving just a Strategic Wing with KC-135 tankers at Kadena AB, Okinawa, in support of PacAF.

At the operational level, the key element

is the "Wing", but the size of these Wings does vary according to equipment and mission. As a rough guide, a typical Bomb Wing will control one Bomb Squadron with either the B-52 Stratofortress or the B-1B and one Air Refueling Squadron with the KC-135 Stratotanker. Unit establishments vary dramatically and a Bomb Squadron may have anything from 10 to 18 aircraft, as indeed can tanker outfits. Inevitably, there are exceptions, some Wings having two Bomb Squadrons and some having two tanker squadrons — in these instances, unit establishment is accordingly greater.

SAC's other bomber aircraft is the FB-111A but this is fast disappearing from the line-up as aircraft are reworked to F-111G configuration and reassigned to Tactical Air Command, and it is now only operational with one Bomb Wing at Plattsburgh AFB, New York. Of the other bomber types, the Stratofortress is still the most numerous asset, with about 250 on charge. In addition to nuclear roles, for which it may carry gravity bombs and the AGM-86B Air-Launched Cruise Missile, it can also be used for conventional bombing operations and maritime missions such as sea surveillance. Maritime attack capability includes the ability to deliver mines and fire the Harpoon sea-skimming, anti-shipping missile. Finally, there are just under 100 B-1Bs — this is now SAC's principal penetrating bomber and it can deliver gravity nuclear bombs, conventional "iron" bombs and the AGM-86B. Both of these bombers do still stand nuclear "alert", SAC maintaining a modest number in a "cocked" configuration, armed and ready to launch within a matter of minutes.

Tanker Wings usually have two squadrons equipped with either the KC-10A Extender or the Stratotanker. Refurbishment of the latter type continues apace and many of the old "stove-pipe" engined KC-135As have now been updated to KC-135R standard with CFM-56 turbofans, offering a huge increase in performance. Once again, some of these aircraft are maintained on ground alert to support operations by deterrent forces should the need arise.

Above: Still providing SAC with a formidable bombing capacity, as witnessed during the Gulf War, one of 200+ B-52 Stratofortresses refuels froma KC-10A Extender aerial tanker.

Below: A pilot's eye view as he guides his fighter into position for a "hook-up" with that other stalwart of SAC's tanking fleet, the ever-dependable KC-135 Stratotanker.

Turning to the half-a-dozen Strategic Missile Wings (SMWs) that control SAC's ICBM resources, these have three or four squadrons, each squadron possessing five flights of 10 missiles. Thus, a three-squadron Wing will have 150 missiles and a four-squadron Wing 200.

Boeing's Minuteman is the most numerous ICBM, the LGM-30F model having a single warhead while the LGM-30G can carry three — respective quantities are 450 and 500 missiles and a very high proportion of these will be on alert at any given time, missile launch crews routinely spending 24-hour periods of duty in the Launch Control Centres deep underground in the upper mid-western USA. In addition, one missile squadron of the 90th SMW at F. E. Warren AFB, Wyoming, operates the LGM-118A, each carrying as many as 10 indepedently-targetable warheads.

At one time it was intended to deploy 100 Peacekeepers, the 50 at F. E. Warren AFB to be joined by 50 rail-mobile weapons. Then, following a Presidential decision to limit procurement to 50, it was decided to redeploy the existing missiles to the rail-garrison with effect from the end of 1992. Now they seem certain to remain in their "holes" in Wyoming.

Other operational forces under SAC control consist of a quartet of Reconnaissance Wings. Two are equipped with some rather weird and wonderful variations on the C-135 theme and one of these (the 55th SRW at Offutt) also manages the SAC and National Command Authorities EC-135 and E-4B flying command posts. The remaining two both utilize the Lockheed U-2R/TR-1 as primary mission equipment, one (the 9th SRW) being stationed in the USA and making extensive use of overseas detachments, and the other (the 17th RW) residing at Alconbury in the United Kingdom, from where it mainly operates in support of NATO.

If SAC is the "heavy hammer", then Tactical Air Command (TAC) might best be likened to the "fire brigade". Certainly, mobility is at the heart of TAC doctrine, as exemplified by this command's massive contribution to Operations *"Desert Shield"* and *"Desert Storm"* to counter Iraq during 1990-91. Combat types like the A-10A Thunderbolt II, F-4G Phantom, F-15C Eagle, F-16 Fighting Falcon and the F-117A stealth fighter relied on in-flight refuelling support furnished by SAC as they were hastily moved from US bases to the Gulf area as part of the build-up and subsequent war, such hurried action confirming the value of annual deployments to conduct out-of-area operational training in both Europe and the Far East.

Below: In addition to the manned strategic bombers, SAC controls the land-based ICBM force, one of whose LGM-30F Minuteman II single-warhead ICBMs is shown here.

Above: With the SR-71 retired from service during 1990, much of the USAF's insatiable reconnaissance needs are satisfied by the Lockheed U-2R/TR-1. Two of the 9th SRW's U-2Rs are seen here prior to take-off.

Below: On its way to strike another set of Iraqi armoured targets as part of Operation *"Desert Storm"*, one of the USAF's Fairchild A-10A Thunderbolt II "tank-busters" gets set to refuel while flying high over the desert.

Bottom: With a healthy stock of air-to-air missiles on board, a 1st TFW F-15C Eagle roars off into the clear blue sky above Saudi Arabia, at the start of a Combat Air patrol to counter the threat posed by the Iraqi Air Force.

As with most major USAF components, with the exception of three direct reporting units, all TAC elements are grouped together within numbered Air Forces so as to facilitate operational and administrative control. There are three, to be precise, all of which are directed from TAC headquarters at Langley AFB, Virginia. In the case of TAC, though, one of the Air Force elements — the 1st Air Force, also with headquarters at Langley — is mission-orientated, being responsible for the air defence of the continental USA. As such, it is closely allied to the North American Air Defense (NORAD) organization at Colorado Springs, Colorado, which oversees US and Canadian efforts in this field.

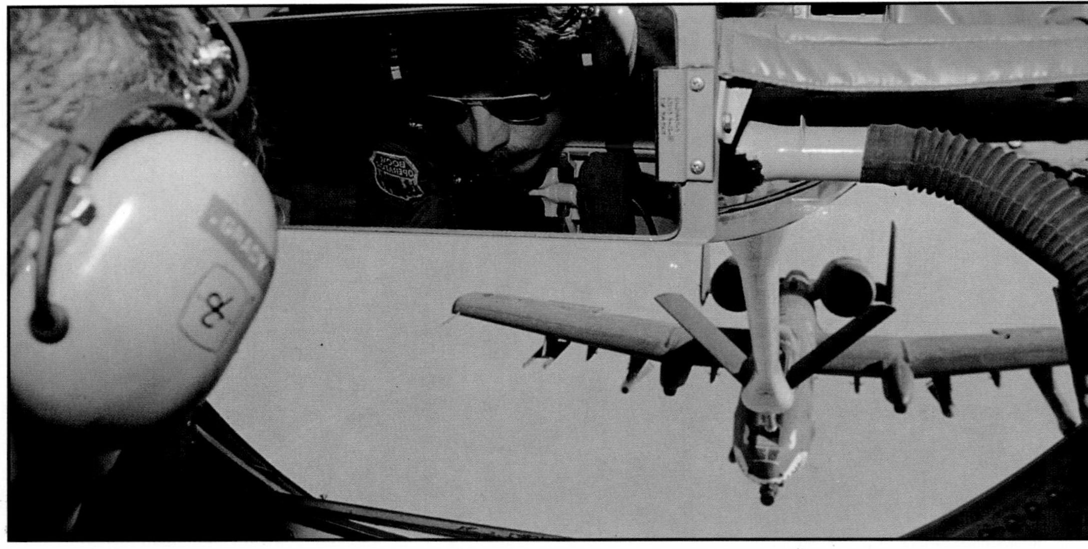

Current organization of TAC elements is primarily based on the one-type Tactical Fighter Wing (TFW), the majority of which oversee the operations of three Tactical Fighter Squadrons (TFS). However, plans now being formulated herald a move away from this structure. As a direct result of operational experience gained by the USAF during Operations *"Desert Shield"* and, more significantly, *"Desert Storm"*, a composite, almost self-contained type of Wing, with several types of aircraft co-assigned, will be evaluated. If this proves successful, it will most likely be adopted within other USAF Commands.

As far as operational hardware is concerned, 1st AF has few resources, these being limited to just two F-15 Eagle-equipped Fighter Interceptor Squadrons. One, by coincidence, is to be found at Langley — the other is at Keflavik, Iceland. In addition, however, 1st AF is able to call on a number

Above: MAC's two great "heavyweight haulers" at work, with a C-5A Galaxy loaded up for despatch as a C-141B Starlifter lands.

"mother-ships" whenever fighters are deployed overseas. In addition, elements at two other bases come under the 28th AD, both using variants of the hugely successful Hercules transport — Keesler AFB, Missouri, hosts the EC-130E airborne battlefield command and control aircraft while Davis-Monthan has the EC-130H "Compass Call" communications jamming version.

Combat forces assigned to SAC and TAC would not be able to function for long without good supply lines, and it is in this area that the Military Airlift Command (MAC) is able to make an important contribution to US defence. Headquartered at Scott AFB, Illinois, MAC provides global airlift of personnel and materiel with a fleet of transport aircraft that ranges in size from the massive Lockheed C-5 Galaxy down to the diminutive Beech C-12 Super King Air. Looking to the future, the McDonnell Douglas C-17 should be able to perform strategic and tactical missions when it starts to enter service in a few years time, but procurement may well be curtailed and it seems unlikely that MAC will acquire all 210 that it says it needs.

Like TAC, MAC has three numbered Air Forces under its control, two being geographically aligned and concerned solely with airlift tasks, while the third is mission-orientated in that it constitutes the USAF contribution to the US Special Operations Command. Between them, they possess a fleet of aircraft that numbers around the 1,000 mark. A number of specialized service agencies also report to MAC, these comprising the Air Weather Service, the Air Rescue Service, the Aerospace Audiovisual Service and the Defense Courier Service.

Dealing with pure airlift tasks first, 21st Air Force has control of resources to the east of the Mississippi and 22nd Air Force those to the west, respective headquarters being located at McGuire AFB, New Jersey, and Travis AFB, California. Strategic airlift assets consist of about 120 C-5 Galaxies and 270 C-141B Starlifters. Both types can be refuelled in flight, eliminating the need for *en route* landing rights and bestowing genuine global capability should the need arise. They are concentrated within half-a-dozen Military Airlift Wings (MAWs), split evenly between the two Air Forces. C-5 and C-141 aircrew training requirements for both Air Forces are met by 22nd AF which maintains a small specialist unit specifically established for this task.

As they have been for three decades now, tactical airlift requirements are satisfied by the hugely versatile Lockheed C-130 Hercules, a type that presently serves with three US-based Tactical Airlift Wings. One is assigned to 21st AF and two to 22nd AF, one of the latter incorporating a training unit at Little Rock AFB, Arkansas.

Right: Cargo flown in by C-5s and C-141s is often dispersed by the third string to MAC's bow, namely the C-130 Hercules. The type is set to serve well into the 21st Century.

Left: Its introduction into service was long delayed, but the "Air Force One" Presidential transport call-sign is now used by one of two converted Boeing 747s, designated VC-25As.

Above: Bristling with firepower, an AC-130H "Spectre" gunship lets rip at ground targets far below. An integral element of the Special Forces, this variation on the Hercules theme is to be joined by the AC-130U in due course.

In addition, however, the "Herky-Bird" is active with a number of overseas-based units that constitute part of MAC. In Europe, overall control of MAC assets is entrusted to the 322nd Airlift Division at Ramstein AB, West Germany. Part of the 21st AF establishment, this directs airlift operations in support of USAFE. Resources include a squadron's worth (about 18 aircraft) of permanently-resident C-130s with the 435th TAW at Rhein-Main and a similar number of rotational C-130s with the 313th Tactical Airlift Group at RAF Mildenhall, UK.

Other 322nd Airlift Division assets consist of a liaison and communications squadron at Ramstein with a mixture of equipment including the C-12F, C-20A, C-21A, C-135, T-43 and UH-1N; a logistics support outfit at Zweibrucken AB, West Germany, with the C-23A; and an aeromedical element at Rhein-Main with the C-9A.

Elsewhere, 21st AF also has control of the 61st Military Airlift Group in Panama. Again, the primary transport aircraft is the C-130 Hercules which serves with one squadron, but this unit also has a solitary C-22 and a couple of CASA C.212s.

Turning to the Pacific theatre, MAC operations in this part of the world are overseen by the 834th Airlift Division at Hickam AFB, Hawaii, which in turn reports to 22nd AF. Elements under the Division's control include C-130 squadrons at Yokota AB, Japan and Clark AB in the Philippines, as well as communications, aeromedical and logistical support elements at Yokota, Clark and Kadena AB, Okinawa. Equipment operated in the latter support roles includes the C-9, C-12 and C-21.

Two more units also figure in the airlift line-up, one being assigned to each Air Force. Located conveniently close to the home of US government, the 89th Special Missions Airlift Wing (89th SMAW) based at Andrews AFB, Maryland, is the USAF's VIP transport outfit. With a diverse fleet that contains examples of the C-9, C-12, C-20, C-135, C-137 and VH-1, as well as two VC-25As (VIP-configured Boeing 747s), this unit's duties include the carriage of politcal and military officials. Its most visible customer is the President himself, with a VC-25A bearing the famous call-sign of "Air Force One" in its role as Presidential transport.

The other unit is the 375th MAW, which reports to 22nd AF and which controls an extensive network of detachments. Using a mix of equipment that is made up of the C-9, C-12, C-21 and C-29, it satisfies aeromedical and communications/liaison needs within the USA and also performs navaid calibration tasks at US military installations on a world-wide basis.

The MAC line-up is completed by 23rd Air Force at Hurlburt Field, Florida. As mentioned earlier, this is intimately associated with special operations and its resources include some weird and wonderfully modified machines. Without doubt the most lethal of these is the AC-130 "Spectre"

Right: A modification programme will result in the USAF's Black Hawk helicopter force being reconfigured to become MH-60G Pave Hawks, for use by US Special Forces.

Above: The "Herky Bird" in another guise, this time an MC-130E "Combat Talon" used for covert insertion of Special Forces.

gunship, soon to be supplanted in front-line service by the AC-130U. Other equipment includes HH-3, MH-53 and MH-60 helicopters which can be used on a variety of tasks such as search-and-rescue (SAR) and covert missions. There is also the MC-130E "Combat Talon" variant of the Hercules which specializes in covert tasks but nobody says too much about the precise nature of its capabilities — again, modernization is in prospect with the fairly imminent arrival of the MC-130H.

Organization of 23rd AF appears to be largely along geographic lines, with three Special Operations Wings being established to control activity in the various major theatres. Thus, one (the 1st SOW) is resident at Hurlburt, another (the 39th SOW) has its main base at Rhein-Main in Germany, and the third (the 353rd SOW) is at Clark AB in the Philippines. In addition, a training element is to be found in the USA at Kirtland AFB, New Mexico.

Two overseas-based commands make up the remainder of the USAF's front-line fighting forces and both are predominantly tactical organizations with regard to hardware. The United States Air Forces in Europe (USAFE) is the larger of the two in terms of operational assets, but the Pacific Air Forces (PacAF) is responsible for a significantly greater area in pure geographical terms. Both also make key contributions to specified commands, USAFE providing tactical air power for European Command (EuCom) and PacAF doing the same for the appropriately titled Pacific Command (PaCom).

USAFE is at present at a very important crossroads in its existence and is all set to contract in size in the near future as two important factors begin to exert their infleunce. First and foremost are talks on Conventional Forces in Europe (CFE), which are set to lead to the withdrawal and/or relocation of various tactical elements as East and West seek to reduce the risk of armed confrontation. Secondly, there are American financial concerns, and these may well have a more immediate effect as the budget cuts bite deeper into the amount of money allocated to the US Air Force. Either way, USAFE faces lean times ahead.

At the present, though, it is organized along classic USAF lines, with the headquarters at Ramstein AB, Germany, directing the activities of three subordinate Air Forces, each with responsibility for a fairly clearly defined geographical area. In the United Kingdom, there is the 3rd Air Force with headquarters at RAF Mildenhall; in Spain, there is the 16th Air Force at Torrejon AB; and in Germany there is 17th Air Force at Sembach AB.

Operational echelons assigned to 3rd AF are to be found at four major stations and are spearheaded by two Tactical Fighter Wings with the General Dynamics F-111. Two different versions are assigned, with the F-111E serving at Upper Heyford and the F-111F at Lakenheath. Nuclear and conventional weapons may be employed, and aircraft from both bases were involved in the 1991 attacks on targets in Iraq and Kuwait, F-111s being employed to bomb targets while EF-111As from Upper Heyford furnished

Right: An F-111F from USAFE's 48th TFW drops its underwing load of Snakeye para-retarded 500lb (227kg) bombs on the target.

elctronic support. It should be noted that even though they are based in England, the EF-111As are actually assigned to the 66th Electronic Combat Wing at Sembach.

In addition, 3rd AF parents two Wings that are equipped with the A-10A Thunderbolt II "tank-buster", these residing at Alconbury and at the "twin-base" complex at Bentwaters and Woodbridge. A sizeable contingent from these two Wings are to be found in Germany at any given time, being deployed to a quartet of forward operating locations (FOLs). Other 3rd AF assets are rounded out by a few EC-135H flying command posts at Mildenhall.

Responsibility for the Mediterranean area is entrusted to 16th AF. Despite the fact that it covers the greatest area, it has few tactical assets, these being limited to a single F-16 Fighting Falcon Wing at Torrejon AB in Spain. The F-16s are slated to move from Torrejon to Crotone, Italy, by mid-1992. Some other 16th AF bases do host tactical aircraft, but these are drawn from other USAFE commands — for instance, UK-based F-111s are normally based at Incirlik AB, Turkey, on a rotational basis. In much the same way, Zaragoza AB, Spain, and Aviano AB, Italy, host rotational fighters, although these mainly deploy for training purposes.

Finally, there is the 17th AF, by far the largest USAFE element in terms of tactical aircraft on charge. Most of the subordinate units report direct but there are a couple of Air Divisions which act as links in the chain of command. Specifically, these are the 65th Air Division which directs units equipped with aircraft that are engaged in various aspects of electronic warfare (EF-111As, EC-130Hs and the "Wild Weasels") from headquarters at Lindsey AB, Germany, while Ramstein AB is home to the 316th Air Division.

Concentrated in Germany, 17th AF operates a fairly mixed bag of hardware. The most numerous single type has to be the F-16 which equips a three-squadron Wing at Hahn AB, Germany, and a two-squadron Wing at Ramstein. In addition, F-16s are also operational alongside F-4G Phantoms in the "Wild Weasel" defence suppression role with a full-size Wing at Spangdahlem AB, Germany — about 40 examples of each type are flown. Air superiority assets comprise an F-15 Wing at Bitburg AB, Germany, and an F-15 Group at Soesterberg AB, in the Netherlands.

Specialized tasks are also performed by 17th AF elements. At Zweibrucken AB, Germany, the remaining examples of USAFE's once-large reconnaissance fleet are assigned to a single-squadron Wing which has about two dozen RF-4C Phantoms, while, as noted earlier, Sembach is home to the 66th ECW which has a single squadron of EC-130H Hercules "Compass Call" communications jammers as well as the UK-based EF-111As.

Above: Although based in the UK, the EF-111A Ravens are operated by the 66th Electronic Combat Wing.

Left: With the aircraft of the 81st TFW set to leave the UK, the 10th TFW will be the sole USAFE A-10A operator.

Left: The new and the old combine in the form of the F-16C and F-4G to form the 52nd TFW's "Wild Weasel" team. Note the HARM missile on the F-4G's inboard pylon.

PacAF is, if anything, even more complex in organizational terms, directing the activities of no fewer than four subordinate Air Forces. It has its headquarters at Hickam AFB, Hawaii, but the only aircraft to be found at that location are a few EC-135J command posts, operational forces being distributed amongst bases in Japan, South Korea, the Philippines and, with effect from August 1990 when Alaskan Air Command was inactivated, the State of Alaska.

Yokota AB on the outskirts of Tokyo is the headquarters of 5th Air Force, which has combat-ready elements equipped with the F-15 Eage and the F-16 Fighting Falcon. The former type serves with a full-size Wing at Kadena AB, Okinawa, while the latter is operational with a two-squadron Wing at Misawa AB in Northern Japan.

USAF resources in South Korea are gathered together within 7th Air Force which has its headquarters at Osan AB, also home for a single-squadron Wing with the F-16C. This type also equips both squadrons of the Wing at Kunsan. Other elements consist of a Tactical Reconnaissance Group at Taegu AB with one squadron of RF-4C Phantoms, and a Tactical Air Control Group at Suwon AB with one squadron of OA-10A Thunderbolts. Some reorganization is due to occur in the near future, with US facilities at Suwon and Taegu being earmarked for closure — as part of this project, the RF-4Cs are to be disposed of but the OA-10As will move to Osan.

PacAF also now has command jurisdiction over US tactical resources in Alaska, having created the 11th Air Force at Elmendorf specifically to direct the activities of the handful of units that until recently constituted the Alaskan Air Command. Air defence of this strategically vital region is the primary mission and is undertaken by a two-squadron Wing equipped with the F-15C Eagle. Resident at Elmendorf AFB, this also maintains permanent alert detachments at King Salmon and Galena airports.

Other 11th AF assets consist of a single-squadron Wing at Eielson AFB equipped with the A-10A, and it is also responsible for managing the Alaskan NORAD Region Operations Control Center. Not surprisingly, operation of long-range surveillance radars figures prominently in that task, which is entrusted to a Tactical ControlWing at Elmendorf on a day-to-day basis.

PacAF's final element is resident in the Philippines, where 13th Air Force functions as the principal command organization with headquarters at Clark AB. This also serves as home to a pair of Phantom squadrons with a mix of conventional F-4Es and "Wild Weasel" F-4Gs on hand. In addition, however, Clark hosts the 6200th Tactical Fighter Training Group which manages nearby range facilities and also organizes "*Cope Thunder*" war game exercises. As a consequence, Clark regularly welcomes other PacAF combat units as well as fighter aircraft from allied nations in the region which regularly deploy to participate in "*Cope Thunder*".

With such a large and dynamic organization as the USAF, the demand for suitably qualified personnel is almost insatiable. Responsibility for meeting this demand is vested in the Air Training Command (ATC) which has its headquarters at Randolph AFB, Texas. In a typical year, ATC will provide 350,000 personnel from the USAF and a number of allied nations with tuition of

Below: Currently in the midst of a considerable reorganization, PacAF will consolidate around the F-16 (foreground). For the A-10As based in South Korea, the future is less assured, but may involve retirement from PacAF duties.

Above: The sleek lines of the T-38A Talon are well-known to thousands upon thousands of USAF pilots past and present, and will be so for thousands more to come. As yet, there is no definite successor to the T-38A in sight.

some form or another, but perhaps its most important job is that of training pilots.

To accomplish that job, it presently has eight Flying Training Wings. Six of them are concerned only with undergraduate pilot training, while one concentrates on "teaching the teachers". All of them are equipped with T-37Bs and T-38As, and students are able to undergo basic and advanced tuition at a single location. ATC's other Wing has T-37Bs and T-43As and turns out navigators for both the USAF and the US Navy. Other ATC facilities offer basic training ("Boot Camp"), technical training (often using redundant aircraft as teaching aids) and survival training.

A number of other major commands also exist although these are generally rather less "visible" since they are for the most part engaged in support tasks which do not involve extensive operation of aircraft. Nevertheless, they are worthy of mention for they also have important roles to fulfil.

Without Air Force Communications Command, for instance, all of the many strands which combine to make up today's USAF would be unable to talk to each other, and this agency currently requires the services of some 55,000 military and civilian personnel at more than 400 locations in order to accomplish its tasks. Electronic Security Command is also heavily involved in the communications game although, as its title implies, it is more concerned with ensuring that military secrets stay that way.

Without the Air Force Logistics Command to ensure that material needed to keep the Air Force combat-ready is available, the service would soon cease to be an efficient fighting machine. Close links are maintained with Air Force Systems Command (AFSC) which is fundamentally concerned with shaping the Air Force of the future by keeping in touch with developments today; but AFSC is also an aircraft-operating agency in its own right, for it directs the activities of establishments like the Air Force Flight Test Center at Edwards AFB, California, and the Aeronautical Systems Division at Wright-Patterson AFB, Ohio. Between them, these agencies are entrusted with test and evaluation of new aircraft and equipment prior to service entry.

Air Force Space Command is tasked with ensuring that good use is made of the new "high ground" of space, managing many systems that are "high-tech" in both a literal and metaphorical sense. Among its responsibilities are providing warning of impending missile attack, and it is also tasked with satellite operations and tracking. As a result, Space Command is a truly global agency, with assets in such far-flung locations as the UK, Turkey, South Korea, Australia, Greenland and the Seychelles.

Last of all, there are the second-line elements of the Air National Guard (ANG) and the Air Force Reserve (AFRes) although one should not be deceived into thinking that they are less capable when it comes to performance, for they are evaluated along identical lines to front-line outfits and frequently outdo regular-force units in competitions and exercises like "*William Tell*" and "*Red Flag*".

Providing a readily-available and well-qualified "second-string", ANG and AFRes units have received an injection of much

Right: Typical of the older types "passed down" to the ANG and now the subject of replacement plans, the A-7 Corsair II will soon give way to an attack-oriented F-16.

more modern equipment in the past decade or so and in many instances operate hardware that is identical to that of the regular Air Force. Under the "Total Force" concept, these second-line units would report to a "gaining command" with a similar mission in the event of mobilization. Thus, transport squadrons would join MAC while fighter outfits would got to TAC and tanker squadrons to SAC.

As far as AFRes is concerned, most of its resources are MAC-gained, this organization possessing 37 squadrons which own and operate equipment like the C-5, C-130, KC-135, C-141, A-10, F-4 and F-16. In addition it also makes extensive use of the "associate" concept, whereby AFRes air crew regularly fly C-5, C-9 and C-141 aircraft that are owned by MAC, as well as SAC's KC-10s. Since AFRes crews are only paid for duty hours, this is an ideal way of increasing utilization at a modest cost. Needless to say, many AFRes crews, principally those in MAC-associated units, saw their flying time soar during the build up to, and conduct of the Gulf War.

Turning to the ANG, this impressive force is primarily intended to function in support of the individual states that constitute the USA, hence the nationwide disposition of its numerous flying elements. However, the ANG can also be called upon to satisfy federal requirements in the event of mobilization, and has assumed an increasing responsibility for specific missions, such as continental air defence.

Like the AFRes, the ANG found itself in the thick of things during the conflict in the Gulf, with tasks ranging from transport to tanking, and from photo-reconnaissance to combat air patrol. That the ANG was able to perform such varied missions is testimony to the wide range of aircraft types — many the same types operated by front-line USAF units — assigned to nearly 100 ANG flying units located at almost as many individual bases throughout the land.

Below: For so long the spearhead of tactical operations, the F-4 Phantom II is now in the twilight of its USAF career as the AFRes and ANG acquire more modern combat types.

EQUIPMENT

Strategic Bombing:
Rockwell B-1B Lancer
Boeing B-52G/H Stratofortress
General Dynamics F-111G
Interdiction/Strike:
General Dynamics F-111C/D/E/F
Interception/Strike:
McDonnell Douglas F-15E Strike Eagle
General Dynamics F-16A/C Fighting Falcon
McDonnell Douglas F-4D/E Phantom II
Attack:
Lockheed F-117A
Fairchild A-10A Thunderbolt II
Vought A-7D Corsair II
Air Superiority:
McDonnell Douglas F-15A/C Eagle
Defence Suppression:
General Dynamics F-16C Fighting Falcon
McDonnell Douglas F-4G "Wild Weasel"
AEW:
Boeing E-3B/C Sentry
Airborne Command Post:
Boeing E-4B
Boeing EC-135G/H/J/K/L/P/Y
Lockheed EC-130E Hercules
Strategic Reconnaissance:
Lockheed U-2R
Boeing RC-135U/V/W Stratotanker
Tactical Reconnaissance:
McDonnell Douglas RF-4C Phantom II
Lockheed TR-1A
Tactical ECM:
Grumman EF-111A Raven
Lockheed EC-130H Hercules
FAC/COIN:
Fairchild OA-10A Thunderbolt II
Rockwell OV-10A Bronco
Cessna OA-37B Dragonfly
Transport:
Lockheed C-5A/B Galaxy
Lockheed C-141A/B Starlifter
Lockheed C-130A/B/D/E/H Hercules
Boeing C-135A/B/C Stratotanker
McDonnell Douglas C-9A Nightingale
Boeing C-22A
Shorts C-23A Sherpa
CASA C.212 Aviocar
Tanking/Transport:
Boeing KC-135A/E/R Stratotanker
McDonnell Douglas KC-10A Extender
VIP Transport:
Boeing VC-25A
Boeing VC-137A/B/C
Boeing VC-135A/B/C Stratotanker
McDonnell Douglas VC-9C Nightingale
Grumman C-20A/B/C
Bell VH-1N Iroquois
Utility/Communications:
LearJet C-21A
Beech C-12A/D/E/F Super King Air
Beech C-12J
Fairchild C-26A/B Metro III
Boeing Canada UV-18B Twin Otter
Utility/SAR:
Lockheed HC-130H/N/P Hercules
Bell UH-1F/HH-1H Iroquois
Sikorsky MH-60G Credible Hawk
Sikorsky CH/HH-3E
SAR/Special Operations:
Lockheed MC-130E/H Hercules
Sikorsky CH-53C/HH-53H/MH-53J
Sikorsky MH-60G Credible Hawk
Weather Reconnaissance:
Lockheed WC-130H Hercules
Boeing WC-135B Stratotanker
Training:
Cessna T-41A/C Mescalero
Cessna T-37B
Northrop T-38A/AT-38B Talon
Boeing T-43A
Vought A-7K Corsair II
McDonnell Douglas F-15B/D Eagle
General Dynamics F-16B/D Fighting Falcon
Lockheed TR-1B
Miscellaneous:
Grumman E-8 J-STARS
Boeing EC-18A ARIA
BAe C-29A
Boeing Canada E-9A
North American QF-100F Super Sabre
Convair QF-106A Delta Dart

CENTRAL AND SOUTH AMERICA

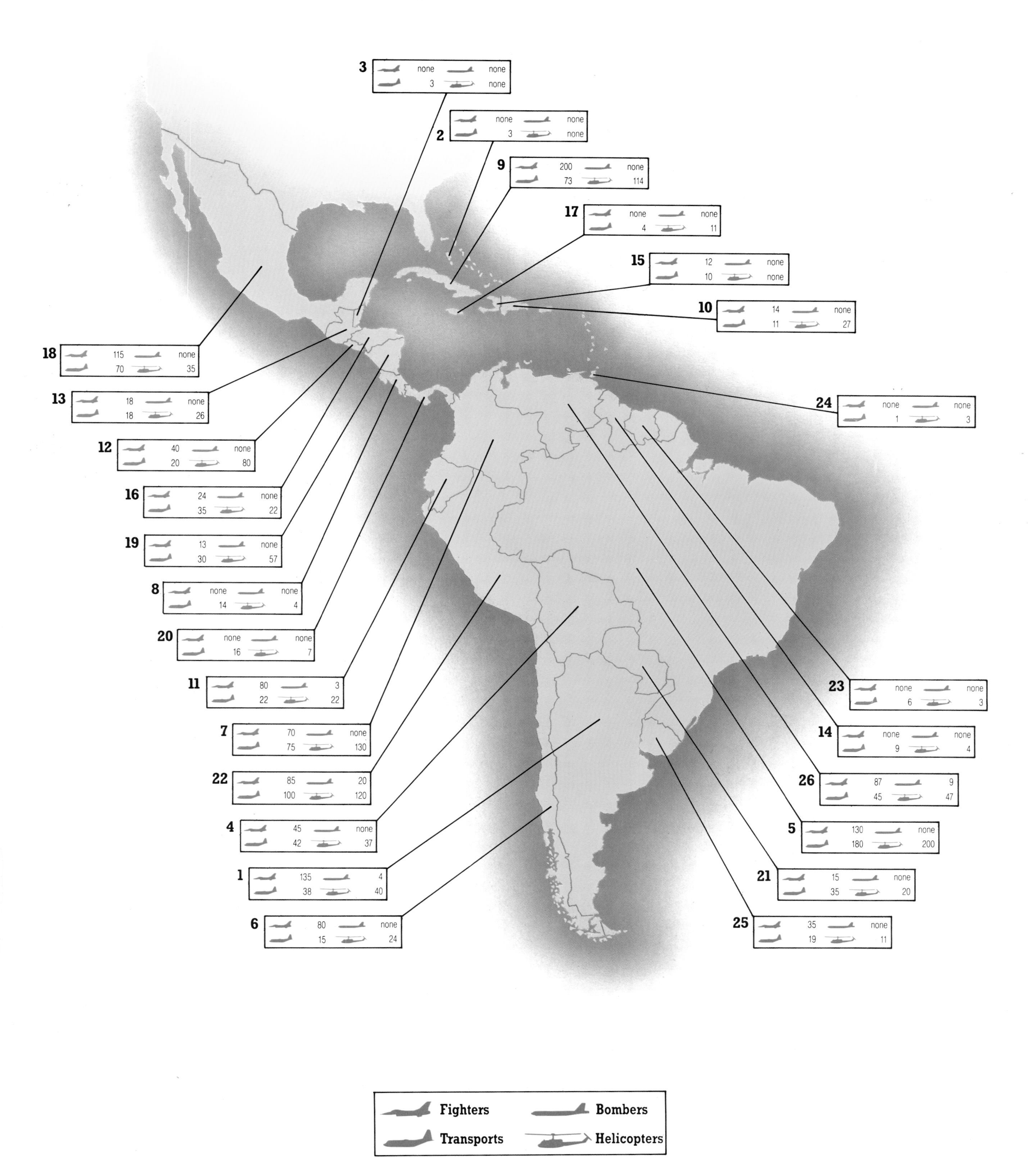

3 none none 3 none
2 none none 3 none
9 200 none 73 114
17 none none 4 11
15 12 none 10 none
10 14 none 11 27
18 115 none 70 35
13 18 none 18 26
12 40 none 20 80
16 24 none 35 22
19 13 none 30 57
8 none none 14 4
20 none none 16 7
11 80 3 22 22
7 70 none 75 130
22 85 20 100 120
4 45 none 42 37
1 135 4 38 40
6 80 none 15 24
24 none none 1 3
23 none none 6 3
14 none none 9 4
26 87 9 45 47
5 130 none 180 200
21 15 none 35 20
25 35 none 19 11
Fighters
Bombers
Transports
Helicopters

Above: A recent and significant addition to the FAA's training inventory is the IA/63 Pampa, 100 of which are currently on order. Initial service examples have been assigned to No.2 Squadron, IV Air Brigade.

Below: Various models of the ever-dependable Fokker F-27 Friendship have been delivered to the FAA since 1968. A total of nine remain in use, their duties including rough-field operations from some unprepared airstrips.

ARGENTINA

SUFFERING substantial losses during the brief but bloody conflict of 1982 over the controversial issue of sovereignty of the Falkland Islands, the *Fuerza Aérea Argentina* (FAA: Argentine Air Force) has been hard hit by President Menem's policy of austerity. Intended to allow the federal government to reverse a financial situation that has at times been dire, economies have been widespread and the FAA has had to endure its fair share of cuts, contracting slightly in size and having to delay long-overdue replacement of front-line combat types such as the veteran Canberra and Skyhawk. Thus far, there is little evidence of improvement with regard to financial matters, and it seems certain that existing hardware will have to soldier on for several more years with no real prospect of relief in the shape of new equipment.

With regard to organization, the FAA is nominally under the control of President Menem in his capacity as Commander-in-Chief of all the armed services, but responsibility for overseeing operations is devolved via the Ministry of Defence to the Air Staff and on to a quartet of executive Command agencies of which the Air Operations Command is by far the most significant. Other Commands are mostly concerned with second-line and support activities and comprise the Material Command, the Training Command and the Air Regions Command.

Elements assigned to the Air Operations Command comprise all combat-ready units plus a modest number of support echelons which are mostly active in transport roles. Some nine Air Brigades are currently in existence and these serve as an intermediate link between the more rarified command levels and the operating forces, it being usual for the Air Groups to utilize an identical numerical designation to that of the parent Air Brigade. Thus, the IV Air Brigade at El Plumerillo Air Base has the 4th Fighter Group as its flying echelon; other components within an Air Brigade generally consisting of a Technical Group and a Base Group. As their titles imply, these satisfy the important aircraft maintenance and base management functions.

Combat forces are spearheaded by a trio of Groups which operate an interesting mix of Mirage-type aircraft obtained from various sources. Initial deliveries took the form of new-build Mirage IIIEA and IIIDA trainer aircraft from Dassault-Breguet but others were obtained second-hand, most notably from Israel which supplied 19 surplus Mirage IIICJs and three IIIBJs in 1982, while Argentina also purchased 10 Mirage 5Ps from Peru in that same year. Israel also furnished a quantity of the broadly similar IAI Dagger, 34 single-seat As and four two-seat Bs being obtained between 1978 and 1981. Combat losses and normal attrition has reduced this fleet to around the four-dozen mark. The 4th Fighter Group at El Plumerillo operates surviving examples of the IIIBJ/CJ models in two Squadrons, while the ex-Peruvian machines serve with a single squadron of the 10th Fighter Group at Rio Gallegos; but the greatest concentration is to be found with the 6th Fighter Group. Stationed at Tandil, near Buenos Aires, this has two squadrons of Mirage IIIEA/DA aircraft and two squadrons of Daggers, the latter having recently been updated with inertial navigation systems and a laser rangerfinder in the so-called *"Finger IIIA"* modification programme.

Remaining combat assets operate a mix of home-grown and imported equipment, but quantities are limited and effectiveness must be low in view of the age of some of this hardware. Numerically most important is the indigenous IA.58 Pucara which serves with two squadrons of the 3rd Attack Group and one squadron of the composite 9th Air Group, but many Pucaras have been placed in storage and the former Group's squadrons actually take turns in flying the limited number of aircraft that are available for their use at Reconquista.

Some 15 or so A-4C and A-4P Skyhawks continue to constitute the teeth of the 5th Fighter Group's two squadrons at Villa Reynolds, while four elderly Canberra B.62s and two T.64s still serve with the Parana-based 2nd Bomb Group. The latter is one of two Groups assigned to II Air Brigade control, the other being the 1st Photo-Reconnaissance Group which utilizes three LearJet 35As and 10 IA.50 Guaranis on reconnaissance and survey tasks although only five of the latter are equipped with cameras. Also worthy of mention are the three squadrons of the 4th Fighter Group which function as a "fighter school": one has the locally-designed IA.63 Pampa basic/advanced jet trainer while the other two continue to operate the MS.760 Paris II, but this machine-gun-armed veteran is gradually to be replaced by the Pampa, Argentina having a requirement for some 63 such aircraft. The 4th Fighter Group also has a fifth squadron equipped with a handful of vividly-coloured SA.315B Lamas for mountain rescue duties.

Fixed and rotary-wing transport echelons complete the Air Operations Command roster and these are mostly assigned to two separate Groups. At El Palomar, Buenos Aires, the 1st Air Transport Group has four squadrons equipped with just over two dozen aircraft, comprising eight assorted Hercules, five F-28 Fellowships, nine F-27 Friendships and five Boeing 707s including two that are configured for the acquisition of electronic intelligence (ELINT). Other fixed-wing transportation comprises three more F-27s and six Twin Otters which serve with the 9th Air Group.

Transport assets are completed by the helicopter-equipped 7th Air Group at Mariano Moreno, Buenos Aires. This has three rotary-wing squadrons and a rather disparate fleet. Medium-lift potential is possessed by one squadron with a brace of UH-1H Iroquois and five Bell 212s; heavylift resources are concentrated in another squadron with two CH-47C Chinooks and one Sikorsky S-61R; and liaison/communications tasks are the preserve of the third squadron, which has about 25 assorted Hughes 369s and McDonnell Douglas Helicopters 500DEs. Additional 7th Air Group elements are engaged on aeromedical evacuation with two Merlin IVAs, and navigation aid (Navaid) calibration with a single LearJet 35 and a pair of Rockwell Aero Commander 560s.

Also under Air Operations Command jurisdiction is the Vice-Comodoro Marambio base in the Antarctic. No permanent flying units reside here but Twin Otters from the 9th Air Brigade and helicopters from 7th Air Brigade are often present on detachment, and C-130s and F-27s are regular visitors in support of scientific and military installations in this inhospitable region.

Pilot training is accomplished by the Military Aviation School at Cordoba, this being the only flying formation within Training Command. Initial instruction is given on the long-serving Beech T-34 Mentor, about 40 of which remain in service. Students then move to the much newer EMB-312 Tucano, thereafter being streamed for the combat, helicopter or transport communities. Those for the combat world will receive advanced instruction on the Paris' and Pampas of the 4th Fighter Group (if they are to fly fast jets), the Canberras of the 2nd Bomb Group or the Pucaras of the 3rd Attack Group, while transport and helicopter aircrew candidates learn "on the job".

EQUIPMENT

Interception/Attack:
Dassault-Breguet Mirage IIICJ/IIIEA/5P
IAI Dagger A
Attack:
McDonnell Douglas A-4C/P Skyhawk II
FMA IA.58A Pucara
Bombing:
BAe Canberra B.62
Reconnaissance/Surveillance:
LearJet 35A
FMA IA.50 Guarani
Elint:
Boeing 707-320B/C
Transport:
Lockheed C-130H/L-100-30 Hercules
FMA IA.50 Guarani
Fokker F-27 Friendship 400/600
Fokker F.28 Fellowship 1000C
Boeing 707-320B/C
Boeing Canada Twin Otter 200
Bell 212
Bell UH-1H Iroquois
Boeing-Vertol CH-47C Chinook
Sikorsky S-61R
Tanker/Transport:
Lockheed KC-130H Hercules
Communications/Liaison:
Piper PA-34 Seneca
Cessna 320
Piper PA-28 Arrow/Dakota
Cessna 150
Cessna 182
Hughes 369
McDonnell Douglas 500D/E
Medical Evacuation:
Swearingen Merlin IVA
SAR:
Aerospatiale SA.315B Lama
Calibration:
LearJet 35A
Rockwell Aero Commander 560
Training:
Beech T-34A Mentor
Embraer EMB-312 Tucano
Morane-Saulnier MS-760B Paris
FMA IA.63 Pampa
Dassault-Breguet Mirage IIIBJ/DA
BAe Canberra T.64

Left: High-visibility paint on this CH-47C Chinook (one of three delivered) identifies its use in support of Argentinian operations in the Antarctic.

Below: E for "Escuela" (School) on the rear fuselage identifies the role of the Beechcraft T-34A Mentor, with the 39th of 90 examples delivered to the FAA leading this trio.

BAHAMAS

PHYSICAL geography dictates that the Royal Bahamas Defence Force is fundamentally a maritime organization, but it does possess a small aviation element. In the normal course of events, this undertakes some surveillance and search-and-rescue duties, and also functions in the liaison and communications role, linking the centre of government in Nassau with some 30 populated outlying islands.

Equipment is modest, being confined to a trio of Cessna light-twins.

EQUIPMENT

General Purpose:
Cessna 404
Cessna 414
Cessna 421C

BELIZE

DEFENCE OF this tiny Latin American state is for the most part provided by British Forces Belize which maintains a garrison of close to 2,000 men, available air support comprising permanent Harrier, Puma and Gazelle detachments stationed at Belize International Airport. Their primary function is to deter neighbouring Guatemala from pursuing territorial claims, and they are supported by a small, locally-organized Defence Force which has an Air Wing equipped with two BN-2B Defenders and an impounded Do27A-1 that fulfil infantry support, reconnaissance and liaison tasks, as well as internal security operations in conjunction with the local police force. The Defenders can also be used on behalf of the Maritime Wing in the search-and-rescue role.

EQUIPMENT

General Purpose:
Pilatus Britten-Norman BN-2B Defender
Dornier Do 27A-1

BOLIVIA

RAMPANT inflation and a notoriously high degree of political instability have conspired to prevent Bolivia from acquiring much in the way of modern military hardware, and nowhere is this more evident than in the *Fuerza Aérea Boliviana* (FAB: Bolivian Air Force), which continues to rely on a few Korean War-vintage F-86 Sabres and approximately three-dozen T-33s as its primary combat equipment; backed up by some 20 Pilatus PC-7 Turbo-Trainers which are compatible with light armament. Missions assigned to these types are predominantly orientated towards counter-insurgency (COIN), with five "Fighter" Groups currently being active. Three are equipped solely with T-33s, one has a mixture of T-33s and F-86s, and the last utilizes the PC-7s which have an important training role to fulfil. A few AT-6G Texans are also in use with a Tactical Group.

Airlift assets are, for the most part, amalgamated into a single Air Transport Group with four subordinate elements, of which perhaps the most important is the

Below: Posing for the camera with the lush jungle of Belize as a backdrop, the second BN-2B Defender to be acquired by the BDF's Air Wing is used to carry out a variety of military duties over both land and water.

Above: Taxying out at the start of another pilot training sortie, the 15th of the 36 PC-7 Turbo-Trainers to be acquired by the FAB to date displays its distinctive "face". Not all FAB PC-7s are painted in camouflage colours.

Below: A fresh coat of paint adds an air of youthfulness to these T-33s, but in truth these are second-hand jets rendered surplus to French Air Force requirements. The FAB has eagerly snapped up such "bargains".

Transporte Aéreos Militar (TAM), which undertakes civilian-type domestic passenger services with a fleet that includes Convair CV.440/580 Metropolitans, Fokker F-27 Friendships and a Lockheed L.188 Electra. In similar fashion, the cargo "airline" *Transportes Aereos Boliviano* (TAB) uses about half-a-dozen Lockheed Hercules on heavy freight operations and may still be flying a single Douglas DC-8 Srs.55F freighter.

Other air Transport Group components consist of an aerial survey unit with two LearJets and a Cessna 402B, plus an executive unit which looks after the Presidential Sabre 65. One other small transport unit also exists at Trinidad, equipped with a couple of C-47 Dakotas, one IAI-201 Arava and an Aero Commander.

Rotary-wing flying is also concentrated within a single Group, which directs the activities of about 10 Aerospatiale Lamas and a similar number of ex-US Army UH-1H Iroquois, while a number of light aircraft satisfy liaison and communications functions. These are dominated by Cessna products, "singles" in use including the Models 185 and 210, with "twins" being represented by the Models 402 and 404.

Pilot training is accomplished by the Military Aviation College, with primary instruction being given on the Uirapuru and Tangara, followed by basic training on the Cessna A152 Aerobat and Cessna 172/T-41D Mescalero. After that, students proceed to the PC-7 for advanced instruction and "streaming" to either jet or transport units for further tuition.

EQUIPMENT

Interception/Attack:
North American F-86F Sabre
COIN:
Lockheed/Canadair T-33AN/SF
Pilatus PC-7 Turbo-Trainer
North American AT-6G Texan
Transport:
Douglas DC-8 Srs.55F
Lockheed C-130H Hercules
Lockheed L-100-20 Hercules
Lockheed L-188A Electra
Douglas C-47 Dakota
Fokker F-27 Friendship
Convair CV.440/580 Metropolitan
IAI-201 Arava
Bell UH-1H Iroquois
VIP Transport:
Rockwell Sabre 65
Communications/Liaison:
Rockwell Turbo Commander 690B
Rockwell Aero Commander 500S
Beech Super King Air 200
Beech King Air 90
Piper PA-31T Cheyenne
Piper PA-31 Navajo
Cessna 421B
Cessna 404
Cessna 402
Cessna 210
Cessna U.206/TU.206
Cessna 185/U-17 Skywagon
Pilatus PC-6B Turbo-Porter
Aerospatiale SA.315B Lama
Helibras HB-315B Gavilan
Aerial Survey:
LearJet 25B/D
Cessna 402B
Training:
Aerotec T-23 Uirapuru
Aerotec A-123 Tangara
Cessna A152 Aerobat
Cessna 172K/T-41D Mescalero
Pilatus PC-7 Turbo-Trainer
Lockheed/Canadair T-33AN/SF

BRAZIL

BY FAR THE largest and certainly one of the best equipped air arms in Latin America, the *Forca Aérea Brasileira* (FAB: Brazilian Air Force) is in the happy position of being able to rely on an indigenous aerospace industry that is tackling increasingly ambitious projects, often in collaboration with other countries. At the moment, this policy is best epitomized by the AMX attack/fighter, which is a joint Italo-Brazilian venture, production being undertaken in both countries for service with the respective air forces. FAB procurement of the AMX is presently pegged at 79 aircraft, including 15 two-seat trainers, but may ultimately rise to as many as 150, some of which could be configured for tactical reconnaissance operations courtesy of an interchangeable sensor pack.

In organizational terms, the FAB actually consists of five of the six Ministry of Aviation departments, the solitary exception being that which is concerned with civil aviation. Of the five departments, the Air General Command is the most important, for it is this which manages most flying units, other elements being responsible for support, research and development, personnel and training respectively.

Returning to the Air General Command, this is further broken down into half-a-dozen sub-sections, most of which are functional agencies tasked in a specific role. Thus, the FAB line-up includes the Tactical Air Command and the Air Defence Command with most combat resources; the Air Transport Command with responsibility for airlift; the Tactical and Crew Training Centre for operational instruction; and the Regional Air Command with seven district headquarters to co-ordinate the activities of aircraft stationed at air bases within their specific area. There is also a Coastal Command but this is under Navy direction even though its operational assets are owned and operated by the FAB.

At the operational level, the FAB employs a Wing/Squadron structure, with the Wings controlling anything from one to four Squadrons. Air Defence Command is the smallest operating agency and has just one subordinate Air Defence Wing with two squadrons of Mirage IIIs at Anapolis, close to the capital city of Brasilia. About 20 single and two-seat Mirages are on hand and these are currently being modernized for service through the 1990s, acquiring new avionics and the now almost obligatory canard foreplanes to enhance handling qualities.

Tactical Air Command is a rather more substantial organization, with a handful of Fighter Aircraft Wings, two Aircraft Wings and a Helicopter Instructional Centre. Combat-capable elements assigned to the Fighter Wings comprise three squadrons equipped with the F-5E Tiger II, three with the licence-built EMB.326GB Xavante and two that have recently begun working up on the AMX. For the most part, these units are employed on ground attack duties but one Xavante squadron specializes in the tactical reconnaissance role.

Mention has already been made of AMX procurement, but Brazil also has about 50 F-5Es and around 60 attack-dedicated Xavantes, with a further 50 or so of the latter employed purely in the training role. Other Tactical Air Command equipment flown by the two Aircraft Wings consists primarily of the Iroquois, Ecureuil, Puma and Super Puma helicopters plus a number of EMBRAER-built U-7 Senecas, which between them fulfil a variety of tasks including

Below: Synonymous with the FAB, the Embraer Bandeirante has proved its versatility in a number of diverse and exacting roles.

Below: Sporting the latest low-visibility grey camouflage, and a pair of prominent canard foreplanes to enhance performance, an FAB Mirage IIIDBR shows off the sleek lines of the popular delta-winged fighter.

observation, search-and-rescue (SAR), liaison, assault, armed attack and support of ground forces. Equipment with the Helicopter Training Centre comprises the Bell Iroquois and JetRanger and McDonnell Douglas OH-6A Cayuse.

Air Transport Command resources are tasked with a variety of airlift missions and the sizeable fleet includes examples of the Hercules (including a pair configured for in-flight refuelling), four Boeing 707 tanker/transports, DHC-5 Buffaloes, a dozen BAe 748s and more than 100 EMBRAER Bandeirantes, some of which are assigned to special duties such as aerial survey, navaid calibration and SAR. VIP and utility tasks are also undertaken, with equipment in use for such operations including 10 BAe125s, a couple of Boeing 737s, some EMBRAER Brasilias and Xingus plus a few helicopters.

Coastal Command has responsibility for all fixed-wing aircraft engaged on maritime operations and relies heavily on suitably configured Bandeirantes to fulfil patrol and surveillance duties, but it does also have a dozen or so S-2E Trackers which are now being re-engined with PT-6A turboprops and given new avionics to extend their lives. Until recently, these were periodically deployed aboard the Navy's carrier *Minas Gerais*, but this is now to be scrapped although it is intended to build a new carrier for service from the mid-1990s.

Pilot training is assigned to the Air Force Academy at Pirassununga and begins on the Neiva T-25 Universal, but the FAB is anxious to retire this type and has been looking closely at the Chilean ENAER Pillan. Students then move on to the EMB-312 Tucano, completing their instruction with operational-type training on the Xavante at the Tactical and Crew Training Centre at Natal if they are destined to join combat elements. Those candidates earmarked for transport units will receive further training on type while helicopter aircrew transfer to Tactical Air Command's Helicopter Instructional Centre for further tuition.

Above: Living up to their name, the FAB's Escuadron de Fume (Smoke Squadron) lays down its "signature" courtesy of its T-27 Tucano trainers.

Right: Designated the C-91 in FAB service, the 12 BAe 748s have proved their abilities time and time again as rugged and reliable medium transports.

EQUIPMENT

Interception:
Dassault-Breguet Mirage IIIEBR
Interception/Attack:
Northrop F-5E Tiger II
Attack:
Embraer AMX
Light Attack:
Embraer EMB.326GB Xavante
Maritime Patrol/ASW:
Embraer EMB-111A Bandeirante
Grumman S-2E Turbo-Tracker
Transport:
Lockheed C-130E/H Hercules
Boeing Canada Buffalo
Embraer EMB-110 Bandeirante
BAe 748
Bell UH-1D/H Iroquois
Aerospatiale SA.330L Puma
Aerospatiale AS.332M Super Puma
VIP Transport:
Boeing 737-2N3
BAe 125
Embraer EMB-120 Brasilia
Embraer EMB-121E Xingu
Aerospatiale AS.355F Ecureuil 2
Bell 206B JetRanger
Tanking/Transport:
Boeing 707-321C
Lockheed KC-130H Hercules
Communications/Liaison:
Embraer EMB-120 Brasilia
Embraer EMB-121 Xingu
Embraer EMB-81DC Seneca II
Grumman US-2A Tracker
Cessna 208 Caravan I
Neiva U-42 Regente
Cessna 0-1 Bird Dog
Aerospatiale SA.350 Ecureuil
Aerospatiale AS.355F Ecureuil 2
Observation:
Bell 206 JetRanger
McDonnell Douglas OH-6A Cayuse
SAR:
Bell SH-1H Iroquois
SAR/Surveillance:
Embraer EMB-110 Bandeirante
LearJet 36A
Training:
Aerotec T-23 Uirapuru
Neiva T-25 Universal
Embraer EMB-312 Tucano
Embraer EMB-326GB Xavante
Northrop F-5B Freedom Fighter
Northrop F-5F Tiger II
Embraer AMX-T
Bell 47G/OH-13 Sioux
Dassault-Breguet Mirage IIIDBR
Miscellaneous:
Embraer EMB-110P1 Bandeirante
Embraer EMB-201 Ipanema
Sailplanes:
Schliecher ASW.20
LET L-13 Blanik
Glasflugel Libelle

CHILE

DEFENCE OF Chile is complicated by its geography, this long and narrow state being bordered on its western side by the Pacific Ocean and on the east by Bolivia and Argentina, relations with the latter nation being by no means entirely amicable although a dispute over the southerly Beagle Channel has been resolved. Further problems have arisen as a result of Chile's poor human rights record which led to several countries embargoing the supply of arms, but the situation does now appear to be improving, with the USA agreeing to resume the supply of spares for the F-5 fleet in late-1988 at a time when Chile was seriously considering purchasing the IAI Kfir from Israel.

Geographical considerations are a key factor in the organization of the *Fuerza Aérea de Chile* (FACh: Chilean Air Force), with the country effectively being split into four zones running from north to south. Each zone is the responsibility of an Air Brigade, each of which will typically manage the activities of one or two air bases and their resident Squadrons. Thus, No.1 Air Brigade is headquartered at Antofagasta/Cerro Moreno air base and also has Iquique/Los Condores air base under its control; No.2 Air Brigade is at Santiago/Los Cerrillos and also has Santiago/Merino Benitez air base; No.3 Air Brigade is at Puerto Montt/El Tepual; and No.4 Air Brigade is at Punta Arenas/Carlos Ibanez, with added responsibility for a facility in Antarctica. Operational elements assigned to each of these Air Brigades varies from one to four squadrons but by no means all possess combat forces, these being concentrated in the northern and southern extremities of Chile with Nos.1 and 4 Air Brigades.

Combat capability is spearheaded by

Above: A four-ship of FACh Hunters, with a photo-reconnaissance FR.71A (coded "734") and a trio of fighter ground attack FGA. 71s in perfect formation over the Pacific.

Below: While some of the FACh's Beech 99A light twins are used for transport duties, this "Petrel Alpha" is the property of No.2 Group's Electronic Warfare Squadron.

Mirage 50s which are currently being updated to *Pantera* (Panther) standard with canard foreplanes and revised avionics. Undertaken locally by ENAER, this project is a joint collaboration with IAI of Israel, and modified aircraft closely resemble the latter company's Kfir. Also the subject of an upgrade effort by ENAER, the F-5E Tiger II has enjoyed a somewhat chequered career with the FACh, serviceability sometimes dipping as low as four aircraft as a result of a spares embargo imposed by the USA. As noted earlier, this has now been lifted and the 15 or so survivors (including three F-5F two-seaters) are again making a worthwhile contribution to the defence of Chile in dual attack/interceptor roles.

Attack is the principal task of the 20-odd Hunters that are generally active at any given time, Chile operating a somewhat varied fleet of aircraft that includes refurbished FGA.71s and FR.71As, as well as ex-RAF FGA.9s and T.67 and T.72 two-seat trainers. Despite their age, there are no plans to retire them in the immediate future. Other hardware with a combat application comprises the A-37B Dragonfly attack/counter-insurgency (COIN) aircraft, but the locally-assembled ENAER A-36 Halcon (licence-built CASA C.101 Aviojet) could also be employed for such tasks although it is actually used as an advanced trainer with emphasis on gunnery and bombing.

Airlift capacity is limited to say the least, but the FACh does have a couple of C-130H Hercules and two Boeing 707-351Cs for medium/long-haul operations and is apparently awaiting the delivery of Airtech CN.235M twin-turboprop freighters. Three Beech A99s are used as staff transports, one being configured for VIP duties, and Twin Otters are employed in the light transport role. Rotary-wing airlift is confined to UH-1H Iroquois and six MBB BO.105CBs which are mainly used for liaison duties, but at least one VIP-configured MBB/Kawasaki BK117 has recently been ordered.

Other second-line equipment is engaged on a variety of tasks including aerial survey, maritime surveillance, search-and-rescue (SAR) and the acquisition of electronic intelligence (Elint).

Pilot training is mostly undertaken at the "*Capitan Avalos*" Aviation School at Santiago/El Bosque and is accomplished on the ENAER T-35 Pillan and Cessna T-37B/C, with operational type training ensuing on the T-36 Halcon at Iquique. In addition, all combat units operate small numbers of two-seat trainer versions of the FACh's primary front-line equipment.

Personnel assigned to non-flying duty at FACh headquarters in Santiago are quite well catered for with regard to maintaining pilot skills, for the Los Cerrillos base has a number of Pillans and some ENAER-built Piper PA-28-236 Dakotas for proficiency and instrument training. At nearby Las Condes, several gliders are active with a special school which uses a trio of 0-1 Bird Dogs as towplanes. Finally, the FACh has a full-time aerobatic display team known as the "*Halcones*" (Hawks). Normally stationed at Los Cerrillos, the team is equipped with six Extra 300s sportplanes.

Above: Six examples of the German-designed BO 105CB helicopter have been constructed by ENAER for service with the FACh.

Below: In addition to the 60 T-35A primary trainers procured, the FACh has detained 20 T-35Bs for instrument training duties.

EQUIPMENT

Interception/Attack:
Dassault-Breguet Mirage 50CN
Northrop F-5E Tiger II

Fighter-Ground Attack:
BAe Hunter FGA.9/.71

Fighter-Reconnaissance:
BAe Hunter FGR.71A

COIN:
Cessna A-37B Dragonfly
ENAER A-36 Halcon

Elint:
Beech A99 "Petrel Beta"

Reconnaissance/Surveillance:
BAe Canberra PR.9
LearJet 35A
Beech King Air 100

Maritime Patrol:
Beech A99 "Petrel Alpha"

Transport:
Boeing 707-351C
Lockheed C-130H Hercules
Boeing Canada Twin Otter 100/300
Beech A99

VIP Transport:
Beech A99

Training:
ENAER T-35A/B Pillan
ENAER PA-28-236 Dakota
Cessna A-37B Dragonfly
Cessna T-37B/C
ENAER A/T-36 Halcon
Northrop F-5F Tiger II
BAe Hunter T.67/72
Dassault-Breguet Mirage 50DCH

SAR/Liaison:
Aerospatiale SA.315B Lama

Utility:
Bell UH-1B Iroquois
MBB BO.105CB

Aerobatic Team:
Extra 300

Glider Tugs:
Cessna O-1A Bird Dog

Gliders:
LET L-13 Blanik
Schempp-Hirth Cirrus
Schempp-Hirth Discus
Schempp-Hirth Janus C

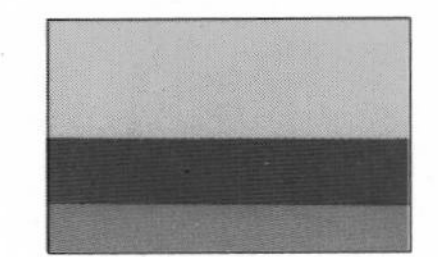

COLOMBIA

THE FIGHTING potential of the *Fuerza Aérea Colombiana* (FAC: Colombian Air Force) received a substantial boost during the course of 1989 when a dozen Kfir C7 fighters (including two TC7 two-seat trainers) were delivered from Israel. Earmarked for service with the Air Combat Command which exercises control over all front-line elements, the Kfirs are supported by a marginally greater number of Mirages, for Colombia still operates most of the 18 aircraft that were delivered as long ago as the early-1970s. At the present time, 12 fighter-bomber Mirage 5COAs, two reconnaissance 5CORs and two trainer 5CODs are still active although these are apparently to be subjected to long-overdue modernization by Israel Aircraft Industries. In the course of this work, it seems likely that they will acquire new avionics and canard flying surfaces.

Other combat equipment is possessed of rather more sedate performance but is perhaps more useful in Colombia's continuing battle against the left-wing guerilla forces and drug cartels that exert considerable power in the country. In the front-line of counter-insurgency (COIN) assets are some three dozen Cessna A-37Bs, OA-37Bs and T-37Cs, these light jets being able to pack quite a powerful punch; but they are by no means the only types conducting such operations, for the FAC also operates about 10 Lockheed AT-33As and a quantity of armed helicopters.

The latter are all assigned to the FAC's Tactical Air Support Command and are dominated by the ubiquitous UH-1 Iroquois, of which close to 50 are presently in service, and there are also some 30 assorted Hughes helicopters including a dozen or so examples of the OH-6A Cayuse and varying quantities of the Model 500MD Defender, 500MG Scout and 500E, most of which may easily be adapted to carry armament. More recent deliveries have seen the FAC add about 10 Sikorsky UH-60A Black Hawks to its inventory, but these are mostly employed on pure transport tasks.

Airlift assets are somewhat mixed, the FAC's own transport fleet consisting of C-47s, DC-4/C-54s, DC-6s, a couple of IAI Aravas and five Lockheed Hercules, but these are often augmented by aircraft of the para-military domestic airline SATENA, Colombia being one of several South American states that employ this concept of air transport operation.

A small VIP unit is tasked with meeting Presidential transportation requirements with a fleet that is composed of one F-28 Fellowship 1000, one Boeing 707 and one Bell 212, while there is also a liaison and communications squadron flying Bell 206B JetRangers. Additional fixed-wing communications assets are many and varied and have recently been bolstered by a substantial number of light aircraft siezed by the authorities in the continuing campaign to curtail the massive drugs trade. Recent reports indicate that close to 400 aircraft have now been impounded and that roughly 180 of these have been taken over by the FAC, but full details of types and quantities are not available.

Primary and basic pilot instruction is entrusted to Training Command and is accomplished at the Military Aviation School at Calion on T-41D Mescaleros and T-34A/B Mentors, with advanced tuition for combat jet aircrew following in the USA as a lead-in to operational conversion back in Colombia. On qualification, it seems likely that aircrew will initially be posted to fly the A/T-37 or T-33 before being allowed anywhere near the Kfir and Mirage force. Those personnel destined for helicopters are trained in-country, as are those selected to fly the FAC's transport aircraft.

Above: No.411 Combat Squadron, FAC, flies this trio of Cessna A-37B Dragonflies.

Below: Similarities between the IAI Kfir (foreground) and its progenitor, the French Mirage, are clear to see in this illustration.

Left: The influence of the USA in the region, and a crackdown on the drug cartels operating from Colombia, has led to the FAC receiving more hardware, such as this UH-60A Black Hawk.

Above: The ubiquitous Douglas C-47 Dakota is an important part of the FAC's motley transport force. The example illustrated flies in logistical support of Colombian Army outposts.

EQUIPMENT

Interception/Attack:
IAI Kfir C7
Dassault-Breguet Mirage 5COA
COIN/Light Attack:
Cessna A/OA-37B Dragonfly
Cessna T-37C
Lockheed AT-33A Shooting Star
COIN/Observation:
Hughes OH-6A Cayuse
McDonnell Douglas 500D/E/MG
COIN/Transport:
Bell UH-1B/H Iroquois
Reconnaissance:
Dassault-Breguet Mirage 5COR
Lockheed RT-33A Shooting Star
Transport:
Lockheed C-130B/H-30 Hercules
Douglas C-54 Skymaster
Douglas DC-6
Douglas C-47 Dakota
IAI Arava
Bell 212
Bell 412
Sikorsky UH-60A Black Hawk
VIP Transport:
Boeing 707-337C
Fokker F-28 Fellowship 1000
Bell 212
Communications/Liaison:
Beech King Air C90
Beech Queen Air
Cessna 210
Cessna 310
Cessna 340
Cessna 404 Titan
Piper PA-31 Navajo
Piper PA-34 Seneca
Piper PA-44 Seminole
Rockwell Aero Commander 560A
de Havilland Canada DHC-2 Beaver
Cessna A185E Floatplane
Bell 206B JetRanger
Training:
Cessna T-41D Mescalero
Beech T-34A/B Mentor
Dassault-Breguet Mirage 5COD
IAI Kfir T7
Bell 47G
Hughes TH-55A Osage
Hughes 300C

SATENA

Fokker F-28 Fellowship 3000
Douglas DC-4/C-54
Douglas C-47 Dakota
BAe 748 Srs.2B
CASA C.212 Aviocar
Pilatus PC-6/6B Turbo-Porter

COSTA RICA

THIS LATIN American state is almost unique in that it does not have a properly constituted air force, since armed forces have been formally banned since the civil war of 1948. However, the para-military Civil Guard organization does feature an Air Section which is equipped with a number of light aircraft and helicopters that are used for border surveillance patrol taks, as well as duties related to internal security and more conventional communications.

Less than 20 aircraft are operated, all being stationed at José Santamaria International Airport, but there are a number of landing sites scattered around the countryside as well as several fully-fledged airfields that can be used.

EQUIPMENT

Observation:
Cessna O-2A Skymaster
McDonnell Douglas 500D
Communications/Liaison:
Rockwell Commander 680FLP
Piper Seneca 200T
Piper Aztec 250
Cessna/Soloy U.206G Stationair 6
Piper Cherokee Six
Grumman American AA-5 Tiger

CUBA

BECOMING increasingly isolated due to its rigid adherence to Communist doctrine, the fortunes of this Caribbean island look to be very much in decline, yet it continues to maintain a substantial air arm. Equipped entirely with material of Warsaw Pact origin, the *Fuerza Aérea Revolucionaria* (FAR: Revolutionary Air Force) is primarily orientated towards air defence but does possess a reasonable attack capability in the formidable shape of the MiG-23 "Flogger".

Contemporary FAR organization is based on the use of Western, Central and Eastern Air Zones, with the bulk of the combat-capable forces being distributed between the former pair. Major air bases are occupied by a Group which directs the activities of from two to four Squadrons, normal unit establishment being around 16 interceptors or 12 fighter-bombers per front-line squadron.

Air defence assets are dominated by the MiG-21, with the FAR presently having a fleet of "Fishbeds" that comfortably exceeds the 150 mark although numbers may now be in decline following receipt of MiG-29 "Fulcrums" Authoritative sources report that some three-dozen "Fulcrums" are to be delivered to Cuba, but that quantity almost certainly includes at least two MiG-29UB two-seaters. Additional interceptors consist of a squadron's worth of MiG-23MF/MS "Floggers", while Cuba also has a large number of air defence sites armed with SA-2 "Guideline", SA-3 "Goa" and SA-6 "Gainful" surface-to-air missiles.

Tactical firepower resources are less numerous and are composed mainly of three squadrons of MiG-23BN "Flogger-Fs" supported by a single squadron of near-obsolescent MiG-17F "Frescos". In addition, some 50 Mi-8/17 "Hip" assault helicopters are operated, as are some 15 Mi-25 "Hind-D" gunships which are compatible with both the AT-2 "Swatter" and AT-3 "Sagger" anti-armour missiles.

Airlift potential is also relatively modest and the most numerous transport aircraft is now the An-26 "Curl", supported by two or three examples of the An-24 "Coke" and An-32 "Cline", while older aircraft comprise as many as 30 An-2 "Colt" biplanes and 20-odd Il-14 "Crates". In addition, two Il-76 "Candids" are reported to be on FAR charge for long-range missions, but these carry civil "identities" and fly in Cubana (the national airline) colours. Allied duties such as communications and liaison are generally satisfied by helicopters such as the ever-dependable Mi-2 "Hoplite" and the larger Mi-4 "Hound".

EQUIPMENT

Interception
Mikoyan-Gurevich MiG-29 "Fulcrum-A"
Mikoyan-Gurevich MiG-23MF/MS "Flogger-B/E"
Mikoyan-Gurevich MiG-21F/PFM/PFMA/bis "Fishbed-C/F/J/L"
Attack
Mikoyan-Gurevich MiG-23BN "Flogger-F"
Mikoyan-Gurevich MiG-17F "Fresco"
Anti-Armour:
Mil Mi-25 "Hind-D"
Transport:
Ilyushin Il-76 "Candid"
Antonov An-32 "Cline"
Antonov An-26 "Curl"
Anotnov An-24 "Coke"
Ilyushin Il-14 "Crate"
Antonov An-2 "Colt"
Mil Mi-8/17 "Hip"
Communications/Liaison:
Mil Mi-4 "Hound"
Mil Mi-2 "Hoplite"
Training:
Zlin Z-326
Aero L-39 Albatros
Mikoyan-Gurevich MiG-15UTI "Midget"
Mikoyan-Gurevich MiG-15 "Fagot"
Mikoyan-Gurevich MiG-21U "Mongol"
Mikoyan-Gurevich MiG-23U "Flogger-C"
Mikoyan-Gurevich MiG-29UB "Fulcrum-B"

DOMINICAN REPUBLIC

LIMITED financial resources mean that the *Fuerza Aérea Dominica* (FAD: Dominican Air Force) has been forced to utilize old and obsolescent equipment for much of its life, and this situation prevails today. Fortunately, US aid has allowed some modernization in recent years, most notably with regard to combat forces, and the FAD now has one counter-insurgency (COIN) squadron equipped with the Cessna A-37B Dragonfly light attack aircraft. A handful of Cessna O-2As is also operated on liaison duties although these are also able to undertake counter-insurgency and forward air control tasks, but the bulk of the inventory is made up of second-line types which satisfy the FAD's training, transport, liaison and communications functions.

EQUIPMENT

COIN:
Cessna A-37B Dragonfly
Cessna O-2A Skymaster
Transport:
Douglas C-47 Dakota
Mitsubishi MU-2J
Bell UH-1H Iroquois
VIP Transport:
Aerospatiale SA.365C Dauphin 2
SAR:
Bell UH-1H Iroquois
Communications/Liaison:
Rallye Commodore
Cessna 210L
Beech Queen Air B80
Piper PA-31 Navajo
Rockwell Aero Commander 680
Aerospatiale Alouette II
McDonnell Douglas 500D

Left: The FAD's almost exclusive reliance on the USA for the supply of military hardware has continued recently with the delivery of some Cessna O-2As for COIN/liaison duties.

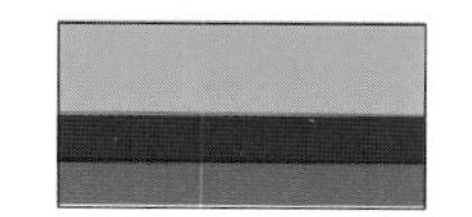

ECUADOR

FOR THE *Fuerza Aérea Ecuatoriana* (FAE: Ecuadorian Air Force), the past 15 years or so have been an era of notable expansion in terms of combat capability, brought about largely in response to aggressive noises coming from neighbouring Peru which erupted into a brief border conflict at the beginning of 1981. Once almost entirely dependent upon the USA as a source of arms, Ecuador has broadened its horizons and currently also operates hardware obtained from France, Israel and the United Kingdom.

Two major command agencies exist within the FAE, namely the 1st Air Zone with control of transport-orientated units, and the 2nd Air Zone which directs all combat-capable resources and the modestly-sized training organization. Combat forces are assigned to three Wing elements at three different bases, although day-to-day operations are actually directed by a subordinate Group, with each Group possessing three flying Squadrons.

Undoubtedly the most important base is that at Taura. Situated close to the major city of Guayaquil, this is home to the 21st Combat Wing and the associated 211th Group which has three squadrons operating very different equipment. Air defence is the principal function of the Mirage F.1JA-equipped No.2112 Fighter Squadron, although this multi-role machine can also be employed on attack duties. Delivery of 16 F.1JAs and two F.1JE trainers was completed during 1978-80 and 14 remain in service, attrition having claimed three F.1JAs and one F.1JE.

Attack is the major mission assigned to the other two Taura-based units, No.2111 Combat Squadron operating Jaguar Internationals (including a couple of two-seaters) and No.2113 Combat Squadron flying a similar quantity of IAI Kfir C2/TC2s. Other equipment which is not presently operational comprises a trio of Canberra B.6 light bombers that have been held in flyable storage for some seven years, but it seems that the FAE is to renovate these veterans for further sevice in the near future.

Air-to-ground attack tasks are also undertaken by the FAE's other front-line formation, this being the 23rd Combat Wing at Manta, but it has rather less potent equipment which is mainly employed on counter-insurgency (COIN) tasks. The three squadrons assigned to the 231st Group all operate suitably modified versions of jet trainer aircraft and consist of No.2311 Combat Squadron with A-37B Dragonflies, No.2312 Combat Squadron with about two dozen Lockheed AT-33As, and No.2313 Combat Squadron with 10 Strikemasters. Apart from their primary combat application, most of these units have a secondary tactical training role to fulfil, the AT-33As, for instance, being used for air combat.

Above: A very mixed echelon of FAE fighters, with a Kfir C2 leading a SEPECAT Jaguar S and, nearest the camera, a Mirage F.1JE trainer.

One other Combat Wing (the 22nd) also exists but this is a combat unit in name only, for it lacks any offensive hardware although the FAE is evidently keen to obtain armed helicopters for this formation. Stationed at the Simon Bolivar air base near Guayaquil, the 22nd Wing's three squadrons are No.2211 Combat Squadron, No.2212 Rescue Squadron and No.2213 Training Squadron. Equipment flown by these three units is drawn from the parent 221st Group and comprises a handful of Alouette IIIs plus single examples of the Bell 212 and Boeing Canada Twin Otter 300.

Transport resources are concentrated with the 11th Transport Wing at Quito's international airport, which is known to the FAE as Mariscal Sucre air base. Barely a dozen aircraft are on hand but by no means all are currently airworthy, for the hostile environment periodically results in accidents necessitating lengthy repair work.

All but the two Sabreliners display dual civil/military identities to permit their use by the para-military airline *Transportes Aereos Militares Ecuatorianos* (TAME) on domestic scheduled services. This practice is, in fact, a "two-way" street, for TAME's own aircraft (one Lockheed Electra, three Boeing 727s, one Boeing 737 and an F-28 Fellowship 4000) can be used by the FAE, as indeed can *Ecuatoriana's* four Boeing 707s and one DC-10 Srs.30 — in consequence, TAME and *Ecuatoriana* aircraft also carry military identities.

Responsibility for pilot training rests with the Military Aviation School at General Ulpiano Paez air base, near Salinas on the coast. Some 19 T-34C Turbo-Mentors are flown by the Air Training Squadron which offers a three-year course culminating in the award of pilot's wings and further training at operational stations. Those destined for combat jets receive further instruction on the Strikemaster at Manta and then usually go to Holloman AFB in the USA for weapons training on the Northrop AT-38B, before assignment to an operational unit.

EQUIPMENT

Interception:
Dassault-Breguet Mirage F.1JA
Attack:
IAI Kfir C2
Dassault-Breguet Mirage F.1JA
SEPECAT Jaguar ES
BAe Strikemaster Mk.89/89A
COIN:
Cessna A-37B Dragonfly
Lockheed AT-33A
Transport:
Lockheed C-130H/L-100-30 Hercules
BAe 748 Srs.2
Boeing Canada Buffalo
Boeing Canada Twin Otter 300
VIP Transport:
Rockwell Sabreliner 40R/60
BAe 748 Srs.2
SAR/Liaison:
Bell 212
Aerospatiale SA.316B Alouette III
Communications/Liaison:
Cessna T-41D Mescalero
Calibration:
Beech King Air E90
Training:
Beech T-34C Turbo-Mentor
IAI Kfir TC2
SEPECAT Jaguar EB
Dassault-Breguet Mirage F.1JE

TAME

Transport:
Boeing 727
Boeing 737
Fokker F-28 Fellowship 4000
Lockheed L.188 Electra

ECUATORIANA

Transport:
McDonnell Douglas DC-10-30
Boeing 707-321

EL SALVADOR

RACKED BY internal conflict between Cuban-backed left-wing guerilla factions and the right-wing government, the *Fuerza Aérea Salvadorena* (FAS: Salvadorean Air Force) has increasingly turned to the USA as a source of equipment but also operates hardware obtained from Israel. Financially improverished, much of the FAS inventory can best be described as elderly, with types like the 1950s-vintage Dassault Ouragan serving alongside the AC-47 Dakota gunship and the UH-1H Iroquois in the Government's continuing anti-guerilla campaign.

Front-line combat capability rests with the survivors of 18 Ouragans acquired from Israel in the 1970s, but attrition and guerilla action has reduced the quantity on hand to about eight. Similar numbers of the Cessna A-37B Dragonfly and the CM.170 Magister form the main counter-insurgency (COIN) strike potential, aided by a handful of Cessna O-2As which also undertake forward air control tasks. Other combat equipment comprises about a dozen SOCATA 235GS Guerriers for light strike duties, close to 50 UH-1H Iroquois helicopters, including some armed examples, and a few McDonnell Douglas 500M Defenders.

Transport resources are, for the most part, also deserving of veteran status, comprising half-a-dozen C-47s (including two that have been fitted with turboprop engines), a trio of IAI-201 Aravas, a couple of C-123K Providers and one Douglas DC-6, while training requirements are satisfied by T-34A Mentors, Cessna T-41C/D Mescaleros and, when they can be spared from combat, the CM.170s. In addition, small numbers of McDonnell Douglas 300 and 500, Alouette III and SA.315B Lama helicopters are utilized for liaison, search-and-rescue (SAR) and training tasks.

Operational bases number about seven, with the international airport at Ilopango being the main centre of activity, although San Miguel is actually home for most of the jet combat aircraft now in service.

EQUIPMENT

Interception:
Dassault Ouragan
Attack:
Dassault Ouragan
COIN:
Cessna A-37B Dragonfly
Douglas AC-47 Dakota
Aerospatiale CM.170 Magister
Cessna O-2A Super Skymaster
SOCATA 235GS Guerrier
Bell UH-1H Iroquois
McDonnell Douglas 500M Defender
Transport:
Douglas DC-6
Douglas C-47 Dakota
Fairchild C-123K Provider
IAI-201 Arava
Bell UH-1H Iroquois
SAR:
Aerospatiale SA.315B Lama
Communications/Liaison:
Cessna 180
Cessna 182
Cessna 185
Aerospatiale Alouette III
Training:
Cessna T-41C/D Mescalero
Beech T-34A Mentor
Aerospataile CM.170 Magister
McDonnell Douglas 300C

GUATEMALA

LIKE MANY Latin American air arms, the *Fuerza Aérea Guatemalteca* (FAG: Guatemalan Air Force) is heavily dependent on US military assistance for much of its hardware, and its offensive capability is modest to say the least, combat forces comprising barely 10 A-37B Dragonflies and a similar number of Pilatus PC-7 Turbo-Trainers, some of which are allocated to training tasks. In dispute with Great Britain over its claims to Belize, Guatemala has recently faced increasing levels of internal dissent from left-wing guerilla forces and it has occasionally employed the A-37s and PC-7s to attack known opposition strongholds with bombs, rockets and gunfire.

In the main, counter-insurgency (COIN) operations are conducted by helicopter, the FAG possessing roughly a dozen Bell 212s, Bell 412s and UH-1D/H Iroquois, all of which can be armed, plus about half as many JetRangers/LongRangers which are mostly used for routine communications. Other elements consist of a few T-33As and PC-7s for training, a motley assortment of old and new transport aircraft including examples of the C-47 Dakota, Douglas DC-6B, IAI Arava and F-27 Friendship, and sundry single-engined Cessnas for liaison and communications duties.

EQUIPMENT

COIN:
Cessna A-37B Dragonfly
Pilatus PC-7 Turbo-Trainer
Assault:
Bell 412
Bell 212
Bell UH-1D/H Iroquois
Transport:
Douglas DC-6B
Fokker F-27 Friendship
Douglas C-47 Dakota
IAI-201 Arava
VIP Transport:
Beech Super King Air 200
Communications/Liaison:
Cessna 172
Cessna 180
Cessna 182
Cessna 185
Cessna 206
Bell 206B/L JetRanger/LongRanger
Training:
Pilatus PC-7 Turbo-Trainer
Lockheed T-33A

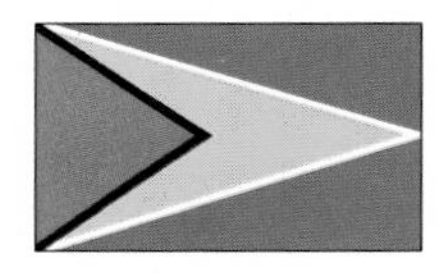

GUYANA

FUNDAMENTALLY a policing force that operates as part of the unified Guyana Defence Force, the Air Corps has little more than a dozen aircraft and helicopters on strength. Combat capability is non-existent, aircraft like the Skyvan, Islander and Cessna U206F operating alongside helicopters such as the Bell 206B JetRanger in transport, communications and liaison roles. Mil Mi-8 "Hip" helicopters were used until recently but are no longer flown due to inadequate performance.

Left: Aircraft for the Guatemalan Air Force has been obtained from a variety of sources, as exemplified by this Dutch-supplied Fokker F-27 Friendship.

Right: The Guyanan Air Corps is one of only a small number of air arms equipped solely with transport types, its largest aircraft being the Skyvan 3M.

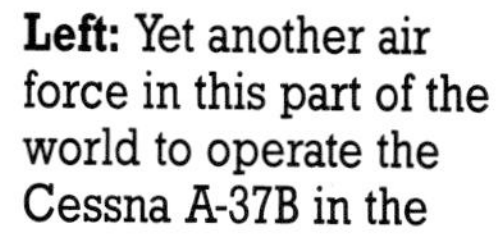

Left: Yet another air force in this part of the world to operate the Cessna A-37B in the COIN role is that of Honduras, with the third example to be supplied shown here.

EQUIPMENT

Transport:
Shorts Skyvan 3M
Pilatus Britten-Norman BN-2A Islander
Bell 412
Bell 212
VIP Transport:
Beech Super King Air 200
Communications/Liaison:
Cessna U206F
Bell 206B JetRanger

HAITI

COMBAT FORCES operational with the *Corps d'Aviation d'Haiti* (Haitian Aviation Corps) are limited to four examples of the SIAI S.211 armed jet trainer and eight Cessna O-2As. Both can be used for counter-insurgency (COIN) missions, but the former also has a secondary training role to fulfil alongside four or five SIAI SF.260TPs and a few single-engined Cessna light planes. Transport elements are spearheaded by a trio of veteran C-47 Dakotas, backed up by single examples of the Twin Otter and Islander, while a couple of DHC-2 Beavers satisfy communications and liaison tasks in concert with single examples of the Beech Baron, Beech Twin Bonanza and Cessna 402. Unusually, no rotary-wing craft have been operated since 1988, when the small fleet of McDonnell Douglas 269/500 helicopters was sold.

EQUIPMENT

COIN:
SIAI-Marchetti S.211
Summit-Cessna 0-2-337
Transport:
Douglas C-47 Dakota
Curtiss C-46 Commando
Boeing Canada Twin Otter 200
Pilatus Britten-Norman BN-2A Islander
Communications/Liaison:
Cessna 402
Beech Baron
Beech Twin Bonanza
Boeing Canada Beaver
Training:
Cessna 150
Cessna 172
Beech F33 Bonanza
SIAI-Marchetti SF.260TP
SIAI-Marchetti S.211

HONDURAS

INVOLVEMENT with US-supported anti-communist operations against the neighbouring Marxist state of Nicaragua resulted in additional military aid for the *Fuerza Aérea Hondurena* (FAH: Honduran Air Force), but the level of activity has declined as assistance to the *Contra* rebels diminished. Nevertheless, Honduras still faces a serious internal threat posed by left-wing guerilla forces, and this has resulted in most new equipment being able to carry armament so as to permit its use should sustained counter-insurgency (COIN) operations be necessary.

Long-overdue modernization of front-line combat elements finally transpired in 1987-89, when the USA supplied a batch of 10 F-5Es and two F-5Fs from surplus stocks, satisfying repeated Honduran requests dating back to 1982. Arrival of these fighters at La Cieba has permitted the FAH to withdraw obsolescent equipment in the form of eight Super Mystere B.2s, eight F-86E/F Sabres, two F-86K Sabres and a handful of T/RT-33As. Other combat-capable hardware is confined to about a dozen A/OA-37B Dragonflies which are used for light attack duties.

Second-line elements are principally concerned with transport and training, the FAH's modest airlift potential being composed of a couple of C-130A Hercules, about half-a-dozen C-47 Dakotas, one C-118A Liftmaster and a pair of IAI-201 Aravas.

VIP and communications transport tasks are undertaken by a Falcon 20, Jet Commander and Westwind, as well as sundry lightplanes including small quantities of the Cessna 172, 180 and 185 plus three Rockwell Commander 114s. Helicopters in service on general purpose airlift tasks comprise some 15 UH-1B/H Iroquois and seven Bell 412SPs.

Training assets are few, the Military Aviation School operating four or five T-41D Mescaleros and a dozen EMB-312 Tucanos as a lead-in to the CASA C.101BB Aviojet. Four of the latter were delivered in 1984 although an option on eight more has never been exercised; but the FAH has recently ordered 10 ENAER T-35 Pillans from Chile.

EQUIPMENT

Interception:
Northrop F-5E Tiger II
Attack:
Cessna A/OA-37B Dragonfly
COIN:
Cessna A/OA-37B Dragonfly
Transport:
Douglas C-118A Liftmaster
Lockheed C-130A Hercules
Douglas C-47 Dakota
IAI-201 Arava
Bell 412SP
Bell UH-1B/H Iroquois
VIP Transport:
IAI-1123 Jet Commander
IAI-1124 Westwind II
Dassault-Breguet Falcon 20
Communications/Liaison:
Rockwell Commander 114
Cessna 172
Cessna 180
Cessna 185
Training:
Cessna T-41D Mescalero
ENAER T-35 Pillan
Embraer EMB-312 Tucano
CASA C.101BB Aviojet
Northrop F-5F Tiger II

JAMAICA

PART OF THE unified Jamaica Defence Force (JDF), the Air Wing is principally concerned with performing missions in support of other JDF elements such as the infantry, Coast Guard and Police. Tasks include observation, search-and-rescue (SAR) patrol, liaison and anti-drugs surveillance, and approximately a dozen aircraft and helicopters are operated.

EQUIPMENT

Maritime Patrol:
Pilatus Britten-Norman BN-2A Islander
Beech King Air 100
SAR:
Bell 206B JetRanger
Transport:
Pilatus Britten-Norman BN-2A Islander
VIP Transport:
Beech King Air 100
Communications/Liaison:
Cessna 210
Cessna 337G Skymaster
Bell 222
Bell 212

MEXICO

BESET BY financial difficulties such as a huge external debt, rampant inflation and declining oil revenues, plans to modernize the *Fuerza Aérea Mexicana* (FAM: Mexican Air Force) have not progressed as smoothly as desired and have lately centred around the procurement of mostly second-hand equipment such as the Lockheed T-33A. For the most part, FAM hardware is optimized for the counter-insurgency (COIN) role, but it does have a small fighter element in the form of the F-5E Tiger II.

Management of the FAM — which is essentially a component of the Mexican Army — is vested in the Ministry of Defence and operations are mainly concentrated at just eight air bases. Of these, by far the most important is Santa Lucia, which is home to five of the nine Air Groups that comprise the operational forces of the FAM. With just one exception, each Air Group controls the activities of two squadrons which normally have similar roles and equipment, even though they may not necessarily be at the same base.

With regard to jet equipment, the FAM is poorly equipped and has chosen to concentrate its limited resources with the 7th Air Group at Santa Lucia. The most potent type is undoubtedly the F-5E Tiger II which serves with No.401 Squadron. Nine of the 10 F-5Es and both F-5Fs that were delivered in 1984 remain in use today, alongside about 30 T/AT-33As that are active with No.202 Jet Fighter Squadron on (COIN) and pure training tasks.

Other combat-capable assets consist of three Air Groups equipped with the Pilatus PC-7 Turbo-Trainer, Mexico having taken delivery of 85 examples of this popular Swiss design between 1979 and 1987. Active with the 2nd, 3rd and 4th Air Groups, the six PC-7 Air Fighter Squadrons (Nos.201 and 203-207) are distributed amongst six different bases so as to extend their operational coverage.

One more Air Group has a limited combat potential, this being the 1st at Santa Lucia with three subordinate squadrons. No.208 Aircraft Squadron operates IAI-201 Aravas which may undertake armed attack missions with machine-guns and rockets, while No.209 Aircraft Squadron is purely helicopter-equipped, using types such as the Bell 47G, UH-1H Iroquois and Bell 206 JetRanger for a variety of tasks. Finally, the 1st Air Group also manages the Mixed Tactical Training Squadron which utilizes the PC-7 and T-28A Trojan for advanced instruction at Zapopan, it being no coincidence that this air base is also home for the FAM's Training School.

Remaining Air Groups are all concerned with facets of the airlift role. Three are at Santa Lucia, No.5 having two Aero Commander squadrons for light transport and aerial survey; No.6 having two heavy air transport squadrons equipped with examples of the DC-4/C-54, DC-6/C-118 and DC-7, although these are gradually being replaced by a batch of 10 second-hand C-130A Hercules; and No.9 having two medium air transport squadrons with about a dozen C-47 Dakotas. The remaining Air Group — No.8 at Mexico City — is a VIP outfit and has separate Presidential and Executive transport squadrons, flying a mixed fleet of fixed-wing aircraft and helicopters that includes the Boeing 727 and 737.

Below: Neatly arranged outside Beech's plant in Wichita, Kansas, a quintet of FAM F33C Bonanzas await their ferry pilots prior to commencing the flight down to Mexico.

EQUIPMENT

Interception:
Northrop F-5E Tiger II
Attack:
Lockheed AT-33A
COIN:
Lockheed AT-33A
Pilatus PC-7 Turbo-Trainer
IAI-201 Arava
Transport:
Lockheed C-130H Hercules
Douglas DC-7
Douglas DC-6/C-118
Douglas DC-4/C-54
Douglas C-47 Dakota
Boeing Canada Buffalo
Fairchild-Hiller FH.227D
Shorts Skyvan 3M
IAI-201 Arava
Pilatus Britten-Norman BN-2A Islander
Cessna 310
Aerospatiale SA.330J Puma
Bell 212
Bell UH-1H Iroquois
VIP Transport:
Boeing 727
Boeing 737
Lockheed Jetstar 8
Grumman Gulfstream II
Rockwell Sabreliner 40/60/75A
Cessna 500 Citation
Aerospatiale AS.332L Super Puma
Bell 212
Agusta A.109A Hirundo
Aerial Survey:
Rockwell Aero Commander 500S
Communications/Liaison:
Rockwell Aero Commander 500S
Rockwell Commander 680
Beech King Air 90/200
Swearingen Metro
Swearingen Merlin III
Beech Queen Air B80
Piper PA-23 Aztec
Training:
Avions Mudry CAP.10
Beech Musketeer
Beech F.33C Bonanza
North American T-28A Trojan
Pilatus PC-7 Turbo-Trainer
Lockheed T-33A
Northrop F-5F Tiger II
Miscellaneous Duties:
Aerospatiale SA.316B Alouette II
Bell 206B JetRanger
Bell 206L LongRanger
Bell 47G

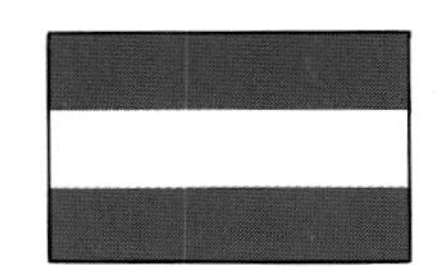

NICARAGUA

WITH the election of a right-wing government accetpable to the USA, in 1990, the long and drawn out war between left-wing *Sandanista* forces and the US-backed *Contra* rebels has all but ended. But the legacy of Nicaragua's decade of left-wing rule is still clear for all to see, especially in the composition of the *Fuerza Aérea Nicaragua* (FAN:Nicaraguan Air Force), which continues to operate an odd assortment of equipment including some that was supplied by Cuba and Libya.

It is now known that the reports of MiG fighters being delivered to the Sandanistas were spurious, and the most potent aircraft in the FAN's inventory is the Czech-built L-39ZO Albatros, half-a-dozen of which are used for both attack and counter-insurgency (COIN) duties. These are backed up by a handful of SF.260WL Warriors donated by Libya, and by a modest number of Mil Mi-25 "Hind-D" gunship helicopters. Approximately three-dozen Mil Mi-17 "Hips" can also be armed, their principal role being that of assault transport.

Remaining FAN transport resources are confined to barely a dozen aircraft, made up in the main of Soviet-built types, the most numerous of which is the An-2 "Colt", with six on charge. No doubt the change of government will affect the composition of the transport fleet in due course, but for now the influence of the USA is confined to 10 Cessna "singles" and a lone OH-6A Cayuse which, on paper at least, form the backbone of the FAN's communications and liaison force. However, the condition of this equipment is in doubt, for the USA's hostility towards the *Sandanista* regime manifested itself in many ways, including an embargo on the supply of spare parts.

EQUIPMENT

Attack:
Aero L-39ZO Albatros
Mil Mi-25 "Hind-D"
Mil Mi-17 "Hip-E/H"
COIN:
SIAI-Marchetti SF.260WL Warrior
Transport:
Antonov An-26 "Curl"
Douglas C-47 Dakota
IAI-201 Arava
Antonov An-2 "Colt"
CASA C-212 Aviocar
Mil Mi-17 "Hip-E/H"
Communications/Liaison:
Cessna 180
Cessna U-17
Mil Mi-2 "Hoplite"
Aerospatiale Alouette III
McDonnell Douglas OH-6A Cayuse
Training:
SIAI-Marchetti SF.260WL Warrior
Aero L-39C Albatros

Above: Prior to the invasion of Panama by US forces during December 1989, the FAP operated this Cessna 421 twin as a communications and liaison aircraft.

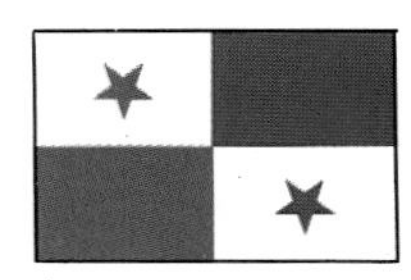

PANAMA

ALTHOUGH IT was at one time expected to receive about 10 Cessna A-37B Dragonflies with which to form a combat element, there is no evidence to show that these have been delivered to the *Fuerza Aérea Panamena* (FAP: Panamanian Air Force). In the wake of the US invasion in December 1989, it now seems unlikely that they will materialize in the immediate future and the status of the (FAP) is still unclear, although it is known that some aircraft and helicopters were damaged by US troops intent on securing airport and airfield installations during Operation "*Just Cause*". Prior to the invasion, the FAP had about 60 aircraft and helicopters on strength, these mostly being used in routine transport tasks from three major bases at Albrook, France Field and Tocumen, as well as other smaller installations.

Surprisingly, despite the close proximity of the USA, few were obtained from that source, either by direct purchase or as part of the Military Assistance Program. Instead, US interests in Panama — and, specifically, the Panama Canal — were protected by a small number of permanently-based Cessna A-37Bs backed up by Air National Guard A-7D Corsair IIs.

EQUIPMENT

Transport:
Airtech CN.235M
CASA C.212 Aviocar
Pilatus Britten-Norman BN-2A Islander
Boeing Canada Twin Otter
Aerospatiale AS.332L Super Puma
Bell UH-1H/N Iroquois
VIP Transport:
Boeing 727-100
LearJet 35
Aerospatiale AS.332L Super Puma
Bell UH-1N Iroquois
Communications/Liaison:
Piper PA-31 Navajo
Piper PA-31T Cheyenne
Cessna 206
Cessna U-17
Cessna 172
Training:
ENAER T-35D Pillan

PARAGUAY

SURVIVING examples of the 10 licence-built Embraer EMB-326GB Xavantes received in 1980-82 constitute the principal combat echelon of the *Fuerza Aérea Paraguay* (FAP: Paraguayan Air Force) which has its headquarters and main base at Campo Grande in Asuncion. Used in counter-insurgency tasks, the Xavantes are complemented by a small number of lightly-armed AT-6G Texans. The FAP also has a sizeable transport component equipped with examples of the long-serving C-47 Dakota and CASA 212 Aviocar plus a solitary C-131D Samaritan, all being operated by *Transportes Aereo Militar* (TAM) which can be augmented by Paraguay's national airline should the need arise. Training equipment has recently been updated with the receipt of half-a-dozen Embraer EMB-312 Tucanos, but some of the older Aerotec T-23 Uirapurus and Neiva T-25 Universals are still active. Communications and liaison tasks are satisfied by a few single and twin-engined Cessnas.

EQUIPMENT

COIN:
Embraer EMB-326GB Xavante
North American AT-6G Texan
Transport:
Convair C-131D Samaritan
Douglas C-47 Dakota
CASA C.212 Aviocar
Boeing Canada Twin Otter
Bell UH-1B Iroquois
Communications/Liaison:
Cessna 421
Cessna 337 Skymaster
Cessna U-17
Helibras HB.350B Ecureuil
Bell 47G
Training:
Aerotec T-23 Uirapuru
Neiva T-25 Universal
North American T-6D/AT-6G Texan
Embraer EMB-312 Tucano

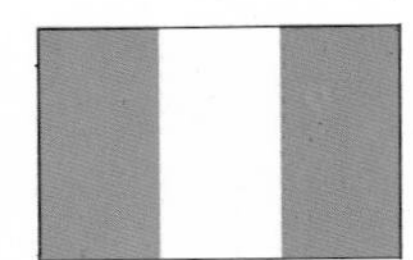

PERU

OPERATING a mixture of hardware obtained from both East and West, the *Fuerza Aerea Peruana* (FAP: Peruvian Air Force) is one of the better-equipped Latin American air arms, and it certainly enjoys quantitative superiority over the neighbouring states of Bolivia, Chile and Ecuador although serviceability of some of the Soviet-supplied equipment is evidently less than ideal.

Combat resources number just over 100 aircraft, these being distributed amongst half-a-dozen Wings, most of which have two Squadrons which usually operate identical equipment. In terms of modernity, the Mirage 2000P tops the list, but funding difficulties have curtailed procurement and Peruvian intentions of purchasing a total of 36 aircraft are unlikely to be satisfied, just 10 2000P single-seaters and two 2000DP two-seat trainers being delivered in 1986-87. These are presently active with one squadron of No.4 Fighter Wing at La Joya, this air base also being home for No.11 Fighter Wing which operates about 12 Su-22 "Fitter-Js" in one squadron as primary equipment, although it may also control A-37B Dragonflies and Mirage 5s detached from other combat outfits.

One other unit has the Sukhoi fighter-bomber, this being No.12 Fighter Wing at Talera, but these are older "Fitter-Fs", about two dozen remaining active along with four examples of the Su-22U "Fitter-E" trainer version. Although principally concerned with pure attack duties, both "Fitter" models have a secondary air-to-air mission for which they are equipped with the AA-2 "Atoll" air defence missile.

Fighter elements are completed by No.6 Wing at Chiclayo, with two squadrons operating Mirage 5Ps and a pair of 5DP two-

Above: A pilot's-eye view of an FAP Cessna A-37B Dragonfly as it lines up for its final approach and landing. Simple and cheap, but highly effective, the A-37B has been used to counter anti-government guerilla forces.

Below: With its highly visible colour scheme signalling its role as a training aircraft, one of the first batch of EMB-312 Tucanos for the FAP formates on the camera-ship.

Right: No.3 Air Wing is responsible for the majority of the FAP's helicopters, many of which, like this pair of Bell 214STs, fly in support of Peruvian Army operations.

seaters which survive from original receipts of 32 and five respectively. Attrition is not the only factor in drastically reducing the size of the Peruvian fleet, for 10 single-seaters were delivered to Argentina as emergency war aid in June 1982 (initially supplied on loan, they were subsequently purchased outright by the FAA).

Like a number of South American air forces, Peru is a long-established user of the Canberra light bomber (receiving its first examples way back in 1956), and No.9 Bomber Wing at Pisco still flies this type today. About 20 aircraft are operational, the FAP's fleet being a rather mixed bag of B(I).8s, B.56s, B(I).68s and B.72s supported by a pair of trainers, and there are no plans to dispose of them in the near future. Another type which has found widespread acceptance within Latin America is the Cessna A-37B Dragonfly light attack/counter-insurgency (COIN) aircraft, and the FAP is no exception, the 7th Attack Wing presently utilizing about 25 survivors of 36 delivered during 1975-77.

Support echelons are consolidated into three Wing organizations, of which arguably the most important is No.3 Air Wing at Lima/Callao. Tasked with managing almost the entire FAP rotary-wing fleet, this has a combat capability in the shape of around two-dozen Mil Mi-24 "Hind" gunships, other helicopters active with the three squadrons of this Wing comprising Mi-6 "Hooks" for heavy-lift tasks, and a variety of smaller types including a trio of Bell 412STs configured for VIP transport. Fixed-wing VIP equipment consists of a pair of DC-8 Srs.62CFs and single examples of the Falcon 20F and F-28 Fellowship 1000, while aircraft employed on tactical transport tasks by No.8 Wing's three other squadrons consist of a single Fairchild-Hiller FH-227, 14 An-32 "Clines" plus similar quantities of the Lockheed Hercules and DHC-5D Buffalo although many of the latter are apparently unserviceable. No.8 Wing's transport assets are completed by a number of light twins including the King Air C90s and the Queen Air A80, and there is also a solitary Boeing 707 tanker which has provided in-flight refuelling support to the FAP's Mirage fleet since 1987.

Also employed in the transport role is No.42 Air Transport Wing at Iquitos with 10 PC-6 Turbo-Porters and 15 DHC-6 Twin Otters, some of which are operated in civil markings. Comprising the *Transportes Aereos Nacionales de la Selva* (TANS: National Jungle Air Transport), these are employed in support of isolated communities in the remote Amazon region and part of the fleet is fitted with floats to permit them to operate from water.

Pilot training is the job of the 51st Air Training Wing at Las Palmas, with T-41A/D Mescaleros, EMB-312 Tucanos and Aermacchi MB.339APs being used to provide primary, basic and advanced flying instruction respectively.

EQUIPMENT

Interception/Attack:
Dassault-Breguet Mirage 2000P
Dassault-Breguet Mirage 5P
Sukhoi Su-22 "Fitter"-F/-J
Mil Mi-24 "Hind"
COIN:
Cessna A-37B Dragonfly
Light Bombing:
BAe Canberra B(I).8/B.56/B(I).68/B.72
Transport:
Lockheed L-100-20/C-130A/D Hercules
Antonov An-32 "Cline"
Boeing Canada Buffalo
Fairchild-Hiller FH-227
Boeing Canada Twin Otter
Pilatus PC-6B/H Turbo-Porter
Mil Mi-6 "Hook"
Mil Mi-8 "Hip"
Bell UH-1H/212/214ST
Tanking/Transport:
Boeing 707-323C
VIP Transport:
Douglas DC-8 Srs.62CF
Fokker F-28 Fellowship 1000
Dassault-Breguet Falcon 20F
Bell 412ST
Aerial Survey:
LearJet 25B/36A
Beech Queen Air A80
Communications/Liaison:
Beech Queen Air A80
Beech King Air C90
Beech 99
Piper PA-31T Cheyenne
Cessna 320 Skynight
Cessna 185 Skywagon
Aerospatiale Alouette III
MBB BO 105CBS
Bell 206B JetRanger
Bell 47G
Training:
Cessna T-41D Mescalero
Embraer EMB-312 Tucano
Aermacchi MB.339AP
Dassault-Breguet Mirage 5DP
Dassault-Breguet Mirage 2000DP
Sukhoi Su-22 "Fitter-E"
BAe Canberra T.4/T.54

SURINAME

ALTHOUGH dignified by the title of Suriname Air Force, this tiny organization is essentially a part of the Army and was only established in 1982, making it one of the most youthful air arms in the world. It has less than 10 aircraft with which to patrol borders and monitor its 240-mile (386km) coastline from airfields at Paramaribo (Zanderij) and Zorg en Hoep; additional tasks including search-and-rescue, transport and liaison. These are undertaken by a motley but reasonably modern fixed- and rotary-wing fleet.

EQUIPMENT

Patrol:
Pilatus PC-7 Turbo-Trainer
Pilatus Britten-Norman BN-2B Defender
Transport:
Pilatus Britten-Norman BN-2B Defender
Bell 205
SAR:
Bell 205
Aerospatiale Alouette III
Communications/Liaison:
Cessna U206
Aerospatiale Alouette III
Training:
Pilatus PC-7 Turbo-Trainer

TRINIDAD & TOBAGO

AT PRESENT, just one aircraft displays the national insignia of the Trinidad & Tobago Defence Force. This is a Cessna 401 which is operated by the tiny air element of the national Defence Force on duties which encompass coastal patrol and liaison. Other equipment with potential military applications consists of three civil-registered helicopters (two Sikorsky S-76s and an SA.341G Gazelle) which are owned and operated by the Ministry of National Security, even though the Gazelle did once carry military markings.

EQUIPMENT

Communications/Liaison:
Cessna 401

URUGUAY

POSSESSING almost exactly 100 aircraft and helicopters, the *Fuerza Aérea Uruguays* (FAU: Uruguayan Air Force) is one of the smaller South American air arms and has only a limited combat potential in the form of a few A-37B Dragonflies and AT-33As obtained from the USA, plus some Pucaras purchased from Argentina. These are assigned to attack and counter-insurgency (COIN) duties.

FAU organization is based upon three major Command agencies, specifically the Tactical Air Command, the Air Training Command and the Air Material Command, but only the first two actually operate aircraft, with the latter looking after maintenance and supply requirements as well as air base infrastructure and communications.

With the exception of a few dedicated trainers, all aircraft and helicopters are assigned to Tactical Air Command which has concentrated its resources as just two air bases. Combat-capable forces are allocated to the II Air Brigade at Santa Bernadina airport, Durazno, which oversees two subordinate squadrons. No.1 Air Squadron operates Pucara turboprop attack aircraft while No.2 Air Squadron is purely jet-equipped, operating the A-37B Dragonflies and Lockheed T/AT-33As, the latter including six that were delivered in 1989. Also resident at this base is the FAU's Advanced Flying Training Centre which utilizes 16 T-34 Mentors, Cessna U-17As and a PA-18 Super Cub as a lead-in for pilots destined to join the ranks of either No.1 or No.2 Air Squadrons.

Other Tactical Air Command equipment is to be found with I Air Brigade and is principally concerned with transport tasks, three of the five squadrons constituting *Transporte Aereo Militar Uruguayo* (TAMU) which is fundamentally a military "airline" that operates in support of the state airline PLUNA. In consequence, most of its aircraft wear dual civil/military insignia.

Elements which make up TAMU are No.3 Squadron with five Queen Air 80s and a trio of CASA C.212 Aviocars (including one with radar for maritime surveillance), No.4

Right: First flown as long ago as 1935, the North American T-6 Texan soldiers on in small numbers around the world. The FAU flew as many as 48 T-6Gs in the past, but now just two are left in military service.

Left: A total of six FMA IA.58A Pucaras form the "teeth" of No.1 Air Squadron (Attack), FAU, the aircraft having been delivered in 1976. Exactly one third of the Pucara force is seen here, with both aircraft carrying 25lb (11.35kg) practice bombs on their centreline racks.

EQUIPMENT

Light Attack COIN:
Cessna A-37B Dragonfly
FMA IA.58A Pucara
Lockheed T/AT-33A Shooting Star
Transport:
Fokker F-27 Friendship 100
Fairchild-Hiller FH-227D
CASA C.212 Aviocar
Embraer EMB-110C Bandeirante
Beech Queen Air 80
Aerial Surveillance:
Embraer EMB-110B1 Bandeirante
Rockwell Commander 680
SAR/Maritime Patrol:
CASA C.212 Aviocar
Training:
Cessna T-41D Mescalero
Beech T-34A/B Mentor
North American T-6 Texan
Cessna U-17A
Communications/Liaison:
Cessna 182A
Cessna U-17A
Piper PA-18 Super Cub
Bell UH-1B/H Iroquois
Bell 212

Squadron with one FH-227 and two F-27s and No.6 Squadron with four EMB-110C Bandeirantes. Remaining units at Carrasco are No.5 Squadron with all of the FAU's helicopters (Bell 212s and UH-1B/H Iroquois) plus one or two Cessna U-17As for liaison and communications, and the Aerial Survey Squadron which operates single examples of the EMB-110B1 Bandeirante and the Rockwell Commander 680, both of which are camera-equipped.

Training activity is undertaken by the *Escuela Militar de Aviacion* (Military Aviation School) at Pando. This offers primary, basic and advanced tuition on T-41D Mescaleros and T-34 Mentors, students thereafter moving to the transport force for "hands on" training or to the Advanced Flying Training Centre if they have been selected to undergo fast jet tuition.

A few other aircraft are currently in service as "hacks" and for liaison duties. At Camina de Mendoza, about half-a-dozen assorted Texans are used for proficiency flying by officers at Air Force headquarters, and there is also a small communications element at Durazno with a single Cessna 182, a Super Cub and one or two Cessna U-17As, although the latter two types are shared with the training unit at this base.

Below: Two of three FH-227Ds remain in FAU service with No.4 Air Squadron, based at Carrasco since 1970-71. The two aircraft serve alongside a pair of standard F-27s, these having been delivered to the FAU in 1970.

VENEZUELA

WITH A combat force made up of equipment obtained from Canada, France, the United Kingdom and the United States, the *Fuerza Aérea Venezolanas* (FAV: Venezuelan Air Force) is keen to implement an ambitious modernization programme although like many South American states it has to keep a fairly tight rein on the financial purse-strings. Nevertheless, it has already taken some steps to enhance capability by purchasing an additional batch of Mirage 50s and setting aside funds to permit upgrading of its existing fleet by Dassault-Breguet in the early-1990s. In addition, it is also negotiating with Holland over the supply of a modest number of surplus NF-5s as attrition replacements for the Canadair-built VF-5s that it presently operates.

FAV organization is based upon the existence of four major Commands, one of which (Air Logistics Command) is purely a support agency with no aircraft of its own. Of the other three, the Air Combat Command is by far the most significant, for it is this which directs day-to-day activity by the six front-line Wings that currently exist, each usually possessing a pair of subordinate Squadrons.

Left: Camouflaged A-27 and silver T-27 Tucanos are used by the FAV for COIN and pilot training tasks respectively.

Below: Nos.161 and 162 Squadrons, FAV, are the only two units in South America to operate the F-16 Fighting Falcon.

Right: The versatility of the helicopter has long been appreciated by the FAV, and they continue to be used in a variety of roles including COIN, SAR and fire-fighting. A sole Bell 412ST (illustrated) acts as a VIP transport.

Three of those six Wings operate fighters, with the FAV's newest and most potent warplane being the F-16 Fighting Falcon. Delivery of 18 F-16As and six F-16B two-seaters was accomplished during 1983-85 for service with No.16 Wing at Maracay, but Venezuela is known to want at least a dozen more such aircraft and would ideally like to obtain as many as 48.

Of older vintage, the ubiquitous Mirage continues to make a worthwhile contribution to national defence, but many of the FAV's original fleet of IIIEVs and 5Vs have been destroyed and only about six remain in use with No.11 Wing along with one 5DV trainer. All are due to be upgraded to Mirage 50 standard once the seven aircraft that formed the subject of a 1988 order have been delivered during 1990-91.

Attrition has also resulted in the once 20-strong fleet of Canadair CF-5A/D fighters being cut, No.12 Wing presently operating 12 aircraft from the air base at Barquisimeto. Updating during the mid- to late-1980s has resulted in the 10 surviving single-seaters being redesignated as VF-5As, but both two-seaters are still referred to as CF-5Ds.

The future of the FAV's sole Bomb Wing (No.13 at Barcelona) is, however, far less assured, for it is known that the surviving Canberras are earmarked for withdrawal. Original deliveries were accomplished between 1952 and 1965 with the FAV obtaining 30 aircraft of various marks, and 18 of these were returned to Britain between 1974 and 1980 for refurbishment although less than 10 remained airworthy in the late-1980s.

Other Air Combat Command resources are primarily concerned with counter-insurgency (COIN), with a Wing at Maracaibo utilizing a mixture of OV-10E Broncos and EMB-312 Tucanos, although the latter may actually function as an operational training element. There is also a helicopter-equipped Wing with Alouette IIIs and Bell UH-1 Iroquois, some being configured for armed border patrol.

Air Transport Command is a somewhat smaller organization but does control three subordinate Wings, one of which is a Presidential Flight that is mainly concerned with VIP tasks. Recent efforts at modernization appear to have resulted in the withdrawal of the last Fairchild C-123B Providers and C-47 Dakotas, with tactical airlift operations now being concentrated within No.5 Wing and No.6 Wing at Caracas-La Carlota and Palo Negro respectively. The former organization has half-a-dozen Aeritalia G.222 cargo aircraft and also maintains a sizeable fleet of light twins for communications, including a few King Airs, Queen Airs, Falcon 20s and Cessna Citation Is, while the latter has six C-130H Hercules. For VIP airlift, No.4 Wing at La Carlota uses single examples of the Boeing 737, Gulfstream II and III and Learjet 24D plus three Cessna 550 Citation IIs and a pair of Bell 412s, although the latter have recently been joined by a small number of AS.332M Super Pumas.

Responsibility for providing aircrew is allotted to the Air Training Command which has a Military Aviation School (No.14 Training Wing) at Maracay. Instruction begins with a primary phase on the T-34A Mentor, with students progressing to the EMB-312 Tucano and the T-2D Buckeye for basic and advanced tuition. Plans to organize a Training and Tactical Support Wing have long been mooted but have evidently failed to reach fruition and are unlikely to do so until such time as the FAV turns its attentions to the purchase of a suitable armed trainer, like the BAe Hawk.

Limited numbers of light planes are employed by the FAV for liaison duties, these for the most part being made up of Cessna "singles" plus a handful of Helibras HB.350B Esquilo helicopters.

EQUIPMENT

Interception/Attack:
General Dynamics F-16A Fighting Falcon
Dassault-Breguet Mirage IIIEV/5V/50
Canadair VF-5A Freedom Fighter
Light Bombing:
BAe Canberra B.82/B(I).88
COIN:
Rockwell OV-10E Bronco
Embraer EMB-312 Tucano
Reconnaissance:
BAe Canberra PR.83
Transport:
Lockheed C-130H Hercules
Aeritalia G.222
Aerospatiale AS.332M Super Puma
Bell UH-1B/D/H Iroquois
Bell 212
VIP Transport:
Boeing 737-2N1
Gulfstream II/III
Cessna 550 Citation
LearJet 24D
Bell 412
Communications/Liaison:
Dassault-Breguet Falcon 20
Cessna 500 Citation I
Beech King Air 200
Beech Queen Air 65/80
Cessna 172/180/182N
Aerospatiale SA.316B Alouette III
Bell 206 JetRanger
Helibras HB.350B Esquilo
Training:
Beech T-34A Mentor
Embraer EMB-312 Tucano
Rockwell T-2D Buckeye
Canadair CF-5D Freedom Fighter
Dassault-Breguet Mirage 5DV
General Dynamics F-16B Fighting Falcon
BAe Canberra T.84

Right: The FAV procured a total of 24 Rockwell T-2D Buckeye advanced trainers in all, half of which were finished in a red and white scheme and assigned to the *Escuela de Aviacion Militar* (EAM: School of Military Aviation).

OCEANIA

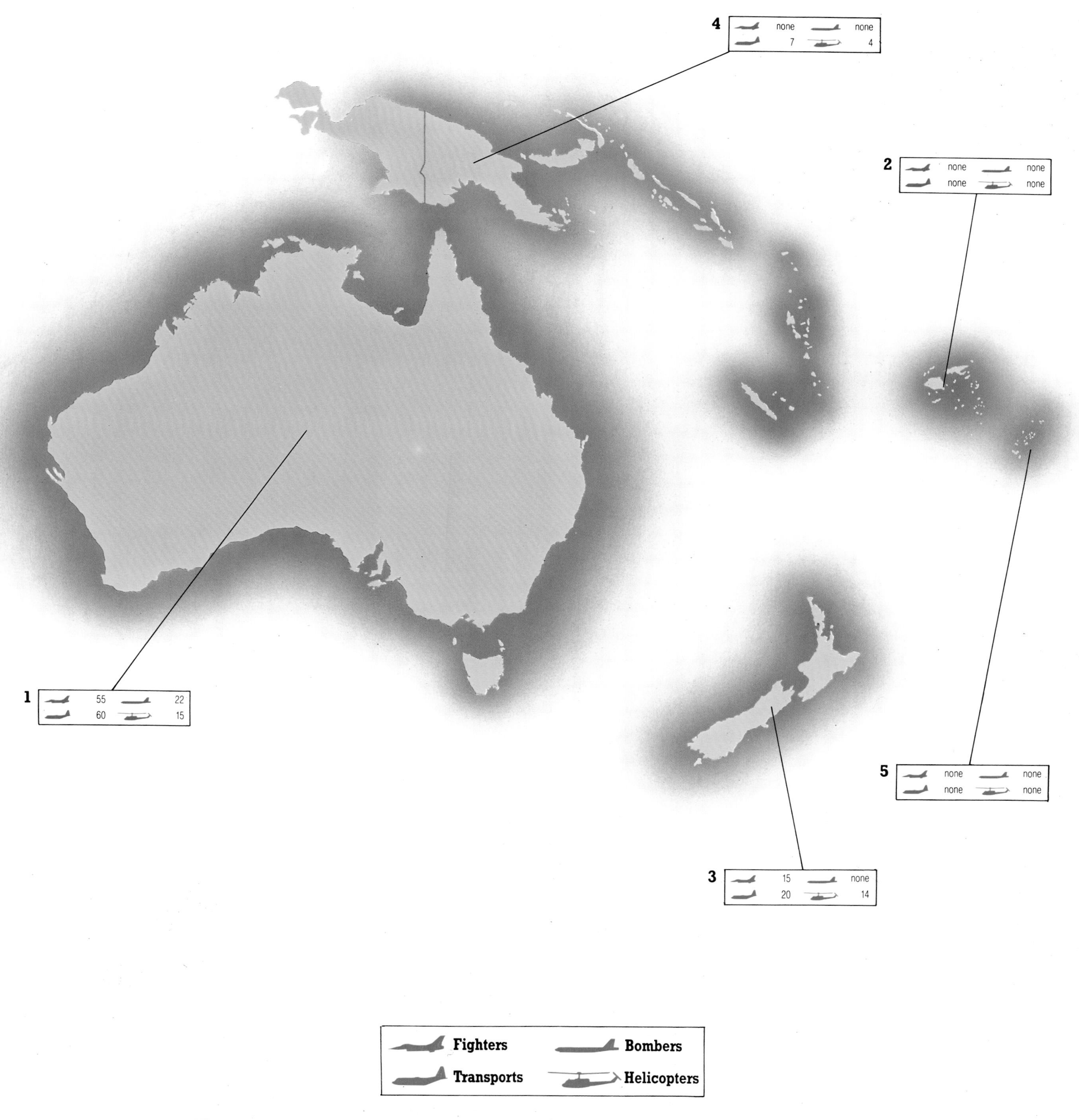
4
none
none
7
4
2
none
none
none
none
1
55
22
60
15
5
none
none
none
none
3
15
none
20
14
Fighters
Bombers
Transports
Helicopters

AUSTRALIA

EASILY THE most powerful air arm in the region, the Royal Australian Air Force (RAAF) has recently been engaged in a fairly major reorganization, and operational assets are now established along functional lines, with separate Group elements controlling the revelant forces engaged in strike/reconnaissance, tactical fighter, maritime patrol, airlift and tactical transport operations.

Strike/reconnaissance capability is vested in two squadrons (Nos.1 and 6) which are equipped with the General Dynamics F-111. Both are resident at Amberley and fly the 18 surviving examples from the original F-111C order plus a quartet of ex-USAF F-111As that were obtained as attrition replacements at a later date. Four of the original machines are now configured for reconnaissance tasks, relying on a pallet-mounted installation featuring cameras, an infra-red linescan sensor and a TV system. Known as RF-111Cs, they are flown by No.6 Squadron. Other RAAF "Aardvarks" (flown by both squadrons) have been fitted with the "*Pave Tack*" forward-looking infra-red and laser designator sensor (FLIR) package which is designed to permit extremely accurate "first-pass" attacks in all kinds of weather, by day or night.

Further updating of F-111 avionics is in prospect so as to ensure that they remain viable and effective well into the 21st Century; compatibility with new weapons such as the AGM-88A high-speed anti-radiation missile (HARM) is also under consideration.

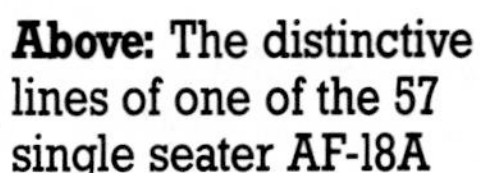

Above: The distinctive lines of one of the 57 single seater AF-18A Hornets supplied to the RAAF, and serving with four squadrons.

Below: Two RAAF units have the distinction of operating the only F-111s ever to have been exported by the United States of America.

All of the 57 AF-18A single-seat and 18 AF-18B two-seat Hornets that were ordered in 1981 have now been delivered, this outstanding aircraft being primarily tasked with air defence, its principal air-to-air weapons being the radar-guided AIM-7 Sparrow and the infra-red homing AIM-9 Sidewinder missiles. However, the Hornet's genuine multi-mission capability means it is equally at home in attack duties and pilots do routinely train to master both of these air warfare disciplines. All four Hornet outfits — which include an Operational Conversion Unit — come under the control of the Tactical Fighter Group.

Maritime reconnaissance and anti-submarine (ASW) warfare is undertaken by a total of 20 Lockheed P-3C Orions. Stationed at Edinburgh, they are evenly distributed between Nos.10 and 11 Squadrons. Airlift resources include a dozen examples of each of the C-130E (No.37 Squadron) and C-130H Hercules (No.36 Squadron), both units being resident at Richmond. Other transport aircraft in RAAF service include six Boeing 707s, four of which are presently being converted to dual tanker/transport configuration by Israel Aircraft Industries, while five Falcon 900s have recently been delivered for the transportation of VIPs.

Tactical transport resources are spearheaded by the long-serving DHC-4 Caribou which serves with two squadrons (No.35 at Townsville and No.38 at Richmond). Plans to replace these veterans have had to be shelved in the immediate future due partly to a lack of finance and partly to the unavailability of a suitable replacement; an alternative under consideration is the re-engining of surviving Caribous with turbine powerplants.

RAAF tactical airlift forces also include an assortment of rotary-winged 'craft, but the heavy-lift Chinooks have been retired and placed in storage pending a decision over their future. As far as other rotary elements are concerned, these are all slated for transfer to the Army (which is to assume responsibility for tactical helicopter operations) over a five-year period which began in 1989 and some of the two-dozen UH-1H Iroquois have already gone, with the balance to follow in due course. In similar fashion, the Army is to operate all 39 Sikorsky Black Hawk helicopters that were originally ordered for RAAF use, as well as about 18 Ecureuils used for training and search-and-rescue (SAR) tasks.

Pilot training begins on the CT-4 Airtrainer, which is used for screening and primary tuition. Those who successfully negotiate the first hurdle move on to the Pilatus PC-9, and the search has begun for a new jet trainer to replace the Macchi MB.326H which is used for the final stage of training at the present time. Candidates for this potentially valuable order include the BAe Hawk, Aermacchi MB.339C and Dassault-Breguet Alpha Jet. Training of navigators is undertaken on eight examples of the Hawker Siddeley HS.748, and the RAAF inventory still includes a couple of C-47 Dakotas which serve with the Air Research and Development Unit (ARDU).

EQUIPMENT

Interception:
McDonnell Douglas AF-18A Hornet
Strike:
General Dynamics F-111C
Attack:
McDonnell Douglas AF-18A Hornet
Reconnaissance:
General Dynamics RF-111C
In-Flight Refuelling:
Boeing 707-320C
Maritime Patrol/ASW:
Lockheed P-3C Orion
Transport:
Lockheed C-130E/H Hercules
Boeing Canada Caribou
Boeing 707-320C
BAe 748
Bell UH-1H Iroquois
VIP Transport:
Dassault-Breguet Falcon 900
Utility/Liaison:
GAF Nomad Mission Master
Training:
CT.4 Airtrainer
HDH (Pilatus) PC-9/A
Aermacchi MB.326H
McDonnell Douglas AF-18B Hornet
BAe 748
Training SAR:
Aerospatiale AS.350 Ecureuil
Test and Evaluation:
Douglas C-47 Dakota

Above: Vast tracts of territorial waters to be patrolled have led the RAAF to procure a sizeable force of P-3 Orion ASW aircraft.

Below: Latest addition to the RAAF's training inventory, the Pilatus PC-9/A is built under licence by the Hawker De Havilland company.

FIJI

THE MODEST defence budget of this small republic allows it to maintain only a token defence force of just over 3,000 personnel, but it is intended to initiate further expansion and plans are in hand to raise personnel levels to around the 5,000 mark. At present, defence of Fiji relies on integrated ground and naval elements and there is no air component. However, as part of the anticipated growth programme, Fiji has indicated that it will buy sufficient helicopters to permit the creation of an airborne battalion. At the time of writing, these helicopters have yet to be chosen, but it is possible that an air arm may be organized to operate them within the framework of the integrated defence force.

Above: Upgraded and updated, the RNZAF's A-4 Skyhawk IIs are likely to continue in front-line use for several more years.

NEW ZEALAND

FROM ITS headquarters in Wellington, the Royal New Zealand Air Force (RNZAF) directs the activities of two subordinate Group organizations with responsibility for day-to-day activities. Of the two, the Operations Group is undoubtedly the most significant, for it is this which controls the limited amount of combat-ready resources from a command post at Auckland.

Front-line forces are headed by No.75 Squadron, which utilizes A-4K Skyhawks for maritime attack and conventional close air support tasks. Resident at Ohakea, it serves alongside No.2 Squadron which functions as an operational conversion and fighter tactics development unit, with a few A-4Ks and most of the TA-4K two-seat trainers. Like many Skyhawk operators, the RNZAF has undertaken extensive updating of this long-serving warplane and its fleet now embodies a revamped avionics suite incorporating much new technology. At the same time, they have acquired the ability to operate with weapons such as the AGM-65 Maverick air-to-surface missile.

Ohakea is also home to No.14 Squadron which is equipped with the survivors of 16 BAe.167 Strikemaster Mk.88s, using these for advanced flying training, a task that includes tuition in the fighter attack mission. After evaluating a number of candidates, New Zealand elected in early-1990 to purchase 18 examples of the Aermacchi MB.339C as a Strikemaster replacement, and delivery of these should be completed by 1992, at which time the Strikemaster will be retired from service.

Other Operations Group assets include No.5 Squadron with half-a-dozen P-3K Orions for maritime patrol and anti-submarine warfare (ASW). Already the subject of one modernization programme since they entered service, these are to be further updated with revised avionics and acoustic processing equipment. Transport resources are also part of the Operations Group empire and include one squadron operating Andover C.1s obtained second-hand from the UK, one squadron with five C-130H Hercules and two Boeing 727-100Cs, and one squadron with about a dozen Bell UH-1H Iroquois helicopters. As well as transport tasks, search-and-rescue (SAR) duties are performed by the UH-1Hs.

Support Group is predominantly concerned with training and second-line functions such as communications and liaison, and virtually all of its flying is performed from the base at Wigram, conveniently close to Group headquarters in Christchurch. Equipment in use with the Flying Training Wing comprises CT-4B Airtrainers, Airtourers and Bell 47Gs for pilot training plus a trio of F-27 Friendship 100s which are used for navigation training. In addition, Support Group operates three Cessna 421Cs for VIP, liaison and communications tasks. Other, non-flying elements within the Support Group are concerned with technical training, logistics and repair functions.

Left: An aircraft that will soon depart from the RNZAF inventory, the Strikemaster Mk.88 is giving way to the Aermacchi MB.339C.

EQUIPMENT

Attack/Close Air Support:
McDonnell Douglas A-4K Skyhawk II
Maritime Patrol/ASW:
Lockheed P-3K Orion
Transport:
Lockheed C-130H hercules
Boeing 727-100C
BAe Andover C.1
Bell UH-1H Iroquois
VIP Transport/Utility:
Cessna 421C
SAR:
Bell UH-1H Iroquois
Training:
Aerospace CT-4B Airtrainer
Victa Airtourer
BAe Strikemaster Mk.88
McDonnell Douglas A-4K/TA-4K Skyhawk II
Fokker F-27 Friendship 100
Bell 47G

Right: A Bell UH-1H Iroquois flown by No.3 Squadron, RNZAF, as it flares for landing.

PAPUA NEW GUINEA

COASTAL and border patrol are the principal missions performed by the air element of Papua New Guinea's integrated Defence Force, but barely a dozen aircraft and helicopters are on charge, these mainly being operated from the international airport at Port Moresby. Routine transport and liaison functions are also satisfied, primarily by a few C-47 Dakotas. Other types comprise four GAF Nomad Mission Masters and three IAI Aravas. The former are fitted with search radar and are mostly tasked with coastal surveillance, while the latter divide their time between transport tasks and patrolling the border with Indonesia.

Australian financial and technical aid was instrumental in the creation of the air component and this support continues, with its most recent manifestation being the supply of a quartet of Bell UH-1H Iroquois utility helicopters. More new equipment is urgently needed, particularly for the transport role since the veteran C-47s are now nearing the end of their useful lives. Two contenders have been short-listed to satisfy Papua New Guinea's needs, namely the Shorts Sherpa and the CASA-Nurtanio CN-235M. The quantity involved in any order that is forthcoming is unlikely to exceed five aircraft.

Below: Support for the PNG Defence Force from Australia has included the delivery of several GAF N22 Nomad Mission Master aircraft. Four of these are currently in use, providing this nation with a coastal patrol capability.

Above: As with so many other small air arms around the world, the PNG Defence Force is reliant on the highly versatile C-47 Dakota to provide a credible transport capability.

EQUIPMENT

Coastal Patrol:
GAF Nomad Mission Master
IAI Arava
Transport:
Douglas C-47 Dakota
IAI Arava
Utility:
Bell UH-1H Iroquois

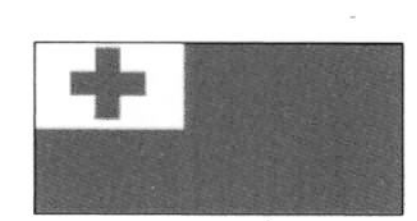

TONGA

TONGA established an independent air arm in 1986, equipping it with a solitary example of the Victa Airtourer. Current status of this machine and, indeed, of Tonga's Air Force is uncertain.

EQUIPMENT

General Purpose:
Victa Airtourer

EUROPE

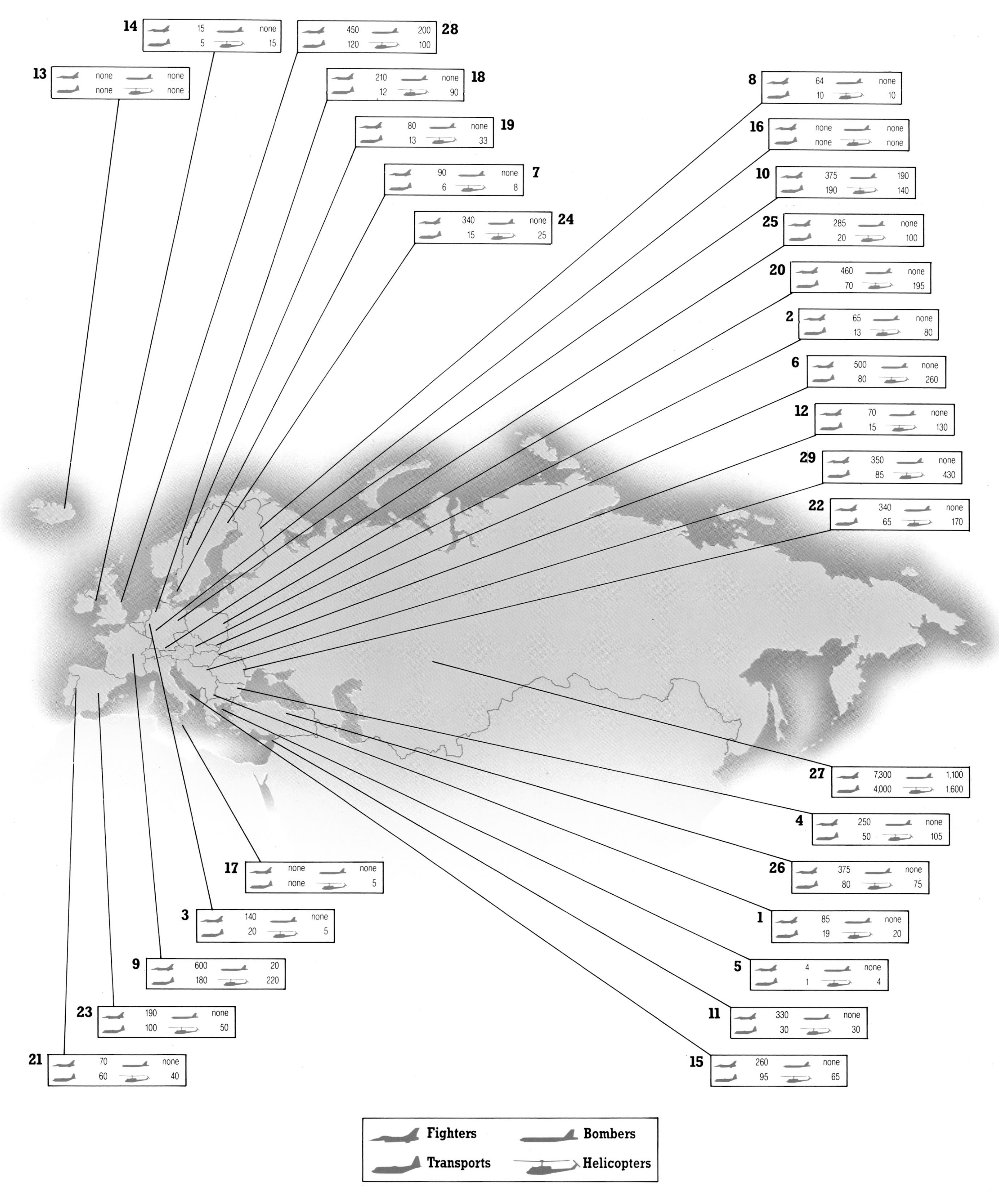

14 15 none 5 15
28 450 200 120 100
13 none none none none
18 210 none 12 90
19 80 none 13 33
7 90 none 6 8
24 340 none 15 25
8 64 none 10 10
16 none none none none
10 375 190 190 140
25 285 none 20 100
20 460 none 70 195
2 65 none 13 80
6 500 none 80 260
12 70 none 15 130
29 350 none 85 430
22 340 none 65 170
27 7,300 1,100 4,000 1,600
4 250 none 50 105
26 375 none 80 75
1 85 none 19 20
5 4 none 1 4
11 330 none 30 30
15 260 none 95 65
17 none none none 5
3 140 none 20 5
9 600 20 180 220
23 190 none 100 50
21 70 none 60 40
Fighters
Bombers
Transports
Helicopters

ALBANIA

DESPITE adhering to Communist political doctrine, Albania has been determinedly isolationist for much of the post-war era, although there are signs that it is at last beginning to emerge from its self-imposed cocoon. As far as military equipment is concerned, the Albanian People's Army Air Force operates hardware of mainly Soviet origin (albeit of Chinese manufacture); a legacy of an association that terminated in the late-1970s after the death of Mao Tse Tung, when the People's Republic of China moved quite a long way towards the implementation of a rather more liberal and certainly less authoritarian political and military regime.

Front-line elements comprise about 90 fighters and fighter-bombers, headed by some 20 Shenyang F-7s which serve as the primary air defence element alongside three dozen or so examples of the Shenyang F-6. These apparently equip three squadrons and an identical number of units are active in ground attack duties, utilizing the Shenyang F-5 and, possibly, a few Shenyang F-2s.

Transport echelons operate an assortment of true veterans, including about six Lisunov Li-2s (licence-built C-47 Dakotas) and ten Pinkiang C-5s. Three Ilyushin Il-14Ms also come under Air Force control even though they are actually assigned to the national airline, Albtransport, since civil aviation is officially non-existent. Further airlift capability is entrusted to a score of Pinkiang H-5 helicopters.

Mirroring Albania's political isolation, pilot-training requirements are satisfied in-country. The reliance on hardware of Eastern origin dictates that the Yak-11 and Yak-18/Nanchang CJ-5 predominate, alongside Shenyang FT-2 jet trainers.

EQUIPMENT

Interception:
Shenyang F-7
Shenyang F-6
Attack:
Shenyang F-5
Shenyang F-2
Transport:
Ilyushin Il-14M "Crate"
Lisunov Li-2 "Cab"
Pinkiang C-5
Pinkiang H-5
Training:
Yakovlev Yak-11 "Moose"
Yakovlev Yak-18/Nanchang CJ-5 "Max"
Shenyang FT-2

AUSTRIA

TECHNICALLY part of the Army, the *Österreichische Luftstreitkrafte* (Austrian Air Force) has a long tradition of obtaining combat equipment from Sweden, which, like itself, is neutral, although part of that tradition clearly stems from the fact that it took close to two decades to finally settle on a "new" fighter aircraft. This is the SAAB J350e Draken, a total of 24 being delivered during 1987-89 for service with air defence units at Linz-Horsching and Graz-Thalerhof. Prior to that, the "front-line" combat force utilized the SAAB 1050e for air defence and ground attack missions as well as training purposes. About 30 of the 40 that were supplied are still active, but their value must be questionable in so far as combat capability is concerned. Some SAAB 1050es are configured for reconnaissance with sensor pods containing cameras and Infra-Red (IR) linescan being fitted.

Other Austrian Air Force equipment is principally concerned with second-line responsibilities, these including transport, observation and forward air control (FAC), communications/liaison, search-and-rescue (SAR) and training. Pure transport duties are the domain of two BAe 146s and Skyvan 3Ms for those "heavy-lift" needs, and a dozen PC-6B Turbo-Porters. Utility-type missions are mostly the preserve of helicopters, and Austria's geography dictates that quite a substantial fleet is operated. Types in service comprise close to two-dozen examples of each of the Alouette III and the Agusta-Bell 212, plus about a dozen Agusta-Bell 206A JetRangers that are mostly used for pilot training and a similar number of OH-58B Kiowas for observation. Finally, eight elderly Agusta-Bell 204Bs are still operational, with a further dozen in storage pending disposal.

Pilot training is undertaken at Zeltweg and begins on the SAAB Safir, students thereafter being "streamed" to rotary- or fixed-wing types.

EQUIPMENT

Interception:
SAAB-Scania J350e Draken
Attack:
SAAB-Scania 1050e
Observation/FAC:
Cessna O-1E Bird Dog
Bell OH-58B Kiowa
Transport:
BAe 146-100
Short Skyvan 3M
Pilatus PC-6B Turbo-Porter
SAR:
Agusta-Bell AB.206A JetRanger
Aerospatiale Alouette III
Communications/Liaison:
Agusta-Bell AB.212
Agusta-Bell AB.204B
Aerospatiale Alouette III
Training:
SAAB-Scania 91D Safir
Pilatus PC-7 Turbo-Trainer
SAAB-Scania 1050e
Agusta-Bell AB.206A JetRanger

Below: The Austrian Air Force's long tradition of purchasing Swedish military hardware was maintained during the 1980s, when two-dozen ex-Swedish Air Force Drakens were overhauled and upgraded for air defence tasks.

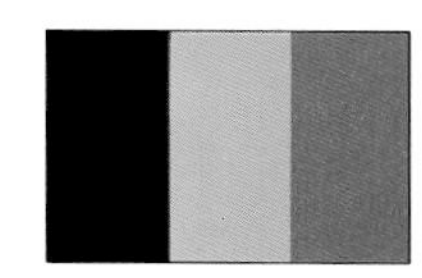

BELGIUM

MAKING a modest contribution to NATO's 2nd Allied Tactical Air Force (2 ATAF), the *Force Aérienne Belge* (FAB: Belgian Air Force) is primarily equipped with the F-16 Fighting Falcon, 138 of which (116 F-16As and 22 F-16Bs) will have been delivered to the FAB when current procurement plans have been completed. These are distributed amongst three double-squadron Fighter Wings and fulfil dual interception and attack duties from air bases at Beauvechain (Nos. 349 and 350 Squadrons/No.1 Wing), Florennes (Nos.1 and 2 Squadrons/No.2 Wing) and Kleine Brogel (Nos.28 and 31 Squadrons/No.10 Wing). Weapons options for use in the interception role are the AIM-9J/M Sidewinder air-to-air missiles (AAMs), and a variety of conventional munitions including cluster-bomb units and airfield denial systems for attack duties. Plans to add the AGM-65 Maverick air-to-surface missile have been shelved on grounds of cost, and budget restraints have also forced the abandonment of a proposal to procure either the General Dynamics Agile Falcon or the Dassault-Breguet Rafale as the next-generation fighter. Instead, surviving F-16s will be subjected to a mid-life update programme.

The Dassault-Breguet Mirage V is the FAB's other current combat type, but the numbers in front-line service have been steadily reduced due to attrition and replacement by the F-16. Plans are in hand to modify a total of 15 VBAs and five VBDs to prolong their service life. Currently, No.3 Wing (Nos.8 and 42 Squadrons) operates a mixed fleet of VBA/D/R models on attack, training and reconnaissance tasks respectively, but the dedicated reconnaissance model is slated for retirement during 1993, when responsibility for such operations will be passed on to Mirage VBAs with pod-mounted sensors. Modified Mirages will serve until the early 21st Century, albeit in quite small numbers.

Pilot training is accomplished in-country, with the basic phase being performed on the SF.260MBs of No.5 Squadron based at Gossoncourt. Students then progress to Brustem for more advanced tuition on the Alpha Jet (Nos.7, 11 and 33 Squadrons), a type also used by No.9 Squadron for the training of instructors.

Financial considerations also look set to reduce the size of the transport force (Nos.20 and 21 Squadrons of No.15 Wing), which is concentrated at Melsbroek. The future of No.21 Squadron look decidedly bleak, since most of its aircraft have been, or will be, disposed of. A dozen C-130H Hercules are operated by No.20 Squadron for tactical airlift purposes. Finally, five Westland-built Sea King Mk.48s are operated by No.40 Squadron, a joint Air Force/Navy unit at Koksjide, to meet SAR requirements in and around Belgian coastal waters.

Above: First ordered by the FAB in 1975, the F-16 Fighting Falcon is quite simply the single most important aircraft type in FAB service.

EQUIPMENT

Interception/Attack:
General Dynamics F-16A Fighting Falcon
Attack:
Dassault-Breguet Mirage VBA
Reconnaissance:
Dassault-Breguet Mirage VBR
Transport:
Lockheed C-130H Hercules
BAe 748 Srs.2A
Dassault-Breguet Falcon 20C
Swearingen Merlin IIIA
Liaison:
Aerospatiale CM.170 Magister
Training:
SIAI-Marchetti SF.260MB
Dassault-Breguet Alpha Jet
Dassault-Breguet Mirage VBD
General Dynamics F-16B Fighting Falcon
SAR:
Westland Sea King Mk.48

Below: The FAB ordered three BAe 748s during 1974, their delivery taking place in 1976

BULGARIA

OPERATING as an element of the Army, the Bulgarian Air Force is entirely equipped with Soviet-supplied hardware (as befits its membership of the Warsaw Pact), and its organization is modelled along Soviet lines with the various operational components being managed by Divisions and Regiments that are task-orientated. Overall command rests with a headquarters in Sofia but many functions are devolved to subordinate echelons. As an example, air defence assets report to a headquarters at Slivan, while tactical resources are directed from Plovdiv.

Air defence is primarily achieved by surface-to-air missile (SAM) forces, but Bulgaria does also have a sizeable contingent of interceptors, the most potent of which are some 30 MiG-23MF "Flogger-Bs". These are supported by just over 100 MiG-21PFM "Fishbed-Fs", while the reconnaissance-dedicated MiG-21RF "Fishbed-H" is also in use although the quantity involved is much smaller, with about 15 examples active on tactical tasks alongside an unspecified number of MiG-25R "Foxbat-Bs" that are employed on strategic reconnaissance. Apart from the USSR, no other Warsaw Pact nation operates this variant of the "Foxbat".

Attack forces have been steadily updated throughout the 1980s, with close to 50 examples each of the MiG-23BN "Flogger-H" and Su-25 "Frogfoot" having been delivered. This has permitted the much older MiG-17 "Fresco" to be progressively withdrawn from the front-line, but as many as 50 are still thought to be in service although their days must now be numbered, as, probably, are those of about a dozen Il-28 "Beagles" used for electronic countermeasures (ECM) tasks.

Battlefield helicopter elements consist of about 40 Mi-24 "Hind" gunships and some 30 Mi-8 "Hips". Other rotary-wing equipment is of a much earlier vintage, but some 20 Mi-4 "Hounds" and a similar number of Mi-2 "Hoplites" are still operated, mostly on a variety of second-line communications and liaison tasks.

Transport duties are satisfied by a somewhat motley assortment of aircraft. Most originate from the Antonov design bureau, with the An-2 "Colt" biplane being most numerous but not necessarily the most useful. About 20 are on hand, backed up by roughly a dozen An-12 "Cubs" and smaller numbers of the An-24 "Coke" and An-26 "Curl", while approximately half-a-dozen An-30 "Clanks" are utilized for aerial survey tasks. In addition, a single Yak-40 "Codling" is employed as a VIP transport.

Training of pilots is undertaken internally, starting on the Yak-11 "Moose" and Yak-18 "Max" piston-engined and progressing via the L-29 Delfin and L-39 Albatros to the MiG-15UTI "Midget". Operational transition is accomplished at squadron level on either the MiG-21U "Mongol" or the MiG-23U "Flogger-C".

A number of Government agencies also operate aircraft and helicopters for civilian-type missions such as aerial spraying, pollution control and fisheries protection. Many of these machines display both civil and military markings.

Above: Though it wears the national insignia of the Bulgarian Air Force for all to see, this elderly Ilyushin Il-14 "Crate" is in fact operated by the Bulgarian Government.

EQUIPMENT

Interception:
Mikoyan-Gurevich MiG-23MF "Flogger-B"
Mikoyan-Gurevich MiG-21PFM "Fishbed-F"
Attack:
Mikoyan-Gurevich MiG-23BN "Flogger-H"
Sukhoi Su-25 "Frogfoot"
Mikoyan-Gurevich MiG-17 "Fresco"
Mil Mi-24 "Hind"
Reconnaissance:
Mikoyan-Gurevich MiG-25R "Foxbat-B"
Mikoyan-Gurevich MiG-21RF "Fishbed-H"
Electronic Warfare:
Ilyushin Il-28 "Beagle"
Transport:
Antonov An-12 "Cub"
Antonov An-24V "Coke"
Antonov An-26 "Curl"
Antonov An-2 "Colt"
Mil Mi-8 "Hip"
VIP Transport:
Yakovlev Yak-40 "Codling"
Aerial Survey:
Antonov An-30 "Clank"
Communications/Liaison:
Mil Mi-4 "Hound"
Mil Mi-2 "Hoplite"
Training:
Yakovlev Yak-11 "Moose"
Yakovlev Yak-18 "Max"
Aero L-29 Delfin
Aero L-39 Albatros
Mikoyan-Gurevich MiG-15UTI "Midget"
Mikoyan-Gurevich MiG-21U "Mongol"
Mikoyan-Gurevich MiG-23U "Flogger-C"

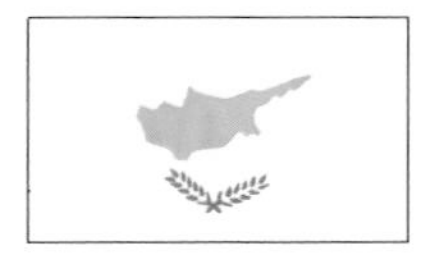

CYPRUS

DESPITE ITS small size, Cyprus has elements of no fewer than five military agencies more or less permanently on its soil, which has been partitioned into Greek and Turkish sectors since the 1974 invasion by Turkey. In consequence, Turkish interests in the north have prompted the Turkish Army to station a substantial garrison on Cyprus, including Cessna U-17 lightplanes and Bell UH-1D Iroquois helicopters at the airfields of Lefkoniko, Nicosia and Salamis. Elsewhere, there is the British sovereign base at Akrotiri which functions as a staging post and armament practice camp in addition to serving as home for a single squadron of Wessex helicopters used for communications and search-and-rescue (SAR) tasks. Other British forces can be found at Dhekelia, where six Army Air Corps Gazelles undertake national and United Nations tasks. US elements are also present in limited quantities, and these usually comprise a single Lockheed U-2R at Akrotiri for strategic reconnaissance of the Mediterranean plus four Army UH-60 Black Hawks for utility transport missions.

Last but by no means least, there is the Cyprus National Guard, a paramilitary organization which protects Greek-Cypriot interests and which includes an air element equipped a single BN-2A Maritime Defender for coastal patrol and utility duties, plus a quartet of SA.342L Gazelles for anti-tank attack. Four Pilatus PC-9s have also been purchased.

EQUIPMENT

Light Attack:
Pilatus PC-9
Anti-Armour:
Aerospatiale SA.342L Gazelle
Maritime Patrol/Utility:
Pilatus Britten-Norman BN-2A Maritime Defender
Training:
Pilatus PC-9

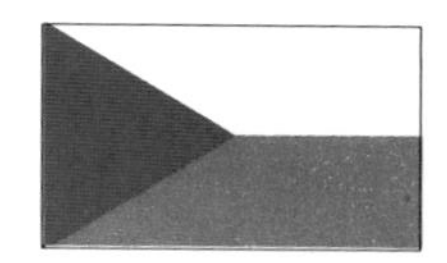

CZECHOSLOVAKIA

As ONE OF the major contributors to the Warsaw Pact, it is hardly surprising that the *Ceskoslovenske Letectvo* (CAF: Czechoslovak Air Force) adheres closely to Soviet practice with regard to organization. Although recent upheavals behind the so-called "Iron Curtain" have led to democratization and a demand for the withdrawal of Soviet forces from its territory, Czechoslovakia is still effectively in the Eastern camp and seems likely to remain so until such time as the Warsaw Pact is formally dismantled.

In terms of structure, CAF operational forces are assigned to one of two Air Armies, depending on mission. Thus, the 7th Air Army is concerned with matters pertaining to air defence and manages a substantial force of interceptors as well as ground-based components with SA-2 "Guideline" and SA-3 "Goa" surface-to-air missiles. Fighter resources are predominantly composed of the MiG-21 "Fishbed" and by far the greater majority of the CAF's 300 or so examples of this versatile fighter are used as interceptors, only about 40 or so being earmarked for attack tasks. Defensive assets are rounded out by about three-dozen MiG-23MF "Flogger-Bs", and some MiG-29 "Fulcrums" are also operated although the CAF is expected to receive only about 20 of the latter type.

Offensive capability is vested in the 10th Air Army which is fundamentally a tactical air arm. Apart from the MiG-21s alluded to earlier, it has some 40 MiG-23BM "Flogger-Hs" and a similar quantity of Su-25 "Frogfoots", but the most numerous type is easily the Su-7 Fitter, at least 80 examples of which are currently in service. Other 10th Air Army resources are tasked with tactical reconnaissance, for which MiG-21RF "Fishbed-Hs" are augmented by camera-equipped versions of the L-39 Albatros.

Above: The sleek lines of a Czech Air Force MiG-21PF "Fishbed-D" are evident in this view. Nearly 300 of these classic Soviet fighters are still in Czech service.

Other combat-capable forces include a sizeable rotary-wing contingent which works closely with the Czech Army. Most potent of these resources is the Mil Mi-24 "Hind", close to 50 of these heavily-armed gunships presently being operated alongside about 50 armed Mi-8/17 "Hip" assault helicopters. Other helicopters that are used are mostly confined to light transport tasks and training, but some Mi-4 "Hounds" may also still be active in an anti-armour capacity courtesy of the AT-3 "Sagger" anti-tank missile.

Backbone of the transport force is the An-24 "Coke" and the An-26 "Curl". A combined total of about 30 examples of these turbine-powered aircraft are flown, the CAF also possessing 15 or so An-2 "Colts", a handful of An-12 "Cubs", a few Avia 14Ts (licence-built Il-14 "Crates") and about 20 L-410 Turbolets. One Tu-134A "Crusty" and a couple of Yak-40 "Codlings" are used on VIP-type duties and as staff transports, although responsibility for this task is mostly entrusted to a few Government-owned aircraft that operate in civil markings.

Pilot training begins on the Aero C.11 (licence-built Yak-11 "Moose") and Zlin Z.526, with pupils then undergoing jet transition on the Aero L-29 Delfin and L-39 Albatros before specialist weapons training on the MiG-15UTI "Midget". Subsequently, fighter pilots will receive further instruction on the MiG-21U "Mongol". Type conversion training (if necessary) is accomplished on two-seat variants of CAF combat aircraft at squadron level.

Below: As in the West, so in the East, with another civilian air transport donning a military guise. In this instance, it is a Czech Air Force Tupolev Tu-154B-2.

EQUIPMENT

Interception:
Mikoyan-Gurevich MiG-29 "Fulcrum"
Mikoyan-Gurevich MiG-23MF "Flogger-B"
Mikoyan-Gurevich MiG-21PF/MF "Fishbed-D/J"
Attack:
Mikoyan-Gurevich MiG-23BM "Flogger-H"
Sukhoi Su-25 "Frogfoot"
Sukhoi Su-7/22 "Fitter"
Mil Mi-24 "Hind"
Assault:
Mil Mi-8/17 "Hip-E/H"
Mil Mi-4 "Hound"
Tactical Reconnaissance:
Mikoyan-Gurevich MiG-21RF "Fishbed-H"
Aero L-39ZA Albatros
Elint/Sigint-Gathering:
Tupolev Tu-134 "Crusty"
Transport:
Tupolev Tu-134 "Crusty"
Yakovlev Yak-40 "Codling"
Antonov An-12 "Cub"
Antonov An-24 "Coke"
Antonov An-26 "Curl"
Avia 14T
LET L-410 Turbolet
Antonov An-2 "Colt"
Mil Mi-6 "Hook"
Communications/Liaision:
Mil Mi-1 "Hare"
Mil Mi-2 "Hoplite"
Training:
Aero C.11
Zlin Z.526
Aero L-29 Delfin
Aero L-39 Albatros
Mikoyan-Gurevich MiG-15UTI "Midget"
Mikoyan-Gurevich MiG-21U "Mongol"
Mikoyan-Gurevich MiG-23U "Flogger-C"
Sukhoi Su-70 "Moujik"
Mil Mi-1 "Hare"

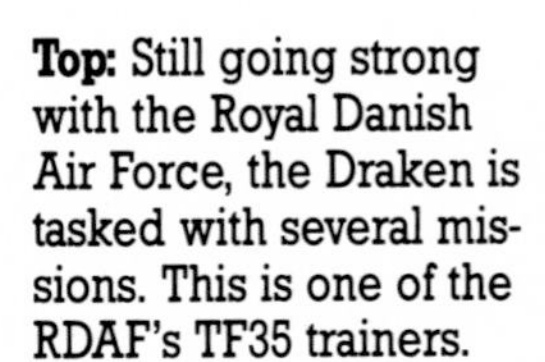

Top: Still going strong with the Royal Danish Air Force, the Draken is tasked with several missions. This is one of the RDAF's TF35 trainers.

Above: Operating from a total of four sites located on the Danish coastline enables the S-61A Sea Kings to provide SAR coverage.

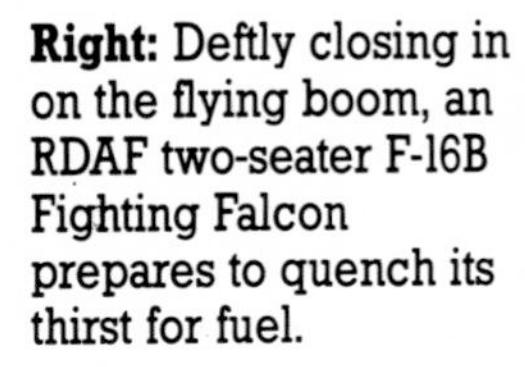

Right: Deftly closing in on the flying boom, an RDAF two-seater F-16B Fighting Falcon prepares to quench its thirst for fuel.

DENMARK

STRATEGICALLY sited astride the entrance to the Baltic Sea, Denmark makes a small but significiant contribution to the NATO alliance, with combat-ready forces being allocated to the Air Commander Baltic Approaches (ComAirBaltAp). In peacetime, those forces are distributed between the three major air bases at Aalborg, Karup and Skrydstrup, but in the unlikely event of war they would be spread far more thinly, dispersed amongst up to a dozen sites.

As in a number of other NATO forces, the General Dynamics F-16 Fighting Falcon is the principal combat type, and the initial contract covered 46 F-16As and 12 F-16Bs. Follow-on orders have raised procurement to 82, of which about a dozen have still to be delivered. Employed in dual interception/attack functions, they are presently allocated to two squadrons (Eskadrille 723 and 726) at Aalborg and two (Eskadrille 727 and 730) at Skrydstrup. Air-to-air weaponry currently consists of the trusty AIM-9 Sidewinder missile, which is available in several versions including the all-aspect AIM-9L. Denmark has also indicated that it wants to buy the AIM-120A AMRAAM for all-weather interception, but this weapon has suffered more than its fair share of development problems and is still far from being a combat-worthy missile. In air-to-ground roles, ordnance includes conventional "iron" bombs and the veteran Bullpup missile, but the latter should give way to the AGM-65G IIR Maverick before long.

Of older vintage, the Saab Draken serves with two units at Karup. One (Eskadrille 725) is equipped with the F35 version which is primarily concerned with attack duties, although it can perform as a secondary day interceptor. The other (Eskadrille 729) is a specialist reconnaissance outfit equipped with the RF35 model — again, this has a secondary role and could be employed for attack missions. Both units also operate a small number of TF35 two-seat trainers.

Upgrading of the nav/attack package in the early 1980s means that the Draken should remain effective until the turn of the century, but current plans anticipate that one squadron will be deactivated during the 1993-95 timeframe, leaving the other to soldier on with about six F35s, eight RF35s and five TF35s.

Operational forces are rounded out by eight Eskadrilles tasked with defence against aerial threats. Equipped with the MIM-23B Improved Hawk surface-to-air missile (SAM), they are distributed between several bases.

Support elements are few. Denmark's limited airlift requirement is satisfied by Eskadrille 721 which utilizes three C-130H Hercules, three Gulfstream IIIs and a few T-17 Supporters on a variety of transport, fisheries protection and SAR operations. Located at Vaerlose, on the outskirts of Copenhagen, they operate alongside eight SAR-dedicated Sikorsky S-61A helicopters of Eskadrille 722.

As far as pilot training is concerned, initial screening of prospective aircrew is undertaken on T-17s of the *Flyveskolen* (Flying School) at Avno, successful candidates thereafter receiving initial jet tuition in the United States of America.

EQUIPMENT

Interception/Attack:
General Dynamics F-16A Fighting Falcon
Attack:
SAAB-Scania F35 Draken
Reconnaissance:
SAAB-Scania RF35 Draken
Transport:
Lockheed C-130H Hercules
Grumman Gulfstream III
SAAB-Scania T-17 Supporter
Training:
SAAB-Scania T-17 Supporter
General Dynamics F-16B Fighting Falcon
SAAB-Scania TF35 Draken
SAR:
Sikorsky S-61A

FINLAND

PERMITTED to possess no more than 60 combat aircraft and 3,000 personnel in accordance with the terms of a 1947 neutrality treaty with the United Kingdom and the Soviet Union, the *Suomen Ilmavoimat* (FAF: Finnish Air Force) has actually marginally exceeded that figure in recent years. Today, it has somewhere in the region of about 65 front-line combat aircraft, a total that easily surpasses the 100-mark if one takes into account the BAe Hawk T.51 jet trainer which does possess the ability to carry armament.

Current front-line fighters are the MiG-21 "Fishbed" and SAAB Draken, but Finland is now looking for new equipment and may obtain a mix of hardware from East and West. Candidates for delivery with effect from the mid-1990s include the F-16 Fighting Falcon, Mirage 2000, MiG-29 "Fulcrum" and SAAB 39 Gripen, with the latter pair being viewed as the probable winners.

Organization is relatively straightforward, with operational forces being distributed among three Air Defence Wings (ADWs), each of which is responsible for a specific geographic area. In consequence, they possess a high degree of autonomy and will typically include front-line fighters, trainers, communications and liaison aircraft in their line-up. Although multi-mission capable, each ADW is principally concerned with air defence in order to preserve Finland's cherished neutrality.

Main operating basis and units are at Rovaniemi (11th Fighter Squadron/Lapland ADW), Tampere/Pirkkala (21st Fighter Squadron/Satakunta ADW) and Kuopio/Rissala (31st Fighter Squadron/Karelian ADW). Both the 11th and 21st Fighter Squadrons rely on the Draken as the principal combat type, operating a mixture of J35BS, J35F, J35FS and locally- assembled J35XS versions. Some 40 Drakens are in service, split more or less equally between these two units which also share a handful of two-seat Sk 35Cs for training.

Both units use a small number of Hawks for follow-on training duties, as does the 31st Fighter Squadron. This last unit operates most of the two-dozen MiG-21bis "Fishbed-N" interceptors that are on charge as its principal equipment, plus five MiG-21UM "Mongol" two-seaters. In addition, each of these three units operates an independent communications element for which types like the Valmet Vinka, Piper PA-28R Cherokee Arrow II, Piper PA-31 Chieftain and Mil Mi-8 "Hip" are used in very small numbers.

One other combat-ready unit which merits brief mention is the Reconnaissance Squadron at Jyvaskyla/Tikkakoski; this comes under the direct control of FAF headquarters and operates a few MiG-21bis and Hawk aircraft which are actually shared with the 31st Fighter Squadron. Pod-mounted sensors are used on intelligence-gathering missions.

Other FAF elements include a solitary Transport Squadron and an associated Helicopter Flight. Both are to be found at Utti, aircraft and helicopters in use including three F-27 Friendships, four PA-31 Chieftains, three LearJet 35As for surveillance and target-towing, four PA-28R Cherokee Arrow IVs for liaison, about five Mi-8 "Hips" for SAR/VIP transport and a couple of McDonnell Douglas 500Ds.

Moving on to training requirements, these are satisfied in-country, students beginning their instruction with the Air Academy at Kauhava on the Valmet L-70 Vinka. Ten Valmet L-90 Redigo trainers are presently on order for 1991-92 delivery to augment the Vinkas, but some of these may well be allocated to liaison duties. On completion of initial training, successful candidates move on to the Hawk for further tuition to "wings" standard, after which they will join the Hawk-equipped training elements attached to the combat squadrons, spending about a year on operational training before transitioning onto the MiG-21 or Draken at the same base.

Above: First ordered by the Finnish Air Force as long ago as 1973, the two-seater Valmet L-70 finally entered service in 1980-82. In all, 30 were acquired for training duties.

Below: Exports of the SAAB-Scania Draken have been relatively modest, but Finland has made the most of this Swedish design. Today, the Finnish Air Force operates no less than five Draken variants in numerous roles.

EQUIPMENT

Interception:
Mikoyan-Gurevich MiG-21bis "Fishbed-N"
SAAB-Scania J35BS/F/FS/XS Draken
Transport:
Fokker F-27 Friendship 400
VIP Transport/SAR:
Mil Mi-8 "Hip"
Communications/Liaison:
Piper PA-28R Cherokee Arrow II/IV
Piper PA-31-350 Chieftain
Surveillance/Target-Towing:
LearJet 35A
Training:
Valmet L-70 Vinka
BAe Hawk T.51
SAAB-Scania Sk 35C Draken
Mikoyan-Gurevich MiG-21UM "Mongol"
McDonnell Douglas 500D

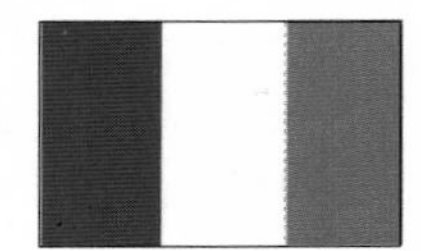

FRANCE

ALTHOUGH it withdrew from the North Atlantic Treaty Organization (NATO) military alliance as long ago as 1966, France does co-operate closely with the armed forces of most of the nations that make up that alliance and is regularly invited to participate in military manoeuvres and exercises; and it has also indicated that it would almost certainly commit forces to action in the increasingly unlikely event of a major attack by the Warsaw Pact. However, as has been the case with most European states, the size of the French military establishment has experienced some decline over the past couple of decades, and this is certainly apparent with the *l'Armee de l'Air* (AdA: French Air Force), although quantitative losses have to some extent been compensated for by qualitative gains through the deployment of much more potent hardware like the Dassault-Breguet Mirage 2000.

Overall responsibility for management is vested in the *Etat Major de l'Armee de l'Air* (Air Force General Staff), which has its headquarters in Paris, but day-to-day control of the various forces and elements that constitute the AdA actually devolves to seven major subordinate Commands. Six of these are engaged in the aircraft-operating business, these consisting of the *Forces Aeriennes Strategiques* (FAS: Strategic Air Forces); *Force Aerienne Tactique* (FATAC: Tactical Air Force); *Commandement Air des Forces de Defense Aerienne* (CAFDA: Air Defence Forces Command); *Commandement du Transport Aerien Militaire* (COTAM: Military Air Transport Command); *Commandement des Ecoles de l'Armee de l'Air* (CEAA: Air Force Schools Command); and the *Commandement des Transmissions de l'Armee de l'Air* (CTAA: Air Force Telecommunications Command). The remaining agency is tasked with engineering support.

Above: With an ASMP nuclear missile on its centreline hardpoint, this Mirage 2000N is armed for a low-level tactical strike sortie.

To facilitate administration, France is divided into four *Region Aerienne* (RA: Air Region), specifically No.1 RA at Metz (alias Tactical Air Command); No.2 RA at Villacoublay; No.3 RA at Bordeaux and No.4 RA at Aix-les-Milles, while flying units are generally organized in *Escardres* (Wings) which may possess anything from one to five *Escadrons* (Squadrons), although not all of these will necessarily occupy the same air base as their parent Wing. At the operating level, it is also usual for an *Escadron* to be further split into *Escadrilles* (Flights), while the combat Wings of FATAC and CAFDA each invariably have a small liaison and training element equipped with a few CM.170 Magisters.

Most important of the AdA formations by virtue of its nuclear strike role is the FAS. From a hardened underground command post at Taverny near Paris, the FAS directs two of the three elements that make up France's nuclear arsenal, namely manned bombers and intermediate range ballistic missiles (IRBMs).

Bomber strength was at its peak in the late-1960s when about 60 Mirage IVAs were active, but barely 20 of these large and impressive deltas remain in service today. Of these survivors, 18 are modified aircraft and are now known as Mirage IVPs, being fitted with improved avionics and penetration aids as well as being configured to carry and launch the Aerospatiale ASMP tactical nuclear missile during the mid-1980s.

Attaining operational status in 1986, the Mirage IVP fleet presently serves with two squadrons of the 91st Bomb Wing and a training outfit. Use of detachments permits alert-dedicated aircraft to be distributed amongst four bases, namely Cazaux, Istres, Mount-de-Marsan and Orange, while the FAS also possesses 11 C-135FR Stratotankers. Based at Avord, Istres and Mont-de-Marsan, these have also recently been updated and will remain in service with the 93rd Flight-Refuelling Wing until well into the 21st Century. Although dedicated to support of the Mirage IVPs, the C-135FRs furnish in-flight refuelling services to a host of

Below: The sight of a rocket-assisted take-off (RATO) by an AdA Mirage IV is all but guaranteed to take the breath away.

Below Right: Hidden beneath the ground, the AdA's IRBM force is small in number, but each warhead has a 1.2-megaton yield.

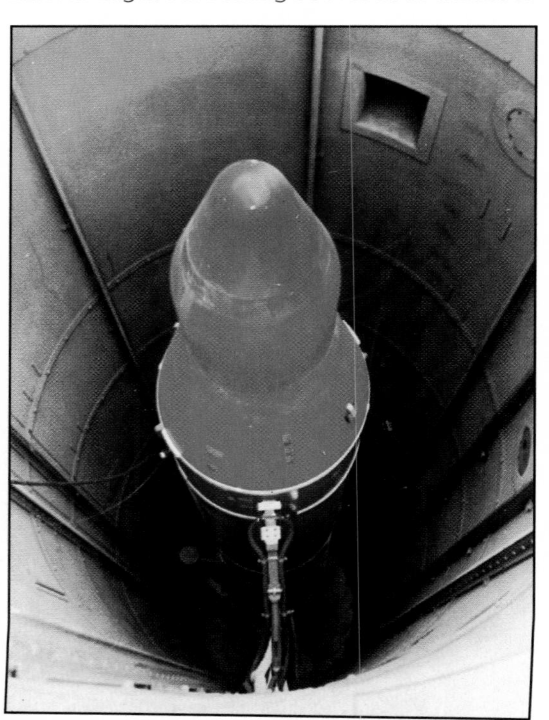

Right: Destined to equip four AdA Wings, each with a trio of squadrons, the Mirage 2000C will remain a prime interception asset throughout the 1990s and beyond.

"customers" and can also be employed on strategic airlift missions.

Training of FAS personnel is centred on Bordeaux and is undertaken by three squadrons of the 328th *Centre d'Instruction des FAS* (CIFAS 328). One squadron has a dual role to fulfil and is equipped with a pair of Mirage IVPs plus four IVAs. Although normally used for peacetime training duties, the latter aircraft have been modified to operate with the CT52 sensor package and would perform strategic reconnaissance in the event of conflict. Both the other squadrons are dedicated solely to training, one operating about 15 Mirage IIIBs for conversion and in-flight refuelling instruction, while the second has a few Alpha Jets, CM.170 Magisters and Mystere 20s for navigation training.

Missile forces are limited to just 18 Aerospatiale SSBS S-3D IRBMs which are allocated to two equal-sized flights of the 95th Missile Wing at Apt. Emplaced in hardened silos in the vicinity of Reilhannette and Rustrel since the early-1980s, each of these weapons is able to deliver a single 1.2 megaton thermonuclear warhead.

FATAC elements are concentrated at a clutch of air bases within north-eastern France and, apart from two Jaguar squadrons, are all assigned to the 1st Tactical Air Command which is also at Metz. Assets consist of six Wings with Mirage IIIE/5F, Mirage 2000N, Mirage F.1CR and Jaguar aircraft, and there are also a few Mystere 20 avionics trainers for pilot training and conversion.

The long-serving Mirage IIIE is now mainly assigned to defence-suppression tasks using the Martel air-to-surface missile (ASM), and remains active with three squadrons of No.3 Wing at Nancy and one squadron of No.13 Wing at Colmar. The latter Wing also possesses a number of Mirage IIIB trainers, as well as two squadrons equipped with the Mirage 5F for attack duties.

Two Wings — No.7 at St. Dizier and No.11 at Toul-Rosieres — each have four squadrons of Jaguars, although one squadron of each Wing is detached (to Istres and Bordeaux respectively). These detached squadrons are the only flying units that are permanently assigned to the Nancy-based 2nd Tactical Air Command, which acts as a rapid response force and which can be augmented by elements drawn from any other unit according to circumstance. Jaguar missions vary, but No.7 Wing generally specializes in tactical nuclear attack, while No.11 Wing performs conventional tasks in support of Army ground forces. Both squadrons of No.2 Tactical Air Command are also orientated towards conventional attack.

FATAC resources are completed by No.4 Wing at Luxeuil and No.33 Wing at Strasbourg. The former was the first operational unit to receive the Mirage 2000N and its primary mission is that of tactical nuclear

Right: Having put much faith in the reliable Transall twin-engined transport aircraft for many years, COTAM has recently enhanced its capabilities with 10 C-130H/H-30 Hercules.

strike with the ASMP missile, while the latter operates the reconnaissance-dedicated Mirage F.1CR.

Production of the Mirage 2000N and the similar, but non ASMP-compatible, 2000D is continuing, with No.7 Wing at St. Dizier being next to undergo transition, during 1990-92. After that date, it was intended to introduce the Dassault-Breguet Rafale as a Jaguar and Mirage replacement, but service entry of this new fighter has now slipped to 1996 and about 50 Mirage F.1C interceptors made redundant by the Mirage 2000C will therefore be modified to F.1CT attack configuration as an interim solution.

CAFDA is tasked with ensuring the security of French air-space and includes anti-aircraft artillery (AAA), Crotale surface-to-air missiles (SAM), interceptors and ground radars in its array of defensive kit, while it is also to manage the four Boeing E-3F Sentries that are on order, delivery of which began in October 1990. Fighter forces are assigned to just four Wings, two of which — the 2nd at Dijon and the 5th at Orange — operate the Mirage 2000C, but procurement is continuing and both Mirage F.1C Wings — the 12th at Cambrai and the 30th at Reims — are almost certain to convert to the newer type during the early-1990s.

Airlift is the preserve of COTAM which has three tactical transport Wings (six squadrons) to operate a fleet of about 70 Transalls (including 10 with tanker capability) and 10 recently acquired Lockheed Hercules, while specialist units also exist to satisfy VIP and liaison requirements, types engaged on these duties including the DC-8, Falcon 900, Nord 262, Twin Otter, Super Puma and Dauphin. Apart from the VIP/liaison examples, most rotary-wing resources are concentrated within a single Wing (the 67th) which maintains five squadrons at different bases to operate a fleet that is dominated by the Puma and Alouette III.

Other transport outfits include a handful of liaison and communications squadrons stationed alongside three of the RA headquarters (at Aix-les-Milles, Bordeaux and Metz), and a mixed aircraft group at Evreux with two or three examples of the Twin Otter, Transall and Puma being flown in support of the French Secret Service. There are also a few overseas-based units at such far-flung locations as Tontouta, New Caledonia; Dakar, Senegal; St. Denis, Reunion. Point-a-Pitre, Guadeloupe; and Faaa, Tahiti. For the most part, these are equipped with light twins and helicopters, but Transalls are also detached from French-based units to St. Denis, Dakar and Point-a-Pitre.

Pilot training for the AdA begins with an aptitude assessment on the single-engined CAP.10, this being conducted by the *Ecole de l'Air* (EA: Flying School) based at Salon de Provence. The vast majority of the 56 CAP.10s supplied to the AdA are based at Salon de Provence, but some are flown from Avord in support of the AdA's navigator training.

On completion of this initial period of assessment, successful candidates progress on to the TB.30 Epsilon. Initial examples of this tandem-seat trainer entered AdA service during mid-1984, being assigned to GE 315 at Cognac/Chateaubernard. Plans to divide the 150 Epsilons ordered amongst several such units have been abandoned, and all of these trainers are now in the hands of GE 315.

Students continue to fly the Epsilon until the award of their "wings", at which time they will be "streamed" according to their recognized abilities. Those deemed suitable for the fast-jet community will then log further hours in the Epsilon as a prelude to their introduction to the Alpha Jet for advanced tuition at Tours and weapons training at Cazaux. The next hurdle comes in the form of operational conversion, this being accomplished on type courtesy of training elements within front-line units, specifically No.5 Wing

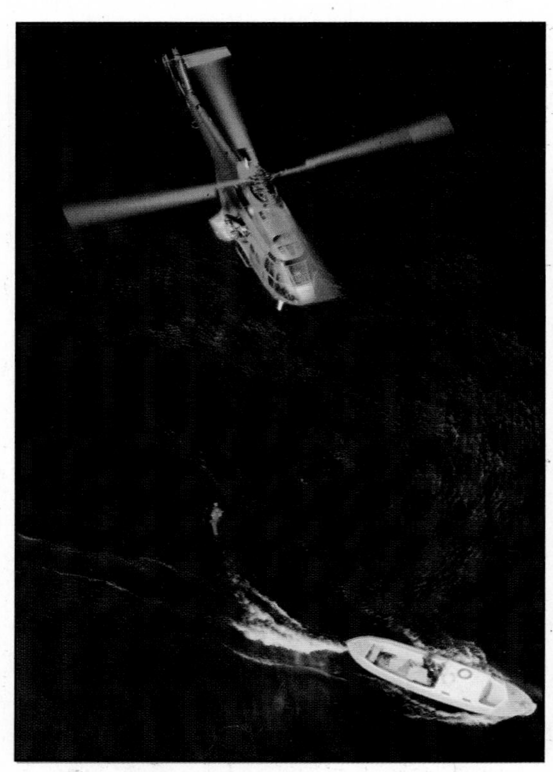

Left: As with several other large air forces, the AdA has numerous overseas commitments, most of which utilize the Puma helicopter in various roles, such as offshore SAR.

Below: No respectable air force is complete in the 1990s without a high-performance turboprop trainer. In the AdA's case, the answer is the TB.30B Epsilon, shown here.

Right: The backbone of the AdA's fast-jet training force is the Alpha Jet, a total of 176 units having been procured primarily for use in the advanced flying tuition role.

(Mirage F.1), No.7 Wing (Jaguar), No.13 Wing (Mirage III) and CIFAS 328 (Mirage IV). Transport pilots also accumulate additional time on the Epsilon before multi-engine training on the EMB-121 Xingu at Avord, while the CEAA organization includes schools for navigators, air traffic controllers, maintenance personnel and other disciplines.

Although it ranks as the smallest AdA component in terms of numbers of aircraft, the CTAA is amongst the most interesting, for its three squadrons all use much-modified equipment. Two of those squadrons reside at Evreux, the 51st *Escadron Electronique* (EE: Electronic Squadron) using a single DC-8 Srs.53 with numerous antennae for acquisition of electronic intelligence, (ELINT), and the 59th EE operating four Transall "ASTARTE" aircraft as very low frequency (VLF) relay platforms with US equipment for communications with nuclear submarines. Finally, at Metz, there is the 54th EE with two Transall "GABRIEL" ELINT-gathering aircraft.

EQUIPMENT

Strategic Strike:
Dassault-Breguet Mirage IVP
Interception
Dassault-Breguet Mirage 2000C
Dassault-Breguet Mirage F.1C/C-200
Strike/Attack:
Dassault-Breguet Mirage 2000N
Attack:
SEPECAT Jaguar A
Dassault-Breguet Mirage IIIE
Dassault-Breguet Mirage 5F
Strategic Reconnaissance:
Dassault-Breguet Mirage IVA
Tactical Reconnaissance:
Dassault-Breguet Mirage F.1CR-200
AEW:
Boeing E-3F Sentry
ECM/Elint-Gathering:
Douglas DC-8 Srs.53 "SARIG"
Transall C.160EL "GABRIEL"
VLF Relay:
Transall C.160H "ASTARE"
Transport:
Douglas DC-8 Srs.55/72
Aerospatiale Caravelle 11R
Lockheed C-130H/H-30 Hercules
Transall C.160F/NG
Nord 262 Fregate
Boeing Canada Twin Otter
Aerospatiale SA.330B Puma
Aerospatiale AS.332C Super Puma
VIP Transport:
Dassault-Breguet Falcon 900
Dassault-Breguet Falcon 50
Dassault-Breguet Falcon 20C
Tanking/Transport:
Boeing C-135FR Stratotanker
Transall C.160NG
Navaid Calibration:
Dassault-Breguet Mystere 20
Target-Towing:
Dassault-Breguet Mystere 20
Communications/Liaison:
Morane-Saulnier MS.760 Paris
Embraer EMB-121AA Xingu
Cessna 411
Cessna 310K/L/N
Nord 260 Super Broussard
Avions Robin HR.100-250
Jodel D.140E/R
CE.43 Guepard
Aerospatiale AS.355F/N Ecureuil
Aerospatiale SE.3130 Alouette II
Aerospatiale SE.3160 Alouette III
Training:
Avions Mudry/CAARP CAP.10/20
Avionis Mudry/CAARP CAP.230
Aerospatiale TB.30B Epsilon
Aerospatiale CM.170 Magister
Dassault-Breguet Alpha Jet E
Dassault-Breguet Mirage IIIB
SEPECAT Jaguar E
Dassault-Breguet Mirage F.1B
Dassault-Breguet Mirage 2000B
Embraer EMB-121AA Xingu
Dassault Mystere 20/20SNA/20SNE/20P
Aerospatiale AS.355F Ecureuil
Aerospatiale SE.3130 Alouette II
Aerospatiale SE.3160 Alouette III
Aerospatiale SA.330 Puma
Test Duties:
Airbus A.300
Aerospatiale Carvelle 11R/III
Sud Vatour IIN
Dassault-Breguet Mystere 20C
CASA C.212 Aviocar
Pilatus PC-9
Gliders:
Centrair C-10A
Janus J2
Janus J38
Schleicher ASW-20
Glider-Towing:
Jodel D.140R

GERMANY

THE UNIFICATION of East and West Germany at the beginning of October 1990 in theory resulted in the size of the *Luftwaffe* (Air Force) being substantially increased. In reality, however, it is evident that the vast majority of units and aircraft which previously operated as part of the German Democratic Republic's *Luftstreitkrafte* (Air Force) have little or no place in the military structure of post-unification Germany. Furthermore, since the USSR has refused to take back any of the military hardware it supplied to East Germany, it seems certain that most will be scrapped or sold off, although a batch of 24 MiG-29 "Fulcrums" is apparently to be retained in the short term. Other selected Soviet-built items, virtually all transport types, have been retained to form the basis of the *Luftwaffe's* newly-constituted 5th Air Division. All such equipment will bear *Luftwaffe* insignia and serials.

With the *Luftstreitkrafte* effectively out of business, this survey will concentrate on those elements that consitute West Germany's *Luftwaffe*. Expected to remain a part of the NATO military alliance for the foreseeable future, the *Luftwaffe* line-up is largely built around the 200 or so Tornado IDS strike fighters that equip four fully-operational *Jagdbombergeschwaders* (Fighter-Bomber Wings) and a training unit.

The Tornado is still in production for the *Luftwaffe* and is expected to equip a fifth such Wing in the mid-1990s, although the continually shifting status of East-West relations could bring about a change. Currently in the process of being deployed are close to three-dozen Tornado ECR (Electronic Combat and Reconnaissance) aircraft which are earmarked for service with two *Staffels* (Squadrons) in different Wings.

Other attack-orientated forces comprise two F-4F Phantom II Wings, one of which has a training element assigned, and there are also three close air support (CAS) Wings equipped with the Dassault-Breguet/Dornier Alpha Jet A, although this small and vulnerable machine seems set to disappear from the *Luftwaffe's* combat inventory before too much longer, since one unit is due to disband and another to convert to the Tornado. Present plans call for redundant Alpha Jets to be assigned to Tornado outfits for second-line continuation training duties. Other Alpha Jets serve in the weapons training role from Beja in Portugal and there is speculation that Portugal might ultimately receive some redundant examples as replacements for veteran G-91s.

Elements tasked with air defence consist of just two *Jagdgeschwaders* (Fighter Wings) equipped with F-4F, over half of which are to be given an expanded operational capability with "look-down/shoot-down" potential through installation of the new AN/APQ-120 radar and the AIM-120A Advanced Medium-Range Air-to-Air Missile (AMRAAM). Tactical reconnaissance is also undertaken by a variant of the Phantom, in this instance the RF-4E version which is operated by two *Aufklarungsgeschwaders* (Reconnaissance Wings) although these will be augmented to some extent by the Tornado ECR and, if all goes according to plan, by just over a dozen Grob Egrett 1 high-altitude surveillance platforms from the mid-1990s.

Above: A total of 175 Alpha Jet as entered operational service with the West German Luftwaffe between 1979 and 1983, their principal role being close air support.

Transport units are mostly equipped with the twin-engined Transall C.160D. Some 89 examples of this Hercules "look-alike" are still in use with three *Lufttransportgeschwaders* (Air Transport Wings), one of which also has a helicopter transport squadron equipped with the UH-1D Iroquois while another includes a crew training unit equipped with Transalls and Dornier Do 28D Skyservants. Further helicopter airlift and search-and-rescue (SAR) requirements are met by a fourth transport Wing which has two squadrons of the versatile "Huey", and there is also a special independent transport unit — the *Flugbereitschaftstaffel* — with a mixed fleet that includes some VIP-configured aircraft and helicopters.

Below: Cloaked in the Luftwaffe's latest tactical camouflage, this JBF 31 Panavia Tornado blends in well as it performs a low-level, run.

In addition, about half-a-dozen Hansa Jets serve with an electronic countermeasures (ECM) training unit and it is also worth mentioning that most combat units also possess a few examples of the twin-engined Do 28D Skyservant "hack" aircraft for general purpose transport tasks such as communications and liaison.

Pilot training is undertaken in the USA on German-owned Cessna T-37s and Northrop T-38 Talons at Sheppard AFB, Texas. These display standard USAF insignia, as do a group of about 10 F-4E Phantom IIs at George AFB, California. Although the latter feature the unit insignia of the 35th Tactical Fighter Wing, they are also German-owned. On completion of US training, students return to Europe for specialized instruction on the equipment that they will eventually fly when posted to an operational unit. This can be accomplished in England (Tornado), in Germany (Phantom II) and in Portugal (Alpha Jet), but will invariably include a period of "Europeanization" so that the students can adjust to the very different conditions that prevail on the eastern side of the Atlantic Ocean.

Other specialized training is accomplished overseas, most notably at Goose Bay in Canada where examples of all combat aircraft types are deployed to permit aircrew to practice low-level flying over this sparsely inhabited region. Climatic conditions prevent this training effort from being conducted on a year-round basis, but during the fine-weather period all *Luftwaffe* units will be rotated through the programme in a typical training season.

Looking to the future, the *Luftwaffe* is slated to obtain some 160-200 examples of the Eurofighter, largely to replace the existing F-4Fs, although the changing international climate and an increasingly vocal anti-defence lobby seem certain to bring about the cancellation of most — and, quite possibly, all — of these aircraft. In the process, it might well do irrevocable damage to the European aerospace business.

In addition to airborne assets, the *Luftwaffe* also manages a substantial force of missiles. Most are tasked with air defence duties, with the American-supplied Patriot and Hawk being the primary weapons, but three units are equipped with the Euromissile Roland system. Some offensive potential also exists in the shape of two Pershing 1A nuclear surface-to-surface missile units (warheads for these are under US control), but these are due to be disbanded by the end of 1991.

Above: The brilliant orange colour of this Canberra B.2 (Mod) makes a refreshing change to the usual low-vis. camouflage worn by the majority of Luftwaffe aircraft.

Below: One of the few NATO air arms not to operate the Lockheed C-130 Hercules, the Luftwaffe relies on the smaller C.160D Transall to meet its transport requirements.

EQUIPMENT

Interception;
McDonnell Douglas F-4F Phantom II
Mikoyan-Gurevich MiG-29 "Fulcrum-A"
Strike/Attack:
Panavia Tornado IDS
McDonnell Douglas F-4F Phantom II
Close Air Support:
Dornier Alpha Jet A
Reconnaissance:
Panavia Tornado ECR
McDonnell Douglas RF-4E Phantom II
Transport:
Transall C.160D
Antonov An-26 "Curl"
LET 410UVP
Mil Mi-8S/T/TB "Hip"
Bell UH-1D Iroquois
VIP Transport:
Ilyushin Il-62M/MK
Tupolev Tu-154M
Canadair Challenger
VFW-614
Dornier Do 28D Skyservant
Bell UH-1D Iroquois
ECM Training:
HFB-320 Hansa Jet
SAR:
Bell UH-1D Iroquois
Ground Mapping:
BAe Canberra B.2 (Mod)
Training:
Cessna T-37B
Northrop T-38A Talon
Dornier Alpha Jet A
McDonnell Douglas F-4E Phantom II
Panavia Tornado IDS

GREECE

ALTHOUGH a full member of NATO, Greece has elected to remove its forces from unified command largely as a result of a long-running dispute with Turkey over Cyprus. Indeed, ill-feeling between these two "allies" is such that Greece has chosen to posture its defences to counter a threat from Turkey rather than from the traditional "enemy", namely the Warsaw Pact (WarPac).

Along with Turkey, Greece was long perceived as a veritable "dustbin" for hand-me-down and redundant military aircraft. In recent times, however, it has been engaged on major updating of its military forces and defence spending has been amongst the highest of all the NATO member states. In consequence, the *Elliniki Aeroporia* (HAF: Hellenic Air Force) now operates considerably more modern and significantly more potent equipment, obtained from France and the USA. Spearheading the new wave of warplanes are the F-16 Fighting Falcon and the Mirage 2000 — 40 examples of each have been purchased so far and one of these types is to be the subject of a further buy of 20 aircraft. It is not inconceivable that further orders will follow in due course. At the moment, both of the new fighters are primarily concerned with air defence tasks although the F-16s do have an important secondary attack role. Two squadrons have been equipped with each type.

Older equipment is dominated numerically by the F-104 Starfighter since Greece has bought many second-hand machines, but it seems as though most of the 130 or so on hand have been placed in reserve and the type is now only operational with a single two-squadron Wing at Araxos.

Above: The HAF now has 36 Dassault-Breguet Mirage 2000CGs, plus a quartet of 2000BG two-seater trainers. All of these aircraft serve in Nos. 331 and 332 Mire (Squadrons), and may be joined by further examples.

Of more recent vintage and also operating in the fighter-interceptor role is the Mirage F.1CG. About 30 remain in use with two squadrons at Tanagra, but these are slated to move to Heraklion and Skiros once the Mirage 2000 has attained full operational status. Interceptor assets are rounded out by single squadrons with the F-4E Phantom and the Northrop F-5A at Larissa.

F-4s and F-5s also serve with surface-attack units at four bases, but the principal warplane used on these duties is the A-7H Corsair II, just under 50 examples being active with three squadrons, including two at Souda Bay in Crete. In concert with one squadron at Larissa, the long-legged Corsair is able to project its anti-shipping attack capability throughout the Eastern Mediterranean and Aegean Seas, and it appears that the HAF is set to acquire a number of redundant US Navy examples — along with more Phantoms — in the near future.

More conventional ground attack tasks are performed by the latter type which serves with a couple of squadrons at Andravidha, and by a solitary F-5A squadron at Thessaloniki in the north, these units operating alongside a tactical reconnaissance squadron operating the RF-5A. Further reconnaissance capability is limited to half-a-dozen RF-4Es and a handful of Republic RF-84F Thunderflashes, the latter type being long overdue for retirement. Another old-timer still in daily use is the Grumman HU-16B Albatross amphibian, 10 of which are used for maritime surveillance. Normally resident at Elefsis, these are likely to be encountered more or less anywhere in the Aegean Sea, but their days might now be numbered since the HAF looks likely to acquire a small number of surplus P-3 Orions from the US Navy before too much longer.

Transport elements utilize a mixture of old and new types, with the turboprop-powered C-130H Hercules and NAMC YS-11 serving happily alongside the piston-powered Do 28D Skyservant and C-47 Dakota in a fleet of airlift aircraft that does not exceed 50 in number, although it is augmented by some two-dozen UH-1H Iroquois and Bell 212 helicopters. Civil-type missions are also undertaken by the HAF, which operates about 15 Canadair CL-215 water-bombers for aerial fire-fighting as well as roughly 20 Grumman AgCats, 25 PZL M-18 Dromaders and some Bell 47Gs for crop-spraying duties on behalf of the Ministry of Works. Interestingly, the presence of the Dromader made Greece the only NATO nation to

Left: Streaming its braking parachute, a Sidewinder-equipped F-4E of No.337 Mira returns to base at Larissa at the end of another practice interception sortie in the skies above the Aegean Sea.

EQUIPMENT

Interception:
Dassault-Breguet Mirage 2000CG
General Dynamics F-16CG Fighting Falcon
Dassault-Breguet Mirage F.1CG
McDonnell Douglas F-4E Phantom II
Lockheed F-104G Starfighter
Northrop F-5A Freedom Fighter
Attack:
Vought A-7H Corsair II
General Dynamics F-16CG Fighting Falcon
McDonnell Douglas F-4E Phantom II
Lockheed F-104G Starfighter
Northrop F-5A Freedom Fighter
Reconnaissance:
McDonnell Douglas RF-4E Phantom II
Northrop RF-5A Freedom Fighter
Republic RF-84F Thunderflash
Maritime Patrol:
Grumman HU-16B Albatross
Transport:
Lockheed C-130H Hercules
NAMC YS-11A
Douglas C-47 Dakota
Dornier Do 28D Skyservant
Boeing CH-47C Chinook
VIP Transport:
Grumman Gulfstream I
Bell 212
Agusta-Bell AB.206A JetRanger
Training:
Cessna T-41D Mescalero
Cessna T-37
Rockwell T-2E Buckeye
Northrop F-5B Freedom Fighter
Vought TA-7H Corsair II
Lockheed TF-104G Starfighter
General Dynamics F-16DG Fighting Falcon
Dassault-Breguet Mirage 2000BG
Breda-Nardi/Hughes NH.300i
Fire-Fighting:
Canadair CL-215
Aerial Spraying:
Grumman AgCat
PZL M-18 Dromader
Bell 47G-3B

operate WarPac equipment until quite recently, but that unique claim has now been rendered invalid in the light of German military unification.

Pilot training is undertaken with a diverse fleet that is of entirely US origin, initial instruction on the Cessna T-41D being followed by basic training on the Cessna T-37 and advanced tuition on the Rockwell T-2E Buckeye. In addition, some 50 Lockheed T-33As are still active, but these are primarily operated as "hack" aircraft on communications and liaison duties.

Below: With its landing gear in the process of being retracted, one of 349 Mira's ageing complement of F-5A Freedom Fighters climbs up and away into the clear blue Mediterranean sky.

Right: Although the Army operates most of the Boeing CH-47 Chinook medium-lift helicopters now in Greek service, the HAF also possesses a small number for logistical support tasks.

HUNGARY

THE SO-CALLED "peace dividend" looks set to have some impact on the size of the *Magyar Legerio* (HAF: Hungarian Air Force) with financial restrictions being responsible for an expected cut in the overall size of this, one of the smallest of the Warsaw Pact air arms. Essentially a part of the Hungarian Army, it adheres strictly to the Soviet model in having a separate Air Defence Command to co-ordinate interceptor and surface-to-air missile (SAM) forces, as well as a series of air defence radars.

Two main types of interceptor are in service with three Fighter Regiments, namely the MiG-21 "Fishbed" and the MiG-23 "Flogger", and each Regiment usually has two squadrons equipped with a combined complement of about 30 aircraft. These share responsibility for defence with Soviet warplanes that are resident at a number of major air bases within Hungary.

The most numerous interceptor is the MiG-21, which equips five of the six air defence-dedicated fighter units, Regiments at Kecskemet and Taszar being solely dependent upon the "Fishbed", although the latter base also supports a single Su-22 "Fitter" squadron which is under Troop Air Command control. The other interceptor base is at Papa and has a mixed fleet made up of single squadrons operating the MiG-21 and MiG-23.

Despite its rather misleading title, Troop Air Command (TAC) is concerned with tactical attack as well as airlift and assault operations. Fixed-wing air power is confined to the "Fitter" squadron mentioned earlier, other TAC combat-capable resources comprising a couple of dozen Mil Mi-24 "Hind" battlefield attack helicopters which equip two squadrons at Veszprem, and roughly twice that number of Mi-8 "Hip" assault helicopters distributed between two squadrons at Veszprem and one based at Szolnok.

Also under TAC management is the HAF's limited transport force which is composed of An-26 "Curls", a pair of An-24 "Cokes", several LET L-410 Turbolets, and a few Zlin Z43s which fulfil utility tasks alongside about 25 Mi-2 "Hoplites". Most of the An-26s serve with a squadron at Szolnok, but a few are resident at Tokol along with the other fixed-wing transports.

Pilot training needs are mostly met in Czechoslovakia and the USSR, but some initial training does take place in Hungary, primarily with a para-military establishment at Bekescaba on assorted Zlin lightplanes. A few L-29 Delfin jet trainers may still be in service. Operational-type training is accomplished at unit level, using two-seat versions of the principal combat types in the case of fighter pilots or, at Veszprem, on Mi-8s for helicopter pilots.

Above: Home-based at Veszprem, the HAF's Mi-24s are used as attack helicopters.

EQUIPMENT

Interception:
Mikoyan-Gurevich MiG-23MF "Flogger-B"
Mikoyan-Gurevich MiG-21MF/bis "Fishbed-J/N"
Attack:
Sukhoi Su-22M-3 "Fitter-H"
Mil Mi-24 "Hind-D/E"
Transport:
Antonov An-24 "Coke"
Antonov An-26 "Curl"
LET L-410 Turbolet
Mil Mi-8TB "Hip-C"
Communications/Liaison:
Zlin Z43
Mil Mi-2 "Hoplite"
Training:
Aero L-29 Delfin
Mikoyan-Gurevich MiG-21UM "Mongol"
Mikoyan-Gurevich MiG-23UB "Flogger-C"
Sukhoi Su-22U "Fitter-G"

ICELAND

HAVING NO formally-constituted armed forces of its own, Iceland is nevertheless a member state of the North Atlantic Treaty Organization (NATO) alliance and does permit air units of other Allied nations to be permanently stationed on its soil. Of these, the USA has the largest presence and, as a result, Icelandic security is mainly guaranteed by US forces, with air defence being entrusted to one squadron of F-15C Eagles. These are based at Keflavik, which is also used by rotational Boeing E-3 Sentry airborne warning and control system (AWACS) aircraft of the USAF, and by Lockheed P-3 Orion maritime patrol aircraft of the US Navy and the Royal Netherlands Navy operating from here on a forward-deployed basis.

Above: Despite the addition of a second cockpit, the smooth lines of the MiG-21 have been preserved, as evidenced by this Hungarian Air Force MiG-21U "Mongol".

Right: With the lush Irish countryside as a backdrop, a pair of Light Strike Squadron CM.170 Magisters lose height as they complete a perfect "loop the loop" manoeuvre.

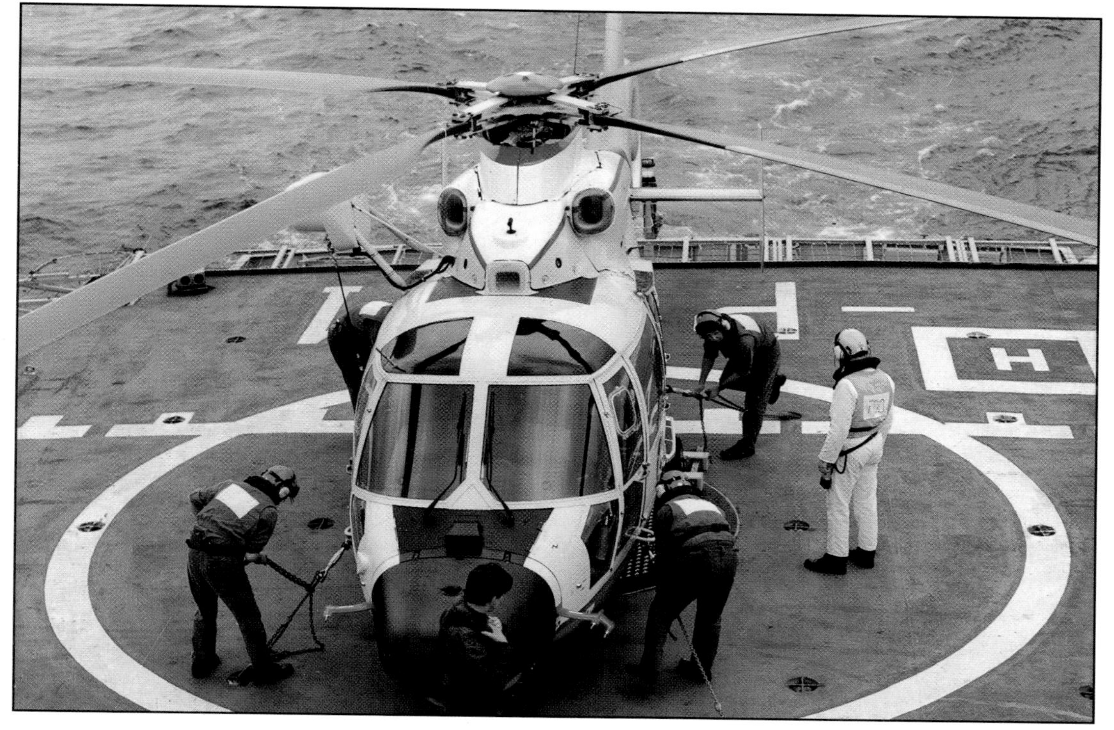

Left: Given the fact that it is surrounded by water, Ireland's need for effective maritime patrol is an obvious one, and the role is performed in part by the Dauphin 2.

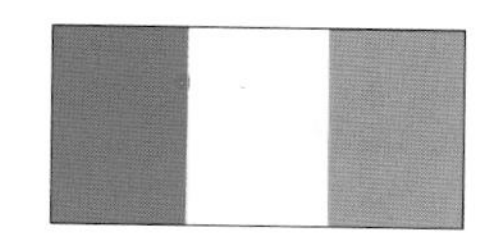

IRELAND

FULFILLING responsibilities which include support of Army ground forces as well as fisheries surveillance and protection, SAR and transport, the operational strength of the Irish Air Corps numbers less than 50 aircraft and helicopters, with most being flown from the principal base at Casement (Baldonnel), located close to the Parkgate headquarters in Dublin.

Combat capability is limited to half-a-dozen Aerospatiale CM.170 Magister armed jet trainers of the Light Strike Squadron and about nine SIAI-Marchetti SF.260WE Warriors which serve with the Training Wing. Between them, they constitute the service's modest COIN component, with Army co-operation duties being performed by eight Reims-Cessna FR.172s.

Transport missions are principally concerned with movement of VIPs and routine liaison, being undertaken by single examples of the BAe 125 Srs.700, the Gulfstream III and the Beechcraft Super King Air 200, two further examples of the latter type being dedicated to maritime duties.

Finally, there is a small collection of helicopters, including eight Aerospatiale Alouette IIIs for liaison and communications, five Aerospatiale Dauphins for maritime surveillance and SAR and a pair of Aerospatiale Gazelles for training.

With the exception of the Reims-Cessna FR.172s which are based at Gormanston, all of these aircraft and helicopters normally operate from Casement, although a SAR detachment is usually to be found at Shannon to provide coverage of Ireland's western seaboard.

EQUIPMENT

COIN/Light Strike:
Aerospatiale CM.170 Magister
SIAI-Marchetti SF.260WE Warrior
Army Liaison:
Reims-Cessna FR.172
Maritime Patrol:
Beech Super King Air 200
Aerospatiale SA.365F Dauphin 2
SAR:
Aerospatiale SA. 365F Dauphin 2
Transport:
Grumman Gulfstream III
BAe 125-700B
Beech Super King Air 200
Utility:
Aerospatiale SA.316 Alouette III
Training:
SIAI-Marchetti SF.260WE Warrior
Aerospatiale SA.342L Gazelle

ITALY

CONSTITUTING NATO's 5th Allied Tactical Air Force (5 ATAF), the *Aeronautica Militare Italiana* (AMI: Italian Air Force) is currently well advanced with an ambitious re-equipment and modernization programme that has seen deployment of brand-new Tornado and AMX strike/attack aircraft, as well as a major revamping of the long-serving Lockheed F-104 Starfighter so as to enable it to fulfil dual attack/interception missions. Italy's strategic location adjacent to the Mediterranean Sea means that a considerable amount of training effort is directed towards maritime attack, with the MBB Kormoran anti-ship missile (ASM) being a prime weapon system. Already compatible with the Tornado and F-104S, it may ultimately be added to the AMX, and plans are in hand to evaluate a suitably-modified aircraft with this potent weapon.

Peacetime operations by the AMI are overseen from a headquarters in Rome by a General Staff which exercises control via a number of subordinate commands. Of these, by far the most important is the National Air Defence Command, which has responsibility for all front-line combat and transport-oriented elements.

As it has been for many years now, air defence continues to be satisfied by the Lockheed F-104S Starfighter, backed up by eight surface-to-air missile (SAM) squadrons equipped with the Nike-Hercules. Just under 150 examples of the ever-impressive Starfighter are assigned to air defence, these being active with some seven squadrons, and they seem sure to remain in use until the Eurofighter EFA becomes available from the late-1990s. Modernization of the F-104S has resulted in the F-104S/ASA which embodies new radar and an internal Vulcan M61 20mm (0.8in) cannon, as well as compatibility with the Selenia Aspide air-to-air missile (AAM), itself a modification of the widely used AIM-7 Sparrow. A secondary air-ground potential is built in and one other F-104S/ASA Starfighter-equipped squadron does function primarily in this role.

Above: Providing the AMI with a respectable "punch", the Panavia Tornado provides the backbone to the strike force. Compatible with a variety of ordnance, its operational duties include anti-shipping strike operations.

For the most part, though, strike/attack duties are entrusted to the Panavia Tornado. Apart from a handful of aircraft which serve with the Trinational Tornado Training Establishment (TTTE) in Britain, all of the 100 machines purchased by Italy serve with three squadrons, but there is a possibility that up to 35 more will be acquired for the specialist electronic combat and reconnaissance (ECR) task. At the moment, however, Tornado missions are confined to strike/attack and, apart from the Kormoran ASM, it may also operate with US-supplied nuclear weapons, German-supplied MW-1 sub-munitions dispensers, and "smart" or "dumb" bombs. A small number of AMI Tornadoes were sent to the Gulf in early-1991, conducting strike missions against Iraqi targets as part of Operation "*Desert Storm*".

Only recently introduced to the AMI's operational inventory, the joint Italo-Brazilian AMX is presently used by a single squadron based at Treviso-Istrana, but will become increasingly important during the next few years as it progressively replaces the Fiat G-91R, RF-104G and G-91Y. Current plans call for procurement of no fewer than 187 single-seaters by the end of 1993, and these will be complemented by at least 51 AMX-T two-seaters.

In the meantime, tactical attack/reconnaissance missions continue to be performed by one squadron with the G-91R, but these veterans are currently being retired from service in anticipation of AMX. Similar tasks are assigned to two squadrons with about 50 F-104G and RF-104G Starfighters, but these are unlikely to remain in use for too much longer since they are next in line

Left: The result of a collaborative venture between Brazil and Italy, the AMX is now well established in service with the AMI. Its range can be extended by means of refuelling from Boeing 707T/T tankers.

Right: While virtually all of its NATO allies have withdrawn their fleets of.Starfighters, the AMI continues to rely heavily on this famous design, with the F-104S/ASA variant shown here likely to continue operating in the interception role for several years.

to be replaced by AMX. Then, the re-equipment programme will be brought to a close when two attack squadrons that now share just under 60 examples of the G-91Y convert to the new warplane.

Two other units with a combat role operate some 18 Breguet Atlantics on maritime surveillance and anti-submarine warfare (ASW). Although actually owned by the AMI due to a somewhat convoluted legal argument, these aircraft are unusual in that they are under the tactical control of the Italian Navy and half of the crew members are naval personnel on secondment. Delivered some considerable time ago, the Atlantics are currently being modernized and are unlikely to be retired from active service in the short term.

Elements engaged in airlift tasks are concentrated at just two bases. Tactical transport duties are undertaken by three squadrons at Pisa, with the Aeritalia G.222 being the main workhorse. Some 42 examples of this twin-engined freighter are operational with two squadrons, AMI airlift potential being completed by a third squadron equipped with 12 C-130H Hercules. Both types may also be called upon to perform civilian missions such as aerial fire-fighting and pollution control.

Specialized missions are also undertaken by two transport squadrons at Rome-Ciampino but these are mostly concerned with the movement of VIPs. Numbers of aircraft are limited, the fleet comprising two Gulfstream IIIs, two Falcon 50s, seven Piaggio-Douglas PD-808s and a couple of Agusta-Sikorsky AS-61A-4s; while two McDonnell Douglas DC-9s which once satisfied VIP airlift duties now mostly function as freighters. One other transport squadron exists, this being equipped with the Piaggio P.166 for communications and liaison tasks, but some of its aircraft are fitted with cameras for aerial survey work.

Other one-off missions performed by the AMI include navaid calibration, electronic countermeasures (ECM) training and acquisition of electronic intelligence (Elint), for which a fleet of variously modified transport aircraft are used by two squadrons. One is concerned principally with calibration work and operates the Aeritalia G.222RM, Piaggio-Douglas PD.808RM and Aermacchi MB.339RM, while the other engages in rather murkier electronic "snooping" tasks courtesy of the Aeritalia G.222VS and Piaggio-Douglas PD.808GE.

The second major aircraft-operating agency is the General Training Command which has the job of satisfying the AMI's need for air and ground crew. Pilot tuition begins on the SIAI-Marchetti SF.260, leading on to the Aermacchi MB.339 which has secondary land/maritime attack and helicopter-interception war roles. The final stage of pilot training is performed on the G-91T, but this is to be replaced by the two-seater AMX-T in due course.

Operational conversion follows, those pilots destined for the Starfighter moving to Grosseto and the TF-104G two-seater while candidates for the Tornado go to the TTTE at Cottesmore in England.

Pilot requirements for helicopters are met by a school at Frosinone which trains aircrew for all three Italian military services on the Nardi-Hughes NH.500. Those who enter the rotary-wing community will almost certainly be assigned to one of five search-and-rescue (SAR) outfits.

Liaison functions are satisfied by the simple expedient of assigning a few "hack" aircraft to most of the operational formations. Declared redundant when the MB.339 entered service, the Aermacchi MB.326 jet trainer is widely used for this purpose and for "refresher" flying, other types employed on these duties comprising the Aeritalia G-91T, SIAI S.208M, Piaggio P.166 and Agusta-Bell 212.

EQUIPMENT

Interception:
Aeritalia F-104S/ASA Starfighter
Strike/Attack:
Panavia Tornado
Aeritalia F-104S/ASA Starfighter
Aeritalia/Aermacchi AMX
Fiat G-91Y
Reconnaissance:
Aeritalia F/RF-104G Starfighter
Fiat G-91R
Maritime Patrol/ASW:
Breguet Atlantic
ECM/Elint-Gathering:
Piaggio PD.808GE
Aeritalia G.222VS
Transport:
Lockheed C-130H Hercules
Aeritalia G.222
McDonnell Douglas DC-9-32
Agusta-Bell AB.212/412
VIP Transport:
Grumman Gulfstream III
Dassault-Breguet Falcon 50
Piaggio PD.808
Agusta-Sikorsky AS-61A-4
SAR:
Agusta-Sikorsky HH-3F Pelican
Agusta-Bell AB.212
Communications/Liaison:
Aermacchi MB.326
Fiat G.91T
Piaggio P.166
SIAI-Marchetti S.208M
Agusta-Bell AB.212
Calibration:
Piaggio PD.808RM
Aeritalia G.222RM
Aermacchi MB.339RM
Training:
SIAI-Marchetti SF.206AM
Aermacchi MB.339A
Fiat G-91T
Aeritalia/Aermacchi AMX-T
Lockheed TF-104G Starfighter
Panavia Tornado
Nardi-Hughes NH.500E

LUXEMBOURG

SINCE THE demise of the small Army air element which utilized a couple of Piper L-18Cs a good few years ago, Luxembourg has been out of the business of operating military aircraft and this tiny North Atlantic Treaty Organization (NATO) member state seems unlikely to resume aerial activity of a military kind. However, it is worth noting that the NATO fleet of Boeing E-3A Sentry Airborne Warning And Control System (AWACS) aircraft and three Boeing 707-329Cs that are used for training and general transport duties all carry Luxembourg civil "registrations" and lion insignia, even though they actually operate from Geilenkirchen, Germany. This is purely to satisfy legal requirements due to NATO's lack of national status.

Below: Registered in Luxembourg but based in Germany, NATO's 18-strong force of Boeing E-3A Sentry aircraft perform a vital role as part of the NATO Airborne Early Warning Force (NAEWF). They will soon be augmented by the seven E-3Ds now joining the UK's Royal Air Force (RAF).

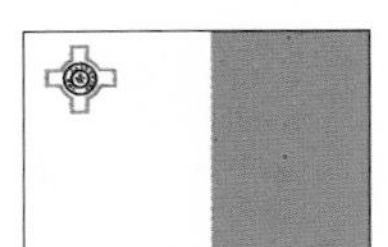

MALTA

THE Helicopter Flight of the Armed Forces of Malta comprises the only aviation element that is presently active, but all five machines on strength actually display civilian identities.

Tasks undertaken by the three Agusta-Bell 47G-2s, one Bell 47G and one Agusta-Bell JetRanger are mainly of a civilian nature at government direction and include search-and-rescue (SAR) and coastal patrol. Close co-operation is maintained with an Italian military mission which provides technical and training assistance and which has a couple of Agusta-Bell 212s to help satisfy Italian obligations as the guarantor of Maltese neutrality.

Malta's once close ties with Libya now seem to have lapsed following a change of government in Valletta.

EQUIPMENT

Miscellaneous Duties:
Agusta-Bell AB.47G-2
Bell 47G
Agusta-Bell AB.206A JetRanger

NETHERLANDS

In the final stages of a major conversion programme which will see it standardize on just one combat aircraft type, the *Koninklijke Luchtmacht* (KLu: Royal Netherlands Air Force) will in future employ the F-16 Fighting Falcon for air defence, nuclear strike, conventional attack and reconnaissance tasks. Procurement is expected to stop in the near future after the delivery of 177 single-seat F-16As and 36 two-seat F-16Bs, and the type is now in service with the eight squadrons that are to survive through the 1990s, a ninth fighter unit (No.316 Squadron) with NF-5A/B Freedom Fighters being due for disbandment in the near future.

Apart from No.306 Squadron, which is allocated to tactical reconnaissance with F-16A(R) aircraft configured to carry the Oude Delft *Orpheus* sensor pod, all Fighting Falcon outfits are dual-capable, devoting about 60 per cent of their mission capability to air-ground tasks, with the remainder being allocated to air superiority.

Weapons used in the former roles mostly consist of "iron" bombs and 70mm (2.8in)

Above: In concert with its fellow European air forces of Belgium, Denmark and Norway, the KLu selected the F-16 Fighting Falcon to replace its fleet of Lockheed F-104 Starfighters during the 1980s. When the re-equipment plan is complete, the F-16 will equip no less than nine squadrons.

rocket pods, but some units are more than likely in possession of the Paveway laser-guided "smart" bomb. Evidence to support this is provided by the fact that No.306 Squadron is ultimately to switch to laser designation when (and, indeed, if) it relinquishes the tactical reconnaissance task in the early-1990s as is currently planned. However, senior NATO commanders have expressed concern over declining reconnaissance resources and pressure is apparently being brought to bear on the Netherlands to reverse this decision. Greater punch is possessed by No.311 Squadron which has a nuclear strike commitment, using US-supplied weapons, but it also devotes training time to interception.

At present, the principal air-to-air weapon is the trusty heat-seeking Sidewinder, the KLu using a mix of AIM-9J, AIM-9L and AIM-9M variants; but some Hughes AIM-120A radar-guided missiles are expected to be acquired so as to bestow an all-weather air defence capability.

Other elements are modest and include a single transport squadron equipped with a dozen F-27 Friendship/Troopship aircraft which are long overdue for retirement. Fokker may well be the source of a replacement since both the Fokker 50 and Fokker 100 have been considered, but no decision has yet been taken. The KLu has also formulated a requirement for three McDonnell Douglas KC-10A Extender tanker/transports in an attempt to enhance strategic mobility, though an official order had not been placed at the time of writing. A quartet of Alouette IIIs serve with a search-and-rescue (SAR) flight at Leeuwarden and the

Below: With disposal of the ageing F-104s complete, attention turned to replacing the survivors of the 75 NF-5As and 30 NF-5Bs operated by the KLu since 1969. Some sixty examples have been transferred to Turkey, 12 have been sent to Greece, and seven are being overhauled for Venezuelan use.

Air Force also flies and maintains a number of helicopters which operate in support of the Army on observation, transport and liaison tasks. Two squadrons share about 60 Alouette IIIs and just under 30 MBB BO.105Cs serve with a third squadron, but none are armed although interest has been expressed in obtaining the AH-64 Apache as a replacement for the Alouettes.

Pilot training begins in-country with elementary instruction on 10 Pilatus PC-7s at Woensdrecht. Thereafter, students destined to fly fighters go to Sheppard AFB, Texas, for jet training on the Cessna T-37s and Northrop T-38s of the Euro-NATO Joint Jet Pilot Training Scheme. Helicopter pilots also travel to the USA for instruction, which is provided by the US Army at Fort Rucker, Alabama, while transport aircrew receive tuition at a Dutch civilian flying school.

Fighter conversion training is now undertaken at Tucson, Arizona, with the Air National Guard's 148th Tactical Fighter Training Squadron which includes 10 Dutch-owned F-16s in its complement, and a Dutch contingent has been using Canadian range facilities adjacent to Goose Bay, Labrador, for low-level flying training for the past few years. During the training "season" about a dozen Fighting Falcons are sent to Goose Bay and these are flown by personnel from all nine KLu fighter squadrons on a rotational basis.

Finally, about 15 units are equipped with the Hawk surface-to-air missile (SAM) for air defence, although plans are in hand to replace most of these with the American Patriot and French Crotale SAMs during the next few years.

EQUIPMENT

Interception:
General Dynamics F-16A Fighting Falcon
Strike/Attack:
General Dynamics F-16A Fighting Falcon
Canadair NF-5A Freedom Fighter
Reconnaissance:
General Dynamics F-16A(R) Fighting Falcon
Transport:
Fokker F-27 Friendship/Troopship
Army Support:
Aerospatiale Alouette III
MBB BO 105C
SAR:
Aerospatiale Alouette III
Training:
Pilatus PC-7
General Dynamics F-16B Fighting Falcon

NORWAY

ONE OF THE smaller air arms within the NATO alliance, the *Kongelige Norske Luftforsvaret* (KNL: Royal Norwegian Air Force) has its headquarters at Huseby, although for ease of operational control this long and narrow country is divided into two regional commands, split by geography between north and south.

Elements assigned to *Luftkommando Nord Norge* (Air Command Northern Norway) are directed from Reitan, near Bodo. Air defence is the primary mission of all four Fighting Falcon squadrons, but close air support is also practised and one of the four (334 Skvadron) has an additional anti-shipping attack capability courtesy of the indigenous NDT Penguin missile. Northern-based fighter units comprise two squadrons with the F-16A/B (331/334 Skv). These are resident at Bodo which is also occupied by a light transport unit equipped with the DHC-6 Twin Otter (719 Skv). Elsewhere, at Andoya, 333 Skv conducts maritime patrol and anti-submarine warfare (ASW) tasks with the P-3C Orion and this unit also has two P-3Ns (P-3Bs with simplified avionics) for coastguard functions. Similar duties are performed by a Lynx-equipped coastguard unit (337 Skv) which is resident at Bardufoss alongside a transport outfit (339 Skv) with Bell 412SPs. In addition, Bodo is home for 330 Skv which operates the Sea King Mk.43 on search-and-rescue (SAR) duties, with subordinate flights being stationed at Bodo and Banak in the north, and at Sola and Orland in the south of the country.

Luftkommando Sor Norge (Air Command Southern Norway) has fewer assets to control from its headquarters in Oslo. Combat-ready assets again consist of two F-16A/B units — 332 Skv at Rygge and 338 Skv at Orland — and there is an F-5A/B outfit for close air support at Rygge (336 Skv) which also hosts a Bell 412SP transport unit (720 Skv). Finally, tactical transport and electronic countermeasures (ECM) tasks are fulfilled by 335 Skv at Gardermoen, equipment used on these very different missions being the C-130H Hercules and Falcon 20.

Pilot screening is performed at Vaernes on the Saab MFI-15. Successful candidates thereafter proceed to the USA for basic and advanced instruction at Sheppard AFB, Texas, and Holloman AFB, New Mexico, followed by a period of European acclimatization with 336 Skv before they are assigned to an operational unit with the Fighting Falcon. Trade training for maintenance and engineering personnel is performed at Kjevik and Kjeller.

KNL responsibilities are completed by providing maintenance support for the fleet of Cessna O-1 Bird Dogs of the *Luftvernartilleriet*. These perform artillery observation and liaison duties from the airfields at Vaernes and Bardufoss and are flown by Norwegian Army pilots.

Although all four F-16 squadrons are committed to NATO's Allied Forces Northern Europe (AFNorth) organization, in the event of conflict Norway would be heavily reinforced by other NATO member states, most notably the UK and the USA.

Right: Norway's rugged coastline is patrolled by four detachments of SAR-dedicated Sea King Mk.43Bs, all part of 330 SKv at Bodo.

EQUIPMENT

Interception:
General Dynamics F-16A Fighting Falcon
Attack:
General Dynamics F-16A Fighting Falcon
Northrop F-5A Freedom Fighter
Maritime Patrol ASW:
Lockheed P-3C/N Orion
Transport:
Lockheed C-130H Hercules
Dassault-Breguet Falcon 20
Boeing Canada Twin Otter
Bell 412SP
Observation:
Cessna 0-1 Bird Dog
SAR:
Westland Sea King Mk.43B
Coastal Patrol
Westland Lynx Mk.86
Training:
SAAB MFI-15
Dassault-Breguet Falcon 20
General Dynamics F-16A/B Fighting Falcon

Below: Carrying pairs of dummy (blue) and live AIM-9 Sidewinder air-to-air missiles,, two KNL F-16As from 334 Skv (foreground) and 331 Skv conduct an air defence sortie.

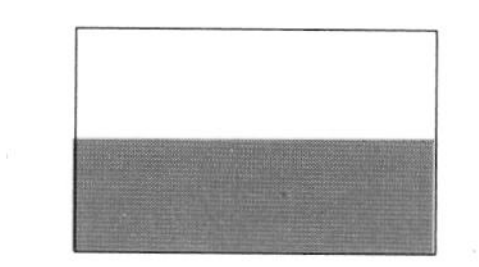

POLAND

OF THE Warsaw Pact nations, Poland is second only to the USSR with regard to the size of its air arm, and organization of the *Polskie Wojska Lotnicze* (Polish Air Force) adheres closely to Soviet lines. Overall command rests with Air Force headquarters in Poznan and combat elements are primarily assigned to two major commands which are concerned with the very different demands of air defence and tactical operations.

Air defence is entrusted to three separate Divisions which manage half-a-dozen Fighter Regiments and the latter will typically control two or three squadrons, each with a complement of around 15-20 aircraft. The classic MiG-21 "Fishbed" is still the most numerous fighter in the inventory and is presently active with four Regiments, a fifth currently being engaged in transition to the newer and much more potent MiG-29 "Fulcrum", while the sixth operates the MiG-23MF "Flogger-B". Until quite recently, air defence resources were reported to be under Soviet control, but the fast-changing political climate behind what used to be the "Iron Curtain" may well have led to a revision of this arrangement.

Tactical components also adhere to the Division/Regiment method of organization, three Divisions controlling a total of nine Regiments between them. Three of the latter are mainly concerned with air superiority, being equipped with the MiG-21, while four are tasked with fighter-bomber duties with the variable-geometry Sukhoi Su-22 "Fitter". The remaining two are essentially training establishments, and utilize the locally-built LIM-5/6 (MiG-17 "Fresco") alongside some Su-7BMK "Fitter-As". There is also a Regiment assigned to the reconnaissance role for which the MiG-21RF "Fishbed-H" is used, but this unit appears to be semi-autonomous and almost certainly operates in support of all three of the tactical Divisions.

Other assets which have a combat capability operate a sizeable fleet of helicopters, many of which are armed. Most lethal must surely be the Mil Mi-24 "Hind" gunship which is currently in service with two Attack Helicopter Regiments. Approximately 60 "Hinds" are on charge, alongside the Mi-2US "Hoplite" which is able to satisfy the "tank-busting" role by virtue of being equipped with AT-2 "Swatter" and AT-3 "Sagger" anti-armour missiles. Other rotary-wing equipment is dominated by close to 50 Mi-8/17 "Hip" assault helicopters which form the main strength of a Transport Regiment that also has a number of Swidnik-built "Hoplites". As with fixed-wing tactical forces, there is a specialist Training Regiment which employs the Mi-2.

Conventional airlift tasks are fulfilled by two Transport Regiments. One operates mainly on tactical duties, being equipped with a fleet that includes about 20 An-12 "Cubs", half-a-dozen An-24 "Cokes", 12 An-26 "Curls" and 10 An-2 "Colts", while the other is a "special" unit which evidently satisfies VIP transport needs. Most of Poland's 20 Yak-40s serve with the latter, alongside a couple of Tu-134As and at least one Tu-154. Utility and communications tasks are performed by PZL-104 Wilgas.

Pilot training is concentrated at Deblin-Irana with the Air Force Officers' School. Instruction begins on the TS-8 Bies, progressing to the jet-powered TS-11 Iskra and the LIM-5/6; but change is underway, with the piston-engined PZL-130 Orlik basic trainer currently entering service. A handful of turbine-powered Turbo-Orliks has been ordered and this type looks set to take over from the Bies, while Poland may also opt to proceed with the PZL I-22 Iryd light jet trainer in due course. Flown in prototype form in 1985, the latter could well replace the Iskra. Operational conversion training is accomplished on two-seat versions of the principal combat types.

EQUIPMENT

Interception:
Mikoyan-Gurevich MiG-29 "Fulcrum-A"
Mikoyan-Gurevich MiG-23MF "Flogger-B"
Mikoyan-Gurevich MiG-21MF/bis "Fishbed-J/N"
Attack:
Sukhoi Su-22 "Fitter-K"
Sukhoi Su-7BMK "Fitter-A"
LIM-5/6
Mil Mi-24 "Hind-D/E"
Mil Mi-2 "Hoplite"
Reconnaissance:
Mikoyan-Gurevich MiG-21RF "Fishbed-H"
Transport:
Antonov An-12 "Cub"
Antonov An-26 "Curl"
Antonov An-24 "Coke"
Antonov An-2 "Colt"
Mil Mi-8/17 "Hip-C/H"
Mil Mi-2 "Hoplite"
VIP Transport:
Tupolev Tu-154 "Careless"
Tupolev Tu-134 "Crusty"
Yakovlev Yak-40 "Codling"
Communications/Liaison:
PZL-104 Wilga
Training:
WSK-Mielec TS-8 Bies
PZL-130 Turbo-Orlik
WSK-Mielec TS-11 Iskra
LIM-1/Mikoyan-Gurevich MiG-15UTI "Midget"
LIM-5/6
Sukhoi Su-7U "Moujik"
Sukhoi Su-22U "Fitter-G"
Mikoyan-Gurevich MiG-21U "Mongol"
Mikoyan-Gurevich MiG-23U "Flogger-C"
Mikoyan-Gurevich MiG-29UB "Fulcrum-B"
Mil Mi-2 "Hoplite"

Above: Like several of its Warsaw Pact allies, the PWL has a fleet of Yak-40 "Codlings" for use in the short-haul VIP transport role.

Right: Caught by the camera as they break formation is a quartet of Sukhoi Su-22M-4 "Fitter-Ks". Note the chaff/flare dispenser racks on the fuselage of the second machine.

PORTUGAL

ONE OF THE smallest and least well-equipped air forces within the NATO framework, Portugal's main contribution to the military alliance is that of making available the air base at Lajes in the Azores. Occupying a key position in the Atlantic Ocean, Lajes is used by P-3 Orion patrol aircraft of the US Navy, and continued availability of this strategically important facility was part of the negotiation process whereby the *Força Aerea Portuguesa* (FAP: Portuguese Air Force) is to receive sufficient F-16 Fighting Falcons to equip a single air defence-dedicated squadron, to be based on the mainland.

Some 20 F-16s are involved in the deal and these will allow the FAP to possess a realistic air defence element for the first time in many, many years. In recent times, this task has been performed by Sidewinder-equipped T-38A Talons, supported by A-7P Corsair IIs and Fiat G-91s. Both of the latter types still figure prominently in the FAP's operational inventory, with the 40-odd A-7s that are presently operated by two squadrons being mainly concerned with maritime attack, while a smaller number of "Ginas" fulfil land attack and close air support (CAS) missions. Obtained second-hand from Germany some years ago, there is a strong possibility that the "Ginas" will be replaced by surplus Alpha Jets from the same source in the early-1990s.

Anti-submarine warfare (ASW) and maritime patrol tasks have long been undertaken by Lockheed products, and half-a-dozen former Australian P-3B Orions are currently being modernized for service with Portugal. Taking over responsibility for this mission from the C-130H Hercules, which served as a stop-gap Neptune replacement, the first P-3P Orion was handed over to the FAP in 1988.

Search-and-resuce (SAR) is entrusted to about 10 Aerospatiale SA.330 Puma helicopters which fly from mainland bases as well as Lajes, and half of the fleet now has *Omera* nose radar offering enhanced surveillance capability. Other helicopters in service comprise some three-dozen Alouette IIIs which are mainly used for light transport, although they can also perform fire support of the Army since they may be armed with 70mm rockets and machine guns. Looking ahead, the FAP is to receive 50 helicopters from the USA during the present decade and this quantity will include some second-hand UH-1H Iroquois.

Other equipment mostly performs second-line tasks and is made up of 30 Reims-Cessna 337 Skymasters for Army co-operation and light transport, a handful of C-130H Hercules for tactical airlift and about 20 CASA Aviocars, including a few that are specially configured for aerial survey work. VIP transport and calibration duties are fulfilled by a trio of Falcon 20s, which are to be joined by two Falcon 50s.

Below: One of only two export customers for the A-7 Corsair II to date, the FAP makes effective use of what is first and foremost an attack-oriented aircraft. However, a distinct lack of a credible interceptor force has resulted in the A-7Ps being used as back-up interceptors.

Pilot training begins in earnest on the Aerospatiale Epsilon, 18 examples of which began to replace the long-serving Chipmunk in 1989, with jet-bound students thereafter moving on to the Cessna T-37C and Lockheed T-33 before operational conversion on the T-38A, TA-7P or G-91T. Helicopter pilots move to the Alouette III after the Epsilon phase, while those who are to fly transport aircraft go to the Aviocar. Some Aerostructure RF-10 powered gliders are also used by the Portuguese Air Force Academy at Sintra.

EQUIPMENT

Attack:
Vought A-7P Corsair II
Aeritalia G-91R
Maritime Patrol/ASW:
Lockheed P-3P Orion
Transport:
Lockheed C-130H Hercules
CASA C.212 Aviocar
VIP Transport:
Dassault-Breguet Falcon 50
Dassault-Breguet Falcon 20
SAR/Sea Surveillance:
Aerospatiale SA.330 Puma
Aerial Survey:
CASA C.212 Aviocar
Communications/Liaison:
Reims-Cessna 337 Skymaster
Aerospatiale Alouette III
Training:
Fournier RF-10
Aerospatiale TB-30 Epsilon
Cessna T-37C
Lockheed T-33
Northrop T-38A Talon
Aeritalia G-91T
Vought TA-7P Corsair II

ROMANIA

DESPITE SOME reduction in defence spending during the last few years of the notorious Ceasusescu regime, the Romanian Air Force (RAF) is still a fairly substantial organization, and one that operates an unusual mixture of equipment. Most front-line hardware is of Soviet origin, but a determined effort has been made to introduce locally-designed and manufactured equipment such as the IAR-93 which stemmed from collaboration with Yugoslavia. Further aerospace expertise stems from licence production of a number of types of Western origin, including the French Puma and Alouette helicopters, both of which have been inducted into military service in reasonable numbers.

Organized along Soviet lines, the RAF's combat capability is dominated by more than 200 interceptors. Most are MiG-21 "Fishbeds", which are reported to be distributed between a dozen squadrons, but close to 50 MiG-23 "Floggers" are assigned to a trio of squadrons which constitute a single Fighter Regiment and some MiG-29 "Fulcrums" are now also in service with a unit at Mihail Kogalniceanu. Delivery of the "Fulcrum" evidently began shortly before Ceasusescu's demise and the type duly became operational during 1990. At least 14 "Fulcrum-As" and a pair of "Fulcrum-B" two-seaters have been handed over so far and Romania has expressed interest in obtaining up to 49, although the fact that payment for future examples will have to be in US dollars may delay the re-equipment programme.

Attack forces continue to operate a steadily diminishing quantity of MiG-17 "Frescos" and fewer than 50 are thought to remain in the front-line, but plans to replace them with close to 200 IAR-93s have taken longer to implement than was originally hoped for due to technical and financial difficulties. At present, though, the RAF is still hoping to obtain a reasonable quantity, with most being to the definitive IAR-93B standard incorporating a locally-designed afterburner for the licence-built Viper turbojet engine. Operational application will be primarily ground attack, but a secondary intercept capability is a feature.

Combat echelons of the RAF are rounded out by 10 Il-28 "Beagles", these obsolete light bombers being used for reconnaissance and electronic countermeasures (ECM) tasks.

Transport resources are quite limited in scope, being confined to modest numbers of An-24 "Cokes", An-26 "Curls", Il-14 "Crates", An-2 "Colts" and a handful of Li-2 "Cabs", although the last type may by now have been retired. Rotary-wing types which fulfil airlift duties are now dominated by the licence-built IAR-330 Puma, of which just about 100 are in service, supported by 20 or so Mi-8 "Hips" and some fairly recently delivered Mi-17s plus about 10 Mi-4 "Hounds" and a few Mi-2 "Hoplites". Other helicopters have more warlike potential, with close to 50 IAR-316 Alouette IIIs being used for anti-armour attack, but work on a much-modified derivative known as the IAR-317 Airfox has now been abandoned after a fairly prolonged period of testing.

Instruction of pilots is accomplished internally and this is one area in which the RAF has sought to move closer to a state of self-sufficiency by developing and deploying a family of trainers. Grading and assessment is accomplished on the IAR-28MA and leads on to primary tuition on the IAR-823. About 40 examples of this indigenous Lycoming-engined design are in use with the RAF, which is also set to obtain the IAR-825 Triumf turboprop trainer following a lengthy evaluation. Greater success already seems to have been achieved by the IAR-99 Soim jet trainer which made its maiden flight in December 1985 and which is now being introduced to service as a replacement for the 60 or so L-29 Delfins obtained from Czechoslovakia. Specialized weapons training is given on the L-39 Albatros and MiG-15UTI "Midget", with operational conversion following on two-seat trainer derivatives of the principal front-line combat types.

Above: The standard medium-lift transport used by Warsaw Pact air forces, including that of Romania, is the An-26 "Curl".

Below: The latest of Romania's indigenous aircraft designs to enter service is the sleek and purposeful IAR-99 Soim trainer.

EQUIPMENT

Interception:
Mikoyan-Gurevich MiG-29 "Fulcrum-A"
Mikoyan-Gurevich MiG-23 "Flogger"
Mikoyan-Gurevich MiG-21F/PF/MF "Fishbed-C/D/J"

Attack:
SOKO/CNIAR IAR-93A/B
Mikoyan-Gurevich MiG-17F "Fresco"
IAR-316 Alouette III

ECM/Reconnaissance:
Ilyushin Il-28 "Beagle"

Aerial Survey:
Antonov An-30 "Clank"

Transport:
Antonov An-26 "Curl"
Antonov An-24 "Coke"
Ilyushin Il-14 "Crate"
Lisunov Li-2 "Cab"
Antonov An-2 "Colt"
Mil Mi-8/17 "Hip"
IAR-330 Puma
Mil Mi-4 "Hound"

VIP Transport:
IAR-330 Puma
Aerospatiale SA.365N Dauphin 2

Communications/Liaison:
Morava L-200
Mil Mi-2 "Hoplite"
IAR-316 Alouette III

Training:
ICA IAR-28MA
ICA-Brasov IAR-823
Aero L-29 Delfin
Mikoyan-Gurevich MiG-15UTI "Midget"
Aero L-39 Albatros
IAR-99 Soim
Mikoyan-Gurevich MiG-21U "Mongol"
Mikoyan-Gurevich MiG-29UB "Fulcrum-B"
SOKO/CNIAR IAR-93

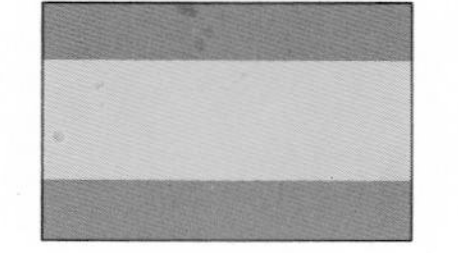

SPAIN

ALTHOUGH ostensibly part of the North Atlantic Treaty Organization (NATO) alliance, the *Ejercito del Aire* (EdA: Spanish Air Force) has not been formally declared to NATO and nor does it seem likely to be in the near to mid-term future. Current organization is based on the establishment of three main Divisions, each of which manages the activities of subordinate elements via a number of Commands. By way of illustration, the General Staff Division is responsible for VIP airlift elements as well as those units that have what could be classed as "civilian" missions, specifically search-and-rescue (SAR) and airborne fire-fighting. Other Divisions comprise the Air Force and Air Logistics, but the distribution of assets between these two is slightly unusual in so far as the latter agency is entrusted with control of Tactical Air Command, which utilizes an odd mix of hardware including Northrop F-5s and Lockheed P-3 Orions.

Combat elements are equipped with fighters of French and US origin. Newest and most significant is the Hornet, some 60 single-seat EF-18As and 12 two-seat EF-18Bs having been purchased for service with two two-squadron Fighter Wings at Torrejon and Zaragoza. Multi-mission capability means that they are almost equally at home in attack and air defence, and the second major combat type is also dual-tasked in these roles. This is the Mirage F.1, which serves with a full-size Wing at Los Llanos on the mainland (F.1CE) and with one squadron at Gando in the Canary Islands (F.1EE). About 24 Mirages of an earlier generation also fulfil attack/air defence roles with a Wing at Valencia (Manises). These are IIIEEs that were slated for retirement but which are to be modernized in order to extend their useful lives.

Dual-mission potential is also possessed by a Wing at Moron, attack and reconnaissance tasks being performed by a mixture of SF-5A and SRF-5A Freedom Fighters from this southern base. About a dozen RF-4C Phantom IIs are also assigned to reconnaissance, these former USAF machines equipping a third squadron of the Torrejon-based Wing.

One other unit with a clear-cut combat role is located at Jerez and this has six P-3A Orions and a brace of CASA Aviocars for anti-submarine warfare (ASW) and maritime surveillance. Most of the P-3As are operated under the terms of a lease agreement and these are soon to be returned to the US Navy; but Spain will continue to fly Orions, henceforth using five former Norwegian P-3Bs alongside its own two P-3As, all of which are to be given P-3C avionics amongst other improvements. In addition, three F-27MPA Friendships and four suitably modified Super Pumas meet maritime requirements in the Canaries, where they fly from Gando.

Transport resources are extensive and include no fewer than 55 Aviocars plus 11 C-130 Hercules, about half of the latter being configured as tanker-transports, and 18 Caribou freighters. A few CASA-Nurtanio CN.235s are also operated and at least 18 are to be purchased to permit retirement of the Caribou fleet, while VIP transport is entrusted to a fleet that includes examples of

Left: Without a shadow of a doubt, the most potent combat asset in service with the EdA is the EF.18 Hornet. Known locally as the CE.15 (single-seat) and CE.15 (two-seat), the Hornet equips a total of four squadrons.

Above: The Northrop F-5 has proved to be especially popular with the air arms of Southern Europe, and the EdA continues to make good use of the type. Illustrated is an AE.9 (SF-5B) trainer.

Right: Adorned with Trainer Yellow paint, this trio of Beech F.33C Bonanzas (known locally as E.24As) are part of a batch of 24 examples acquired in the 1970s for use in the training role.

the Falcon 20, Falcon 50/900, Douglas DC-8 and Boeing 707 in its composition, although at least two of the last type are to be fitted out for in-flight refuelling duties. Communications and liaison tasks are dealt with by a number of light aircraft types including close to 40 Dornier Do 27s and licence-built CASA 127s.

Pilot training begins with basic tuition on the CASA-ENAER T-35C Tamiz, or Pillan as it is probably better known, some 40 having been delivered to Spain's Air Academy at San Javier. Advanced instruction follows on the locally-designed CASA Aviojet before students move to the SF-5B for training relating to tactics and weapons delivery. Thereafter, operational instruction is performed at Wing level using two-seat versions of the principal combat types. Transport and helicopter instruction is also undertaken, types employed including the Aviocar, Bell 47G, Hughes 300 and Iroquois. Other aircraft engaged on specialist training are the Piper Aztec and Navajo, and the Beech Bonanza and Baron.

Civilian-type missions are headed by SAR, with mainland-based units operating Aviocars, Super Pumas and Alouette IIIs, while two Torrejon-based squadrons have about a dozen Canadair CL-215 fire-fighting water-bombers which are to be updated to CL-215T standard and retro-fitted with turboprop powerplants in due course.

EQUIPMENT

Interception-Attack:
McDonnell Douglas EF-18A Hornet
Dassault-Breguet Mirage F.1CE/EE
Dassault-Breguet Mirage IIIEE
Attack:
Northrop SF-5A Freedom Fighter
Reconnaissance:
McDonnell Douglas RF-4C Phantom II
Northrop SRF-5A Freedom Fighter
Maritime Patrol/ASW
Lockheed P-3A Orion
Fokker F-27MPA Friendship
CASA C.212 Aviocar
Transport:
Boeing 707-331C
Douglas DC-8 Srs.52
Lockheed C-130H Hercules
Airtech CN.235
Boeing Canada Caribou
CASA C.212 Aviocar
Aerospatiale SA.330 Puma
Aerospatiale AS.332 Super Puma
VIP Transport:
Dassault-Breguet Falcon 20
Dassault-Breguet Falcon 50/900
Tanking-Transport:
Boeing 707-331C
Lockheed KC-130H Hercules
ECM:
CASA C.212 Aviocar
Communications/Liaison:
Beech King Air
SAR:
CASA C.212 Aviocar
Aerospatiale AS.332 Super Puma
Aerospatale Alouette III
Aerial Survey:
CASA C.212 Aviocar
Fire-Fighting:
Canadair CL-215
Utility:
Dornier Do 27
CASA 127
Training:
ENAER T-35C Tamiz
Beech Bonanza
CASA C.101 Aviojet
Northrop SF-5B Freedom Fighter
Dassault-Breguet Mirage IIIDE
Dassault-Breguet Mirage F.1BE
McDonnell Douglas EF-18B Hornet
Beech Baron
Piper PA-23 Aztec
Piper PA-31P/T Navajo
CASA C.212 Aviocar
Bell 47G
McDonnell Douglas 300C
Agusta-Bell AB.205A/UH-1H Iroquois

Above: At the heart of the Swedish Air Force is the Viggen, with a trio of JA 37s (149 built in all) holding line for the camera-ship.

SWEDEN

ONE OF the small number of neutral states within Europe, Sweden has demonstrated an impressive degree of self-reliance with regard to armaments, and nowhere is this more apparent than in the *Svenska Flygvapnet* (Swedish Air Force) which relies totally on home-grown aircraft to equip its combat echelons. It has, nevertheless, been greatly reduced in size over the past couple of decades and may well contract still further since the forthcoming SAAB-Scania JAS 39 Gripen multi-role fighter is already running well behind schedule and is being troubled by increasing costs. Between them, these factors may result in the requirement for some 355 aircraft being reduced by quite a wide margin.

At present, the principal warplane is the SAAB-Scania Viggen which, like Gripen, is a multi-role fighter. Production finally terminated in June 1990 when the last of 329 aircraft was handed over to the *Flygvapnet*. Destined to remain in service until at least 2010, five basic versions were manufactured, made up of 110 attack-optimized AJ 37s, 26 reconaissance SF 37s, 26 maritime attack/reconnaissance SH 37s, 149 interceptor JA 37s and 18 two-seater Sk 37 trainers. Attrition has reduced the size of this fleet to the 290 mark, with most of the casualties being AJ 37s.

Surviving aircraft are currently distributed amongst eight of the nine *Flygflottiljer* (Combat Wings), each of which controls the activities of two or three *Divisionen* (Squadrons), with a typical unit establishment of around 18 aircraft. In the case of the Viggen, some 17 squadrons use the type, although one is effectively a half-sized unit since it also operates the two-seater Sk 37s in the pilot transition role on behalf of the entire Viggen force.

As the most numerous version, it is hardly surprising that the AJ 37 is flown by no less than eight squadrons, while the older attack-dedicated AJ 37 is now used by just six, one being the half-sized unit. Remaining Viggen-equipped combat units are fundamentally composite organizations, with three squadrons sharing the four dozen or so examples that remain of the pure reconnaissance SF 37 and maritime attack/reconnaissance SH 37 models.

Combat-capable forces are completed by a ninth Wing, again with three squadrons, which fly the uniquely distinctive SAAB-Scania Draken, a recently completed upgrade programme resulting in the transformation of 64 J 35Fs to J 35J standard. Work entailed structural changes to permit the provision of extra external stores stations as well as avionics improvements, with revised radar and infra-red sensors being key aspects. Modification in this manner should enable these Drakens to remain operational until at least the mid-1990s when the Gripen is expected to become available. About 10 two-seater Sk 35Cs have been retained for training duties in support of the J 35Js.

Second-line and support elements are engaged in a variety of tasks, ranging from airlift through communications to target-towing and electronic countermeasures (ECM) training. Pure transport potential is

Below: Another product from the SAAB-Scania company to bear the three crowns insignia of the Swedish Air Force is the SF.340B, one of which has been configured to enable it to be used as a VIP transport aircraft.

confined to just eight examples of the Lockheed Hercules which serve with one squadron, while most combat wings do possess a communications element which usually operates a handful of Sk 50 Safirs and Sk 60 jet trainers, these being augmented by a single Cessna 404 Titan. Other utility transport equipment includes two Super King Airs, one Swearingen Merlin, and a single SAAB SF.340 for use by the Air Force Chief-of-Staff.

Also normally a part of each combat wing is a search-and-rescue (SAR) component with two or three examples of the Agusta-Bell 204, MBB BO 105CBS or Aerospatiale AS.332M Super Puma. Other "one-off" roles are concentrated at Malmslatt and mainly relate to electronic missions, for which a pair of former Scandinavian Airlines System Caravelles and a motley assortment of much-modified J 32 Lansens are utilized by a special outfit. This base is also home for the *Forsokcentralen* (Test Centre) which has a few Lansens, Drakens and Viggens plus a brace of Rockwell Sabre 65s for research and development duties.

Pilot training is concentrated at Ljungbyhed and is now accomplished throughout on the SAAB-Scania Sk 60, a type that could be employed for light attack duties by four mobilized squadrons in the event of Sweden becoming embroiled in combat. BAe Bulldogs that were previously used for primary instruction are still active, although they are mainly used for the training of civilian pupils. Operational-type instruction is undertaken on two-seater versions of the Draken and Viggen.

EQUIPMENT

Interception:
SAAB-Scania JA 37 Viggen
SAAB-Scania J 35J Draken
Attack:
SAAB-Scania AJ 37 Viggen
Maritime Attack/Reconnaissance:
SAAB-Scania SH 37 Viggen
Reconnaissance:
SAAB-Scania SF 37 Viggen
SAAB-Scania Sk 60C
ECM/Elint-Gathering:
Aerospatiale SE.210 Caravelle III
SAAB-Scania J 32E Lansen
Rockwell Sabre 65
AEW (Trials):
Swearingen Metro III
Transport:
Lockheed C-130H Hercules
Cessna 404 Titan
Swearingen Merlin IVC
Beech Super King Air
VIP Transport:
SAAB-Scania SF. 340B
Target-Towing:
SAAB-Scania J 32D Lansen
SAR/Utility:
Aerospatiale AS.332M Super Puma
Agusta-Bell AB.204B
MBB BO 105CBS
Training:
BAe Bulldog 101
SAAB-Scania Sk 60
SAAB-Scania J 32B Lansen
SAAB-Scania Sk 35C Draken
SAAB-Scania Sk 37 Viggen
Communications/Liaison:
SAAB-Scania Sk 60
SAAB-Scania Sk 50 Safir

Above: One Metro III with a dorsal Ericsson PS-890 radar housing is under evaluation. Note also the complex "splinter" camouflage.

Below: Numbers may be dwindling, but SAAB's Sk 60 jet trainer is still an important element in the pilot training programme.

SWITZERLAND

Above: The final home for BAe Hunters on the European mainland is Switzerland, where over 100 survivors of another era continue to provide a highly respectable "punch".

OFFICIALLY known as the *Kommando der Flieger- und Fliegerabwehrtruppen* (Swiss Air Force and Anti-Aircraft Command) to use its rather wordy title, but usually alluded to as simply the *Flugwaffe* (Air Force), this organization is actually a part of the Army and is tasked with directing the activities of the five Brigades which constitute the 5th Army Corps in both peace and war. Most significant of these is *Flugwaffenbrigade* (Air Force Brigade) 31 which has responsibility for all flying operations and air traffic control.

In peacetime, operating philosophy is based largely on the use of reservist (Militia) personnel. In consequence, only six of the 19 combat squadrons are fully-constituted formations and these make up the Surveillance Wing. However, personnel assigned to these six squadrons invariably include some members of the Militia on annual active duty training.

In the event of full-scale mobilization, combat-capable elements are augmented by four more F-5E units and no fewer than nine with Hunters, annual training of the latter 13 squadrons ensuring that they can very quickly be brought to a full state of operational readiness.

Longest-serving of the front-line types is the Dassault-Breguet Mirage, high-altitude interception being the primary function of the IIIS model 30 or so of which remain in service at Payerne with Nos. 16 and 17 Squadrons. A recent upgrade programme should extend their lives until well into the 21st Century, the IIIS sprouting canards and nose strakes as visible evidence of the transformation. Less obvious improvements are the provision of new Martin-Baker Mk.6 ejection seats, *Dalmo Victor* radar warning receivers, VHF radio and a new set of chaff/flare dispensers.

Also part of the Surveillance Wing is No.10 Squadron at Dubendorf which flies the Mirage IIIRS on tactical reconnaissance tasks, and it is a remarkable tribute to Swiss pilot and maintenance skills that all 18 aircraft delivered in the late-1960s are still active today. A few two-seat Mirages are employed for pilot training at Payerne, the Swiss having taken delivery of four IIIBSs and two IIIUDSs between 1963 and 1983, but operational attrition has claimed a couple of victims over the years.

Three regular units fly the Northrop F-5E Tiger II, deliveries to Switzerland comprising 98 F-5Es and 12 F-5F two-seaters, with most of the F-5Es being assembled locally from Northrop-supplied kits. About 90 F-5Es survive, Surveillance Wing units that operate the Tiger II consisting of No.1 Squadron at Payerne, No.11 Squadron at Meiringen and No.18 Squadron at Dubendorf; and it also equips four reserve outfits (Nos.6, 8, 13 and 19 Squadrons).

The remaining combat type is no longer employed by front-line echelons but some 125 Hunter F.58/58As and seven T.68 two-seaters would undoubtedly have an important role to play in any conflict. Missions assigned to the nine reserve units that fly these veterans (Nos.2, 3, 4, 5, 7, 15, 20, 21 and 24 Squadrons) include interception (with the well-proven AIM-9 Sidewinder missile) and air-to-ground attack, for which a variety of ordnance including AGM-65 Maverick missiles, BL755 cluster-bomb units, "iron" bombs and 80mm rockets may be employed. The remaining operational task

Below: A more modern Swiss Air Force asset is the sleek Northrop F-5E Tiger II, 98 of which were acquired to equip a total of seven units (plus an eighth with two-seater F-5Fs).

Right: Counted amongst the Swiss Air Force's day-to-day duties is SAR among the peaks and valleys that form the Alps. Helicopters are the best platform for such operations, as illustrated here by an Alouette III.

is electronic countermeasures (ECM), No.24 Squadron having formed in the mid-1980s with at least three modified two-seater Hunters, these being fitted with radar warning receivers, chaff/flare dispensers and other specialized "kit".

Looking to the future, in October 1988, Switzerland revealed it was to purchase the McDonnell Douglas F-18 Hornet as its next fighter. Initial planning called for the procurement of 34 aircraft (26 F-18Cs and eight F-18D trainers), but this quantity was later cut to 24 and more recent developments in East-West relations have thrown a veil of doubt over Swiss intentions, for the Mirage 2000-5 is to be re-evaluated and even the USSR is trying to get in on the act by offering the MiG-29 "Fulcrum" for assessment.

Second-line liaison and communications assets are known as *Lichtfliegerstaffeln* (Light Aviation Squadrons) and are manned by a mix of regular and reserve crews. Resources in use comprise 18 PC-6B Turbo-Porters, two Dornier Do 27H-2s, 24 Alouette IIs and just under 80 Alouette IIIs. Four of these squadrons (Nos.1 to 4) function in direct support of Swiss Army ground forces, with one being assigned to each Corps. Equipment operated by this quartet consists solely of Alouette IIs and IIIs.

Three of the remaining four squadrons (Nos.5, 6 and 8) use only the Alouette III and come under *Flugwaffe* control, but Aerospatiale AS.332M Super Pumas are now being added to the inventory, Switzerland having thus far ordered a total of 15 for service with Light Aviation Squadrons 5, 6 and 8.

The last Light Aviation Squadron (No.7) specializes in covert-type insertion of parachute troops and operates in support of a Parachute-Grenadier Company with 18 Pilatus PC-6B Turbo-Porters. This unit also has both Do 27s, one of which features a mapping camera for aerial survey tasks.

There is also the *Transportfliegerkorps* (Air Transport Corps) with two civil-registered LearJet 35As for general purpose transport duties from Dubendorf, and the *Zeilfliegerkorps 5* (5th Aerial Target Corps) which has a small number of Pilatus PC-9s. These are used to tow targets for anti-aircraft gunnery practise from Sion, along with a few Vampire FB.6s, but more PC-9s are in prospect and the fleet is eventually expected to number around 14 aircraft.

Pilot training begins at Magadino with basic military and technical instruction before students get airborne in the Pilatus PC-7 Turbo-Trainer for selection and basic tuition, which culminates in streaming to either jets or helicopters. Until recently, jet pilots then encountered the Vampire T.55 and FB.6 but these have now given way to the much more modern BAe Hawk T.66, with 19 of the 20 that have been ordered to date being assembled locally at Emmen.

Final streaming into ground attack and intercept disciplines then occurs as a prelude to operational-type instruction on F-5s, Hunters and PC-7s, but the Hawk is expected to assume responsibility for at least part of this phase in due course. Helicopter pilots complete their training on Alouette II/IIIs, Pilatus P-3s and PC-7s.

Not all pilots will become part of the permanent air force, however, for some may choose to enter civil aviation, but they will have to complete six weeks of Militia service during each succeeding year until released from this obligation.

EQUIPMENT

Interception/Attack:
Northrop F-5E Tiger II
Dassault-Breguet Mirage IIIS
BAe Hunter F.58/.58A
Reconnaissance:
Dassault-Breguet Mirage IIIRS
ECM Training:
BAe Hunter T.68
Transport:
LearJet 35A
Pilatus PC-6B Turbo-Porter
Dornier Do 27H-2
Aerospatiale AS.332M Super Puma
Target-Towing:
Pilatus PC-9
de Havilland Vampire FB.6
Training:
Pilatus P-3
Pilatus PC-7 Turbo-Trainer
BAe Hawk T.66
Northrop F-5F Tiger II
BAe Hunter T.68
Dassault-Breguet Mirage IIIBS/DS
General Duties:
Aerospatiale Alouette II
Aerospatiale Alouette III

TURKEY

THE recipient of a substantial amount of military aid from the USA, Turkey has a seemingly inexhaustible requirement for surplus military hardware from other NATO nations and has in recent years obtained Lockheed F-104 Starfighters from Belgium, Canada, Holland and West Germany, as well as Northrop F-5 Freedom Fighters from Holland and Norway. More significantly, it has also embarked on a modernization programme centred around the General Dynamics F-16 Fighting Falcon, with current plans anticipating procurement of 136 F-16Cs and 24 F-16Ds. Initially, this entailed assembly of kits supplied by General Dynamics, but the TUSAS organization is destined to progress to fully licenced manufacture at its Murted factory.

Organizationally, combat-ready units of the *Turk Hava Kuvvetleri* (THK — Turkish Air Force) are assigned to one of two Tactical Air Forces, air bases to the west of the 35th Meridian belonging to the Inci THKK with headquarters at Eskisehir, and those to the east constituting the 2nci THKK headquartered at Diyarbakir. In addition, there is a Transport Command which reports directly to THK headquarters in Ankara, and a Training Command with its headquarters at Gaziemir.

As already noted, much of the hardware has been obtained second-hand and two basic types — the McDonnell Douglas F-4 Phantom II and the F-104 Starfighter — form the principal combat equipment. The latter is probably marginally more numerous and is active with seven squadrons although it is now beginning to give way to the F-16 which equips at least two squadrons. It is probably no coincidence that these are both based at Murted, close to the TUSAS factory. Starfighter variants in use include F-104G, F-104S and CF-104 single-seaters, and there is also a substantial number of two-seater TF-104Gs and Canadair-built CF-104Ds. Turning to the rather more potent Phantom II, the F-4E version is in use with seven squadrons while one squadron has a small number of RF-4Es for reconnsissance, a task that is also undertaken by one RF-5A squadron. The basic F-5A version of the diminutive Freedom Fighter is far from defunct, for it remains operational with three squadrons. Some F-5Bs are also operated on training tasks.

Airlift requirements are satisfied by four squadrons which utilize an assortment of somewhat elderly transport aircraft, including the Lockheed C-130E Hercules, Transall C.160D and Douglas C-47 Dakota. One of this quartet of squadrons is tasked with VIP and calibration missions; Vickers Viscount 794Ds and Cessna Citation IIs are used for the former duty, with a small number of suitably configured C-47s undertaking the latter. Transport elements are in sore need of modernization and it seems likely that the CASA-Nurtanio CN-235 will be acquired, although a proposed order for 52 examples has still to be confirmed.

Training needs are satisfied in-country and the THK operates a sizeable fleet of aircraft dedicated to meeting the need for aircrew. Students log about 250 flying hours before being awarded their "Wings".

One other squadron, at Topel, is equipped with the Grumman S-2E Tracker for maritime surveillance and ASW missions. These tasks are performed on behalf of the Turkish Navy, which is believed to retain operational control.

EQUIPMENT

Interception:
General Dynamics F-16C/D Fighting Falcon
Lockheed F-104S/CF-104 Starfighter
Attack:
Lockheed F-104G/CF-104 Starfighter
McDonnell Douglas F-4E Phantom II
Northrop F-5A Freedom Fighter
Reconnaissance:
McDonnell Douglas RF-4E Phantom II
Northrop RF-5A Freedom Fighter
Transport:
Douglas C-47 Dakota
Lockheed C-130E Hercules
Transall C.160D
Transport (VIP):
Cessna Citation II
Vickers Viscount 794D
Survey/Mapping:
Pilatus Britten-Norman BN-2A Islander
SAR/Liaison:
Bell UH-1H Iroquois
Maritime Reconnaissance/ASW:
Grumman S-2E Tracker
Training:
Cessna T-41D Mescalero
Beech T-34A Mentor
Cessna T-37B/C
Lockheed T-33A
Northrop T-38A Talon
Northrop F-5B Freedom Fighter

Above: Caught seconds after take-off from its base at Eskisehir, this F-4E Phantom II is a typical example of the hardware that has been supplied to the THK by the United States.

Right: A THK C-130E Hercules taxies out at the start of a return flight to Turkey from the UK, where it had picked up urgently needed engine spares.

Left: Quality is just as vital as quantity when it comes tot he modern-day air force, and the THK is set to acquire in excess of 200 F-16 fighters during the coming years.

USSR

EFFORTS to modernize Soviet military capability continued apace throughout the last decade, the closing stages of which were marked by steadily improving relationships between the two great superpowers. One of the first tangible manifestations of this process was the Intermediate Nuclear Forces (INF) treaty, but efforts aimed at reducing armaments are continuing in both the nuclear and conventional warfare fields and deep cuts appear to be imminent in the latter area, although the initial phases will almost certainly be satisfied by the scrapping of old and obsolescent hardware.

As far as air power is concerned, the so-called "quality gap" between East and West has been steadily eroded over the past decade or so, with the USSR deploying a number of potent new warplanes. Perhaps best epitomized by the Sukhoi Su-27 "Flanker", MiG-29 "Fulcrum" and MiG-31 "Foxhound", the latest generation of warplanes to be developed is possessed of capabilities that closely match — and, in some cases, surpass — those of contemporary Western hardware.

Not surprisingly, the North Atlantic Treaty Organization (NATO) expressed mounting anxiety over such developments for much of the 1980s, although the worst fears appear to have been allayed by recent events behind what used to be commonly known as the "Iron Curtain". Nevertheless, the USSR is still possessed of formidable fighting potential, whether it be in the air, on the ground or at sea.

As well as receiving much new military equipment, the overall structure of the Soviet armed forces has also been subjected to change, this change embracing all of the five major elements that make up Soviet military power. Two of those elements — namely the Ground Forces and the Navy — lie outside the scope of this study; but the other three all have air components and do merit attention, these being the Strategic Nuclear Forces, the National Air Defence Force and the Air Force.

Before looking more closely at those commands, it is worth presenting brief details of overall military structure since this is one area that has undergone fairly significant change, with the USSR establishing what might fairly be described as "unified commands" to co-ordinate the activities of land, sea and air echelons. Known as *Teatr Voyennykh Destivy* (TVD: Theatre of Military Operations), these come under the control of a single commander and are further grouped into *Teatr Voyny* (TV: Theatre of War) establishments. Three of the TVs are constituted on purely geographic lines, these consisting of the Western TV, the Southern TV and the Far East TV, while the fourth is fundamentally a strategic reserve.

Elements assigned to the Western TV are composed of forces of the North-Western TVD centred on the Leningrad Military District (MD); the South-Western TVD (Odessa MD, Kiev MD plus the Southern Group of Forces with assets in Hungary, Bulgaria and Romania), the Western TVD (Baltic MD, Byelorussian MD, Carpathian MD plus the Group of Forces in Germany, the Northern Group of Forces in Poland and the Central Group of Forces in Czechoslovakia) and the Atlantic and Arctic TVDs which are purely naval in make-up. Air power available to the Western TV is truly massive, with some 3,000 tactical aircraft on hand.

Southern TV components consist of the Southern TVD (North Caucasus MD, Trans-Caucasus MD, Turkestan MD and the Caspian Flotilla). This has some 700 tactical aircraft at its disposal, with roughly twice that number available to the Far East TV which is made up of the Far-East TVD (Central Asia MD, Siberian MD, Trans-Baikal MD, Far Eastern MD and Mongolia) and the Pacific Ocean TVD, which again is purely naval. Finally, there is the Strategic Reserve with just under 150 aircraft distributed amongst the Moscow, Ural and Volga MDs.

Overall control of air power elements assigned to most of the Military Districts referred to is entrusted to the Air Forces of the Military District (AFMD), or to the Air Forces of Group of Forces (AFGF) in the case of components stationed on the territory of allied nations such as Mongolia and Romania. Each of the 20 AFMDs and AFGFs that exist comes under a single commander with deputies who specialize in air defence and tactical activities, but they are also able to enlist significantly heavier fire power from home-based Air Armies (AA) of the Central Reserve.

In excess of 1,500 aircraft are controlled by the five Central Reserve Air Armies at Irkutsk, Legnica, Moscow, Smolensk and Vinnitsa, with a force that is composed of strategic and tactical attack bombers and fighters as well as assorted MiGs for escort duty. In the normal course of events, Central Reserve assets report to Moscow for operational control, but they would come under the direction of an AFMD or AFGF commander if reassigned.

Below: Continually shadowed by a USAF F-15A Eagle as it heads south over the Atlantic Ocean on its way to Cuba, this Tu-142K "Bear-H" is an example of the latest production version of an aircraft that first flew in 1954. This model, of which over 70 are now in service, can carry at least 10 long-range "cruise" missiles, such as the AS-15 "Kent".

Left: Quite capable of attacking the United States — if refuelled *en route* — this Tu-26 "Backfire-B" had its refuelling nose probe deleted to exempt it from SALT 2 cuts.

Possessing awesome destructive capability, the Strategic Nuclear Force conforms closely to American philosophy in that it is a three-pronged weapon, with delivery systems being composed of manned bombers as well as land-and sea-based missiles. Bomber echelons are assigned to the five Air Armies alluded to earlier and these are collectively known as the Strategic Air Armies (formerly *Dal'naya Aviatsiya* or Long-Range Aviation). Between them, they possess some 1,650 aircraft, roughly a quarter of which are Sukhoi Su-24 "Fencers" for interdiction, while about 250 MiG-21 "Fishbed", MiG-23 "Flogger" and Su-27 "Flanker" fighters are available for escort duties.

Rather heavier metal includes a substantial quantity of the turboprop-powered Tupolev "Bear" which, remarkably, is still in production, being viewed as a "cruise" missile platform rather than as a "penetrator". In this role, it is believed that the Tu-142 "Bear-H" may carry up to 14 AS-15 "Kent" cruise missiles, each with a range of up to 1,684 miles (2,700km) and able to deliver a nuclear warhead with a yield of around 200 kT. Other versions are configured for strategic reconnaissance and electronic warfare (EW), and the USSR shows no sign of being in a hurry to retire this remarkable machine.

Manned bomber forces also operate a considerable fleet of Tu-16 "Badgers", Tu-22 "Blinders" and Tu-26 "Backfires" on various strategic tasks, with the "Badger" being amongst the most versatile despite its age, for it is employed as an electronic countermeasures (ECM) and reconnaissance platform as well as an in-flight refuelling tanker and remains operational as a bomber, although, like the "Bear", it mostly relies on missiles to deliver nuclear or conventional warheads.

Of rather more recent origin is the Tu-160 "Blackjack" variable-geometry bomber, which began to enter service during mid-1988 and which was expected to achieve an initial operational capability at the start of the present decade, although problems encountered during development may delay its wide-scale deployment. Essentially a Soviet counterpart to the USA's Rockwell B-1B Lancer, "Blackjack" may be used to deliver either gravity bombs (weapons payload capacity is reportedly in the 36,000lb [16,3454kg] class) or "cruise" missiles like the AS-15 "Kent" and, ultimately, the supersonic AS-19 which is currently under development.

Air elements available to the Strategic Air Armies are rounded out by about 15 Il-78 "Midas" tanker versions of the Il-76 "Candid" freighter. A small number of Il-22 "Coot" airborne command posts are also in service, but these will almost certainly soon be replaced by a suitably-configured version of the Il-96 airliner as the present decade progresses.

Strategic Rocket Forces is responsible for managing the USSR's land-based missiles and currently possesses six Rocket Armies organized into Divisions, Regiments, Battalions and Batteries to operate well over 1,000 Intercontinental Ballistic Missiles (ICBMs). Principal types in service are the SS-11 "Sego" (being withdrawn), SS-13 "Savage", SS-17 "Spanker", SS-18 "Satan", SS-19 "Stiletto", the rail-mobile SS-24 "Scalpel" and the road-mobile SS-25 "Sickle"; but at least two more fifth-generation ICBMs (SS-26 and SS-27) are now under development and may eventually be placed in service. On a brighter note, the INF treaty of December 1987 resulted in an agreement to scrap some 1,752 shorter-range weapons although not all of these were deployed, and there is reason to believe that on-going talks with the USA will eventually lead to a significant reduction in strategic missile arsenals.

Responsibility for the protection of the USSR from air attack is the *raison d'etre* of the *Voyska-Protiyovozdushnoy Oborony* (V-PVO: Troops of Air Defence), which exercises control over most radar, gun and missile elements as well as a substantial interceptor force, although there is considerable doubt as to just how interceptor elements are split between the *Voyenno-Vozdushnyye Sily* (VVS: Soviet Air Force) and the V-PVO. What is clear, however, is that much attention has been devoted to finding a less unwieldy chain of command so as to avoid a repetition of the destruction of the Korean Airlines Boeing 747 in 1983 and the arrival of Matthias Rust and his Cessna 172 in Moscow's Red Square during 1987. Both events were hugely embarrassing to the USSR and both were responsible for changes, the extent of which have still to be fully explained.

While there may be confusion as to the precise organization of Soviet defences, there is certainly less room for doubt when it comes to the matter of equipment. Well-established fighters like the MiG-23 "Flogger", MiG-25 "Foxbat" and Su-15 "Flagon" form the heart of the system, these currently being joined by an increasing number of MiG-31 "Foxhounds" and Su-27 "Flankers"

Right: Some 900 or so MiG-23 "Floggers" are in Soviet service as interceptors, and a similar quantity (of which this trio of MiG-23M "Flogger-Bs" is an example) serve in the tactical role. An immensely versatile basic design has led to a host of variants since the early 1970s, many of which have acted as successors to the MiG-21 "Fishbed".

as smaller quantities of the Tu-28P "Fiddler" and Yak-28P "Firebar" are progressively retired from service.

A limited airborne early warning (AEW) capability also exists in the form of the Tu-126 "Moss", but less than 10 of these aircraft are in service and efforts are being directed towards improvement in AEW, most notably through the recent deployment of the Il-76 "Mainstay". Essentially an Il-76 "Candid" with a dorsal rotodome similar to that of the Boeing E-3 Sentry, the "Mainstay" is now in limited production with at least a dozen examples having been delivered to date.

In terms of numbers of aircraft on charge, the VVS is easily the largest command and has responsibility for controlling elements that were previously assigned to *Frontovaya Aviatsiya* (FA: Frontal Aviation) and *Voyenno-Transportnaya Aviatsiya* (VTA: Transport Aviation). As already noted, tactical assets are gathered together into theatre formations known as Frontal Air Armies, but it should be noted that the airlift force does retain a certain degree of operational autonomy.

Close to 10,000 aircraft and helicopters are available to the VVS, with virtually all of that huge quantity being capable of undertaking combat operations in support of ground forces. Missions performed by VVS elements embrace the entire spectrum of tactical air operations, including air superiority, close air support (CAS), interdiction/strike, tactical reconnaissance, electronic countermeasures (ECM) and acquisition of electronic intelligence (Elint).

In terms of attack capability, the Su-24 "Fencer" is arguably the most lethal item of VVS hardware, with just over 300 being available for interdiction tasks, plus about 100 or so examples of the "Fencer-E" variant which are assigned to reconnaissance and ECM support. Also dedicated to ground attack tasks is the MiG-27 "Flogger-D/J", but this is much more widely used, with over 800 in service, a quantity that is slightly exceeded by the Su-17 "Fitter" which is able to perform both CAS and interdiction.

Battlefield air superiority resources are dominated by some 600 MiG-23 "Flogger-B/Gs" and the VVS also possesses a fairly substantial contingent of dedicated interceptors, including about 100 MiG-25 "Foxbats", 50 MiG-31 "Foxhounds", 200 Su-15 "Flagons", 20 Tu-28P "Fiddlers", at least 100 Su-27 "Flankers" and more than 400 MiG-29 "Fulcrums". Of an earlier generation and now in sharp decline, the MiG-21 "Fishbed" is still operated in reasonable quantities, with about 400 late-production specimens being available for air superiority and attack operations.

For reconnaissance, the VVS has a somewhat mixed collection of equipment, the 500-plus strong fleet being mostly composed of tactical types. Numerically in the ascendant is the MiG-25R "Foxbat", about 200 being on hand, and they are supported by the "Fencer-Es" mentioned earlier as well as about 100 Yak-28 "Brewer-Ds" and 65 MiG-21R "Fishbed-Hs". Strategic reconnaissance is also performed by VVS elements but resources are somewhat more

Above: A rare view of life on a Soviet air base, with a trio of Su-15 "Flagon-F" single-seat, twin-jet interceptors seen undergoing preparation for another combat air patrol.

Below: Designed as a heavily-armed assault transport for a squad of troops, the Mil Mi-24 "Hind" is a fearsome machine armed with an undernose cannon and underwing rockets.

modest, with about 40 Tu-16 "Badgers", 15 Tu-22 "Blinders", four Tu-95 "Bears" and 20 MiG-25R "Foxbats" available.

Specialist missions such as defence suppression are also undertaken and have almost certainly gained in importance over the past decade or so, recent years having seen the appearance of the MiG-25 "Foxbat-F" and its AS-9 "Kyle" and AS-11 "Kilter" missiles. Less likely to be seen directly over the battlefield but still capable of making a worthwhile contribution are the ECM and Elint gatherers, resources in this area being confined to about 75 Yak-28 "Brewer-Es" and some An-12 "Cub-Cs".

Last but certainly by no means least of the VVS forces are those which would operate in and around the immediate field of battle, and these are no less substantial. Foremost among them is the Su-25 "Frogfoot" close support aircraft, somewhere in the region of 250 examples of this rugged and rather unsophisticated warplane being operational. In any major land battle, however, the "Frogfoot's" contribution is almost certain to be far outweighed by that of armed helicopters, for the USSR has invested heavily in procurment of dedicated "gunships" and their weaponry. Most fearsome is the Mil Mi-24 "Hind" and the VVS inventory currently includes around 1,300, as well as at least 1,200 examples of the Mi-8 "Hip-E".

Employed primarily for the rapid movement of troops and equipment in large scale assault operations, there are close to 2,000 Mi-8/17 "Hips", VVS heavy-lift capability being provided by some 450 Mi-6 "Hooks" and a growing number of Mi-26 "Halos". For scout/observation and liaison tasks, roughly 700 Mi-2 "Hoplites" are still in service and the VVS also operates about a score of ECM/Elint-dedicated Mi-4 "Hound-Cs".

Pure airlift capability is increasingly being dominated by the Il-76 "Candid" and well over 400 examples of this jet-powered freighter are active with the VVS, which continues to operate a declining number of An-12 "Cub" tactical transports along with modest numbers of the An-22 "Cock", An-124 "Condor", An-24 "Coke" and An-26 "Curl" freighters.

Most candidates for pilot training learn the rudiments with DOSAAF, a para-military organization that specializes in sport-flying. Formal military instruction begins on the Yak-11 "Moose", with students thereafter progressing via the Yak-18 "Max" to basic jet training on the L-29 Delfin and L-39 Albatros. Advanced phases of training are undertaken on the MiG-15UTI "Midget" and MiG-17 "Fresco", and the fledgling pilot will have accumulated about 250 flying hours by the time he completes the course and begins conversion training on a two-seater equivalent of the type that he will fly when assigned to operational forces.

Below: It may bear the markings of Aeroflot, but aircraft from the quasi-military state airline, such as this An-124 "Condor", are just as likely to be used by military units.

EQUIPMENT

Strategic Strike:
Tupolev Tu-160 "Blackjack"
Tupolev Tu-26 "Backfire"
Tupolev Tu-22 "Blinder"
Tupolev Tu-95/142 "Bear"
Tupolev Tu-16 "Badger"
Maritime Strike:
Tupolev Tu-22M "Blinder"
Tupolev Tu-16 "Badger"
Interception:
Mikoyan-Gurevich MiG-31 "Foxhound"
Mikoyan-Gurevich MiG-25 "Foxbat"
Sukhoi Su-15/21 "Flagon"
Sukhoi Su-27 "Flanker"
Mikoyan-Gurevich MiG-29 "Fulcrum"
Mikoyan-Gurevich MiG-23 "Flogger"
Mikoyan-Gurevich MiG-21 "Fishbed"
Tupolev Tu-28P/128 "Fiddler"
Yakovlev Yak-28P "Firebar"
Attack:
Sukhoi Su-24 "Fencer"
Sukhoi Su-25 "Frogfoot"
Mikoyan-Gurevich MiG-25 "Foxbat"
Mikoyan-Gurevich MiG-27 "Flogger"
Sukhoi Su-17 "Fitter"
Mikoyan-Gurevich MiG-21 "Fishbed"
Anti-Armour/Assault:
Mil Mi-24 "Hind"
Mil Mi-8/17 "Hip"
Reconnaissance:
Mikoyan-Gurevich MiG-25 "Foxbat"
Tupolev Tu-95 "Bear"
Tupolev Tu-16 "Badger"
Tupolev Tu-22 "Blinder"
Sukhoi Su-24 "Fencer"
Mikoyan-Gurevich MiG-21R "Fishbed"
Yakovlev Yak-28 "Brewer"
Sukhoi Su-17 "Fitter"
AEW:
Tupolev Tu-126 "Moss"
Ilyushin Il-76 "Mainstay"
ECM/Command Post:
Ilyushin Il-20/22 "Coot"
Antonov An-30 "Clank"
ECM/Elint-Gathering:
Yakovlev Yak-28 "Brewer"
Antonov An-12 "Cub"
Tanking:
Ilyushin Il-78 "Midas"
Tupolev Tu-16 "Badger"
Transport:
Antonov An-124 "Condor"
Ilyushin Il-76 "Candid"
Antonov An-22 "Cock"
Ilyushin Il-62 "Classic
Antonov An-12 "Cub"
Tupolev Tu-134 "Crusty"
Ilyushin Il-18 "Coot"
Antonov An-26 "Curl"
Antonov An-24 "Coke"
Ilyushin Il-14 "Crate"
Antonov An-8 "Camp"
Antonov An-2 "Colt"
Mil Mi-26 "Halo"
Mil Mi-10 "Harke"
Mil Mi-6 "Hook"
Mil Mi-8/17 "Hip"
Observation/Liaison:
Mil Mi-2 "Hoplite"
Mil Mi-4 "Hound"
Training:
Yakovlev Yak-11 "Moose"
Yakovlev Yak-18 "Max"
Yakovlev Yak-50/52/53
Aero L-29 Delfin
Aero L-39 Albatros
Mikoyan-Gurevich MiG-15UTI "Midget"
Mikoyan-Gurevich MiG-17 "Fresco"
Mikoyan-Gurevich MiG-19 "Farmer"
Mikoyan-Gurevich MiG-21U "Mongol"
Mikoyan-Gurevich MiG-23UM "Flogger"
Mikoyan-Gurevich MiG-29UB "Fulcrum"
Sukhoi Su-27UB "Flanker"
Mikoyan-Gurevich MiG-25 "Foxbat"
Yakovlev Yak-28 "Brewer"
Sukhoi Su-7U "Moujik"
Sukhoi Su-17UM "Fitter"
Sukhoi Su-25UB "Frogfoot"
Ilyushin Il-28U "Beagle"
Mil Mi-2 "Hoplite"

UNITED KINGDOM

NUMBERING around 60 squadrons, the Royal Air Force (RAF) makes a substantial contribution to the NATO alliance and is now nearing the end of an extensive re-equipment programme aimed at enhancing combat posture. Key elements of this programme concern the large-scale deployment of strike and air defence dedicated versions of the Panavia Tornado, as well as improved BAe Harriers, Lockheed Tristar tanker/cargo aircraft and the Boeing E-3D Sentry AEW.1. Looking ahead, it is still hoped to introduce the EFA in the late-1990s as a replacement for McDonnell Douglas F-4 Phantoms and SEPECAT Jaguars, but the future of this new warplane looks far from assured in the light of recent changes to the political map of Europe.

The bulk of the operational forces are distributed between two major command organizations. In the UK, Strike Command exercises control over a diverse collection of equipment engaged in a variety of roles from its headquarters at High Wycombe, but day-to-day management is entrusted to subordinate Group elements responsible for tactical, air defence and maritime missions. Most of the operational assets under Strike Command reside in the UK, but this agency also acts as parent to the "outstations" located at Belize, Cyprus, Hong Kong and the Falkland Islands.

The other major command is RAF Germany which makes a major contribution to NATO's 2nd Allied Tactical Air Force. From its headquarters at Rheindahlen, RAF Germany directs tactical and air defence forces located at four air bases, two of which are expected to close as the so-called "peace dividend" becomes ever more apparent and the overall size of the British presence in Germany is significantly reduced.

Tactical operations within the UK are co-ordinated by No. 1 Group at Upavon and embrace a miscellany of tasks, ranging from strike/attack through close air support and reconnaissance to airlift and in-flight refuelling. Strike/attack is now solely the prerogative of the Tornado GR.1 which serves with two squadrons (Nos. 27 and 617), while a third (No. 13) utilizes suitably modified Tornado GR.1As for reconnaissance. During the recent Gulf crisis, men and machines from this trio of units were actively engaged in operations against the Iraqi forces. An equally important contribution was made by the Jaguar GR.1As, the RAF having three units equipped with this rugged warplane. Two of the units (Nos. 6 and 54) are normally tasked with offensive support of the British Army, a mission they share with a single Harrier GR.5-equipped squadron (No.1).

Other Strike Command assets comprise single squadrons of Tristar (No. 216), VC-10 (No. 101) and Victor (No. 55) tankers for in-flight refuelling, and the VC-10 also serves with another squadron (No. 10) in the pure transport role although this is due to pick up a secondary air refuelling task with eight of the 13 aircraft on charge being earmarked to serve as two-point tankers.

Staying with transport duties, four squadrons (Nos. 24, 30, 47 and 70) are equipped

with a mixture of standard and stretched examples of the versatile C-130 Hercules, and there are also three tactical helicopter squadrons, operating the Boeing-Vertol Chinook (No. 7), the Westland Puma (No. 33) and the Westland Wessex (No. 72), mainly in support of Army forces. In addition, one squadron (No.32) utilizes a mixture of BAe 125s, Andovers and Westland Gazelles on routine communications and VIP tasks. Andovers also serve with a rather unusual squadron (No. 115) at Benson, the E.3 model

Below: Caught by the camera over the Saudi Arabian desert during the war to liberate Kuwait, a pair of RAF Tornado GR.1s hold formation as an F.3 breaks off to port.

being employed to calibrate navigation aids. This Oxfordshire airfield is also home to Strike Command's final flying outfit — the Queen's Flight which employs the Andover, BAe 146 and Wessex on Very, Very Important Person (VVIP) airlift.

No. 11 Group at Bentley Priory has a rather more myopic mission, being entrusted with air defence of the UK, for which it uses a mixture of aircraft and missile-equipped formations. Two basic fighter types are assigned to this role, namely the Tornado F.3 and the Phantom. The former is easily in the ascendancy by virtue of equipping seven squadrons (Nos. 5, 11, 23, 25, 29, 43 and 111) at three bases, but Phantoms remain active with a further two squadrons (Nos. 56 and 74) at Wattisham, Suffolk, although these are set to be disbanded before too much longer in the wake of a recent review of UK forces. Air defence missile elements include one squadron (No. 85) with Bloodhound dispersed amongst six subordinate flights, while there are also two RAF Regiment squadrons equipped with Rapier. The only other regular squadron within the No.11 Group line-up (No.8) operates in the airborne early warning (AEW) role, and has recently completed conversion from the aged Avro Shackleton AEW.2 to the Boeing E-3D Sentry AEW.1.

Maritime capability is vested in No. 18 Group which has its headquarters at Northwood. Long-range maritime patrol/anti-submarine warfare (ASW) is performed by four squadrons (Nos. 42, 120, 201 and 206)

Above: The bulky but familiar outline of a Lockheed Hercules, the RAF's principal transport. Some 60 examples are in use, equipping a total of four squadrons.

Above: Additional transport capacity is provided by a trio of helicopter-equipped squadrons, one of which (No.7) flies the double-rotored Chinook HC.1.

Below: A dramatic overwater study of a Harrier GR.5, one of the most recent additions to the RAF's combat force, as it fires one of its Sidewinder air-to-air missiles.

of BAe Nimrods, and three examples of a much modified variation on the Nimrod theme equip a unique and little-publicized squadron (No. 51) engaged in the acquisition of electronic intelligence (Elint). Anti-shipping strike is entrusted to two squadrons (Nos. 12 and 208) which use the rugged BAe Buccaneer although they are expected to re-equip with Tornados made redundant by cutbacks elsewhere.

Two of No. 18 Group's other squadrons are employed on tasks of a more humanitarian nature, specifically search-and-rescue (SAR). Both units make use of detached Flights based at coastal airfields, those of No. 22 Squadron being equipped with the Westland Wessex, whereas No. 202 has Westland Sea Kings. Alsopart of No. 18 Group are three English Electric Canberra-equipped units which perform tasks that cannot really be classified as being of a truly maritime nature. All are resident at Wyton, No. 100 primarily satisfying target facilities requirements with a variety of Canberra models; No. 360 engaging in ECM provision with the T.17 and T.17A; and No.1 Photographic Reconnaissance Unit undertaking exactly what its designation implies with the PR.9 variant.

Overseas-based echelons under Strike Command comprise the Wessex-equipped squadrons in Cyprus (No.84) and Hong Kong (No.28), as well as the Belize-based Harrier Flight (No.1417) and Puma Flight (No.1563). Sea Kings and Chinooks form a composite squadron (No.78) operating from the Falkland Islands alongside a Phantom-equipped air defence Flight (No.1453) and a Hercules-equipped tanker/transport Flight (No.1312).

Turning to RAF Germany, the rapid changes that have been taking place to the east of the "Iron Curtain" mean that the *raison d'etre* for its existence is fast disappearing. In view of that, the command is unlikely to remain at its present strength for long, plans to disband three of RAFG's

Above: Armed with Sidewinder and Sky Flash missiles, as well as an internal cannon, the RAF's seven Tornado F.3 squadrons provide air defence for the United Kingdom.

Below: A much-needed replacement for the Avro Shackleton in the AEW role, the Boeing Sentry AEW.1 officially entered service with the RAF in July 1991, at RAF Waddington.

Tornado squadrons (Nos. 15, 16 and 20), as well as the surviving Phantom units (Nos. 19 and 92) having been announced.

Numerically, the Tornado GR.1 is by far the cornerstone of RAFG, seven squadrons (Nos. 9, 14, 15, 16, 17, 20 and 31) using this model in the strike/attack role, while another (No. 2) has the GR.1A for reconnaissance. Offensive support of the British Army Of the Rhine is entrusted to two squadrons (Nos. 3 and 4) of Harriers, with two helicopter squadrons mainly engaged on Army support, these being equipped with Chinooks (No. 18) and Pumas (No. 230). Air defence is performed by two Phantom squadrons (Nos. 19 and 92) and there is a limited transport capability in the shape of No. 60 Squadron which operates a few BAe Andovers.

Training of air and ground crew is the responsibility of Support Command, which is headquartered at Brampton. Many pilot training candidates will already have gained some flying experience courtesy of the Bulldog-equipped University Air Squadrons, but a few Chipmunks remain in service with the Elementary Flying Training School. In the past, basic training would then be conducted on the BAe Jet Provost, but replacement of this trainer by the turboprop-powered Shorts Tucano is now well advanced.

On completion of basic training, successful candidates are "streamed" before moving on to receive advanced tuition. Those destined for the fast-jet world progress to the BAe Hawk, a type they also fly during advanced operational training with one of two Tactical Weapons Units. Subsequent to that, they proceed to a specialist element equipped with the type that they will eventually fly at squadron level. By way of illustration, Tornado GR.1 aircrew move first to the Trinational Tornado Training Establishment at Cottesmore and then to the Tornado Weapons Conversion Unit at Honington. In much the same way, aircrew destined for the Harrier proceed to No. 233 Operational Conversion Unit while those for the Phantoms go to No. 228 OCU.

Multi-engine training is given on the BAe Jetstream and rotary wing instruction on the

Gazelle and Wessex. In both instances, the path to squadron assignment involves further instruction with an OCU.

Navigator training is presently accomplished on the Jet Provost and BAe Dominie, but a new syllabus is to be introduced during the 1990s involving tuition on the Tucano and Hawk. Finally, training of instructors is accomplished by the Central Flying School, an organisation which is equipped with a few examples of most RAF trainer types.

EQUIPMENT

Strike:
Panavia Tornado GR.1
SEPECAT Jaguar GR.1A
Interception:
Panavia Tornado F.3
McDonnell Douglas Phantom FGR.2
Attack:
BAe Harrier GR.5/GR.7
Maritime Strike:
BAe Buccaneer S.2A/B
Reconnaissance:
Panavia Tornado GR.1A
SEPECAT Jaguar GR.1A
BAe Canberra PR.9
Maritime Reconnaissance/ASW.
BAe Nimrod MR.2/.2P
AEW:
Boeing E-3D Sentry AEW.1
Tanking:
BAe VC-10 K.2/.3
BAe Victor K.2
Lockheed Hercules C.1K
Tanking/Transport:
Lockheed Tristar K.1/KC.1/500
Lockheed Hercules C.1K
Transport:
Lockheed Hercules C.1/.1P/.3/.3P
BAe VC-10 C.1
BAe 125 CC.1/.2/.3
BAe Andover C.1/CC.2
Pilatus Britten-Norman BN-2T Islander
Boeing-Vertol Chinook HC.1
Westland Puma HC.1
Westland Wessex HC.2/.5C
VIP/VVIP Transport:
BAe 146 CC.2
BAe 125 CC.1/.2/.3
Westland Gazelle HT.3
Westland Wessex HCC.4
Elint-Gathering:
BAe Nimrod R.1P
Radar Calibration:
BAe Andover E.3/.3A
Training:
de Havilland Canada Chipmunk T.10
BAe Bulldog T.1
BAe Jet Provost T.3/.3A/.5A/.5B
Shorts Tucano T.1
BAe Hawk T.1/.1A
BAe Hunter T.7/.7A/.7B/.8B/.8C
BAe Dominie T.1
BAe Jetstream T.1
BAe Canberra B.2/.2(T)/T.4
Westland Gazelle HT.3
Westland Wessex HC.2
ECM Provision:
BAe Canberra T.17/.17A
SAR:
Westland Sea King HAR.3
Westland Wessex HC.2

Above: Providing a vital SAR-dedicated force around the British coastline, the easy-to-spot Sea King HAR.3s winch victims to safety all year round, but especially summer.

Below: At the heart of the RAF's fast jet syllabus is the BAe Hawk T.1, one of which is seen here proving just how manoeuvrable and highly nimble this little jet really is.

YUGOSLAVIA

WHILE IT may be non-aligned, Yugoslavia is firmly wedded to Communist doctrine, yet obtains military equipment from both East and West for its armed forces which include the *Jugoslovensko Ratno Vazduhoplovstvo i Protiv-Vaszdusna Obrana* (JRV/PVO: Yugoslav Air Force and Anti-Aircraft Defence). Grave economic difficulties experienced during the past few years have necessitated cuts in defence spending and have prompted Yugoslavia to look more to its own resources when seeking new equipment. Manifestations of this are the Galeb/Jastreb families, which are of wholly indigenous origins, and a collaborative venture with Romania has resulted in the Orao. Another indigenous design — the *Novi Avion* (New Aircraft) — is currently under development and this lightweight fighter may enter JRV service later in the present decade.

Combat assets number around 300 aircraft, with roughly a third of the force being composed of MiG-21 "Fishbed" variants that are employed in the interceptor role by about eight squadrons; but at least 14 MiG-29 "Fulcrums" have also been received since the spring of 1988 to equip a single squadron, and the JRV has apparently ordered 28 more to replace some older "Fishbeds". Other defensive resources comprise ground-based missile and artillery elements (PVO) which are under JRV control even though they are manned by Army personnel. Missiles in use are the SA-2 "Guideline" and SA-3 "Goa".

Attack-capable units are slightly more numerous, with about a dozen squadrons currently in existence. Equipment is a mixture of SOKO J-1 Jastrebs and SOKO/IAR-93 Oraos, although problems experienced with the latter have delayed service introduction. Two basic versions of Orao exist and the JRV has acquired both, using some 30 examples of the non-afterburning Orao 1 for reconnaissance and approximately 100 of the definitive Orao 2 for attack with weapons that include AGM-65 Maverick and AS-9 "Kyle" air-to-surface missiles, Durandal anti-runway bombs, BL.755 cluster bomb units and various unguided rockets.

Additional tactical reconnaissance capabilities are entrusted to the RJ-1 Jastreb, about 30 having been completed for service with two squadrons, in addition to 200 or so pure attack models and about 20 JT-1 two-seaters for training duties.

Transport elements are confined to just a couple of squadrons which rely mainly on Soviet types such as the An-12 "Cub" and An-26 "Curl", but three C-130H Hercules are currently on order and these may well replace the "Cubs". Also active is a small VIP-dedicated contingent with one Falcon 50, one LearJet 25B and about six Yak-40 "Codlings", while routine communications and utility tasks are mostly the province of the locally-designed UTVA-66 light plane. Rotary-wing airlift capability is spearheaded by almost 100 Mi-8 "Hip-C/E" assault helicopters, but these are outnumbered by the Gazelle which fulfils anti-armour attack, observation/reconnaissance and liaison duties. Known locally as the Partizan, initial deliveries consisted of 21 SA.341Hs from Aerospatiale, but it has also been built under licence by SOKO, with local manufacture raising the number of SA.341Hs received to around 100. These are now being joined by 100 SA.342Ls. The AT-3 "Sagger" is the primary anti-tank weapon used by armed Gazelles, which can also carry the SA-7 "Strela" air-to-air missile for anti-helicopter use.

Pilot training is mainly entrusted to the Air Force College at Mostar, and begins on the UTVA-75 which is used for initial assessment and basic instruction, leading up to the SOKO G2-A Galeb and G-4 Super Galeb. Both of the latter have armament capability for weapons training purposes and could also be used for light attack and counter-insurgency (COIN) operations should the need arise.

A limited aerial fire-fighting capacity also exists in the form of the Canadair CL-215 amphibian. Four such aircraft are presently operated and there is a strong possibility that these will be upgraded to CL-215T standard with PW.120 turboprop engines.

Above: Representing a considerable upgrade in operational terms, the MiG-29 "Fulcrum" is the face of the future for the JRV's interceptor force, replacing older MiG-21 "Fishbeds".

Below: Built as a two-seat basic trainer, the indigenous SOKO G2-A Galeb can also be used for armament practice courtesy of underwing stores pylons and two nose-mounted cannon.

Above: Although these particular examples are unarmed, many of the SOKO SA.341H/342L Partizans used by the JRV tote AT-3 "Sagger" and SA-7 "Grail" anti-armour missiles.

Below: A pair of JRV SOKO G-4 Super Galebs on a training sortie. Substantial numbers of this sleek two-seater trainer are operated by basic and advanced JRV training units.

EQUIPMENT

Interception:
Mikoyan-Gurevich MiG-29 "Fulcrum-A"
Mikoyan-Gurevich MiG-21 "Fishbed-F/J/L/N"

Attack:
SOKO J-22 Orao 2
SOKO J-1 Jastreb

Anti-Armour:
SOKO SA.341H/342L Partizan

Reconnaissance:
SOKO J-22 Orao 1
SOKO RJ-1 Jastreb

Observation:
SOKO SA.341H/342L Partizan

Transport:
Antonov An-12 "Cub"
Antonov An-26 "Curl"
Mil Mi-8 "Hip-C/E"

VIP Transport:
Dassault-Breguet Falcon 50
Yakovlev Yak-40 "Codling"
LearJet 25B

Fire-Fighting:
Canadair CL-215

Communications/Liaison:
UTVA-66
SOKO SA.341H/342L Partizan

Training:
UTVA-75
SOKO JT-1 Jastreb
SOKO G2-A Galeb
SOKO G-4 Super Galeb
SOKO J-22 Orao 1/2
Mikoyan-Gurevich MiG-15UTI "Midget"
Mikoyan-Gurevich MiG-21U/US "Mongol-A/B"
Mikoyan-Gurevich MiG-21F "Fishbed-C"
Mikoyan-Gurevich MiG-29UB "Fulcrum-B"

ASIA AND FAR EAST

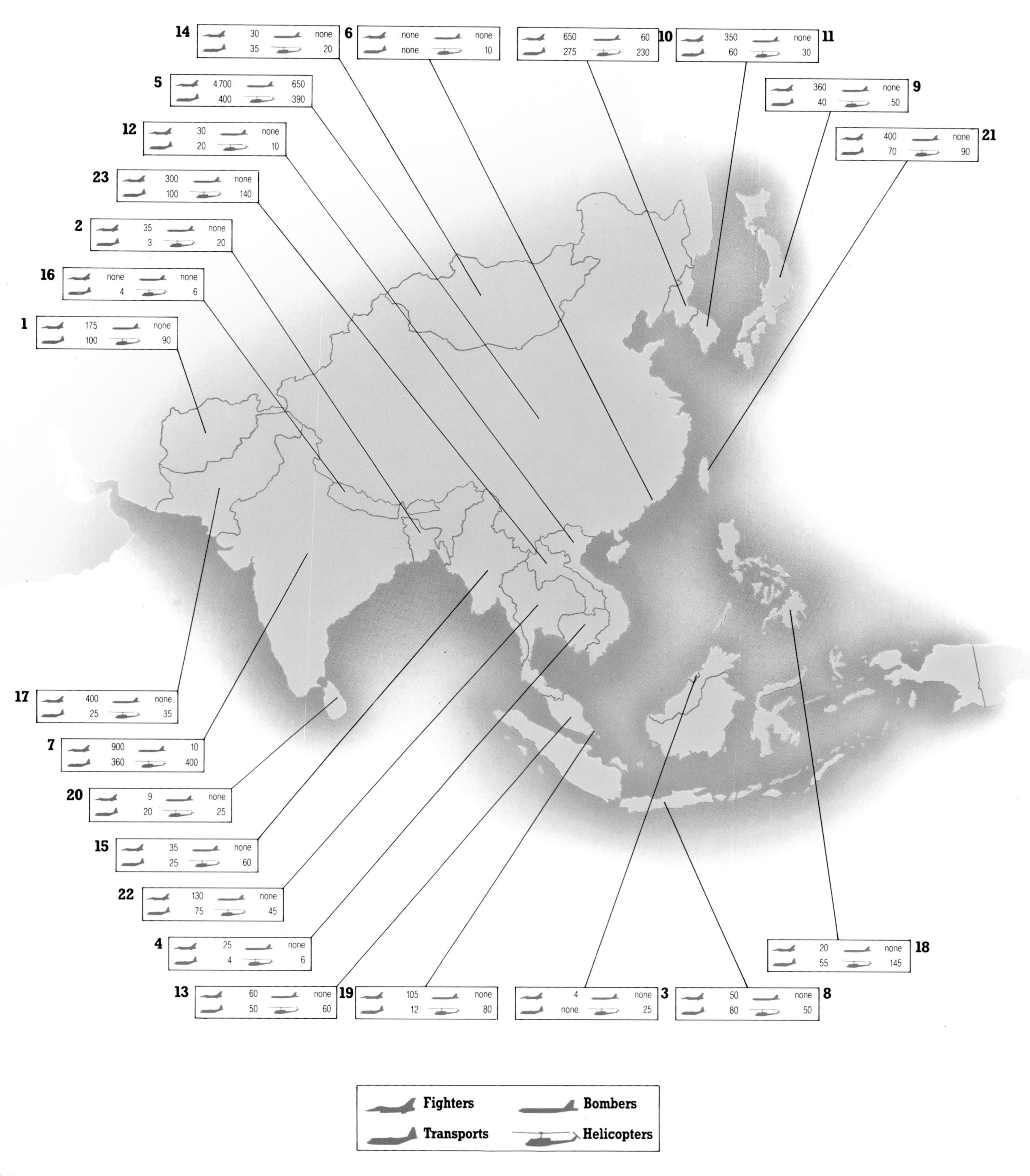

14 30 none 35 20
6 none none none 10
650 60 275 230 10
11 350 none 60 30
5 4,700 650 400 390
9 360 none 40 50
12 30 none 20 10
21 400 none 70 90
23 300 none 100 140
2 35 none 3 20
16 none none 4 6
1 175 none 100 90
17 400 none 25 35
7 900 10 360 400
20 9 none 20 25
15 35 none 25 60
22 130 none 75 45
4 25 none 4 6
18 20 none 55 145
13 60 none 50 60
19 105 none 12 80
3 4 none none 25
8 50 none 80 50
Fighters
Bombers
Transports
Helicopters

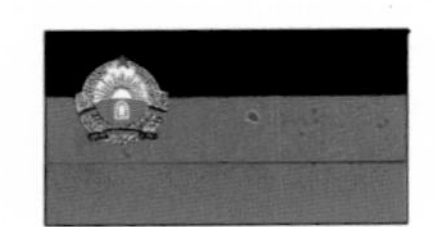

AFGHANISTAN

CONFRONTATION between the Afghanistan government and the *Mujahideen* guerilla forces continues more or less unabated following the Soviet withdrawal, but neither side seems to be able to gain a decisive advantage. For the Afghan Republican Air Force (ARAF), this has resulted in considerable combat attrition with many aircraft and helicopters falling victim to surface-to-air missiles (SAM) such as the US-supplied FIM-92A Stinger.

In the wake of the USSR's decision to withdraw from the fray, the ARAF received a substantial amount of "new" equipment by virtue of inheriting much of the hardware previously operated by Soviet units resident in Afghanistan. This influx included at least two-dozen MiG-23 "Floggers" with a dual air defence/attack capability and perhaps as many as 50 Su-25 "Frogfoots" for close air support (CAS) operations. Other combat equipment is entirely of Soviet origin, the most numerous type being the MiG-21F "Fishbed" interceptor, about 45 of which are operational.

Less numerous but probably more valuable in the context of the struggle against the guerilla forces are some 20 MiG-17 "Frescos", about 40 Su-7/20 "Fitters", close to three dozen Mil Mi-25 "Hind" attack helicopters and roughly 60 Mi-8/17 "Hip" assault helicopters. Combat losses are periodically made good by the USSR and it appears that the ARAF is in line to receive some examples of the latest generation of Soviet fighters, including MiG-29 "Fulcrums" and Su-27 "Flankers".

Transport aircraft are concentrated at Kabul, which is one of eight major air bases, although at least 30 smaller airfields are used regularly by combat and support echelons. In numerical terms, the An-24 "Coke" and An-26 "Curl" provide the mainstay of Afghanistan's airlift potential. A combined total of about 40 is operated alongside a dozen or so specimens of each of the An-12 "Cub", An-14 "Clod", Il-14 "Crate" and An-2 "Colt", with smaller quantities of the Il-18 "Coot", An-30 "Clank" and An-32 "Cline" also figuring in the ARAF's transport fleet.

As far as training is concerned, this appears to be undertaken in-country, students receiving tuition on the Yak-11 "Moose", Yak-18 "Max", Aero L-29 Delfin, Aero L-39 Albatros and MiG-15UTI "Midget" before joining operational outfits for transition training on two-seater equivalents of the primary combat types. In addition to their use in pure training roles, both the Delfin and the Albatros have secondary counter-insurgency (COIN) applications.

Below: For the MiG-21 (foreground) and the Su-22 seen here, the war ended when their pilots defected to the safety of Pakistan.

EQUIPMENT

Interception:
Mikoyan-Gurevich MiG-21F "Fishbed"
Mikoyan-Gurevich MiG-23 "Flogger"
Attack:
Sukhoi Su-25 "Frogfoot"
Sukhoi Su-20 "Fitter-C"
Sukhoi Su-7 "Fitter-A"
Mikoyan-Gurevich MiG-23 "Flogger"
Mikoyan-Gurevich MiG-17 "Fresco"
Mil Mi-25 "Hind-A/B
Assault:
Mil Mi-8 "Hip-E"
Mil Mi-17 "Hip-H"
Transport:
Ilyushin Il-18 "Coot"
Antonov An-12 "Cub"
Antonov An-24 "Coke"
Antonov An-26 "Curl"
Antonov An-30 "Clank"
Antonov An-32 "Cline"
Ilyushin Il-14 "Crate"
Antonov An-14 "Clod"
Antonov An-2 "Colt"
Training:
Yakovlev Yak-11 "Moose"
Yakovlev Yak-18 "Max"
Aero L-29 Delphin
Aero L-39 Albatros
Mikoyan-Gurevich MiG-15UTI "Midget"
Mikoyan-Gurevich MiG-21U "Mongol"
Sukhoi Su-7U "Moujik"

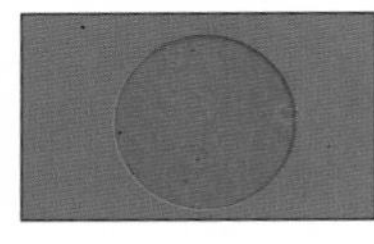

BANGLADESH

CURRENTLY heavily dependent on the People's Republic of China for military assistance and equipment, the Bangladesh Air Wing (BAW) still utilizes some Soviet-supplied hardware that was obtained during the 1970s, although the MiG-21s that constituted the principal interceptor have long since been withdrawn. Retirement of the MiG-21s arose largely as a result of spares shortages, an affliction that is apparently also suffered by current BAW equipment.

Operating as an independent echelon of the integrated Bangladesh Defence Force, the BAW's only truly combat-capable type is the Shenyang F-6. About 20 are on charge and these equip fighter squadrons at Tezgaon and Jessore, being used in both the interception and attack roles.

Chinese-built warplanes of more recent origin may, however, now be in service in limited quantities, for there are reports that some Nanchang A-5 Fantans have been delivered for attack duties, and the BAW has also expressed interest in the Xian F-7 (Chinese-built MiG-21).

Other operational units are principally engaged in transport tasks. Few aircraft are operated, but at least one An-24 "Coke" is still used, as, possibly, are a Yak-40 "Codling" and a Douglas DC-6. For the most part, the BAW relies on helicopters for airlift and has a reasonably large rotary-winged fleet, made up of half-a-dozen Mi-8 "Hips" and 13 or so Bell 212s, plus a couple of Bell 206L LongRangers for communications and liaison duties.

Training resources are much more numerous, the Flying Training School at Jessore being able to provide a comprehensive course of instruction, starting with assessment on the Cessna 152. This is followed by about 25 hours' on the Nanchang BT-6 piston-engined primary trainer, some 20 examples of which are in service.

Above: A significant number of the BAW's aircraft operate in the training role, as exemplified by this Shenyang FT-2.

Students then progress to the CM.170 Magister, some 15 examples of this French jet trainer having been obtained from West Germany, France and Togo. On award of "wings", pilots move to Tezgaon for advanced work on the Shenyang FT-2 (Chinese-built MiG-15UTI "Midget") although some Shenyang FT-5s may now be in use as replacements. Subsequent pilot tuition is at squadron level on the FT-6 two-seater derivative of the F-6.

EQUIPMENT

Interception/Attack:
Shenyang F-6
Transport:
Yakovlev Yak-40 "Codling"
Douglas DC-6
Mil Mi-8 "Hip"
Bell 212
Communications/Liaison:
Bell 206L LongRanger
Training:
Cessna 152
Nanchang BT-6
Aerospatiale CM.170 Magister
Shenyang FT-2
Shenyang FT-5
Shenyang FT-6

BRUNEI

THE AIR Wing of the Royal Brunei Armed Forces was initially established some 25 years ago with British equipment and assistance and has been fundamentally a helicopter-operating agency for much of its existence, although it is now beginning to purchase more potent, fixed-wing hardware, having ordered a batch of 16 British Aerospace Hawk 100 and 200 attack/trainers in October 1989, as well as four turboprop trainers which will presumably be Shorts Tucanos. Other new equipment in prospect includes a maritime surveillance variant of the Airtech CN-235, up to four of which may be purchased, as well as a few Lockheed C-130H Hercules tactical transports.

At present, however, the Air Wing is still heavily rotor-orientated, with three flying units, two of which are operational. No.1 Squadron has around a dozen Bell 212s for transport, casualty evacuation (CASEVAC) and search-and-rescue (SAR). One Bell 214ST also serves with this unit on SAR tasks, having previously been assigned to VIP airlift. No.2 Squadron operates six BO 105s including one in VIP configuration, and these are potentially more lethal since they can be fitted with door-mounted machine-guns and unguided rocket pods.

Lastly, there is No.3 Squadron with a mixture of SIAI-Marchetti SF.260 Warriors and Bell 206 JetRangers. Quantities on hand are four and two respectively, and these are mainly used for pilot training from Brunei International airport, although the Warriors can fulfil a secondary counter-insurgency (COIN) mission. Prospective pilots begin their tuition on the SF.260, accumulating about 120 flight hours before adding up to 100 more on the JetRanger. Subsequently, they proceed to No.1 Squadron as co-pilots.

EQUIPMENT

COIN:
SIAI-Marchetti SF.260W Warrior
MBB BO 105CB
VIP Transport:
MBB BO 105CBS
Miscellaneous Duties:
Bell 212
Bell 214ST
Training:
SIAI-Marchetti SF.260W Warrior
Bell 206B JetRanger

Below: Although it has taken the appropriate measures to boost its fixed-wing force, the Brunei's Air Wing is still heavily reliant on helicopters for its day-to-day functions. Shown here is a No.2 Squadron BO 105CB.

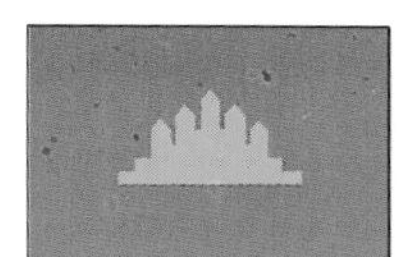

CAMBODIA

CAMBODIA'S air force has had a somewhat chequered history, being more or less non-existent between 1979 and 1985. It reappeared in the latter year with a few helicopters, adding a modest combat jet capability in 1986 when it resumed using some Shenyang F-6s that were originally supplied in the 1970s. Vietnamese aid was instrumental in restoring these elderly fighters to airworthy status, and the size of the Cambodian Air Force (CAF) has been further increased following the withdrawal of Vietnamese troops during 1988-89.

Today, the CAF's principal combat equipment takes the form of the MiG-21 "Fishbed" interceptor, some 20 of which were obtained in 1988-89. These are flown by pilots who received their training in the USSR and Vietnam, other combat-ready resources comprising a handful of Shenyang F-6s used for attack tasks and a trio of Mil Mi-24 "Hind" gunship helicopters.

Cambodia also has a few transports, including a couple of An-24 "Cokes", a similar number of Yak-40 "Codlings", and about six Mi-8/17 "Hips" which can also be used for assault operations.

As far as the future is concerned, this must be considered uncertain at best, since the various factions that are seeking power seem to be unable to come to any agreement on its division in this troubled country.

EQUIPMENT

Interception:
Mikoyan-Gurevich MiG-21 "Fishbed"
Attack:
Shenyang F-6
Mil Mi-24 "Hind"
Transport:
Yakovlev Yak-40 "Codling"
Antonov An-24 "Coke"
Mil Mi-8/-17 "Hip"

CHINA

WITH SOMEWHERE in the region of 5,000 tactical aircraft, the People's Republic of China (PRC) certainly possesses a substantial air arm, although the Air Force of the People's Liberation Army (AFPLA) lags far behind both East and West with regard to qualitative refinements, continuing to rely on hardware that is basically of 1950s vintage to equip most of its combat echelons. Improved relations with the technically much more sophisticated West have brought about some improvement, especially in the avionics field, but those relations were damaged by the Tiananmen Square massacre of 1989, with the USA being just one of several nations that suspended technology transfer and weapons sales in protest at the slaughter of the students. As a result, progress has slowed.

Although the AFPLA has expressed considerable interest in obtaining combat aircraft such as the F-16 Fighting Falcon and Mirage 2000 from the West, this has not yet occurred and modernization plans remain firmly wedded to the deployment of local developments of Soviet designs. However, the PRC is displaying an increasing degree of self-reliance and is presently working on a new interdictor/strike fighter — the Xian H-7 — which is destined to enter service with the AFPLA during the early part of this decade. Until such time as the H-7 becomes available, it will continue to rely on old and obsolescent bomber aircraft like the Xian H-6 and Harbin H-5, which are locally-built copies of the Soviet Tupolev TU-16 "Badger" and the Ilyushin Il-28 "Beagle" respectively.

AFPLA organization is along geographical lines with eight Military Air Regions exercising operational control over forces situated in specific areas of this massive country. By way of illustration, the Southern Air Region is responsible for elements stationed along the boundaries with Laos and Vietnam, while the Northern Air Region handles those that lie adjacent to the USSR and Mongolia.

At lower levels of command, the AFPLA generally follows Soviet practice quite closely, with the basic fighting formation being the Battalion. Essentially the Chinese equivalent of a squadron, each Battalion will possess from 10 to 15 aircraft (including spares) and it is usual for three Battalions to make up an Air Regiment, with three Air Regiments constituting an Air Division. Thus, a typical Air Division will possess around 100 aircraft with some 135 pilots as well as the various logisticals and maintenance support facilities that are necessary to give them a reasonable degree of independence with regard to day-to-day operations. Air Divisions also invariably possess a tactical bomber echelon but these are spread rather more thinly, the AFPLA presently possessing somewhere in the region of a dozen Regiments with light bomber aircraft.

Following the ideological split during the 1960s, the PRC has perceived the USSR as the main threat and has positioned a substantial proportion of AFPLA assets along its borders with the Soviet Union and Mongolia. Most of these forces remain in place even though relations have taken a turn for the better in recent times. The PRC also keeps a close watch on its southern borders with India, with which it has clashed sporadically over the past couple of decades, further fuel for Sino-Indian hostilities being supplied by the PRC's close ties with Pakistan. Taiwan also merits consideration as a possible troublespot, but the PRC's emergence from self-imposed isolation has led to a diminution of the "sabre-rattling" that was so commonplace at the height of the Cold War.

Above: A licence-built version of the Tu-16 "Badger", the Xian H-6 can carry a pair of C-601 missiles on its underwing pylons for use in anti-shipping operations.

As far as equipment is concerned, the backbone of the AFPLA is the Shenyang J-6. Production of this copy of the MiG-19 "Farmer" was launched during the 1960s and is apparently still under way, several thousand having been completed for both its own use and export. About 3,000 examples remain in front-line service and versions that have been deployed by interceptor/attack formations of the AFPLA during the past quarter of a century include the baseline J-6 (MiG-19S/SF), the J-6A (MiG-19F), J-6B (MiG-19PM), J-6C (enhanced MiG-19S/SF) and J-6Xin (MiG-19PF), while specialized versions have been evolved to satisfy tactical reconnaissance (JZ-6) and pilot training (JJ-6) requirements.

Possessing superior performance, but available in far fewer numbers, about 350 Xian J-7s are on charge, some of which incorporate Western-supplied equipment, including an avionics package obtained from GEC in the United Kingdom which features a lightweight radar as well as a head-up display unit and a radar altimeter. J-7 manufacture is continuing, with later versions of this MiG-21 "Fishbed" copy being akin to the all-weather MiG-21MF interceptor, and there is also a two-seat JJ-7 derivative for training.

Broadly based on the MiG-21/J-7, the J-8 "Finback" is the latest Chinese-developed variation on the "Fishbed" theme and

Left: With up to ten external hardpoints available, plus a 23mm internal cannon, the Nanchang Q-5 "Fantan" is a key player in the AFPLA's potent team of attack aircraft.

Right: Unglamorous but vital resupply flights to far-flung outposts are often performed by Mi-4 "Hound" helicopters, as witnessed here in a winter setting.

embodies twin engines, a somewhat longer fuselage and a bigger delta wing. Production was initially of the basic J-8, but only about 50 examples were completed before the J-8-II made its debut in 1984.

Other tactical components of the AFPLA are equipped with close to 700 MiG-17 "Frescos", the majority of which are of the locally-built Shenyang J-5 version although about 150 reconnaissance-dedicated JZ-5s are evidently also in use. Any realistic appraisal of the AFPLA must question the value of these old and obsolete warplanes, but there is less doubt when it comes to the Nanchang Q-5 "Fantan" attack aircraft. Evolved from the J-6, this possesses a revised forward fuselage section with side air intakes and an internal weapons bay that is normally confined to the carriage of additional fuel cells. Some 500 examples are reported to be in AFPLA service.

The AFPLA's airlift capability is for the most part entrusted to a large fleet of mostly obsolete equipment, much of which is of Soviet origin. Without doubt the most modern type is the Antonov An-26 "Curl", but numbers are limited to barely 10 and there are only about twice as many examples of the similar Xian Y-7 (An-24 "Coke") and Shaanxi Y-8 (An-12 "Cub"), other equipment consisting of about 250 Huabei Y-5s (An-2 "Colt"), 30 or so Il-14 "Crates", about 10 Il-18 "Coots", a dozen or so Harbin Y-11s and around 50 Li-2 "Cabs". Jet-powered resources are even more modest, centering around 16 Trident 2Es, while there is also a trio of Cessna 500 Citations which fulfil communications duties. Some of this equipment may well have been reassigned to civil operations.

Rotary-wing elements are in better shape, the AFPLA having taken delivery of a modest amount of Western equipment over the past decade, including two dozen Sikorsky S-70C-IIs, six AS.332 Super Pumas and eight HOT-armed SA.342L Gazelles for evaluation in the anti-armor role. It also ordered six CH-47D Chinooks in January 1989, but there is real doubt as to whether this contract is to be fulfilled.

Pilot instruction appears to be concentrated in Manchuria and begins with basic training on the Nanchang CJ-5 and CJ-6 (variations on the Yak-18 "Max" theme) before students progress to jet-conversion on the MiG-15UTI "Midget" and Shenyang JJ-5 (a two-seater version of the MiG-17 "Fresco"), this phase of tuition probably also including some weapons training. However, the PRC is presently developing a new jet trainer — the Nanchang K-8 — in co-operation with Pakistan. The AFPLA has indicated an initial requirement for 150 K-8s although ultimate procurement is likely to rise to around the 1,000 mark for service with a number of training establishments.

Operational training is the final stage and is undertaken on the JJ-6 and other two-seat equivalents of the principal types to be found in the front-line inventory.

EQUIPMENT

Strategic Strike:
Xian H-6
Tupolev Du-4 "Bull"
Light Bombing:
Harbin H-5
Interception:
Chengdu/Xian J-7 Skybolt
Shenyang J-8 "Finback"
Shenyang J-6
Shenyang J-5
Attack:
Nanchang Q-5 "Fantan-A"
Chengdu/Xian J-7 Skybolt
Shenyang J-8 "Finback"
Shenyang J-6
Shenyang J-5
Tupolev Du-2 "Bat"
Anti-Armour Attack:
Aerospatiale SA.342L Gazelle
Reconnaissance:
Shenyang JZ-6
Shenyang JZ-5
Harbin HZ-5
Transport:
BAe Trident IIE
Cessna Citation I
Ilyushin Il-18 "Coot"
Shaanxi Y-8
Antonov An-26 "Curl"
Ilyushin Il-14 "Crate"
Lisunov Li-2 "Cab"
Harbin Y-11
Huabei Y-5
Mil Mi-8 "Hip"
Aerospatiale AS.332 Super Puma
Sikorsky S-70C-II
Harbin Z-5
Communications/Liaison:
Harbin Z-9 Haitun
Mil Mi-1 "Hare"
Training:
Nanchang CJ-5/6
Shenyang/Mikoyan-Gurevich MiG-15UTI "Midget"
Shenyang JJ-5
Shenyang JJ-6
Guizhou JJ-7
Harbin HJ-7

HONG KONG

CONCERNED mainly with policing and communications tasks, the Royal Hong Kong Auxiliary Air Force presently has a fleet of about 10 aircraft and helicopters, all of which are stationed at Kai Tak International Airport. "Front-line" elements are headed by a single BN-2A Islander and a pair of Beech Super King Airs, the latter being equipped with surveillance radar and forward-looking infra-red (FLIR). These tools are extremely useful for maritime surveillance in support of Hong Kong's police force, which is extremely active in attempting to eradicate smuggling. A third Super King Air is to be acquired, possibly as a replacement for the Islander which was delivered to the RHKAAF some 20 years ago.

Inshore patrol and search-and-rescue (SAR) duties are undertaken by a pair of SA.365C Dauphin 2s, but eight Sikorsky S-76s are now in the process of being delivered. Three will be SAR-dedicated S-76+s, while the others (three S-76+s and two S-76Cs) will perform generally utility missions as Hong Kong moves towards its return to China in 1997, by which time the RAF Wessex of No.28 Squadron will have been withdrawn.

A limited training capability also exists in the shape of four Slingsby T.67M-200 Fireflies delivered in 1987-88, and these are expected to move to a new base at Sek Kong before too long.

EQUIPMENT

Maritime Patrol/Surveillance:
Beech Super King Air 200
Maritime Patrol/SAR:
Aerospatiale SA.365C Dauphin 2
Surveillance/SAR Cover:
Pilatus Britten-Norman BN-2A Islander
SAR/Utility:
Sikorsky S-76+/C
Training:
Slingsby T.67M-200 Firefly

INDIA

PERIODIC outbreaks of hostilities with neighbouring Pakistan and sporadic interludes of violent altercation along the border with China are responsible for the Indian Air Force (IAF) maintaining a substantial presence in the northern provinces, and for an on-going effort directed at modernizing combat-ready elements. The source of much new military hardware has been the USSR, and licence production has been undertaken of such Soviet types as the MiG-21 "Fishbed" and, more recently, the MiG-27 "Flogger". However, India remains staunchly non-aligned and is by no means solely dependent upon the USSR for armaments, having also obtained warplanes from the West.

Most notable amongst these are the Dassault-Breguet Mirage 2000 and the SEPECAT Jaguar, with local manufacture of the latter continuing, but India is increasingly anxious to develop an indigenous combat aircraft design capability. This is now beginning to take a more tangible form in the shape of the Light Combat Aircraft (LCA) project, although serious development delays have been encountered recently, resulting in plans to deploy the first of 200 or so examples of this type in 1996 slipping by about four years. Of greater import, however, is the fact that this delay is almost certain to result in further arms purchases from overseas.

From its headquarters in New Delhi, the IAF maintains control of the various forces at its disposal by means of seven major Command agencies. Five of these are concerned with managing operational echelons and are all established on purely geographical lines, consisting of Southern Air Command, South-Western Air Command, Western Air Command, Eastern Air Command and Central Air Command. Tactical Air Centres exist within each Air Command, these being attached to key Army headquarters so as to permit co-ordinated air/ground operations to be undertaken. Remaining command agencies consist of Training Command and Maintenance Command, but these are purely functional in nature and are concerned with support in those areas implied by their titles.

At the operational level, the basic unit is the squadron, and the IAF order of battle is currently spearheaded by around 40 combat-capable outfits, backed up by about a dozen transport squadrons and a similar number of rotary-wing units, some of which also have a combat role to perform in support of the Army, although most light helicopter units (equipped with the locally-built SA.315B Lama/Cheetah and SA.316B Alouette III/Chetak) were transferred to the newly-constituted Indian Army Air Corps (IAAC) during 1986-87. Unit establishment varies from 12 to 18 aircraft depending upon role, but the IAF currently has in excess of 1,700 aircraft if training and support equipment is taken into account. However, a shortage of technical skills means that a fair proportion of this force is probably non-effective at any given time.

Air defence requirements are mainly satisfied by fighters of Soviet origin, with the ubiquitous MiG-21 "Fishbed" being the most widely used interceptor, and it presently serves with around half-a-dozen squadrons. IAF procurement of the "Fishbed" has been undertaken on a massive scale, with more than 800 examples reportedly delivered, and the lion's share of those were either assembled or manufactured by Hindustan Aeronautics Ltd (HAL) at its Nasik factory between the mid-1960s and the late-1980s.

Interceptor versions in use comprise the MiG-21FL "Fishbed-D" and the rather more numerous MiG-21bis "Fishbed-N", with the latter sub-type having been configured to fire the MATRA 550 Magic infra-red (IR) homing air-to-air missile (AAM). An improved version of this weapon also forms part of the armoury of the considerably more potent Dassault-Breguet Mirage 2000. IAF use of the latter type is confined to just two squadrons, some 42 2000H single-seaters and seven 2000TH trainers having been received between October 1984 and late-1987, but plans to obtain further aircraft by means of local assembly and manufacture were abandoned due to the high production costs involved.

As a result, the IAF again turned to the USSR for interceptors and ordered 44 MiG-29 "Fulcrums" (including four two-seaters), all of which were supplied in

Above: Having received an interim batch of SEPECAT Jaguars from the United Kingdom, the IAF set about acquiring a further 76 examples. They are used in both the attack and anti-shipping roles.

Left: Illustrating a variety of camouflage schemes worn by IAF fighters, this trio of MiG-21 "Fishbeds" was supplied direct from the USSR. Subsequent IAF requirements led to local assembly of this potent fighter.

knocked-down "kit" form between December 1986 and May 1987, for assembly at Nasik. Now in service with two squadrons, they are to be joined by a further 20 examples that were ordered in 1989, and the IAF may ultimately acquire more to update its interceptor fleet, possibly by embarking on licence production. In the meantime, the survivors of 40 MiG-23MF "Flogger-Bs" delivered in the early-1980s continue in service with the two other interceptor outfits, but this type is evidently earmarked for early retirement from service.

Offensive capability is largely the preserve of two very different types obtained from two very different sources, both of which form the subject of ambitious manufacturing programmes. From the West, India selected the Anglo-French SEPECAT Jaguar International to satisfy its requirement for a deep penetration strike aircraft in October 1978, and this warplane entered IAF service very quickly, thanks to Great Britain's Royal Air Force agreeing to loan 18 aircraft (including two trainers) to the IAF with effect from July 1979. Most were eventually returned to the UK in the early-1980s, following delivery of 40 British-built machines.

Since then, HAL has undertaken local production, initially of aircraft supplied in kit form and ultimately of wholly indigenous origin. Further orders have increased the IAF buy to 131 aircraft (including just five two-seaters), and the Jaguar is now in service with five squadrons in the strike role. In addition, eight aircraft have been fitted with the nose-mounted Thomson-CSF *Agave* radar for anti-shipping attack duties, and these operate alongside a limited number of similarly-tasked Canberra B(I).12s in a single squadron at Poona. Maritime attack Jaguars are apparently armed with the Aerospatiale AM.39 Exocet missile, and it appears that about nine further examples are to be similarly configured to permit retirement of the elderly Canberras.

The other major manufacturing effort concerns the MiG-27 "Flogger-J", some 165 copies of which were ordered in the early-1980s. Once again, the programme was to begin with assembly, leading up to eventual total fabrication, and the first aircraft to be completed emerged from the Nasik factory in October 1984, with deliveries getting under way at the beginning of 1986. Thus far, about half-a-dozen squadrons have received the MiG-27, but the IAF also operates a sizeable number of MiG-23BN "Flogger-Hs", three squadrons using the survivors of 95 aircraft that were obtained direct from the USSR in 1980-83, along with 15 MiG-23UM "Flogger-Cs" for pilot training duties.

Above: Designed from the outset to meet an Indian armed forces requirement for a lightweight general purpose helicopter, the SA.315B Lama has since been produced under licence by HAL Ltd. as the Cheetah.

Remaining attack-capable forces consist of around 10 squadrons with the "Fishbed-J", the IAF having apparently received 30 MiG-21PFMAs and 30 MiG-21MFs from the USSR before undertaking production of 160 MiG-21Ms between 1973-81. Many of these machines are now somewhat ancient and the older examples are obviously prime candidates for replacement by the MiG-27, but it seems likely that some will have to remain in use until such time as the LCA becomes available, although, as noted earlier, the IAF has indicated that it will need to procure an interim fighter as a result of delays to the LCA project.

Other equipment with a combat role to perform is concerned mainly with reconnaissance duties, for which the MiG-25R "Foxbat-B" and the Canberra PR.57 are employed. Delivery of half-a-dozen examples of the former type took place in about 1981, but attrition has since claimed at least two victims and it is not known if these have been replaced. As for the Canberra, about eight aircraft continue to give good service alongside a small number of suitably modified HAL-built BAe 748s with one squadron at Agra, while another Agra-based unit operates B(I).58s, B.66s and T.4/13s on IAF electronic countermeasures (ECM) and target-towing support tasks. Like many air arms, the IAF has found the Canberra to be a hard act to follow and these veterans are unlikely to be retired until at least 1995.

Last but by no means least, a single squadron has been engaged in evaluating the Mil Mi-25 "Hind-E" gunship helicopter, using a dozen examples that were delivered in 1984 and evidently placing a follow-on order for about twice that quantity of improved Mi-35s shortly before the end of 1988. However, there has been some acrimony between the IAF and the IAAC as to just who should operate this type. The solution adopted in 1988 was to assign the gunships to the IAF and to give operational control to the Army — a course of action which seems certain to result in more friction at some time in the future.

Modernization efforts have by no means been confined to combat forces, for the IAF's respectably-sized transport fleet has been more or less transformed over the past

Left: A truly massive transport helicopter, the Mil Mi-26 "Halo" has a payload capacity similar to that of a C-130 Hercules. The IAF received two of these helicopters in 1986, against an initial order for 10.

Left: Combining the IAF's ever-necessary pilot training needs with a light attack capability led to the design of the HAL HJT-16 Kiran II, a development of the Kiran I/IA, which is used by the IAF as a two-seat light attack trainer aircraft.

decade, when old and obsolescent equipment such as the C-47 Dakota, C-119G Flying Boxcar, Boeing Canada Caribou and An-12 "Cub" were steadily phased out in favour of much more modern turboprop and turbofan-powered types. Today, the backbone of the IAF's tactical transport force is the twin-engined An-32 "Cline", which serves with at least five squadrons and a training unit. Deliveries began in 1984 and are continuing, but early intentions to produce the type under licence were shelved and all 118 aircraft that have been ordered to date have originated from the Soviet assembly line.

Heavy-lift capability has also been greatly improved through the procurement of 24 examples of the Il-76MD "Candid" from 1985 on and these now equip two squadrons, while the IAF requirement for a new light transport has been met by the Dornier Do 228. The IAF expects to obtain around 70 of these twin-engined aircraft, most of which will be of wholly Indian origin, for a licence agreement was part of the deal. Service entry took place shortly before the end of 1987 and the type is primarily intended to replace Otters and the few remaining Doves and Devons on such tasks as communications and liaison, although some are destined for miscellaneous support duties such as aerial target-towing.

Other transports in service consist of about 50 locally-manufactured BAe 748s, but these are assigned to a number of roles, with delivery being effected over some two decades from the early-1960s. In addition to pure airlift BAe 748Ms active with a single transport squadron, about 15 are used as staff and VIP transports, seven serve as navigation trainers, four are used as signals trainers and about 15 are active with the Transport Training Wing which offers multi-engine pilot conversion courses. Also VIP-configured are a quartet of Boeing 737s, and two former Air India Boeing 707s have been on IAF charge since 1987.

Rotary-wing transport resources now primarily consist of the Mil Mi-8, which is active with about nine squadrons, the IAF possessing some 80 Mi-8s (including a few VIP-configured machines) and 50 or so Mi-17s, with the latter, improved version mainly being concentrated in the Himalayas and Karakorams where its superior high-altitude performance is greatly appreciated. A limited heavy-lift potential also exists, one squadron being equipped with 10 Mi-26 "Halos" delivered during 1986-88, but the IAF has stated that a requirement exists for at least 10 more. Turning to light helicopters, most Cheetahs and Chetaks have been transferred to the IAAC, but limited quantities are still employed on communications and liaison duties, as well as in the training role.

Pilot training is also in a state of flux at the present time, largely due to delays experienced in development of the HPT-32 Deepak primary trainer, but this type is apparently now active although it may eventually give way to a turboprop derivative known as the HTT-34 which itself is also encountering delays. The situation regarding basic and advanced tuition is brighter, but the indigenous Kiran jet trainer also faced problems during development and early service, prompting the IAF to obtain 50 TS-11 Iskra 100s from Poland, about 40 of which are still in IAF service alongside some 200 Kiran Is and IIs.

On completion of advanced instruction, operational-type training ensues. Until quite recently this was accomplished on either the Hunter or the MiG-21, but the recent retirement of the former type from the front-line inventory may well also have led to its demise in the training role. At the operational level, most IAF fighter squadrons possess two-seater equivalents of combat equipment for conversion training and proficiency checking.

In addition to fast jet training establishments, there are also specialist "schools" for transport and rotary-wing aircrew, using the BAe 748/An-32 and HAL Chetak respectively.

EQUIPMENT

Interception:
Mikoyan-Gurevich MiG-29 "Fulcrum-A"
Dassault-Breguet Mirage 2000H
Mikoyan-Gurevich MiG-23 "Flogger-G"
Mikoyan-Gurevich MiG-21FL/bis "Fishbed-D/N"

Attack:
Mikoyan-Gurevich MiG-27ML "Flogger-J"
Mikoyan-Gurevich MiG-23BN "Flogger-H"
SEPECAT Jaguar International IS
Mikoyan-Gurevich MiG-21M/MF/PFMA "Fishbed-J"

Maritime Attack:
SEPECAT Jaguar International IS

Light Bombing:
BAe Canberra B(I).12/B(I).58/B.66

Anti-Armour:
Mil Mi-25 "Hind E"
Mil Mi-35 "Hind"

Reconnaissance:
Mikoyan-Gurevich MiG-25R "Foxbat-B"
BAe Canberra PR.57

Transport:
Boeing 707-337C
Ilyushin Il-76MD "Candid"
Antonov An-32 "Cline"
Boeing Canada Caribou
BAe 748M
Dornier Do 228-201
Boeing Canada Otter
Mil Mi-26 "Halo"
Mil Mi-8/17 "Hip"

VIP Transport:
Boeing 737-2AB
BAe 748
Aerospatiale SA.365N Dauphin 2

Communications/Liaison:
de Havilland Dove/Devon
HAL SA.316B Chetak
HAL SA.315B Cheetah

Training:
HAL HT-2
HAL HPT-32 Deepak
HAL HJT-16 Kiran I/IA/II
PZL TS-11 Iskra
HAL Ajeet Mk.2
Mikoyan-Gurevich MiG-21U/UM "Mongol-A/B"
Dassault-Breguet Mirage 2000TH
Mikoyan-Gurevich MiG-29UB "Fulcrum-C"
Mikoyan-Gurevich MiG-25U "Foxbat-C"
SEPECAT Jaguar International IT
Mikoyan-Gurevich MiG-23UM "Flogger-C"
BAe 748

Left: A diverse fleet both in origin and age equips today's TNI-AU. Literally the largest aircraft in service is this Boeing 707-3MC1.

INDONESIA

ONCE virtually entirely dependent upon the USSR for military equipment, Indonesia now looks to the West and is steadily building up an indigenous aircraft manufacturing capability which presently involves licence production of light transport aircraft and helicopters such as the CASA C.212 Aviocar, MBB BO 105 and Aerospatiale Super Puma, as well as joint international collaborative ventures like the Airtech CN.235M.

Not surprisingly, the *Tentara Nasional Indonesia — Angkatan Udara* (TNI-AU: Indonesian Armed Forces — Air Force) is a customer for most of these projects, and in conjunction with the Navy and Army now uses a fair quantity of locally-manufactured equipment. As yet, though, it still has to look overseas for most of its combat resources, which are predominantly of US origin.

TNI-AU organization was significantly altered in the mid-1980s and is now based upon two operational commands. KOOPSAU I looks after the west from a headquarters in Jakarta, and KOOPSAU II deals with the east from Ujung Pandang. The principal combat formation is the National Air Defence Command, while other elements that are active include Training Command and Materiel Command.

Air defence potential will be greatly enhanced when the Fighting Falcons that are currently on order eventually arrive after a period of pilot training in the USA. Indonesia has indicated a requirement for as many as 36 examples of the General Dynamics warplane, but has so far only ordered eight F-16As and four F-16Bs, delivery of which was understood to be imminent at the time of writing.

Until such time as the F-16 attains operational status at Malang, responsibility for air defence is entrusted to the Northrop F-5E Tiger II, about a dozen aircraft being in service with a single squadron at Madiun. Once the F-16 is in service, these will probably devote more time to attack tasks. Other combat hardware comprises just over two-dozen A-4E Skyhawks which are used for attack. All were obtained from Israel via the USA, a quartet of TA-4H trainers being provided as part of the package. Today, the Skyhawks — which are almost all Middle East combat veterans — are active with squadrons at Madiun and Pekanbaru.

Combat elements are completed by a single squadron at Baucau, on Timor, with just over a dozen Rockwell OV-10F Bronco counter-insurgency (COIN) aircraft, survivors of 16 delivered in the late-1970s.

Should the situation dictate, however, most of the Hawk T.53s that were obtained from Great Britain could be pressed into service on light attack duties, and even the humble Beech T-34C-1 Turbo-Mentor has the ability to carry light armament.

Nevertheless, the TNI-AU has an emphatically long "tail", which is perhaps partly explained by local geography, Indonesia being composed of no fewer than 13,000 islands scattered across a vast area of sea. In view of this, a large assortment of aircraft and helicopters are employed on second-line duties. Many of these are primarily related to military operations, but there are some which are civil-orientated, TNI-AU resources being allocated to such diverse tasks as transport, maritime surveillance, in-flight refuelling, search-and-rescue (SAR), pilot and navigator training and even crop spraying, this last task being the responsibility of a special Agricultural Air Unit.

EQUIPMENT

Interception:
General Dynamics F-16A Fighting Falcon
Northrop F-5E Tiger II
Attack:
McDonnell Douglas A-4E Skyhawk
Northrop F-5E Tiger II
COIN/FAC:
Rockwell OV-10F Bronco
Maritime Patrol/SAR:
Boeing 737-2X9 Surveiller
Lockheed C-130H-MP Hercules
Grumman HU-16 Albatross
Transport:
Lockheed C-130B/H/H-30 Hercules
Lockheed L-100-30 Hercules
Airtech CN.235M
Fokker F-27 Friendship 400M
Douglas C-47 Dakota
CASA-Nurtanio Aviocar
Aerospatiale SA.330J/L Puma
Nurtanio NAS.332B/L Super Puma
Sikorsky S-58T
VIP Transport:
Boeing 707-3MC1
Lockheed Jetstar 6
Tanking/Transport:
Lockheed KC-130B Hercules
Communications/Liaison:
Cessna 180
Cessna 172/T-41D
Cessna 207
Cessna 401/402
Nurtanio-MBB NBO 105
McDonnell Douglas 500
Aerospatiale SE.3160 Alouette III
Bell 206B JetRanger
Utility:
Shorts Skyvan 3M
Bell 204B
Crop-Spraying:
Cessna 188 Ag-Wagon
Pilatus PC-6 Turbo-Porter
PZL-104 Gelatik
Training:
FFA AS.202 Bravo
Beech T-34C-1 Turbo-Mentor
BAe Hawk T.53
Northrop F-5F Tiger II
McDonnell Douglas TA-4H Skyhawk
General Dynamics F-16B Fighting Falcon
Beech King Air 100
Douglas C-47 Dakota

Right: Although it is to be used in the same air superiority role as many other nations' F-16s, those of the TNI-AU are unique in terms of the quite bizarre camouflage adopted.

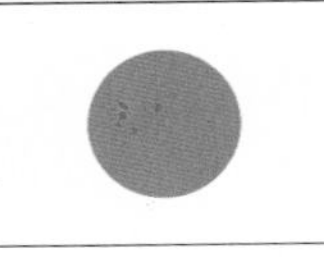

JAPAN

RECENT re-organization of the *Nippon koku Jieitai* (JASDF: Japanese Air Self-Defence Force) means that resources assigned to this modern and well-equipped air arm are now distributed among five major air commands, specifically Air Defence Command, Support Command, Training Command, Research and Development Command and Supply Command, of which all bar the last are aircraft-operating agencies.

Most significant of these, in that it is responsible for the management of all combat-ready forces, is Air Defence Command (ADC). This has its headquarters at Fuchu, from where it directs the operations of air and ground elements that include air defence and attack fighters as well as surface-to-air missile (SAM) forces, airborne early warning (AEW) aircraft and surveillance radars that monitor airspace above and around the homeland. Force size dictates the necessity for subordinate elements to manage day-to-day activities. Four of these elements are established on geographic lines and comprise the Northern Air Defence Force (ADF) at Misawa; the Central ADF at Iruma; the Western ADF at Kasuga; and the Southwest Composite Air Wing at Naha, on Okinawa. In addition, separate elements exist to control tactical reconnaissance assets (the Reconnaissance Air Wing at Hyakuri) and communications and electronic warfare (EW) training (the Air Defence Command Flight at Iruma).

ADF organization typically includes two Air Wings (each with two squadrons) at different bases, one or two Air Defence Missile Groups with from two to four Nike squadrons, and an Aircraft Control and Warning Wing with several radar squadrons. In addition, there is usually a support or headquarters flight for communications duties, although the Iruma-based Central ADF lacks this feature and instead relies on aircraft of the Air Defence Command Flight which reside at the same location. The Southwest Composite Air Wing at Naha adheres broadly to this pattern in so far as it has an Air Defence Missile Group, an Aircraft Control and Warning Wing and a Support Flight (with Queen Airs and T-33As), but it has just one F-4EJ Phantom II squadron which is the sole combat-ready air element of No.83 Air Unit.

Looking more closely at hardware, the JASDF's principal fighter is the F-15J/DJ Eagle. Over 130 of the 187 that are planned are now in service, with most originating from a local manufacturing programme undertaken by Mitsubishi. At the moment, the Eagle equips six squadrons, but a seventh is due to form during FY1991 and about half-a-dozen examples (mostly F-15DJ two-seaters) are also active with Japan's "aggressor" training unit at Tsuiki, these having replaced the Mitsubishi T-2 in 1990. Principal weapons are the radar-guided Sparrow and infra-red (IR) homing Sidewinder air-to-air missile (AAMs).

Also originating from McDonnell Douglas and the subject of local manufacture by Mitsubishi, the F-4 Phantom II is the JASDF's second most numerous warplane, with about 140 presently featuring in the inventory. Most are F-4EJ fighters, four squadrons using this sub-type primarily as an interceptor. Just under 100 are to be updated for further service as the F-4EJ *Kai*, modification including structural strengthening as well as revised avionics systems and additional weapons to bestow enhanced capability in air-to-air and air-to-surface roles. In addition, 14 reconnaissance-dedicated RF-4EJs were obtained from the parent company and these continue to give good service with a single squadron of the Reconnaissance Air Wing. However, they will almost certainly be replaced by 17 F-4EJs that are to be modified during the mid-1990s, conversion for reconnaissance tasks involving fitment of a Thomson-CSF *Raphel* side-looking airborne radar (SLAR) sensor package.

Japan's modest attack capability is vested in three squadrons that operate some 70 examples of the indigenous Mitsubishi F-1. Often thought of as a Jaguar "look-alike", these are mainly tasked with anti-ship attack using the Mitsubishi ASM-1 missile, but they can also perform air defence duties with the trusty Sidewinder AAM. Replacement of the F-1 is targeted for the late-1990s when the Mitsubishi SX-3 derivative of the General Dynamics F-16 begins to enter service, and this type is also expected to take over from the Phantom II at a later date. Thus far, planning calls for the acquisition of 130 SX-3s, but this quantity will almost certainly rise to near the 200 mark.

Other ADC aircraft-operating outfits

Below: Illustrating two very different tactical camouflage patters, a pair of Mitsubishi F-1 fighters lift off from Misawa Air Base. Note the pilots' high-vis. orange flying suits.

Left: Unique amongst the world's users of the F-4 by virtue of the fact that its F-4EJs were built outside the USA, the JASDF still make good use of this rugged machine. With over 130 remaining in service, just under 100 of which are to be updated, it is not beyond the realms of possibility that the F-4EJ *Kai* will still be in service with the JASDF in the 21st Century.

comprise the Misawa-based Surveillance Unit which has a single squadron equipped with eight E-2C Hawkeyes (five more are on order) and the ADC Flight with Queen Airs and T-33As for communications work plus a quartet of NAMC YS-11Es and one Kawasaki EC-1A that serve with the subordinate Electronic Warfare Training Unit.

Second-line elements are tasked with airlift, training and flight test, and are spearheaded by Support Command, which has three transport squadrons operating a fleet of about 40 aircraft. Most are of indigenous design, comprising nine NAMC YS-11s and 26 Kawasaki C-1As, but Lockheed's C-130H Hercules is assuming greater importance and about half of the planned 15 examples have now been delivered. Other Support Command resources consist of the Flight Check Squadron which uses YS-11s, T-33As and Mitsubishi MU-2Js to check and calibrate navigation aids (BAe 125s are on order); the Air Rescue Wing which has Kawasaki-Vertol KV-107 and MU-2 detachments at most major bases for search-and-rescue (SAR) tasks (Sikorsky UH-60J Night Hawks and BAe 125s are on order); and Helicopter Transport Units with a few CH-47J Chinooks at Iruma and Misawa for support of outlying JASDF radar installations.

Training Command's function is fairly clear cut, for this agency is tasked with satisfying JASDF pilot requirements, but it also provides instruction for technicians and maintenance personnel as well as air traffic control specialists. Pilot training is undertaken by five flying Wings using a varied fleet. Instruction begins with an initial stage of primary tuition on the Fuji T-3 at either Shizuhama or Hofu, followed by streaming into specialities, transport pilots receiving the next stage of their training with the Maritime Self-Defence Force (MSDF) and helicopter candidates with the Ground Self-Defence Force (GSDF).

Those fortunate enough to be selected for combat jets receive further primary instruction (including jet transition) on the much older Fuji T-1A/B at Ashiya before transferring to Hamamatsu for basic training on the T-33A (now being replaced by the indigenous Kawasaki T-4). Advanced instruction follows on the Mitsubishi T-2 at Matsushima, operational conversion being accomplished at either Misawa (for the F-1) or at Nyutabaru (F-4EJ/F-15J). Eventually, all Training Command T-1A/Bs and T-33As are to be replaced by the T-4, and this type may also take the place of the T-2 although that would necessitate much revision of the pilot training syllabus.

The only other aircraft-operating agency is the Research and Development Command which manages the Air Proving Wing (APW) at Gifu. The APW's fleet is quite diverse and includes examples of all of the major types in the JASDF inventory for follow-on testing and trials of new items of equipment such as weapons, and it may also "borrow" aircraft from operational units for use in special test projects.

EQUIPMENT

Interception:
McDonnell Douglas F-15J Eagle
McDonnell Douglas F-4EJ Phantom II
Attack:
Mitsubishi F-1
Reconnaissance:
McDonnell Douglas RF-4EJ Phantom II
AEW:
Grumman E-2C Hawkeye
Transport:
Lockheed C-130H Hercules
Kawasaki C-1A
NAMC YS-11
Kawasaki CH-47J Chinook
Calibration:
NAMC YS-11
Mitsubishi MU-2J
Lockheed T-33A
BAe 125-800
Training:
Fuji T-3
Fuji T-1A/B
Lockheed T-33A
Kawasaki T-4A
Mitsubishi T-2
McDonnell Douglas F-15DJ Eagle
ECM Training:
NAMC YS-11E
Kawasaki EC-1A
SAR/Liaison:
Kawasaki-Vertol KV-107-II
Mitsubishi MU-2J/S
Sikorsky UH-60J Night Hawk
BAe 125-800
Communications/Liaison:
Beech Queen Air
Lockheed T-33A

Right: The acquistion of military equipment, no matter that it may be unarmed, has always been a sensitive issue for the Japanese, and may in part help to explain the fact that the C-130H Hercules only began to enter JASDF service during the mid-1980s.

KOREA (NORTH)

WITH MORE than 600 fighters — including some 30 MiG-29 "Fulcrums" and about twice as many MiG-23 "Floggers" — the Korean People's Army Air Force (KPAAF) is indeed a formidable military organization which outnumbers South Korea's air force in terms of quantity if not quality. Despite some efforts at reaching more amicable relations between these two diametrically-opposed states, little headway has been made and it looks as if this localized "arms race" will continue for some time to come.

Headquartered in Pyongyang, the KPAAF has around 15 major bases, including several that are located close to the demilitarized zone from where attacks could be mounted deep into the south in the event of a sudden air offensive being launched. Apart from the aforementioned "Fulcrums" and "Floggers", fighter forces which are primarily concerned with air defence are for the most part equipped with the MiG-21 "Fishbed". At least 150 examples of this interceptor are operated, variants in service including the MiG-21F, MiG-21PF and MiG-21PFM, but some 50 Chinese-built Shenyang F-6s also fulfil air defence duties. At least another 100 F-6s are employed as fighter-bombers for ground attack, as are about 150 Shenyang F-5s, 40 Nanchang A-5 Fantans, a score of Sukhoi Su-25 "Frogfoots" and approximately 30 rather elderly Su-7BM "Fitter-As".

Of older vintage and unlikely to be too effective in a modern aerial battlefield are about 50 Harbin H-5 (Il-28 "Beagle") light bombers, offensive firepower being rounded out by some 50 Mil Mi-24 "Hind-D" gunships and some (possibly as many as 60) McDonnell Douglas 500 light helicopters that were obtained in what can best be described as "dubious circumstances". Of particular concern to South Korea is evidence that these machines can carry the AT-3 "Sagger" anti-armour missile; a concern heightened by the fact that South Korea also operates helicopters of this type, which renders the latter country vulnerable to the "false flag" border incursions — a serious concern given the tense political and military stand-off that still exists between these nations.

Airlift assets are less numerous but about a dozen An-24 "Cokes" are supported by a handful of piston-engined Il-12 "Coach" and Il-14 "Crate" light transports, as well as a few Li-2G "Cabs" and small numbers of the turbine-powered Il-18D "Coot" and jet-powered Tu-134B "Crusty", Il-62M "Classic" and Tu-154B "Careless".

At least 200 Fong Shu C-2s (An-2 "Colts") are also active and these have a special forces insertion mission as well as the more conventional transport applications. Helicopters used for various transport-related tasks comprise about 20 Mil Mi-4 "Hounds" and 70-odd Mi-8/17 "Hips", while five Mi-14 "Hazes" perform anti-submarine warfare (ASW) tasks.

Training equipment comprises the Nanchang BT-5/6, Yakovlev Yak-11 "Moose", Shenyang FT-2, Aero L-39A Albatros, Shenyang FT-6 and MiG-21U "Mongol", while a few Harbin HJ-5s (Il-28U "Beagle") may still serve as operational trainers with light bomber units.

EQUIPMENT

Interception:
Mikoyan-Gurevich MiG-29 "Fulcrum"
Mikoyan-Gurevich MiG-23 "Flogger"
Mikoyan-Gurevich MiG-21 "Fishbed"
Shenyang F-6
Attack:
Sukhoi Su-25 "Frogfoot"
Sukhoi Su-7BM "Fitter-A"
Nanchang A-5 Fantan
Shenyang F-6
Shenyang F-5
Mil Mi-24 "Hind"
McDonnell Douglas 500D/E
Light Bombing:
Harbin H-5
Maritime Patrol:
Mil Mi-14PL "Haze"
Transport:
Tupolev Tu-134B "Crusty"
Ilyushin Il-18 "Coot"
Antonov An-24 "Coke"
Ilyushin Il-14 "Crate"
Ilyushin Il-12 "Coach"
Lisunov Li-2G "Cab"
Fong Shu C-2
Mil Mi-8/17 "Hip"
Mil Mi-4 "Hound"
VIP Transport:
Ilyushin Il-62M "Classic"
Tupolev Tu-154B "Careless"
Communications/Liaison:
McDonnell Douglas 500D/E
Training:
Nanchang BT-5
Nanchang BT-6
Yakovlev Yak-11 "Moose"
Shenyang FT-2
Aero L-39 Albatros
Shenyang FT-6
Mikoyan-Gurevich MiG-21U "Mongol"
Harbin HJ-5

KOREA (SOUTH)

HEAVILY dependent on the USA as a source of military hardware for many years, South Korea receives less aid than it used to, but this is more than compensated for by a booming economy and an expanding defence industry. Between them, these factors give South Korea the necessary financial clout and technological skill to buy or build most of the weapons that it requires.

The most recent manifestation of this concerns selection of the McDonnell Douglas F/A-18 Hornet to satisfy the FX-1 fighter requirement. Some 120 Hornets are involved in this deal, of which the first dozen will be supplied from US production. Thereafter, 36 will follow as "kits" for local assembly, clearing the way for complete manufacture of the remaining 72 by Samsung. Ultimately, up to 300 may be obtained to meet the follow-on FX-2 requirement, although later examples could well be of the upgraded Hornet 2000 derivative. Earlier production programmes undertaken in South Korea by the engineering division of Korean Airlines have involved licenced production of the Northrop F-5E/F Tiger II and the McDonnel Douglas 500 light helicopter.

At present, however, the backbone of the *Hankook kong Goon* (RoKAF: Republic of Korea Air Force) is provided by the diminutive Tiger II and the rather more solid F-4 Phantom II. Close to 150 F-5Es figure in the front-line inventory, these being a mixture of locally-assembled and US-supplied aircraft. In terms of quantity, the F-4 is slightly less numerous, with approximately 60 examples of the F-4D and E

Below: Given the high proportion of hardware supplied by the USA, the only real surprise concerning the RoKAF's order for 36 F-16s was that it took so long to be placed.

being in use, and it seems likely that more of the latter will be obtained from surplus USAF stocks. In view of the fact that the F-4Ds are decidedly elderly, with around 25 years' of service behind them, it appears probable that future F-4E deliveries will be used as replacements rather than to equip additional front-line fighter units.

Considerably newer and much more potent is the General Dynamics F-16 Fighting Falcon, which began to enter RoKAF service in 1986 when the first of 36 aircraft (30 F-16Cs and six F-16D two-seaters) arrived at Taegu. Speculation about a follow-on order for a similar-sized batch persists, but this now seems unlikely following selection of the F/A-18 Hornet.

Other front-line equipment comprises the RF-4C Phantom II for tactical reconnaissance and the Cessna A-37B Dragonfly for counter-insurgency (COIN) and light attack. Just over two dozen of the latter remain in service, but RF-4C numbers are still growing, with the dozen machines supplied in 1989 due to be joined by up to nine further examples during the course of 1990. Most of the additonal aircraft are expected to come from the Pacific Air Forces stock since this major USAF command is set to deactivate its solitary reconnaissance outfit in early-1991.

Support and second-line components operate an interesting mixture of old and not so old equipment. This includes modest quantities of the Cessna O-1 Bird Dog and O-2A Skymaster on forward air control (FAC) and liaison duties. Another Skymaster of much earlier vintage still figures in the transport fleet, for about 10 Douglas C-54Ds remain in RoKAF service. Other airlift assets are limited to a similar number of jet-augmented Fairchild C-123 Providers, a solitary C-118A Liftmaster and about 10 C-130H-30 Super Hercules, although more of the latter are expected to enter service during the next few years as the RoKAF undergoes long overdue modernization of its airlift capability. As part of this effort, some Airtech CN.235s may also be purchased, although an announcement in 1986 of an order for 10 seems to have been founded more on optimism than reality, for it has certainly never been confirmed. VIP transport tasks are satisfied by a pair of BAe 748s obtained in 1974 and a single Boeing 737-328 delivered in 1985.

Communications and liaison duties are mostly the province of rotary-winged craft, with limited numbers of the Bell 212, Bell 412, Bell UH-1D Iroquois and McDonnell Douglas 500 being in service, but at least three Aero Commanders are also flown.

Pilot training begins with grading on the Cessna T-41D Mescalero, with basic tuition being undertaken on the same manufacturer's T-37C. Advanced tuition is still given on the long-serving T-33A, while operational conversion follows on the two-seat F-5F version of the Tiger II. Once again, though, the RoKAF has plans for modernization and is set to receive an initial batch of 20 BAe Hawks which will combine the Mk.60's Adour 861 turbofan engine with the Mk.100's nose and combat wing. Likely to be the forerunners of as many as 120 aircraft, it is probable that South Korea will demand local production rights.

Left: The reliance on US-supplied hardware is just as obvious in the RoKAF's rotary-winged force, where the Bell UH-1 Iroquois (and variations thereof) tend to predominate.

Above: In addition to US-supplied examples, the RoKAF operates a substantial number of F-5E (illustrated) and F-5F Tiger IIs that were assembled by Korean Airlines (KAL).

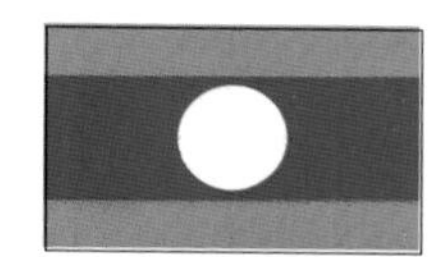

LAOS

NOW FIRMLY in the Communist camp, Laos's Air Force of the People's Liberation Army is entirely equipped with Soviet-supplied hardware, headed by 30 MiG-21 "Fishbeds" and a few MiG-21U "Mongol" two-seat trainers which apparently serve with two fighter squadrons located at Wattay Airport, near the capital city of Vientiane.

In addition to these fighter forces, Laos has a modest fleet of transport aircraft, including seven An-24 "Cokes", three An-26 "Curls", half-a-dozen An-2 "Colts" and a pair of VIP-configured Yak-40 "Codlings". Rotary-wing support is mainly entrusted to 10 or so examples of the Mi-8 "Hip", while one Mi-6 "Hook" is evidently still in service for heavy-lift taskings.

Older equipment dating back to the era of US assistance has now been withdrawn from use, but some of these transports — including a few C-123K Providers and some C-47 Dakotas — may still be operated by the government airline, Lao Aviation.

EQUIPMENT

Interception:
General Dynamics F-16C Fighting Falcon
McDonnell Douglas F-4D/E Phantom II
Attack:
McDonnell Douglas F-4D/E Phantom II
Northrop F-5E Tiger II
COIN:
Cessna A-37B Dragonfly
Reconnaissance:
McDonnell Douglas RF-4C Phantom II
FAC:
Cessna O-2A Super Skymaster
Cessna O-1 Bird Dog
Transport:
Lockheed C-130H-30 Super Hercules
Douglas C-118A Liftmaster
Douglas C-54D Skymaster
Fairchild C-123J/K Provider
VIP Transport:
Boeing 737-328
BAe 748 Srs.280
Communications/Liaison:
Rockwell Aero Commander 520/560F
Cessna 0-1 Bird Dog
Bell 412
Bell 212
Bell UH-1D Iroquois
McDonnell Douglas 500
Training:
Cessna T-41D Mescalero
Cessna T-37C
Lockheed T-33A
Northrop F-5F Tiger II
General Dynamics F-16D Fighting Falcon

EQUIPMENT

Interception:
Mikoyan-Gurevich MiG-21F/PF "Fishbed-C/D"
Attack:
Mikoyan-Gurevich MiG-21F/PF "Fishbed-C/D"
Transport:
Antonov An-26 "Curl"
Antonov An-24 "Coke"
Antonov An-2 "Colt"
Mil Mi-8 "Hip"
Mil Mi-6 "Hook"
VIP Transport:
Yakovlev Yak-40 "Codling"
Training:
Mikoyan-Gurevich MiG-21U "Mongol"

MALAYSIA

AT ONE time expected to purchase a dozen Panavia Tornadoes, the *Tentara Udara Diraja Malaysia* (TUDM: Royal Malaysian Air Force) has now abandoned its plans to operate this sophisticated strike aircraft, although other elements of the deal — most notably acquisition of the Rapier surface-to-air missile (SAM) system — may well go ahead.

For the immediate future, then, the TUDM will continue to rely on the Northrop F-5E Tiger II as its primary — indeed, its only — interceptor asset, the dozen or so survivors of 17 examples that were received in the 1980s currently serving with No.12 Squadron at Butterworth in dual air-to-air and air-to-ground roles. At the same base, No.11 Squadron has the RF-5E Tigereye, Malaysia having obtained two specimens of this reconnaissance-dedicated variation on the popular Tiger II theme, and these two units also share a trio of F-5F two-seat operational trainers.

Remaining combat forces consist of two squadrons (Nos.6 and 9) at Kuantan with the McDonnell Douglas A-4 Skyhawk, Malaysia having purchased 63 A-4Ls and 25 A-4Cs that were held in long-term storage in the USA during 1979. Initial plans called for Grumman to refurbish about 70 of these and fit a costly and sophisticated suite of avionics as part of the remanufacturing programme.

As it transpired, financial constraints eventually led to a less ambitious rework project involving fewer aircraft and a rather simpler avionics kit, and only 40 Skyhawks were ultimately destined to reach Malaysia. New equipment incorporated in the 34 A-4PTM and six TA-4PTM two-seaters that were delivered in the mid-1980s included a Ferranti gunsight and the Hughes angle-rate bombing system (ARBS), as well as new radios and a drag 'chute. Additional weapons options were also built-in, with the Skyhawks being able to carry AIM-9 Sidewinders, and 20 of them were also "wired" for the Hughes AGM-65 Maverick air-to-surface missile (ASM) although this weapon has yet to be made available to Malaysia. Despite such upgrading of the Skyhawk's combat capabilities, the TUDM is looking to the future, with an order for 28 BAe Hawks (18 Hawk 100s and ten Hawk 200s) having been placed in December 1990. In due course, the Hawks will replace the Skyhawks in front-line TUDM service. TUDM support elements are for the most part engaged in routine transport and training tasks. Starting with the former, Malaysia continues to operate about 15 DHC-4

Above: Time is against the TUDM's force of A-4PTM (Peculiar To Malaysia) Skyhawk IIs, three-dozen of which entered service in the mid-1980s. They are to be replaced by at least 28 examples of the BAe Hawk 100/200.

Below: Sandwiched by an F-5E (foreground) and an F-5F, one of two RF-5E Tigereye recce aircraft holds tight formation at 30,000ft (9,150m) above the Strait of Malacca.

Caribou short take-off and landing (STOL) transports with two squadrons, but is keen to replace these ageing machines and has looked closely at the Airtech CN.235M although no order has yet been placed. Two other transport squadrons use the Lockheed Hercules, Malaysia operating six standard C-130Hs and three maritime-capable C-130H-MPs, while other airlift assets are mostly concerned with communications, liaison and and VIP taskings.

Such missions are entrusted to a single squadron at Kuala Lumpur's Subang International Airport, and this has a mixed fleet of aircraft and helicopters that includes a single Dassault-Breguet Falcon 900, two BAe 125 Srs.400Bs, about 10 Cessna 402Bs and one Nurtanio/Aerospatiale NAS.332M Super Puma, although two Grumman HU-16E Albatross amphibians obtained in 1985 for re-supply of offshore garrisons are now apparently unserviceable.

A number of helicopters are also employed on transport duties. Most numerous and perhaps most in need of replacement is the Sikorsky S-61A-4 "Nuri", about 30 examples operating mainly on Army resupply duties with four squadrons at different locations. Those four squadrons also share just under 20 Aerospatiale Alouette IIIs which are used for utility, search-and-rescue (SAR) and forward air control (FAC), some of them being fitted with armament in the form of machine-guns.

Four more "Nuris" and eight Alouettes are active alongside seven Bell 47Gs with a helicopter pilot training school at Keluang (No.2 Flying Training Centre), this being one of three establishments that presently satisfy the TUDM's aircrew requirements. Regardless of eventual speciality, pilot tuition begins on the Pilatus PC-7 Turbo-Trainers of No.1 Flying Training Centre (FTC) at Alor Setar. "Wings" are awarded and "streaming" takes place on completion of the 14-month course, with those earmarked for rotary-wing aircrew duties moving to No.2 FTC, while those destined for the transport world will learn "on the job".

Candidates fortunate enough to be chosen for the "fast-jet" community go first to No.3 FTC at Kuantan for specialist training and jet transition on a fleet that includes the PC-7 and the Aermacchi MB.339A. Eventually, they will undergo operational transition at squadron level on either the F-5F or TA-4PTM Skyhawk II.

One other training unit exists, but this is principally concerned with allowing former aircrew to maintain a degree of currency in flying skills. Equipped with 10 BAe Bulldog 102s, it functions under the title "Voluntary Pilot Training" at Simpang Air Base in the suburbs of Kuala Lumpur.

EQUIPMENT

Interception:
Northrop F-5E Tiger II
Attack:
McDonnell Douglas A-4PTM Skyhawk II
Northrop F-5E Tiger II
Reconnaissaince:
Northrop RF-5E Tigereye
Maritime Patrol:
Lockheed C-130H-MP Hercules
Transport:
Lockheed C-130H Hercules
Boeing Canada Caribou
Grumman HU-16E Albatross
Cessna 402B
Sikorsky S-61A-4 "Nuri"
VIP Transport:
Dassault-Breguet Falcon 900
BAe 125-400B
Nurtanio/Aerospatiale NAS.332M Super Puma
SAR/Communications/Liaison:
Aerospatiale Alouette III
Training:
Pilatus PC-7 Turbo-Trainer
Aermacchi MB.339A
McDonnell Douglas TA-4PTM Skyhawk II
Northrop F-5F Tiger II
Bell 47G
Aerospatiale Alouette III
Sikorsky S-61A-4 "Nuri"
Refresher Training:
BAe Bulldog 102

Right: As with so many other air forces around the globe, the TUDM is a highly appreciative operator of the C-130 Hercules, nine of which are in use. Illustrated on a mission over the South China Sea is one of three C-130H-MPs based at Suban Air Base, and used by No.4 Squadron for maritime patrol tasks.

MONGOLIA

LITTLE MORE than a token force with headquarters in Ulan Bator, the Mongolian People's Republic Air Force is heavily dependent upon Soviet patronage, as befits its status as the smallest of the USSR's satellite nations. Responsibility for air defence is largely satisfied by some 90 Soviet combat aircraft, although these are to be withdrawn and it is probable that some expansion will occur to give Mongolia greater autonomy with regard to defence.

At the moment, combat elements are restricted to just one fighter squadron. This operates about 20-30 MiG-21 "Fishbed" interceptors, but Mongolia also has an SA-2 "Guideline" surface-to-air missile (SAM) unit. Training is undertaken internally, Mongolia's limited pilot requirements being met by half-a-dozen Yak-11 "Moose" and Yak-18 "Max" plus three MiG-15UTI "Midgets" and, rather appropriately, three MiG-21U "Mongols".

Other than that, it is essentially a transport force and the military air arm also doubles as Mongolair, which operates a limited domestic freight and passenger network. Transport aircraft resources are entirely of Antonov origin and consist of An-24 "Cokes", An-2 "Colts" and single examples of the An-26 "Curl" and An-32 "Cline". Rotary-wing types with airlift roles comprise 10 Mi-4 "Hounds" and 10 Mi-8 "Hips". Finally, three PZL-104 Wilgas obtained from Poland are used for utility and liaison.

EQUIPMENT

Interception:
Mikoyan-Gurevich MiG-21 "Fishbed"
Transport:
Antonov An-32 "Cline"
Antonov An-26 "Curl"
Antonov An-24 "Coke"
Antonov An-2 "Colt"
Mil Mi-8 "Hip"
Mil Mi-4 "Hound"
Utility:
PZL-104 Wilga
Mil Mi-4 "Hound"
Liaison:
PZL-104 Wilga
Training:
Yakovlev Yak-11 "Moose"
Yakovlev Yak-18 "Max"
Mikoyan-Gurevich MiG-15 UTI "Midget"
Mikoyan-Gurevich MiG-21U "Mongol"

MYANMAR

OFFICIALLY renamed in 1989, but still widely known as Burma, this small nation's air arm is primarily concerned with counter-insurgency (COIN) and interdiction of drug traffic routes. Marxist doctrine perhaps helps to explain the persistant refusal to accept more capable combat equipment from the USA, and undoubtedly has quite a lot of influence on the continuing conflict with Communist guerilla forces based in the north and along the Laotian border.

Correctly titled *Tamdaw Lay* (Defence Force Air), the small air arm is predominantly equipped with armed trainers which are in many ways ideally suited to COIN operations in this part of the world by virtue of being relatively unsophisticated and reasonably durable. Types and quantities in the inventory consist of half-a-dozen or so Lockheed AT-33As, 15 SIAI-Marchetti SF.260s, a dozen Pilatus PC-7 Turbo-Trainers and a quartet of Pilatus PC-9s. All have seen combat at some time or another and some have fallen victim to accurate and sometimes heavy small arms fire originating from guerilla forces. Looking to the future, Myanmar recently ordered a batch of 20 SOKO Super Galeb G4s from Yugoslavia, and their arrival should significantly improve COIN capability.

Transport elements are few, with "heavy-lift" requirements being satisfied by five Fairchild-Hiller Friendships, one of which is configured for VIP missions. Smaller but perhaps more useful in support of anti-guerilla operations are the Pilatus Porter and Turbo-Porter, Myanmar operating a combined total of eight of these machines alongside 10 UH-1H Iroquois helicopters that survive from a batch of 18 supplied by the USA in the mid-1970s. Other helicopters in service are confined to about eight Alouette IIIs, a handful of Kawasaki-Bell 47G-2s and a brace of Kawasaki-Vertol KV-107-IIs, air force equipment being completed by a VIP-configured Cessna 550 Citation II and four Cessna 180s that are used for communications.

EQUIPMENT

Light Attack/COIN:
SOKO G-4 Super Galeb
Lockheed AT-33A Shooting Star
Pilatus PC-9
Pilatus PC-7 Turbo-Trainer
SIAI-Marchetti SF.260MB/WB
Transport:
Fairchild-Hiller FH-227 Friendship
Pilatus PC-6 Porter
Pilatus PC-6B Turbo-Porter
Kawasaki-Vertol KV-107-II
Bell UH-1H Iroquois
VIP Transport:
Cessna 550 Citation II
Fokker F-27 Friendship
Communications/Liaison:
Cessna 180
Aerospatiale Alouette III
Kawasaki-Bell 47G-2
Training:
SIAI-Marchetti SF.260MB/WB
Pilatus PC-7 Turbo-Trainer
Pilatus PC-9

NEPAL

WITH JUST nine aircraft and helicopters, the Royal Nepalese Air Force functions mainly in support of the Army although civilian-type missions are also undertaken, with the trio of Shorts Skyvans being particularly useful in resupplying outlying villages in this extremely mountainous state.

Although it has expressed the desire to acquire more potent hardware in the shape of an attack-capable trainer aircraft, limited finance has thus far prevented realization of this wish and it seems unlikely to be fulfilled in the near-term. As a result, transport is expected to remain the principal function, other equipment consisting of a single BAe 748 Srs.275 turboprop, a pair of SA.330 Puma medium helicopters and three Alouette IIIs, the latter originating from Aerospatiale's production line as well as licence manufacture in India (HAL) and Romania (IAR). New equipment may be added shortly.

EQUIPMENT

Transport:
BAe 748 Srs.275
Shorts Skyvan 3/3m
Aerospatiale SA.330C/G Puma
Communications/Liaison:
Aerospatiale SA.316B Alouette III
HAL.316B Chetak
IAR.316 Alouette III

PAKISTAN

ALTHOUGH India has been perceived as the traditional enemy for many years, an often uneasy peace has prevailed between these two nations for the best part of two decades; but Pakistan Air Force (PAF) aircrew have had several opportunities to display their skill against another neighbouring air arm, namely the Afghan Air Force, and have succeeded in destroying a number of aircraft engaged on cross-border intrusions.

Equipment operated by combat elements of the PAF is a novel mixture of "high-tech" Western hardware and rugged but less complex Eastern types, some of which have been modified to incorporate weapons such as the AIM-9 Sidewinder air-to-air missile (AAM). China has been a source of much of this equipment, and the PAF presently operates substantial quantities of the Shenyang F-6, Nanchang A5-III "Fantan" and Chengdu F-7P Skybolt alongside Dassault-Breguet Mirages from France and General Dynamics F-16 Fighting Falcons from the USA.

PAF headquarters are located in Chaklala, with organization being broadly split into three main spheres of activity, namely Operations, Administration and Maintenance. At the operational level, squadrons are grouped together into Wing establishments at the various air bases, but Wing size may vary although the fighter squadrons generally have a unit establishment of 16 aircraft.

As far as day-to-day activities are concerned, Pakistan is divided into three regional Air Commands, directing ground-based surveillance radars as well as flying elements, missile units and anti-aircraft artillery forces. In time of war, however, Air Defence Command would be responsible

Right Typical of the Chinese-built hardware in PAF service is the Chengdu F-7TP trainer version of the F-7P Skybolt day fighter.

Above: The PAF is yet another air force to use old airliners as VIP transports, in this instance a pair of Boeing 707s.

for the protection of Pakistan with the forces detailed above; but ADC does also exist in peacetime, albeit primarily in an advisory and supervisory capacity.

As already noted, operational forces are equipped with an unusual mix of warplanes. Longest-serving and now in decline is the Shenyang F-6, basically a Chinese-built MiG-19 "Farmer", but this type is still active in reasonable numbers and functions in dual attack/interceptor roles (using AIM-9 Sidewinders for the latter) and three front-line squadrons, an operational conversion unit (OCU) and a squadron of the Combat Commanders' School.

Other equipment of Chinese origin includes the A5-III "Fantan", close to 60 having been delivered during the early to mid-1980s, and the survivors continue to serve with three squadrons, primarily in the attack role, although, like all PAF types, they are also called upon to undertake air defence duties.

The newest Chinese hardware to be acquired is the F-7P Skybolt, with current planning anticipating procurement of 95 aircraft, including 15 F-7TP two-seaters for training tasks. European avionics are fitted as standard and the principal air-to-air weapon is once again the AIM-9, although these aircraft are also compatible with the French Matra Magic AAM. F-7Ps now equip four squadrons, including a training unit.

Undoubtedly the most potent fighter in PAF service is the F-16 Fighting Falcon, which possesses dual attack/interceptor capability. A total of 40 aircraft comprising 28 F-16As and 12 F-16Bs has so far been delivered and the 37 survivors presently serve with three squadrons, one of which has a secondary training function. Procurement was expected to continue through the 1990s, with the PAF having a requirement for a further 71, but the USA has embargoed these and there is no likelihood of any additional Fighting Falcons being handed over in the immediate future.

Combat assets are completed by the Dassault-Breguet Mirage, Pakistan having purchased a total of 96 examples between 1967 and 1979. Delivery of these aircraft was completed in 1982, but the PAF has since obtained 50 more examples second-hand from Australia and will almost certainly add these to the inventory following rebuild by the Pakistan Aeronautical Complex.

Four basic variants of Mirage are now in service, with the dozen or so remaining IIIEP interceptors (of 18 originally supplied) being used by one squadron alongside a similar quantity of IIIRP reconnaissance-dedicated aircraft. The most numerous version is the Mirage 5PA, 58 examples of three basic sub-types having been delivered. Acquistion of the standard 5PA derivative was limited to 28 aircraft and most of these remain active with one squadron of the Combat Commanders' School as well an OCU. They were followed by eight of the improved 5PA2, most of which still serve with the OCU, procurement being completed by 22 Exocet-capable 5PA3s which now equip a single maritime attack-dedicated squadron. In addition, a few IIIEP and 5DP two-seaters are operated, mostly by the OCU on pilot training tasks.

As with many air arms, the Lockheed C-130 Hercules is the prime airlift tool and the PAF presently has about a dozen examples on hand with one squadron, while another transport unit is engaged on VIP tasks, for which it operates a pair of Boeing 707-320s as well as some smaller, twin-engined types. Communications resources are spearheaded by a single squadron with a few Cessna 172s plus single examples of the Beech Baron and Piper Seneca. In addition, regional Air Commands and air bases also possess their own liaison aircraft, with this duty generally being undertaken by locally-produced Mushshaks although Southern Air Command has one Aero Commander 680S.

Other missions are also the preserve of specialist squadrons. One operates as a composite unit, with a combat component utilizing the F-7P and a target tug element flying a handful of T/RT-33As. Another is an ECM training organization with a brace of Falcon 20s. Finally, there are roughly half-a-dozen SAR squadrons, each of which is equipped with a pair of Aerospatiale Alouette IIIs.

Pilot training is concentrated within the PAF Academy at Risalpur and begins with primary instruction on the locally-produced Mushshak, leading up to basic training on the Cessna T-37 and the award of a pilot's "wings". Newly-qualified pilots then move to No.1 (Fighter Conversion) Unit a Mianwali for advanced tuition on the Shenyang FT-5, after which they usually progress to the co-located No.25 Squadron which functions as an OCU with the F-6 and FT-6. Students who are "chopped" along the way generally end up with transport and helicopter-equipped units.

Below: A locally-built Mushak (foreground) holds formation with a vividly-painted T-37.

EQUIPMENT

Interception:
General Dynamics F-16A Fighting Falcon
Chengdu F-7MP Skybolt
Dassault-Breguet Mirage IIIEP
Shenyang F-6

Attack:
Nanchang A-5C "Fantan-A"
General Dynamics F-16A Fighting Falcon
Dassault-Breguet Mirage 5PA
Shenyang F-6

Reconnaissance:
Dassault-Breguet Mirage IIIRP

Maritime Patrol/ASW:
Lockheed P-3C Orion

Transport:
Lockheed C-130B/E Hercules
Lockheed L-100-20 Hercules

VIP Transport:
Boeing 707-320
Fokker F-27 Friendship 200
Dassault-Breguet Falcon 20

SAR/Liaison:
Aerospatiale Alouette III

Target-Towing:
Martin B-57B/C Canberra

Utility/Survey:
Lockheed T-33A/RT-33A

Communications/Liaison
Rockwell Aero Commander 680
Beech Baron
Piper PA-34 Seneca II
Cessna 172

Training:
PAC (AMF) MFI-17 Mushshak
Cessna T-37
Shenyang FT-5
Shenyang FT-6
Dassault-Breguet Mirage IIIDP/5DPA
General Dynamics F-16B Fighting Falcon
Dassault-Breguet Falcon 20

Left: Assigned to the 6th Tactical Fighter Squadron, 5th Fighter Wing, PAF, this F-5B Freedom Fighter has given years of solid service as a two-seat advanced trainer.

PHILIPPINES

THE OUSTING of the corrupt Marcos regime in February 1986 has failed to bring about a lasting peace and there have been numerous coup attempts aimed at overthrowing President Aquino since then, although none has yet succeeded in its aims. Further difficulties faced by the present administration concern the Libyan-supported Moro Liberation Front guerilla forces that are active in Mindanao, and opposition to US military installations has also been increasingly vocal and violent, resulting in attacks on US military personnel during 1990. Against this background, Philipino military forces have mostly remained loyal throughout a long period of financial restraint.

This austerity has hit the Philippine Air Force (PAF) quite hard, economy measures being partly responsible for premature retirement of the F-8H Crusader in 1988, although corrosion and low in-commission rates were also influential factors. As a result, the long-serving Northrop F-5A remains the only effective fighter, about a dozen such aircraft equipping a single fighter squadron at Basa. Tasked with air defence of the entire country, the value of this unit must be considered questionable since its primary armament is the old and virtually obsolescent AIM-9B version of the heat-seeking Sidewinder air-to-air missile (AAM), but there seems to be little likelihood of an early replacement.

Other combat hardware recently in use consisted of the even older North American T-28D Trojan. As few as seven were reported to be in use in the closing months of 1987 and at least five were destroyed in 1989, victims of various accidents and a December coup attempt. The sale of 20 surplus examples in August 1989 may be indicative of this veteran's withdrawal from service. If that is indeed so, then responsibility for counter-insurgency (COIN) operations may conceivably have passed entirely to helicopters, the PAF inventory including a dozen or so armed versions of the Sikorsky S-76, 100 Bell UH-1 Iroquois (some of which are armed) and about 10 locally-assembled and lightly armed MBB BO 105Cs; while there are unconfirmed reports that as many as 20 McDonnell Douglas 500MDs are in use as "gunships".

Remaining elements of the PAF are mostly concerned with transport duties, for which a mixture of fixed-wing aircraft and helicopters are used. Heavy-lift capability is entrusted to a trio of C-130H Hercules at Mactan Air Base, which is also home for about 15 GAF N22B Nomads that mainly satisfy utility functions. Other transport equipment comprises 10 F-27 Friendships (including one with a VIP interior for Presidential journeys and three maritime-dedicated machines), a few C-47 Dakotas, about 20 locally-built BN-2A Islanders and the Iroquois alluded to earlier, plus pairs of the Sikorsky S-70 Black Hawk, Bell 212 and Bell 214B. A civil-registered Fokker F-28 Fellowship is apparently also under the auspices of the PAF.

One area of activity which has been subjected to recent efforts at modernization is that of pilot training, some 18 locally-assembled examples of the SIAI S.211 jet trainer having been delivered in 1990, and the arrival of this type has had quite a marked effect on the syllabus.

Tuition is concentrated at Fernando and begins with a primary phase on the Cessna T-41D Mescalero, half of the 20 aircraft originally supplied still being in service. Until recently, basic instruction was accomplished on the SIAI-Marchetti SF.260, which also served in the weapons training role. Pilots destined to fly jets then moved to Basa for transition on T-34A Mentors and Lockheed T-33As of the 105th Combat Crew Training Squadron, this outfit also having a trio of RT-33As which constitute the PAF's sole reconnaissance capability. Now, however, it is likely that the S.211 has taken over responsibility for more advanced parts of the programme, and its influence could grow since a further 18 aircraft are the subject of an option taken out when the initial contract was signed in September 1989.

Remaining PAF resources are limited to a few light aircraft that are used for communications and liaison duties. All of the U-6 Beavers have apparently now been disposed of, but two-dozen assorted Cessna "singles" and "twins" are still flown.

EQUIPMENT

Interception:
Northrop F-5A Freedom Fighter
Attack/COIN:
North American T-28D Trojan
Sikorsky AUH-76 Spirit
McDonnell Douglas 500MD
Reconnaissance:
Lockheed RT-33A
Maritime Patrol:
Fokker F-27MPA Friendship
Transport:
Lockheed C-130H Hercules
Fokker F-28 Fellowship
Fokker F-27 Friendship
Douglas C-47 Dakota
GAF N22B Nomad
Pilatus Britten-Norman BN-2A Islander
VIP Transport:
Fokker F-27 Friendship
Sikorsky S-76 Spirit
Communications/Liaison:
Cessna 310/210/180
Cessna U-17B
Utility:
Sikorsky S-70 Black Hawk
Bell 214B
Bell 212
Bell 205/UH-1 Iroquois
MBB BO 105C
Training:
Cessna T-41D Mescalero
SIAI-Marchetti SF.260MP/WP
Beech T-34A Mentor
SIAI-Marchetti S.211
Lockheed T-33A
Northrop F-5B Freedom Fighter

Right: Given the long and drawn out conflict with guerilla forces, the COIN abilities of the SF.260MP/WP have been fully tested.

SINGAPORE

ESTABLISHED little more than 20 years ago in the wake of Singapore's decision to leave the Federation of Malaysian States, the Republic of Singapore Air Force (RoSAF) began operations with just eight Cessna 172Ks, but has since expanded in a most dramatic fashion to a position where it now ranks as one of the most potent air arms in South-East Asia. Today, it has some 15 aircraft-operating squadrons in total, these operating a mixture of fighter, attack, transport and training aircraft from five major air bases.

The newest addition to the RoSAF line-up is the General Dynamics Fighting Falcon, eight of the J79-engined F-16/79 model being ordered in 1984, although the contract was subsequently changed and the RoSAF machines are now standard F-16As and F-16Bs. Four examples of each sub-type have been obtained, with formal handover of the first taking place at General Dynamics' Fort Worth factory in February 1988; but it was only at the beginning of 1990 that they eventually arrived in Singapore, the interval being taken up by extended training at Luke AFB, Arizona, which culminated in participation in a *"Red Flag"* exercise at Nellis AFB, Nevada, during November 1989.

On arrival in Singapore, they were immediately assigned to No.140 Squadron, which was declared operational at Tengah in February 1990. Eventually, it is possible that as many as 20 Fighting Falcons will be procured, but later machines will almost certainly have to be to F-16C/D standard unless second-hand early-model specimens are obtained.

The RoSAF's principal attack warplane is the McDonnell Douglas Skyhawk, in service with three squadrons at Tengah. Extensively remanufactured to produce the A-4S and TA-4S, over 80 aircraft were eventually received, with the bulk of the modification project being undertaken in Singapore. Most of them remain in service, with 72 earmarked for further updating. Some 50 aircraft are to be brought up to so-called Super Skyhawk standard, with the major change relating to fitment of the General Electric F404 turbofan, and the first squadron to receive the re-engined aircraft became operational in March 1989. The remaining 22 examples will acquire new avionics during the course of 1990 but will not receive the new engine.

Other combat-capable units are equipped with the F-5E Tiger II, the last Hunter-equipped squadron (No.140) having effectively disbanded on arrival of the F-16, but there is little doubt that this classic fighter served Singapore well for the best part of two decades. About 30 F-5Es are active with two squadrons and these function in dual attack/interceptor roles, weaponry including AIM-9 Sidewinders for air-to-air tasks and AGM-65 Mavericks for air-to-ground work, as well as conventional iron bombs and rockets. Looking ahead, the RoSAF will add a reconnaissance capability in the near future, for eight F-5Es are to be modified to RF-5E Tigereye configuration.

Equipment that operates in direct support of combat forces consists of a quartet of Grumman E-2C Hawkeye airborne early warning (AEW) aircraft (two more are on order) and four KC-130B Hercules aerial tankers. The former are tied into an integrated air defence system operated in conjunction with Malaysia that includes interceptors, ground radars and surface-to-air missiles (SAM), while the latter serve alongside half-a-dozen standard C-130H tactical transports in a single squadron at Paya Lebar.

Transport capability is completed by six Skyvan 3Ms and an assortment of light and medium helicopters including just over a dozen UH-1H Iroquois, a similar number of Bell and Agusta-Bell 205As and 22 Super Pumas, although procurement of the latter is continuing with at least six more scheduled for delivery. A heavy-lift potential is also due to be added shortly in the shape of eight Boeing-Vertol CH-47D Chinooks.

Above: Pilot training to "wings" standard in the RoSAF is achieved on two SIAI-Marchetti designs. Illustrated are five S.211s used for advanced tuition, 30 of these aircraft having been ordered. The first six were supplied as component kits, while the rest have been built in Singapore by the SAMCO Corporation.

Below: An Aerospatiale AS.332B Super Puma operated by No.120 Squadron, RoSAF, and sporting a white and red SAR colour scheme.

EQUIPMENT

Interception:
General Dynamics F-16A Fighting Falcon
Northrop F-5E Tiger II

Attack:
Northrop F-5E Tiger II
McDonnell Douglas A-4S/A-4S-1 Skyhawk/Super Skyhawk

AEW:
Grumman E-2C Hawkeye

Transport:
Lockheed C-130H Hercules
Short Skyvan 3M
Aerospatiale AS.332M Super Puma
Bell UH-1H Iroquois
Bell/Agusta-Bell AB.205A

Tanking/Transport:
Lockheed KC-130B Hercules

Training:
SIAI-Marchetti SF.260MS/W
SIAI-Marchetti S.211
Northrop F-5F Tiger II
McDonnell Douglas TA-4S/TA-4S-1 Skyhawk/Super Skyhawk
General Dynamics F-16B Fighting Falcon
Aerospatiale AS.350B Ecureuil
Bell UH-1B Iroquois

SRI LANKA

WITH A fleet of aircraft numbering around the 70 mark obtained from a variety of disparate sources, the Sri Lanka Air Force (SLAF) is predominantly concerned with transport and maritime missions, although it does also possess a modest counter-insurgency (COIN) capability which has been employed in combat against Tamil separatist forces active on the Jaffna Peninsula throughout much of the past decade.

Fixed-wing COIN potential is limited to a handful of SF.260TP trainers which can be configured to carry rocket and gun armament, but the Bell 206 JetRanger and Bell 212/412 helicopters have also been committed to combat in addition to undertaking more conventional Army support tasks and lucrative commercial tourist flights.

Operations are conducted from just four main flying bases, each of which has a fairly clearly defined function. No.1 Flying Training Wing resides at Anuradhapura, while No.2 Transport Wing can be found at Ratmalana. Elsewhere, China Bay is home for No.3 Maritime Squadron, and almost all of the SLAF's 20 or so rotary-wing craft serve with No.4 Helicopter Wing at Katunayake.

EQUIPMENT

COIN/Assault:
Bell 212
Bell 412
COIN/Liaison:
Bell 206A/B JetRanger
Maritime Patrol:
Aerospatiale SA.365C Dauphin 2
de Havilland Heron/Riley Heron/Dove
Cessna 337
Transport:
Shaanxi Y-8
BAe 748
Douglas C-47 Dakota
Harbin Y-12
Beech Super King Air 200
Beech 18
Aerial Survey:
Ceessna 421C
Training:
SIAI-Marchetti SF.260TP
Cessna 150
de Havilland Canada Chipmunk

Right: A No.2 Squadron Bell 212 in full gunship configuration, complete with three machine-guns and one 2.75in (70mm) rocket launcher pod.

TAIWAN

Above: One air force to benefit from the NATO withdrawal of Lockheed F-104 Starfighters, the CNAF now has over 100 examples in service. The majority are flown by the 2nd Tactical Fighter Wing, based at Hsinchu Air Base.

FORCED TO fall back ever more on its own resources by the USA's rapprochement with the People's Republic of China, Nationalist China (Taiwan) is currently endeavouring to develop self-sufficiency with regard to armaments. Perhaps the most ambitious manifestation of this is provided by the indigenous Ching Kuo fighter, which is at the heart of a $1 billion, six-year development programme that was launched in 1985 when it had become clear that the USA was no longer prepared to act as a source of fighter aircraft. Flown for the first time in May 1989, single and two-seat versions of the Ching Kuo are currently under test, and the Chinese Nationalist Air Force (CNAF) has indicated that it is to enter service during 1993 against a requirement for some 256 aircraft (including at least 50 two-seaters) to replace existing stocks of F-5E Tiger IIs and F-104 Starfighters.

Until such time as the new fighter becomes available, the latter two types will continue to equip CNAF combat units which are fundamentally organized in similar fashion to the US Air Force. Consequently, fighter elements are distributed amongst seven Wings, each of which usually has three 18-aircraft squadrons, although one of these Wings is more correctly known as the Tactical Training and Development Centre (TTDC).

Assembled locally under licence by the Aero Industry Development Centre (AIDC), the F-5E Tiger II is the principal combat type and is known locally as the Chung Cheng. Procurement has now ended following the "production" of no fewer than 288 aircraft (231 F-5Es and 57 F-5F two-seaters), the majority of which remain operational with units at Tainan (the 1st Tactical Fighter Wing [TFW]), Chi Ayl (4th TFW), Tao Yuan (5th Tactical Combined Wing [TCW]), Taitung (TTDC, alias the 7th TFW) and Hualien (8th TFW). Of these, the most interesting is the TTDC, which includes an "aggressor" squadron with F-5E and F-5F variants in its operational line-up.

Less numerous but still making a worthwhile contribution to the defence of this island state is the Lockheed F-104 Starfighter. The original F-104As and F-104Bs have long departed from the scene, but well over 100 Starfighters continue in service with the 2nd TFW at Hsin Chu and the 3rd TFW at Ching Chuan Kang. Many are F-104Gs obtained from the USA via the Military Assistance Program, but these veterans have been "topped-up" more recently by surplus German and Danish examples. Other variants in service include half-a-dozen RF-104Gs that are active with a reconnaissance-dedicated element of the 5th TCW, while six ex-USAF F-104Ds and about 35 TF-104Gs are utilized in the pilot training role.

Airlift capability has been modernized to some extent in recent years through the acquisition of a dozen C-130H Hercules which began to join the 6th Troop Carrier and Anti-Submarine Warfare Combined Wing at Pingtung in the latter half of the 1980s, and which are probably used for maritime surveillance in addition to more conventional airlift. Other equipment is of much earlier vintage, for the CNAF still operates about 40 C-119G Boxcars, but no C-47 Dakotas remain in service with the Pingtung-based unit.

Other transport resources are concentrated within the Sung Shan Air Base Com-

Right: Caught on film a split-second before touchdown, one of the CNAF's 60-odd AT-3A advanced jet trainers returns to base at the end of another sortie. The entire fleet now wears the red, white and blue colour scheme of the "Thunder Tiger" aerobatic team.

mand which has control of two squadrons, both of which fulfil special airlift tasks, including the transportation of VIPs. One operates a few Boeing 727s plus some VH-1H Iroquois helicopters and at least one C-47, while the other has 11 recently-acquired Beech 1900C-1s, these twin-engined aircraft also being used for navaid calibration duties.

Rotary-wing elements with the CNAF are fairly limited and appear to be concentrated within a special squadron that forms part of the 4th TFW. Concerned mainly with search-and-resuce (SAR), it almost certainly maintains a number of detachments and is known to operate most of the 14 Sikorsky S-70C Black Hawks obtained in 1986, plus a number of UH-1H Iroquois and about eight HU-16B Albatross amphibians.

Pilot training is concentrated at Kang Shan and has become increasingly dependent on locally-designed equipment, with the AIDC AT-3 Tse Tchan having replaced the Lockheed T-33A in basic and advanced jet trainer tasks. An initial order for 60 AT-3s has been completed, the majority of which are AT-3As, but the AT-3B is now also in service. The latter model differs by virtue of its radar-ranging equipment, but both variants can be used just as effectively for weapons training duties.

Further development of the AT-3 has led to the A-3 Lui Meng single-seater, which is equipped with a rather more sophisticated navigation-attack system including a Westinghouse AN/APG-66 radar and fire control system. This variant also has a maximum external stores load in the region of 6000lb (2,721kg), thus offering the CNAF a potent addition to its close air support, night attack and maritime strike capabilities. Two AT-3s have been modifed to act as A-3 prototypes.

Other trainers that are presently in use comprise the Beech T-34C Turbo-Mentor for primary instruction at Kang Shan and the A-CH-1B Chung Shing turboprop-powered derivative of the T-28 Trojan which now fulfils weapons training tasks as part of the 1st TFW. Some T-33As and at least one C-47 Dakota are also thought to remain in use on training duties.

EQUIPMENT

Interception/Attack:
Lockheed F-104G Starfighter
Northrop F-5E Tiger II/Chung Cheng
Reconnaissance:
Lockheed RF-104G Starfighter
Transport:
Lockheed C-130H Hercules
Fairchild C-119G Boxcar
Douglas C-47 Dakota
VIP Transport:
Boeing 727-109/121
Beech 1900C-1
Calibration:
Beech 1900C-1
Training:
Beech T-34C Turbo-Mentor
AIDC AT-3A/B Tse Tchan
AIDC A-CH-1B Chung Shing
Lockheed T-33A
Lockheed F-104D/TF-104G Starfighter
Northrop F-5F Tiger II/Chung Cheng
Douglas C-47 Dakota

Below: A sight to set the heart of any aviation enthusiast racing, as a pair of the CNAF's elderly C-119G Flying Boxcars trundle out at the start of another transport mission. The C-119Gs equip three squadrons of No.6 Troop Carrier and ASW Combined Wing.

THAILAND

EFFORTS AT updating the combat potential of the Royal Thai Air Force (RTAF) have been spearheaded by the recent acquisition of the General Dynamics Fighting Falcon, and delivery of 10 F-16As and two F-16B two-seaters to No.103 Squadron at Korat was accomplished during 1988-89. The subject of a contract placed in 1985, they are to be joined in 1991 by four more F-16As and two F-16Bs which were ordered in 1987, and Thailand may ultimately obtain as many as 36 examples of this potent multi-role fighter, although it has also been linked with the Chinese A-5C "Fantan" and F-7M as well as Panavia's Tornado and surplus USAF A-10A Thunderbolt IIs. Cost will, however, be an influential factor on future procurement plans.

Other RTAF fighter elements continue to operate variants of the highly successful Northrop F-5 family, the current operational inventory including a dozen F-5As and three times as many F-5Es. These are presently active with two squadrons and the F-5Es seem set to remain in service for some considerable time to come, thanks to an ongoing update project which entails the fitment of radar warning receivers (RWR), chaff/flare dispensers and a head-up display (HUD), as well as providing compatibility with new weapons. Other models in service are the F-5B and F-5F trainers (two and six respectively) and Thailand also retains four reconnaissance-dedicated RF-5As delivered in the late-1960s. Reconnaissance may also still be performed by a few antiquated Lockheed RT-33As.

Combat-capable forces are rounded out by a sizeable counter-insurgency (COIN) force which has been committed to action against Laotian, Vietnamese and Cambodian forces over the past decade, as well as guerilla elements intent on destabilizing the government. Types employed on COIN tasks include a dozen A-37B Dragonflies, 20 AU-23 Peacemakers, a handful of AC-47 Dakota "gunships" and about 25 OV-10C Broncos, although the latter quantity might well be increased to nearer the 40 mark since the RTAF has shown interest in obtaining the OV-10BZs that were employed by Germany's *Luftwaffe* as aerial target tugs until recently.

Top: Adorned with the lightning strike motif worn by the aircraft of No.103 Squadron, RTAF, one of the 10 F-16As delivered for use on interception duties poses for the camera.

Support elements utilize a somewhat motley collection of aircraft and helicopters although once again there is evidence of modernization. As far as the transport resources are concerned, this is best exemplified by acquisition of the Lockheed Hercules, the RTAF having taken delivery of three C-130Hs and three C-130H-30s during the 1980s. At least one more C-130H was added in 1990 and the RTAF has indicated a requirement for up to 12; but older types continue to figure prominently in the transport fleet which includes C-123 Providers, BAe 748s (including two with the Royal Flight), C-47 Dakotas and more than 20 GAF N-22B Nomads.

Apart from the BAe 748s referred to earlier, Royal Flight VIP airlift duties are mainly entrusted to a couple of Boeing 737s, (with a third on order) but an A310 is due for delivery to this unit in the autumn of 1991. Other Airbus Industrie products in RTAF service consist of a pair of A300Bs obtained to replace a trio of DC-8 Srs.62s in the transport and VIP roles with No.601 Squadron, while helicopters engaged in airlift functions are confined to just under 20 turbine-engined Sikorsky S-58T Twin-Pacs and close to 30 Bell UH-1H Iroquois.

Pilot training has also been undergoing significant change during the past few years with the syllabus being modified to accommodate the German-designed RFB Fantrainer. Some 31 Srs.400s and 16 Srs.600s are due to enter RTAF service, but problems experienced with the local assembly programme have delayed introduction and by early-1988 only the more powerful Srs.600s had been completed.

In the past, primary instruction was accomplished on the CT-4A Airtrainer, students destined to fly jet equipment thereafter progressing via the SIAI-Marchetti SF.260 and Cessna T-37 to the Lockheed T-33A and Northrop F-5B/F before being declared combat ready. Now, it appears probable that the Fantrainer has taken over from the CT-4A and SF.260, for a number of the latter have recently transferred to a liaison and refresher training unit that operates as part of the transport wing based at Don Muang. Other training equipment consists of eight Grob G.109 and 14 Hoffman Dimona motor gliders.

Miscellaneous duties such as forward air control (FAC), liaison, aerial survey and electronic surveillance are performed by types such as the Cessna 0-1 Bird Dog, LearJet (three) and IAI Arava (three).

Below: Hood up, slats down, an RTAF F-5E Tiger II taxies in at the end of another sortie conducted as part of a joint US-Thai exercise. Note the triple-colour tactical camouflage.

EQUIPMENT

Interception:
General Dynamics F-16A Fighting Falcon
Attack:
Northrop F-5A Freedom Fighter
Northrop F-5E Tiger II
COIN:
Cessna A-37B Dragonfly
Rockwell OV-10C Bronco
Douglas AC-47 Dakota
Fairchild AU-23 Peacemaker
Reconnaissance:
Northrop RF-5A Freedom Fighter
Lockheed RT-33A
ECM/Elint-Gathering:
LearJet 36A
IAI-201 Arava
Transport:
Airbus Industrie A300B Airbus
Lockheed C-130H Hercules
Lockheed C-130H-30 Super Hercules
BAe 748
Fairchild C-123 Provider
Douglas C-47 Dakota
GAF N-22B Nomad MissionMaster
Sikorsky S-58T Twin-Pac
Bell UH-1H Iroquois
VIP Transport:
Boeing 737-200/-300
BAe 748
Bell 412
Training:
Aerospace CT-4A Airtrainer
Hoffman H-36 Dimona
Grob G.109
RFB Fantrainer 400/600
SIAI-Marchetti SF.260MS/MT
Cessna T-37B/C
Lockheed T-33A
Northrop F-5B Freedom Fighter
Northrop F-5F Tiger II
General Dynamics F-16B Fighting Falcon
FAC/Liaison:
Cessna O-1 Bird Dog
Communications/Liaison:
Cessna T-41D Mescalero
SIAI-Marchetti SF.260MS/MT
Cessna 411
Miscellaneous:
Rockwell Commander 690
Beech King Air E90
Swearingen Merlin IVA
LearJet 35A

Above: Given its close ties with the USSR, the appearance of the MiG-21 "Fishbed" in the markings of the VPAAF is no surprise.

VIETNAM

FOLLOWING a split with its one-time ally, China, the *Khong Quan Nhan Dan* (VPAAF: Vietnamese People's Army Air Force) has been almost entirely re-equipped with Soviet-supplied hardware and is currently organized along Soviet lines, with elements committed to defence being assigned to a separate agency. This co-ordinates the activities of surface-to-air missile (SAM) sites, anti-aircraft artillery (AAA), surveillance radars and a substantial force of interceptors. Looking more closely at the latter, most of the dozen or so squadrons that are allocated to four Regiments are equipped with variants of the MiG-21 "Fishbed". Approximately 200 examples of this classic Soviet fighter are thought to be in service, with other air defence resources being confined to about 30 MiG-23 "Floggers" obtained in the latter half of the 1980s.

Attack capability is rather more limited and is mainly confined to just under 50 examples of the Sukhoi Su-20 "Fitter-C", a batch of about 30 Su-7B "Fitter-Bs" having evidently been placed in storage along with 100 MiG-17/Shenyang F-5 "Frescos" and 50 MiG-19SF/Shenyang F-6 "Farmers". Of the American equipment "inherited" in 1975, spares shortages have necessitated grounding and some 200 aircraft — predominantly F-5A/Es and Cessna A-37Bs plus some A-1 Skyraiders, C-7 Caribous, UH-1H Iroquois and CH-47 Chinooks — are also in store, efforts to sell some of this large collection for much-needed foreign currency having met with little success.

A few A-37B Dragonfly light attack aircraft may still be active, but other attack-capable assets are confined to 30 Mi-24 "Hind-Ds", while a limited anti-submarine warfare (ASW) and patrol capability exists in the form of a dozen or so Beriev M-12 "Mail" amphibians and close to 20 Kamov Ka-25 "Hormone-A" helicopters.

Transport units are now dependent mostly on Soviet types, with the An-26 "Curl" being the backbone of the force. Approximately 50 are understood to be in service alongside a few An-12 "Cubs", roughly a dozen An-24 "Cokes", 20 Li-2 "Cabs" and C-47 Dakotas, 20 An-2 "Colts", two Il-18 "Coots" and some Yak-40 "Codlings". These resources may still be augmented by a few elderly Hercules, although most are now stored due to lack of spares. Rotary-wing elements assigned to transport duties have about 60 Mi-8 "Hips", with smaller quantitites of the Mi-6 "Hook" for heavy-lift operations and the Mi-4 "Hound" for utility and search-and-rescue (SAR) tasks.

Pilot training is generally conducted in the Soviet Union, but some trainer aircraft are also present in Vietnam. Again, these are mostly of Soviet origin, including limited numbers of the Yak-11 "Moose", Yak-18 "Max", MiG-15UTI "Midget" and MiG-21U "Mongol", but there are reports that some two dozen Aero L-39 Albatros' are in use although these could be committed to light attack duties rather than pure training.

EQUIPMENT

Interception
Mikoyan-Gurevich MiG-23 "Flogger"
Mikoyan-Gurevich MiG-21 "Fishbed"
Attack:
Sukhoi Su-20 "Fitter-C"
Mil Mi-24 "Hind-D"
ASW:
Beriev M-12 "Mail"
Kamov Ka-25 "Hormone-A"
Transport:
Ilyushin Il-18 "Coot"
Antonov An-12 "Cub"
Antonov An-26 "Curl"
Antonov An-24 "Coke"
Douglas C-47 Dakota
Lisunov Li-2 "Cab"
Yakovlev Yak-40 "Codling"
Antonov An-2 "Colt"
Mil Mi-6 "Hook"
Mil Mi-8 "Hip"
Aerial Survey:
Antonov An-30 "Clank"
SAR/Utility:
Mil Mi-4 "Hound"
Liaison:
Cessna O-1 Bird Dog
Training:
Yakovlev Yak-11 "Moose"
Yakovlev Yak-18 "Max"
Mikoyan-Gurevich MiG-15UTI "Midget"
Aero L-39 Albatros
Mikoyan-Gurevich MiG-21U "Mongol"

IN STORE

Attack:
Sukhoi Su-7B "Fitter-B"
Mikoyan-Gurevich MiG-17 "Fresco"
Shenyang F-5
Mikoyan-Gurevich MiG-19SF "Farmer"
Shenyang F-6
Northrop F-5A Freedom Fighter
Northrop F-5E Tiger II
Cessna A-37B Dragonfly
Douglas A-1 Skyraider
Reconnaissance:
Northrop RF-5A Freedom Fighter
Transport:
Lockheed C-130A/B Hercules
Boeing Canada C-7 Caribou
Boeing CH-47 Chinook
Bell UH-1H Iroquois
Training:
Northrop F-5B Freedom Fighter

NORTH AFRICA AND MIDDLE EAST

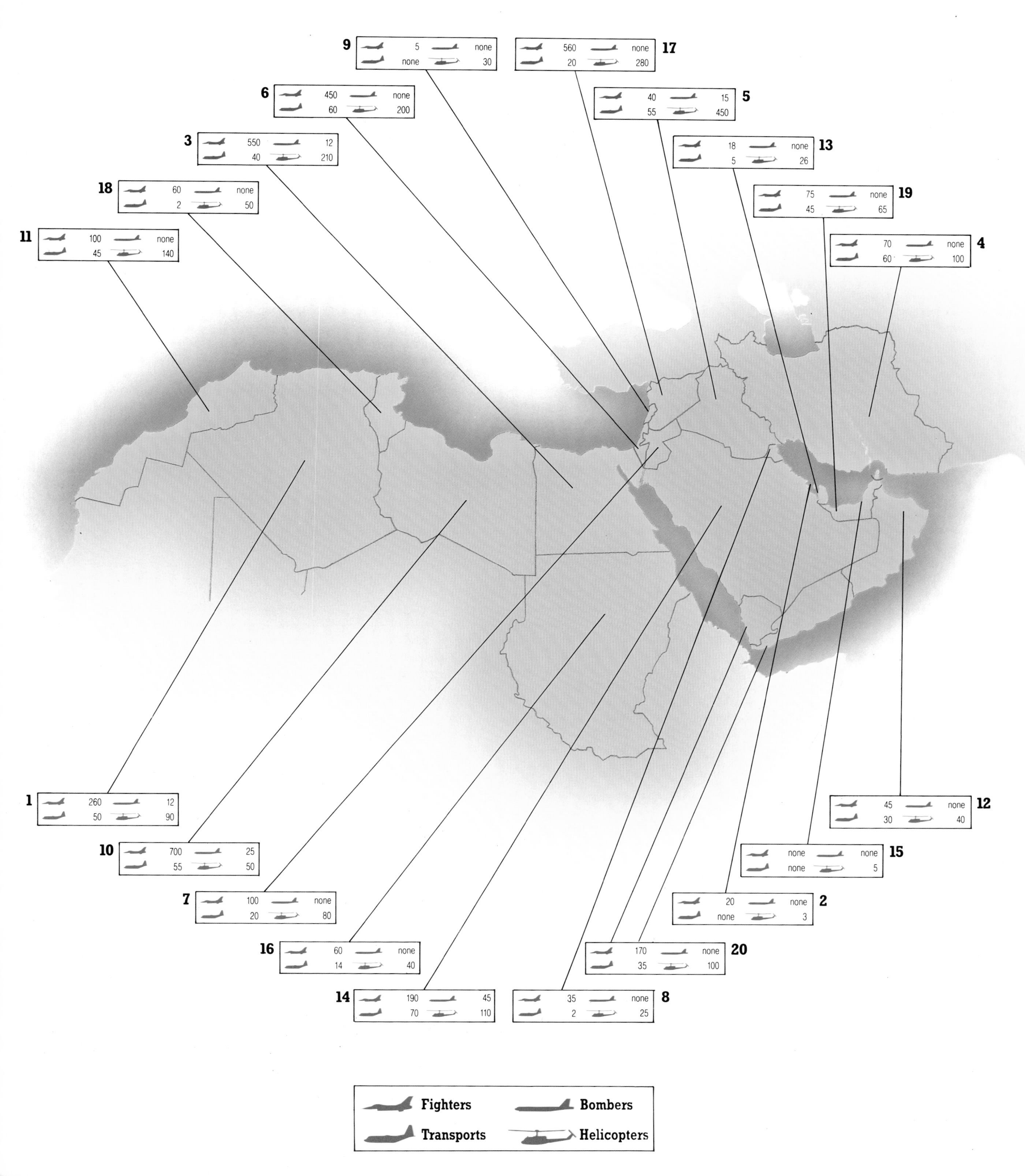

9 5 none none 30
17 560 none 20 280
6 450 none 60 200
5 40 15 55 450
3 550 12 40 210
13 18 none 5 26
18 60 none 2 50
19 75 none 45 65
11 100 none 45 140
4 70 none 60 100
1 260 12 50 90
12 45 none 30 40
10 700 25 55 50
15 none none none 5
7 100 none 20 80
2 20 none none 3
16 60 none 14 40
20 170 none 35 100
14 190 45 70 110
8 35 none 2 25
Fighters
Bombers
Transports
Helicopters

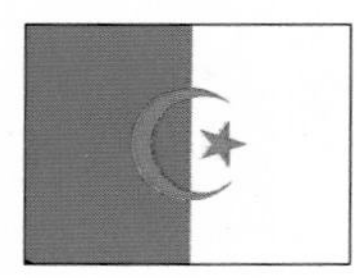

ALGERIA

ALTHOUGH formerly a French colony, the long and often bloody struggle for independence presaged a shift into the Soviet sphere of influence, and this is clearly evident in the Algerian Air Force (AAF) line-up which is predominantly composed of equipment obtained from the Soviet Union. The latter nation's position as Algeria's principal source of arms has, however, been eroded slightly in recent years, and some second-line types obtained from Western sources, most notably France and the United States, are now in service.

Air defence is entrusted to a mixed missile/fighter force, with the interceptor fleet being largely composed of the MiG-21 "Fishbed". Close to 100 are in service with three fighter squadrons and the AAF also has a single unit equipped with about two dozen MiG-25 "Foxbat-As". Other "Foxbat" variants are operated, these comprising a quartet of MiG-25R "Foxbat-Bs" for strategic reconnaissance tasks and at least three MiG-25U "Foxbat-C" operational trainers.

Ground attack and close air support resources are rather more numerous although the 50 or so MiG-17F "Fresco-Cs" that remain in service may well have been relegated to advanced training duties, leaving 40-50 Sukhoi Su-7 "Fitters" and a similar quantity of MiG-23 "Floggers" to constitute the "sharp end" of the AAF's offensive air power. The latter type can and often does augment the AAF's dedicated air defence elements.

Combat capability is also possessed by about 30 Mil Mi-24 "Hind" gunship helicopters, with similar quantities of the Mi-4 "Hound" and Mi-8 "Hip" being employed as assault transports. Other airlift assets are spearheaded by some 20 examples of the Lockheed Hercules. Two basic models of the four-engined transport are operated in equal quantities, although seven of the C-130H-30s are nominally civil-registered even though they display AAF titles. Remaining transport aircraft are principally of Soviet origin and include An-12 "Cubs", An-26 "Curls" and, with effect from 1989, four Il-76 "Candids". Two F-27 Friendship 400Ms are also operated and there is reason to believe that these perform maritime surveillance in concert with the Algerian Navy, as indeed do a pair of Beech Super King Air 200Ts. Other aircraft and helicopters engaged on transport-related tasks such as liaison and communications include a handful of Beech light "twins" and half-a-dozen Romanian-built Alouette IIIs. There are also three Gulfstream IIIs for VIP missions.

EQUIPMENT

Interception:
Mikoyan-Gurevich MiG-25 "Foxbat-A"
Mikoyan-Gurevich MiG-21F/MF/bis "Fishbed"
Attack:
Mikoyan-Gurevich MiG-23 "Flogger"
Sukhoi Su-20 "Fitter-C"
Sukhoi Su-7 "Fitter-A"
Mikoyan-Gurevich MiG-17F "Fresco"
Mil Mi-24 "Hind"
Reconnaissance:
Mikoyan-Gurevich MiG-25R "Foxbat-B"
Maritime Patrol:
Fokker F-27 Friendship 400
Beech Super King Air 200T
Transport:
Ilyushin Il-76 "Candid"
Lockheed C-130H/H-30 Hercules
Antonov An-12 "Cub"
Antonov An-26 "Curl"
Fokker F-27 Friendship 400
Mil Mi-6 "Hook"
Mil Mi-8 "Hip"
Mil Mi-4 "Hound"
VIP Transport:
Grumman Gulfstream III
Communications/Liaison:
Beech Super King Air 200
Beech Queen Air B80
IAR-319 Alouette III
Training:
Helwan Gomhouria
Aero C.11
Beech T-34C Turbo-Mentor
Aerospatiale CM.170-2 Magister
Mikoyan-Gurevich MiG-15UTI "Midget"
Mikoyan-Gurevich MiG-15 bis "Fagot"
Mikoyan-Gurevich MiG-17F "Fresco"
Sukhoi Su-7 "Moujik"
Mikoyan-Gurevich MiG-21U "Mongol"
Mikoyan-Gurevich MiG-23U "Flogger-C"
Mikoyan-Gurevich MiG-25 "Foxbat-C"

Right: Amongst all the Soviet hardware, clues to the AAF's colonial history, such as this French-supplied CM.170 Magister, can be found.

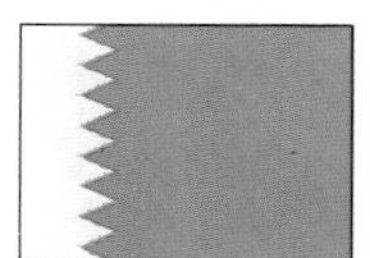

BAHRAIN

SINCE gaining independence from the United Kingdom in 1971, Bahrain has gradually expanded the size and scope of its defence establishment to include ground and naval elements as well as the Bahrain Amiri Air Force (BAAF) which was organized in 1976 with a couple of MBB BO 105C helicopters for routine communications duties. These were joined by a third example in 1977 and all three remain in service to this day.

Early intentions to acquire more capable hardware took some time to reach fruition, but the BAAF does now have a limited fighter-bomber capability, having taken delivery of eight F-5Es and four F-5F two-seat trainers during 1986-87, these being amongst the last Tiger IIs to be produced by Northrop. Even more potent equipment is on the horizon, however, for Bahrain has been cleared to receive the General Dynamics F-16 Fighting Falcon. A total of 16 aircraft is involved, most of which will be F-16C single-seaters, but a few F-16D two-seaters are to be included in the deal to satisfy training requirements.

Dual-mission capability will exist with these aircraft, AIM-9L Sidewinder and AIM-7 Sparrow air-to-air missiles (AAM) being supplied for air-to-air tasks, along with AGM-65D Maverick air-to-surface missiles (ASM), GBU-10/12 laser-guided bombs (LGB) and Rockeye cluster bomb units for air-to-ground applications.

EQUIPMENT

Interception:
General Dynamics F-16C Fighting Falcon
Northrop F-5E Tiger II
Attack:
General Dynamics F-16C Fighting Falcon
Northrop F-5E Tiger II
Communications/Liaison:
MBB BO 105C
Training:
Northrop F-5F Tiger II

EGYPT

ONCE HEAVILY dependent upon the Soviet Union for the supply of military equipment and assistance, Egypt shifted its allegiance to the West — and, in particular, to the USA — in a remarkable *"volte face"* during the mid-1970s. Following hard on the heels of the Camp David peace accord with Israel, this has resulted in a massive re-equipment programme, and today's combat aircraft operated by the Egyptian Air Force (EAF) are primarily of US origin.

Some of the Soviet-supplied hardware is still in service but efforts to modify this and incorporate western avionics and other equipment have met with mixed success, although the MiG-21 (and its Chinese-manufactured Xian F-7 equivalent) has benefited from new avionics and fitment of the AIM-9P Sidewinder heat-seeking air-to-air missile. As a result, the EAF looks set to operate a near-unique mixture of combat equipment for some time to come.

Organization is still apparently based on the Soviet model, with major bases being home to an Air Brigade. In the past, these Brigades typically controlled three squadrons, each with a complement of from 16 to 20 aircraft, but today it is more usual for each to manage the activities of just two squadrons, each of which usually operates identical equipment.

Air defence is a paramount concern and consumes a substantial portion of annual military expenditure, being entrusted to the appropriately named Air Defence Command (ADC) which is in fact a separate entity responsible for controlling Egypt's large missile force as well as anti-aircraft artillery and supporting radars. At around the 80,000 mark, ADC personnel levels handsomely exceed the EAF's more modest 25,000 level, and EAF interceptors are subordinate to ADC in so far as overall operational control is concerned.

Types presently employed include the Mirage 2000EM (16 received, with the prospect of a similarly-sized second batch to follow), assorted MiG-21s (about 100 in use), Xian F-7 (100 or so), Mirage 5SDE/E2 (52 received) and the F-16 Fighting Falcon. To date, two groups of Fighting Falcons have been delivered, starting in 1982 with 34 F-16As, these being supplemented in 1986 by the first of 34 F-16Cs. A further contract, negotiated in 1987, will result in 34 more F-16Cs being received by the EAF from 1991 on and there is a strong possibility that more will follow in due course. Accompanying these single-seaters have been a number of two-seat trainer aircraft, the EAF having obtained six examples of each of the F-16B and F-16D with six more of the latter model due to arrive in 1991.

Initially compatible only with the AIM-9 Sidewinder air-to-air missile (AAM), the Fighting Falcons will be "wired" for the AIM-7F Sparrow radar-guided missile, and this capability is to be retrospectively incorporated in earlier aircraft.

Other US-supplied combat equipment includes 35 former USAF F-4E Phantom IIs, delivery of which began during 1979 in conjunction with Sparrow/Sidewinder AAMs and AGM-65A Maverick air-to-surface missiles, permitting them to be used in interception and ground attack roles. For a time, it seemed as if a dismally poor operational-readiness rate would result in their disposal to Turkey, but US assistance brought about such an improvement that the EAF has requested seven more surplus F-4Es to augment the 33 survivors from the original batch.

Attack and close air support (CAS) duties are also undertaken by about 40 MiG-17F "Fresco-Cs", roughly twice that number of Shenyang F-6s (Chinese-built MiG-19 "Farmer") and just over a dozen locally-assembled Helwan Alpha Jet M22s. A dozen or so Tupolev Tu-16 "Badgers" are apparently also still in service, being used in the bombing, maritime surveillance and anti-shipping attack roles.

In addition to a comprehensive network of ground surveillance radars, Egypt also possesses an airborne early warning (AEW) capability. This is vested in five Grumman E-2C Hawkeyes delivered between late 1985 and late 1988, but this modest fleet is to be increased to six. The EAF will also soon be adding an in-flight refuelling tanker capability for its fighters through conversion of three former Egyptair Boeing 707s. Funding for this programme is to come from the USA.

Remaining front-line resources are completed by a modest tactical reconnaissance force composed of five Mirage 5SDRs and about 20 MiG-21R "Fishbed-Hs", with the closely allied acquisition of electronic intelligence (Elint) being performed by a quartet of suitably-modified Beech 1900Cs, two more examples of this type being configured for maritime patrol missions.

Above: Built in Italy under licence, this is one of the 14 CH-47C Chinooks acquired by the EAF to bolster its diverse transport fleet.

Below: After a quite nightmarish induction into EAF service, the F-4E Phantom II is now a well-liked and very effective combat asset.

Turning to transport elements, these are relatively few, although the EAF continues to receive the C-130H Hercules and has indicated an eventual requirement for as many as 40 such aircraft. At the moment, it operates about 25 on pure airlift duties as well as two EC-130Hs that have been fitted out to undertake ECM and airborne control duties. A handful of Boeing Canada Buffalo STOL freighters are also in service while four others now perform navigation training, and two or three An-12 "Cubs" may still be operational although the recent Hercules deliveries have probably led to their retirement.

Airlift tasks are also performed by helicopters, the EAF possessing quite a substantial force of these versatile machines. This includes some 14 Italian-built CH-47C Chinooks for heavy-lift tasks and close to 30 Westland Commandos, some of which are fitted out for VIP and electronic countermeasures (ECM) duties. Soviet-supplied equipment is also still active although numbers may well be in decline — at least 50 Mi-8 "Hips" are probably operational, but there is doubt about the current status of the larger Mi-6 "Hook", with few of the half-a-dozen or so that are on charge likely to be in an airworthy condition.

Most numerous of all the helicopter types is the Gazelle, at least 90 having been delivered, including some that were assembled locally. A few SA.342Ks are employed on communications duties, but the majority are armed SA.342Ls optimized for various roles including anti-armour attack with HOT missiles, anti-ship attack with AS-12 missiles (for the Navy) and assault support with the French-built 20mm GIAT cannon.

Looking to the future, Egypt has received a couple of UH-60A Black Hawks for evaluation and may well opt for the Desert Hawk variant. It has also expressed interest in acquiring about two-dozen TOW-armed AH-1W SuperCobras as well as Hellfire-armed McDonnell Douglas 500MDs, but no firm order has yet been placed for either type although the USA has supplied 20 Hiller UH-12Es for helicopter pilot training tasks.

Pilot training is in a state of flux at the moment, with much new equipment obtained to replace Soviet-supplied types like the L-29 Delfin and MiG-15UTI "Midget", both of which are still in use. In essence, tuition begins at the EAF Academy with a primary phase on the Gomhouria, students then moving on to intermediate and advanced training on the EMB-312 Tucano and Alpha Jet MS1. Both of these types have been assembled locally and production of the Tucano is continuing to satisfy a requirement for 54. Tactics and weapons training is mostly accomplished on the Alpha Jet, but a batch of 10 Aero L-39 Albatros jet trainers donated by Libya in 1990 may also now be used in this role. Operational conversion usually occurs at squadron level, using two-seater variants of front-line types.

EQUIPMENT

Interception:
Dassault-Breguet Mirage 2000EM
General Dynamics F-16A/C Fighting Falcon
Xian F-7
Mikoyan-Gurevich MiG-21F/FL/PFS/PFM/MF "Fishbed-C/D/E/F/J"
Dassault-Breguet Mirage 5SDE/E2

Attack:
McDonnell Douglas F-4E Phantom II
Shenyang F-6
Mikoyan-Gurevich MiG-17F "Fresco-C"
Dassault-Breguet Alpha Jet MS2
Aerospatiale SA.342L Gazelle

Bombing/Anti-Shipping:
Tupolev Tu-16 "Badger-D/G"

Reconnaissance:
Dassault-Breguet Mirage 5SDR
Mikoyan-Gurevich MiG-21R "Fishbed-H"

Elint-Gathering:
Beech 1900C

ECM Command Post:
Lockheed EC-130H Hercules

ECM:
Westland Commando 2E

AEW:
Grumman E-2C Hawkeye

Maritime Patrol:
Beech 1900C

Transport:
Lockheed C-130H Hercules
Boeing Canada Buffalo
Mil Mi-6 "Hook"
Boeing-Vertol CH-47C Chinook
Mil Mi-8 "Hip"
Westland Commando
Sikorsky UH-60A Black Hawk

VIP Transport:
Agusta-Sikorsky AS-61
Westland Commando 2B

Communications/Liaison:
Beech Super King Air
PZL-104 Wilga
Aerospatiale SA.342K Gazelle
Aerospatiale SA.316B Chetak

Training:
Helwan Gomhouria
Embraer EMB-312 Tucano
Dassault-Breguet Alpha Jet MS1
Aero L-29 Delfin
Mikoyan-Gurevich MiG-15UTI "Midget"
Aero L-39 Albatros
Shenyang FT-6
Mikoyan-Gurevich MiG-21U/US "Mongol"
Dassault-Breguet Mirage 5SDD
General Dynamics F-16B/D Fighting Falcon
Dassault-Breguet Mirage 200BM
Boeing Canada Buffalo
Hiller UGH-12E

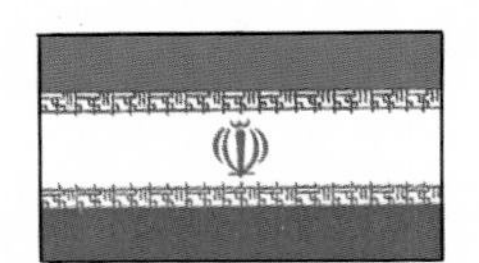

IRAN

ONCE THE possessor of one of the most powerful air arms in this volatile part of the world, Iran severed its links with the USA following the success of the revolution that culminated in the ousting of the Shah in 1979 and the creation of an Islamic Republic. Eight years of war with Iraq ensued, but despite the ceasefire of August 1988 it is only recently that a formal cessation of hostilities has occurred, this no doubt being inspired by Saddam Hussein's wish to realign forces following the seizure of Kuwait. The current operational status of the Islamic Republic of Iran Air Force (IRIAF) is hard to establish for certain, but it is clear that most of the massive amount of US-supplied equipment is no longer in use. High combat attrition during the war with Iraq was partly responsible, as was the US embargo on spare parts. In consequence, it is doubtful if more than a handful of F-14A Tomcats and about 20 examples of each of the F-4 Phantom II and F-5 Tiger II are still operationally effective. Significantly, Iran's attempts to rebuild its air power now centre around Soviet and Chinese types, most notable of which is the MiG-29 "Fulcrum", at least 14 of which have been supplied. Reports linking

Left: A very useful legacy of the pre-revolution days when Iran was a trusted ally of the West, this Bell 214 Isfahan is just one reminder of the huge stocks of US-supplied hardware acquired by the Shah of Iran.

the Yugoslavian-built IAR-93 Orao 2 and the Chinese-built F-7M Airguard with the IRIAF would appear to be speculative at the present time.

Other than that, the IRIAF functions principally as a transport force, with the remaining elements of a once large fleet now being reduced to about nine Boeing 747Fs, 14 Boeing 707 tanker-transports plus about 15 examples of the Fokker Friendship and C-130E/H Hercules and a couple of CH-47C Chinooks. Communications and liaison duties are fulfilled by an assortment of light aircraft and helicopters, while there is a small VIP element with a Boeing 727, two Lockheed Jetstars, a pair of Agusta-Sikorsky AS-61As and, possibly, a Bell 214.

Training capability is limited to say the least, although there are signs of improvement for the future since the IRIAF ordered a batch of 15 EMB-312 Tucanos in December 1988. Some years earlier, in 1983-84, it had taken delivery of 35 Pilatus PC-7 Turbo-Trainers, but these were evidently earmarked for operation by the "*Pasdaran*" (Revolutionary Guard) and may therefore not come under IRIAF control. Other training assets include the survivors of a batch of 49 Beech F33A/C Bonanzas delivered before the revolution plus about 10 Lockheed T-33As and a similar quantity of Northrop F-5B/Fs.

In addition, a pair of Lockheed P-3F Orions are reportedly still airworthy and undertake maritime patrol tasks from Bandar Abbas on the Gulf coast.

EQUIPMENT

Interception:
Mikoyan-Gurevich MiG-29 "Fulcrum-A"
Grumman F-14A Tomcat
Xian F-7
Attack:
McDonnell Douglas F-4D/E Phantom II
Shenyang F-6
Northrop F-5E Tiger II
Maritime Patrol:
Lockheed P-3F Orion
Transport:
Boeing 747F
Boeing 707-3J9C/386C
Lockheed C-130E/H Hercules
Fokker F-27 Friendship 400M/600
Meridionali-Vertol CH-47C Chinook
VIP Transport:
Boeing 727
Lockheed Jetstar
Agusta-Sikorsky As-61A
Bell 214 Isfahan
Communications/Liaison:
Dassault-Breguet Falcon 20F
Rockwell Commander 681B
Cessna 310L
Agusta-Bell Ab.212
Agusta-Bell Ab.206 JetRanger
Training:
Beech F33A/C Bonanza
Pilatus PC-7 Turbo-Trainer
Embraer EMB-312 Tucano
Lockheed T-33
Northrop F-5F Tiger II
Mikoyan-Gurevich MiG-29 "Fulcrum-B"

IRAQ

UNDOUBTEDLY one of the major military powers within the Gulf region, courtesy of Eastern and Western arms suppliers, Iraq is now in a state of turmoil following its defeat at the hands of the Western coalition. As witnessed around the world, the Iraqi Air Force played a very limited role during the conflict, and over 100 front-line aircraft escaped to Iran to avoid possible destruction. A similar quantity were destroyed, either on the ground or in a series of limited air-to-air engagements with Coalition air elements tasked with liberating Kuwait.

Just what constitutes the post-war Iraqi Air Force is uncertain, although it is known that helicopter gunships such as the Mi-24 "Hind" have been used against rebel elements as President Sadam Hussein struggles to keep his grip on power. There can be little doubt that the West would like to impose stringent curbs on the future composition of all Iraqi military forces, but just what form any such curbs will take, and how they will affect the Iraqi Air Force in particular, is uncertain.

Above: A pair of Iraqi Air Force Mirage F.1s formate with an Il-76 configured for tanking duties, during a fly-past over Baghdad.

EQUIPMENT

Interception:
Mikoyan-Gurevich MiG-25 "Foxbat-A"
Mikoyan-Gurevich MiG-29 "Fulcrum-A"
Mikoyan-Gurevich MiG-23MS "Flogger-E"
Dassault-Breguet Mirage F.1EQ
Chengdu F-7B
Mikoyan-Gurevich MiG-21MF/bis "Fishbed"
Attack:
Tupolev Tu-22 "Blinder"
Tupolev Tu-16 "Badger"
Xian H-6D
Sukhoi Su-24 "Fencer"
Mikoyan-Gurevich MiG-23BN "Flogger-F"
Sukhoi Su-22M-3/-4 "Fitter-J/K"
Sukhoi Su-20 "Fitter-C"
Sukhoi Su-25 "Frogfoot"
Anti-Armour:
Mil Mi-24 "Hind"
MBB BO 105
Aerospatiale SA.342L Gazelle
Aerospatiale SA.316C Alouette III
Anti-Shipping/ASW:
Aerospatiale SA.321GV Super Frelon
Aerospatiale AS.332L Super Puma
Agusta-Bell AB.212ASW
Agusta A.109 Hirundo
Reconnaissance:
Mikoyan-Gurevich MiG-25R "Foxbat-B"
AEW:
Ilyushin Il-76 "Adnan-I"/"Baghdad I"
Transport:
Ilyushin Il-76MD "Candid-B"
Antonov An-26 "Curl"
Antonov An-24 "Coke"
Antonov An-2 "Colt"
Mil Mi-6 "Hook"
Mil Mi-8 "Hip"
Bell 214ST
Aerospatiale SA.330 Puma
VIP Transport:
Agusta-Sikorsky AS-61TS
Aerospatiale SA.330 Puma
SAR/Liaison:
MBB-Kawasaki BK 117B
Mil Mi-4 "Hound"
Training:
FFA AS-202 Bravo
Pilatus PC-7 Turbo-Trainer
Pilatus PC-9
Embraer EMB-312 Tucano
Mikoyan-Gurevich MiG-15UTI "Midget"
Aero L-29 Delfin
Mikoyan-Gurevich MiG-17 "Fresco"
Aero L-39 Albatros
Shenyang F-6
Mikoyan-Gurevich MiG-21U "Mongol"
Sukhoi Su-7BM "Fitter-A"
Dassault-Breguet Mirage F.1BQ
Mikoyan-Gurevich MiG-29UB "Fulcrum-B"
McDonnell Douglas 300C/500D/530F

ISRAEL

SECOND TO none in terms of combat experience, the *Heyl HA'Avir* (IDF/AF: Israeli Defence Force/Air Force) is without doubt one of the best equipped and most potent air arms in the Middle East, operating a force of around 450 warplanes of US and indigenous manufacture, with a further 150 or so in storage. A near-impenetrable cloak of security means that precise details of the order of battle are unavailable although it is believed that combat elements include two squadrons equipped with the F-15 Eagle, six with the F-16 Fighting Falcon and four each with the Kfir, F-4E Phantom II and A-4 Skyhawk, supported by a tactical reconnaissance element with the RF-4 Phantom II. Other resources include a sizeable anti-armour force of about 40 AH-1 HueyCobra and McDonnell Douglas 500MD helicopters.

The leading air superiority fighter is the McDonnell Douglas F-15 Eagle, with the IDF/AF being the first export customer for the type when it took delivery of its initial aircraft in December 1976. Subsequent contracts have increased procurement to 56, comprising 38 F-15As (four of which have been lost in accidents), two F-15Bs, nine F-15Cs and seven F-15Ds, with five of the last variant still to be delivered at the time of writing. Plans are in hand to update some of the Eagles by incorporating airframe and avionics changes.

Arriving on the scene somewhat later, the General Dynamics F-16 Fighting Falcon is now arguably the most important warplane in IDF/AF service, and procurement is expected to continue in the wake of cancellation of the indigenous Lavi. At present, the IDF/AF expects to receive no fewer than 210 F-16s, but this figure may yet rise still higher since options do exist on a further 15. Deliveries kicked off in 1980 and to date have included 67 F-16As, eight F-16Bs, 51 F-16Cs and 24 F-16Ds (including some with additional avionics for *"Wild Weasel"* defence-suppression duties), while an outstanding contract will add a further 60 F-16C/D aircraft.

Air-to-air and air-to-ground missions are performed with near equal facility and, like the F-15, the F-16, may be used to deliver nuclear weapons from Israel's apparently substantial stock of warheads.

Nuclear capability is also possessed by the much older McDonnell Douglas F-4 Phantom II, just over 100 of which remain in front-line service in the attack role. Having served the IDF/AF well since it joined the inventory in the late-1960s, the trusty F-4 looks like being around for some time to come and is set to benefit from the *"Phantom 2000"* update project whereby most remaining aircraft are to receive new avionics including a computerized nav/attack system at the same time as they are rewired and structurally strengthened. Originally, it was hoped that refurbishment would also include fitment of a new engine (the Pratt & Whitney PW1120), but this idea appears to have been abandoned.

Also from the McDonnell Douglas stable, the A-4 Skyhawk is still around in worthwhile numbers, with about 100 A-4E/H/N aircraft in front-line service and 60 more in reserve; but the IDF/AF has been steadily disposing of this diminutive attack warplane and has shown little interest in exploring further the upgrade possibilities.

The remaining combat type is the IAI Kfir and this too appears to be in decline, since only about 75 are now in regular service with just under 100 more in store. However, most have been updated to Kfir C7 standard since the mid-1980s, endowing them with

Below: Israel may be a small nation, but the IDF/AF's transport requirements are many and varied. Illustrated is one of the C-130H Hercules at the heart of the transport force.

Above: The acquisition of the USA's principal front-line fighters by the IDF/AF has led to the supply of well over 100 F-16 Fighting Falcons, including this fully-armed F-16C.

more power and a greater payload capability, and they could continue to give good service for many years to come.

The IDF/AF also has quite a long "tail", with support elements being engaged in a multiplicity of tasks including conventional transport duties, in-flight refuelling, airborne early warning (AEW), acquisition of electronic intelligence (Elint) and training. Pure transport requirements are satisfied by about 20 C-130E/H Hercules, a slightly smaller number of long-service C-47 Dakotas, 30-odd Sikorsky CH-53D Sea Stallions and sundry smaller types which include a few Aravas and Islanders as well as some two dozen Bell 212s and 10 Bell 205s.

Airlift tasks are also undertaken by a quartet of Boeing 707s and this basic type serves with the IDF/AF in other roles, Israel Aircraft Industries having converted about six for tanker duties and a similar quantity for Elint-gathering and communications jamming.

AEW is the domain of a quartet of Grumman E-2C Hawkeyes that were delivered in the late-1970s, while additional ECM/Elint capability comes in the shape of Beech RU-21/RC-12D King Airs received in the 1980s. A pair of Grumman EV-1E Mohawks obtained a long ago as 1976 may also still be active on similar tasks.

Pilot training begins with grading and assessment on the Piper Super Cub, about 20 currently being operated. Students then move to the IAI Tzukit (an updated CM.170 Magister with new avionics and the more powerful Marbore 6 turbojet engine) for basic jet training. Some 80 Magisters have been modified in this way, but the IDF/AF is now casting around for a replacement and has evaluated Promavia's Jet Squalus, although no decision has been reached.

Above: Converted from airliner to dual-role tanker/transport, this Boeing 707 (seen here with a trio of thirsty TA-4Js) represents a significant boost to IDF5AF capabilities.

Advanced pilot tuition is given on 20 TA-4H/J Skyhawks, with those who complete the tough course receiving operational conversion at unit level, and the efficacy of IDF/AF pilot training is perhaps best revealed by studying its combat record which is nothing short of remarkable. As an illustration, the F-15 Eagle has to date scored close to 60 confirmed "kills" in aerial combat at no loss to itself.

Finally, several types are employed for communications and liaison. These include varying numbers of the Dornier Do 28B, Cessna 172 and Bell 206 JetRanger, although an unspecified quantity of Beech A36 Bonanzas has been ordered to replace 20 Queen Airs and some two dozen single-engined Cessna U206s.

Above: While other air arms have retired their F-4 fleets, Israel is determined to get the most out of its F-4Es. Updating will allow them to operate into the 21st Century.

EQUIPMENT

Interception:
McDonnell Douglas F-15A/C Eagle
General Dynamics F-16A/C Fighting Falcon
IAI Kfir C2/C7
Attack:
General Dynamics F-16A/C Fighting Falcon
McDonnell Douglas F-4E Phantom II
IAI Kfir C2/C7
McDonnell Douglas A-4E/H/N Skyhawk
Anti-Armour Attack:
McDonnell Douglas AH-64A Apache
Bell AH-1S HueyCobra
McDonnell Douglas 500MD
Defence Suppression:
General Dynamics F-16D Fighting Falcon
Tactical Reconnaissance:
McDonnell Douglas RF-4E/F-4E(S)/F-4P Phantom II
AEW:
Grumman E-2C Hawkeye
Elint-Gathering:
Boeing 707
Grumman EV-1E Mohawk
Beech RC-12D/RU-21 King Air
IAI-201 Arava
Maritime Patrol:
IAI Westwind 1124N
Observation:
Bell OH-58A/D Kiowa
Transport:
Boeing 707
Lockheed C-130H Hercules
Douglas C-47 Dakota
Sikorsky CH-53D Sea Stallion
Sikorsky S-65C
Bell 212 Twin Huey
Bell 205 Iroquois
VIP Transport:
IAI Westwind 1123
Tanker/Transport:
Boeing 707
Lockheed KC-130H Hercules
Utility Transport:
Pilatus Britten-Norman BN-2A Islander
Dornier Do 28B
SAR:
Aerospatiale HH-65A Dauphin 2
Bell 212 Twin Huey
Communications/Liaison:
Cessna 152/172/U.206C
Piper PA-31 Navajo
Beech Queen Air 80
Bell 206 JetRanger
Training:
Piper PA-18 Super Cub
IAI Tzukit/Magister
McDonnell Douglas TA-4H/J Skyhawk
IAI Kfir TC2/TC7
General Dynamics F-16B/D Fighting Falcon
McDonnell Douglas F-15B/D Eagle
Beech Queen Air 80

Above: Symbolizing the close relationship that existed between Jordan and the USA prior to the Gulf Crisis, one of the RJAF's Northrop F-5F Tiger IIs flies as wingman to a USAF F-16C Fighting Falcon while on exercise.

JORDAN

CLOSE TIES with Iraq and the proximity of Israel means that Jordan is caught between "a rock and a hard place", as evidenced by its efforts to steer a fine line between diplomacy and the desire to maintain good relations with Iraq and its opponents during the crisis that followed the invasion of Kuwait.

Traditionally, this Arab nation has looked to the West for military equipment, and the Royal Jordanian Air Force (RJAF) currently operates a mix of US and French warplanes. Numerically in the ascendant is the Northrop F-5E Tiger II, just over 50 examples of this widely used fighter-bomber being active with two squadrons (Nos.9 and 17), while the earlier F-5A still serves with another squadron (No.6) that functions primarily as a fast jet training establishment.

France's Mirage F.1 is the other main combat type and this too serves with a pair of squadrons (Nos.1 and 25). Three basic variants are operated, specifically the F.1CJ which is a dedicated interceptor model, the F.1EJ which has multi-mission capability and can also be employed for attack duties and, finally, the F.1BJ two-seat conversion trainer. Looking to the future the RJAF has placed a contract for a dozen Mirage 2000CJM interceptors, but plans to obtain eight Panavia Tornado IDS multi-role fighters have been shelved due to financial difficulties. As part of the deal with Dassault-Breguet for Mirage 2000s, about 15 Mirage F.1CJs are to be given ground attack capabilities similar to those of the F.1EJ.

One other combat type can be found in the RJAF's front-line inventory, this being the Bell AH-1S HueyCobra, which utilizes the Hughes BGM-71A TOW anti-armour missile in the "tank-busting" role. Again, sufficient aircraft have been received to equip two RJAF squadrons (Nos.10 and 12), all 24 HueyCobras being delivered during the course of 1985. Combat-ready forces are to be found at three major air bases, namely Azraq (Mirages), Prince Hassan (F-5s) and Jafr (AH-1Ss), while the support elements (including the F-5As alluded to earlier) are concentrated at two others.

Four more squadrons exist, all being located at Mafraq which is home for the King Hussein Air College and the Arab Air Academy. As noted earlier, some F-5As and F-5Bs are used by No.6 Squadron for fast jet experience, but pilot tuition really begins on the BAe, Bulldog, some 20 of which are assigned to No.2 Squadron for initial grading and primary training. Basic instruction is undertaken by No.11 Squadron which operates 16 CASA Aviojets delivered to replace the Cessna T-37 during the late-1980s, and this phase takes students to the "Wings" stage at which point they are streamed. Those destined for the fast jet world move to No.6 Squadron, whereas future helicopter pilots join No.5 Squadron for conversion and advanced tuition on the McDonnell Douglas 500D.

EQUIPMENT

Interception:
Dassault-Breguet Mirage F.1CJ
Northrop F-5E Tiger II
Attack:
Dassault-Breguet Mirage F.1EJ
Northrop F-5E Tiger II
Anti-Armour
Bell AH-1S HueyCobra
Transport:
Lockheed C-130B/H Hercules
CASA C.212 Aviocar
Aerospatiale AS.332M Super Puma
Aerial Survey:
CASA C.212 Aviocar
Communications/Liaison:
Sikorsky S-70A Black Hawk
Sikorsky S-76A/B Spirit
Training:
BAe Bulldog 125/125A
CASA C.101 Aviojet
Northrop F-5A/B Freedom Fighter
Northrop F-5E Tiger II
Dassault-Breguet Mirage F.1BJ
McDonnell Douglas 500D

KUWAIT

THE exact operational status of the Kuwaiti Air Force is uncertain in the wake of the recent Gulf War, but it appears that the core of what has always been a modestly-sized air force is still intact. It is somewhat ironic to note that plans formulated during the 1980s to enhance the KAF's fighting capabilities were influenced by concern about Iranian intentions in the Gulf region. Part of the plan involved the purchase from the USA of 40 McDonnell Douglas F/A-18C/D Hornets, and it is likely that their delivery will be accelerated given recent events.

Turning to hardware on strength at the time of the Iraqi invasion, the KAF was able to muster barely 100 aircraft in all. Principal combat types were — and are — the F.1CK Mirage and the A-4KU Skyhawk. In addition, about a dozen BAe Hawk T.64 trainers possess a secondary light attack capability.

The KAF's pre-invasion transport fleet was limited to four Lockheed L-100-30 Hercules, a pair of DC-9 Srs. 32CFs and a pair of Gulfstream IIIs. At least one of the Hercules was destroyed during the war. Helicopters active with the KAF included French-built Pumas and Super Pumas, these being tasked with transportation and anti-shipping attack duties respectively. The smaller Gazelle helicopter was — and is — operated in the dual roles of anti-armour attack and air borne observation.

Examples of all KAF combat types are known to have escaped capture during the invasion by flying south to Saudi Arabia, and some, most notably the Skyhawks and the Mirages, were used (albeit sparingly) during Operation "*Desert Storm*". In time the KAF will undoubtedly be strengthened.

EQUIPMENT

Interception:
Dassault-Breguet Mirage F.1CK
Attack:
McDonnell Douglas A-4KU Skyhawk
BAe Hawk T.64
Anti-Armour Attack:
Aerospatiale SA.342K Gazelle
Anti-Shipping Attack:
Aerospatiale SA.332AF Super Puma
Observation:
Aerospatiale SA.342K Gazelle
SAR:
Aerospatiale SA.330H Puma
Transport:
Lockheed L-100-30 Hercules
Douglas DC-9 Srs.32CF
Grumman Gulfstream III
Aerospatiale SA.330H Puma
Training:
BAe Hawk T.64
McDonnell Douglas TA-4KU Skyhawk
Dassault-Breguet Mirage F.1BK

LEBANON

WHILE internal and external forces continue to tear Lebanon apart, the *Al Quwwat al Jawwiya al Lubnaniya* (LAF: Lebanese Air Force) has for the most part endeavoured to steer clear of the factional conflicts that continue to rage around the capital of Beirut, although some BAe Hunters have flown combat strikes, with at least four being destroyed by ground fire.

Today, the LAF's combat capability is restricted to about half-a-dozen surviving Hunters and 10 Mirages. The former are now flown only rarely and the LAF is to all intents and purposes a non-starter when it comes to combat potential, since all of the surviving Mirages (nine IIIELs and one IIIBL trainer) have been in storage for a number of years.

Other equipment is perhaps more fortunate and the helicopter fleet does remain operational, as do some of the modest number of trainers and one or two communications aircraft. Rotary-wing equipment is mostly of French origin and consists of nine SA.330L Pumas and seven Agusta-Bell 212s for transport tasks plus a couple of Alouette IIs and seven or eight Alouette IIIs which are allocated to communications work. There is also a quartet of SA.342L Gazelles which can be used for anti-armour attack (courtesy of the HOT missile) and observation.

Trainers comprise five Bulldog 126s for primary instruction, three CM.170-2 Magisters for basic tuition and a single Hunter T.66C for operational conversion, but it seems doubtful if many student pilots are currently under instruction.

EQUIPMENT

Interception:
Dassault-Breguet Mirage IIIEL
Attack:
Dassault-Breguet Mirage IIIEL
BAe Hunter F.5/F.70/FGA.70
Anti-Armour:
Aerospatiale SA.342L Gazelle
Transport:
Aerospatiale SA.330L Puma
Agusta-Bell AB.212
Communications/Liaison:
Rockwell Shrike Commander
de Havilland Dove
Aerospatiale SE.3130 Alouette II
Aerospatiale SE.3160/SA.316B Alouette III
Training:
BAe Bulldog 126
Aerospatiale CM.170-2 Magister
BAe Hunter T.66C
Dassault-Breguet Mirage IIIBL

LIBYA

MILITARY adventures such as that in Chad and occasional bouts of "sparring" with the USA have proved somewhat expensive for the Libyan Arab Republic Air Force (LARAF), which has lost a significant amount of equipment over the past few years. It is, nevertheless, still one of the largest of the Arab air arms.

Organization appears to be along Soviet lines, with a separate Air Defence Command being responsible for ground-based missile and artillery elements as well as command and control systems and surveillance radars. Air elements are evidently grouped in Regiments, each of which typically manages the activities of around three subordinate fighter squadrons, and a sizeable force is committed to defence. Soviet-supplied equipment functioning in the interceptor role includes close to 50 MiG-25 "Foxbat-As", three times as many MiG-23MS "Flogger-Es", some 50 MiG-21 "Fishbeds" and just under 100 Su-22 "Fitter-Js" which may also be used for attack duties. In addition, the LARAF has 30 or so Mirage 5DEs and three-dozen Mirage F.1EDs, both types possessing a dual attack/interceptor capability.

Offensive elements are fewer, but dual capability is a compensatory factor and the LARAF could assemble a respectable attack force if it so desired. Apart from the "Fishbeds", "Fitters" and Mirages mentioned earlier, there are also just under 40 MiG-23BN "Flogger-Fs", 50 Mirage 5Ds and about a dozen Mirage F.1ADs which are configured for in-flight refuelling. Libyan attempts to obtain a dedicated tanker force have centered around the Hercules and Boeing 707, but there is doubt as to whether they have succeeded although they may have obtained French-supplied "buddy" packs. A heavier "clout" is possessed by just under 10 Tu-22 "Blinders" and more recent hardware obtained from the USSR includes at least 15 Su-24 "Fencer-Ds".

Offensive firepower is rounded out by somewhere in the region of 20 Mi-25 "Hind" battlefield helicopters and could also be augmented by a number of trainer aircraft with light attack and counter-insurgency (COIN) potential. Foremost among these are about 50 Aero L-39ZO Albatroses and close to 200 SIAI-Marchetti SF.260WL Warriors, both of these types being committed to combat in Chad during 1983-87.

Candidates for pilot training are graded and assessed on about half-a-dozen SOCATA Rallyes, with those who successfully clear this hurdle moving on to the SF.260 for basic instruction. Jet transition ensues on a dozen or so CM.170 Magisters or about 90 SOKO G2-A Galebs, with advanced work being accomplished on the Aero L-39ZO Albatros. Operational conversion is undertaken on two-seat proficiency trainers.

EQUIPMENT

Interception:
Mikoyan-Gurevich MiG-25 "Foxbat-A"
Mikoyan-Gurevich MiG-23MS "Flogger-E"
Interception/Attack:
Dassault-Breguet Mirage F.1ED
Mikoyan-Gurevich MiG-21 "Fishbed"
Sukhoi Su-22 "Fitter-J"
Dassault-Breguet Mirage 5DE
Strike/Attack:
Tupolev Tu-22 "Blinder-A"
Sukhoi Su-24 "Fencer-D"
Mikoyan-Gurevich MiG-23BN "Flogger-F"
Dassault-Breguet Mirage F.1AD
Dassault-Breguet Mirage 5D
Anti-Armour:
Mil Mi-25 "Hind-D"
COIN:
SIAI-Marchetti SF.260WL Warrior
Reconnaissance:
Mikoyan-Gurevich MiG-25R "Foxbat-B"
Dassault-Breguet Mirage 5DR
Transport:
Lockheed C-130H Hercules
Aeritalia G.222L
Antonov An-26 "Curl"
Douglas C-47 Dakota
LET L-410UVP Turbolet
Boeing-Vertol CH-47C Chinook
Mil Mi-8 "Hip"
Communications/Liaison:
Aerospatiale SA.316B Alouette III
Mil Mi-2 "Hoplite"
Training:
SOCATA Rallye
SIAI-Marchetti SF.260WL Warrior
Aerospatiale CM.170-2 Magister
SOKO G2-A Galeb
Aero L-39ZO Albatros
Mikoyan-Gurevich MiG-21 "Mongol"
Mikoyan-Gurevich MiG-23U "Flogger-C"
Dassault-Breguet Mirage F.1BD
Dassault-Breguet Mirage 5DD
Mikoyan-Gurevich MiG-25U "Foxbat-C"
Tupolev Tu-22 "Blinder-D"

Right: Interception of Libyan fighters, such as this MiG-23, has become almost routine for US Navy pilots on air defence missions.

MOROCCO

SPORADIC outbreaks of fighting with Algerian-supported *Polisario* guerilla forces continue over the disputed territory of the Western Sahara, despite a UN-backed ceasefire and the construction of a 1,300-mile (2,092km) long wall by Morocco. Topped with barbed wire and heavily mined, it has partly succeeded in containing *Polisario* forces, but the Royal Moroccan Air Force (RMAF) still mounts regular air surveillance missions.

Equipment operated by the RMAF reflects this long-running conflict with the guerillas, since much of it is optimized for counter-insurgency (COIN) and attack duties. Potentially the most lethal assets are the Mirages, the RMAF presently using about 40 survivors of 50 aircraft received during the late-1970s and early-1980s. Two basic variants were acquired, 30 F.1CH interceptors being complemented by 20 F.1EH multi-role aircraft, some of which were configured for in-flight refuelling. Apart from interception and attack, the latter variant can also undertake tactical reconnaissance duties with a variety of pod-mounted sensors.

Able support is furnished by an assortment of Northrop F-5s, the RMAF currently using a handful of F-5As and close to 20 F-5Es as fighter-bombers plus a couple of RF-5As on fighter-reconnaissance duties.

In addition to these pure combat types, the RMAF operates a sizeable fleet of armed trainers which have frequently been employed on light attack/COIN operations. Primarily of French origin, they comprise about 15-20 CM.170 Magisters and a similar quantity of Alpha Jets, while a trio of US-supplied Rockwell OV-10A Broncos fulfil dual forward air control (FAC)/COIN duties. Remaining equipment with an offensive combat application consists of 20 SA.342L Gazelle light helicopters which can be used in the "tank-busting" role with the Euromissile HOT, or for more conventional COIN operations courtesy of the GIAT 0.8in (20mm) cannon.

Past and present preoccupation with anti-guerilla warfare means that the RMAF also has a considerable number of helicopters to permit the rapid movement of ground forces and support equipment. Most versatile is the Agusta-Bell 205A-1 Iroquois and about 40 remain operational, along with seven Agusta-Bell 212s and about 20 Agusta-Bell JetRangers. Heavier RMAF metal consists of some 30 SA.330 Puma utility helicopters, and there are also just under 10 Italian-built Meridionali/Boeing-Vertol CH-47C Chinooks.

Fixed-wing transport assets are somewhat less numerous and are headed by the ubiquitous Lockheed C-130 Hercules, the RMAF currently operating about 15. Most are standard C-130H tactical transports, but a pair of KC-130H tankers are on charge and at least two C-130Hs have been fitted with side-looking airborne radar (SLAR) for surveillance of the Sahara Wall. One tanker-configured Boeing 707 is also in use, this machine having been given Beech 1800 hose-drogue pods in a local conversion project. A second 707 obtained in 1983 is employed as a VIP transport.

As far as the job of training aircrew is concerned, this actually begins on the FFA AS.202 Bravo and Beech T-34C Turbo-Mentor, with about 10 examples of each type being in service. On completion of primary and basic training, students proceed to the Magister and Alpha Jet. Subsequenfly, those destined to fly the Northrop F-5 will receive advanced instruction on the appropriate two-seat model, while candidates for the Mirage F.1 almost certainly have to travel to France for conversion training since the RMAF has no examples of the F.1B two-seater in its inventory.

Above: Despite being granted independence some 35 years ago, Morocco retains many ties with its French ex-masters, as exemplified by the two RMAF Alpha Jets seen flying outboard of two French Air Force examples.

Below: The virtues of the T-34C Turbo-Mentor have been appreciated by countless students undertaking the RMAF's pilot training course. Students graduate to the type from the AS.202 Bravo.

EQUIPMENT

Interception:
Dassault-Breguet Mirage F.1CH/.EH
Northrop F-5A Freedom Fighter
Northrop F-5E Tiger II
Attack:
Dassault-Breguet Mirage F.1EH
Northrop F-5A Freedom Fighter
Northrop F-5E Tiger II
Dassault-Breguet Alpha Jet H
Aerospatiale SA.342L Gazelle
COIN/FAC:
Rockwell OV-10A Bronco
Aerospatiale CM.170 Magister
Reconnaissance:
Northrop RF-5A Freedom Fighter
Radar Surveillance:
Lockheed (E)C-130H Hercules
ECM:
Dassault-Breguet Falcon 20
Maritime Patrol:
Dornier Do 28D-2 Skyservant
Transport:
Lockheed C-130H Hercules
Airtech CN.235M
Meridionali Boeing-Vertol CH-47C Chinook
Aerospatiale SA.330F/G Puma
Agusta-Bell AB.212
Agusta-Bell AB.205A-1 Iroquois
VIP Transport:
Boeing 707-3W6C
Dassault-Breguet Falcon 50
Grumman Gulfstream IITT
Cessna Citation 560
Airtech CN.235M
Tanker/Transport:
Boeing 707-138B
Lockheed KC-130H Hercules
Training:
FFA AS.202 Bravo
Beech T-34C-1 Turbo-Mentor
Aerospatiale CM.170 Magister
Dassault-Breguet Alpha Jet H
Northrop F-5B Freedom Fighter
Northrop F-5F Tiger II
Communications/Liaison:
Agusta-Bell AB.206A/B JetRanger
Beech King Air 100/200

OMAN

PLANS TO acquire a batch of eight Tornado ADV interceptors have now been abandoned on grounds of cost, but the Royal Air Force of Oman (RAFO) has opted to purchase a mixed force of 16 BAe Hawk 100 two-seat trainers and Hawk 200 single-seat fighters as replacements for the elderly BAe Hunters, most of which were obtained from Jordan in the mid-1970s. Recent events in the Gulf could lead to further expansion of RAFO air power, which has traditionally operated British equipment since its formation in 1959.

Today, RAFO elements fly from four principal bases, that on Masirah Island being home for most of the modestly-sized combat force. This is headed by two squadrons (Nos. 8 and 20) with the SEPECAT Jaguar, the RAFO having taken delivery of 20 single-seat Jaguar OS attack-interceptors and four two-seat Jaguar OB trainers between March 1977 and November 1983. Attrition has been light, with two OS and one OB having been destroyed, but these losses have largely been made good through the supply of single examples of the GR.1 and T.2 variants obtained from surplus British stocks. Also resident at Masirah, No. 1 Squadron has around a dozen BAe Strikemasters which are employed purely as trainers, although they were involved in combat operations against the Dhofar Liberation Front during the 1970s and 1980s, as also were the Jaguars and Hunters.

The latter type also fulfils dual interceptor/attack duties and is concentrated within No. 6 Squadron at Thumrait. About 14-15 Hunters are still active, comprising several variants: most are FR.73A/Bs, but some examples of the F.6 and FR.10 are also flown, as are four T.66/67 two-seat trainers.

Second-line units are, for the most part, transport-orientated and are distributed between the airfields at Salalah and Seeb. Three squadrons operate from Salalah: No. 2 has 15 Skyvan 3Ms, including seven that are fitted with surveillance radar for maritime missions and search-and-rescue (SAR) coverage; No. 3 has Agusta-Bell 205A-1s and Bell 214Bs for SAR and utility duties; and No. 5 has half-a-dozen BN-2A Defenders which can perform counter-insurgency (COIN) missions, although they are mostly kept busy on coastal patrol and transport activities. Seeb is more thinly populated but does have two squadrons, specifically No. 4 flying three BAe One-Eleven 485GDs and three C-130H Hercules, and No. 14 with AB.205A-1s and AB.206 JetRangers for SAR/liaison.

In addition, the Rapier Blindfire missile defence system is operated by two squadrons (Nos. 10 and 12) which deploy fire units to all of the major air bases by way of perimeter air defence.

EQUIPMENT

Interception/Attack:
SEPECAT Jaguar OS/GR.1
BAe Hunter F.6/FR.10/FR.73A/B
COIN:
BAe Strikemaster Mk.82/.82A
Training:
BAe Strikemaster Mk.82/.82A
BAe Hunter T.66/.67
SEPECAT Jaguar OB/T.2
Coastal Patrol:
Pilatus Britten-Norman BN-2A-21 Defender
Short Skyvan 3M
Transport:
Lockheed C-130H Hercules
BAe One-Eleven Srs. 485GD
Short Skyvan 3M
Pilatus Britten-Norman BN-2A-21 Defender
Miscellaneous:
Bell 214B
Agusta-Bell AB.205A-1 Iroquois
Agusta-Bell AB.206B JetRanger

Below: Hurtling low over the Omani coast, four missile-toting SEPECAT Jaguar OS fighters are caught on film as they set off on another Combat Air Patrol sortie.

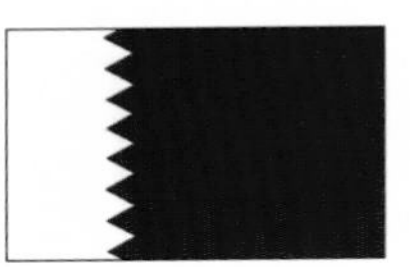

QATAR

THE QATAR Emiri Air Force (QEAF) expanded quite significantly in terms of size and capability during the course of the 1980s, but financial concerns have forestalled further growth and the construction of a dedicated military airfield at Al Ghariyeh. In consequence, QEAF aircraft continue to use Doha International Airport as their base.

Organization is fairly straightforward, with aircraft and helicopters being gathered together into just two Wings, specifically No.1 Fighter Wing and No.2 Rotary Wing. As the principal combat formation, No.1 Fighter Wing controls the activities of two squadrons. All of the dozen Mirage F.1EDAs and two F.1DDA trainers serve with No.7 (Air Superiority) Squadron, an outfit which, as its title implies, is tasked with air defence. Half-a-dozen Alpha Jets of No.11 (Close Support) Squadron constitute the QEAF's limited fixed-wing attack capability, but an offensive potential is possessed by a number of the helicopters that are presently assigned to the three squadrons of No.2 Wing.

Anti-armour tasks are performed by 12 SA.342L Gazelles of No.6 (Close Support) Squadron, these helicopters relying on the Euromissile HOT as the main anti-tank weapon. Two other Gazelles with this unit (both SA.341Gs) are used for liaison duties and in support of Qatar's Police force. Other helicopters comprise eight Westland Commando 3s of No.8 (Anti-Surface Vessel) Squadron, these being compatible with the Aerospatiale AM.39 Exocet anti-ship missile (ASM); but they can also be used for anti-armour operations should the need arise. Three Commando 2As and one Commando 2C with a VIP interior equip No.9 (Multi-Role) Squadron, missions undertaken including assault transport.

Unfortunately, the QEAF has no fixed-wing transport aircraft; nor does it yet train pilots beyond the initial screening stage, basic tuition being undertaken in Saudi Arabia, with advanced instruction following in the UK or Jordan. However, the Gulf War, spurred by Iraq's invasion of Kuwait, may well result in considerable change with regard to future training requirements and operational procedures.

Above: An interesting array of combatants from the recent Gulf conflict, with a QEAF camouflaged Alpha Jet and Mirage F.1EDA flanking French, US and Canadian fighters, all operating from Qatar during the Gulf War.

EQUIPMENT

Interception:
Dassault-Breguet Mirage F.1EDA
Attack/Close Air Support:
Dassault Breguet Alpha Jet
Anti-Armour Attack:
Aerospatiale SA.342L Gazelle
Anti-Shipping Attack:
Westland Commando 3
Transport:
Westland Commando 2a
VIP Transport:
Westland Commando 2C
Communications/Liaison:
Aerospatiale SA.342G Gazelle
Training:
Dassault-Breguet Mirage F.1DDA

SAUDI ARABIA

ONE OF THE wealthiest nations in the world by virtue of its massive oil revenues, Saudi Arabia has recently been pursuing a vigorous build-up of its armed forces, and this process will be accelerated following the involvement of its armed forces as part of Operation "*Desert Storm*". Congressional opposition in the USA and the terms of the Camp David peace agreement have had some influence on procurement policy, and Saudi Arabia has consequently turned to the United Kingdom as a source of additional armaments, placing contracts for Tornado and Hawk aircraft, amongst other hardware. However, events in the Gulf have already resulted in relaxation of US restrictions and paved the way for further purchases, including more F-15 Eagles, some of which have already been transferred from USAFE stocks. Doubt over follow-on orders for Tornadoes may also be resolved as a result of recent events both inside and outside Saudi Arabia's borders.

At present, US-supplied equipment constitutes the backbone of the Royal Saudi Air Force (RSAF), with the principal interceptor being the McDonnell Douglas F-15 Eagle. Some 74 examples have been ordered to date, but until recently only 60 were allowed to be present in-country at any given time, this amount being composed of 45 F-15Cs and 15 F-15Ds. As a result, additional aircraft had to be stored outside Saudi Arabia, to be supplied piecemeal as attrition replacements whenever necessary. Now, however, it looks as if that restriction has been lifted. In RSAF service, the Eagle fleet has been distributed amongst three squadrons at Taif, Khamis Mushayt and Dhahran air bases.

Augmenting the Eagle, Panavia's Tornado ADV has been purchased in more modest

Below: The RSAF has for many years made good use of Northrop's F-5 in a variety of roles. Illustrated is one of the F-5F Tiger II two-seat aircraft used for fast jet training purposes.

quantities, two dozen forming the subject of the initial order under the "*Al Yamamah*" programme, most of which have now been delivered. Initial aircraft went to Dhahran but there is evidence to indicate that the Tornado ADV is in service with two squadrons and the second may well be at a different base. "*Al Yamamah 2*", agreed in 1988, was to have included 36 more Tornado interceptors, but this order has still to be confirmed.

Ground-based air defence radars are augmented by the RSAF's airborne warning and control system (AWACS), which relies on five Boeing E-3A Sentries delivered between July 1986 and June 1987, although it took some considerable time for the RSAF to achieve an operational capability with this highly sophisticated kit. Support for the E-3As and fighter elements is furnished by eight KE-3A tankers, two of which reportedly have additional equipment to allow them to undertake electronic reconnaissance duties. Regardless of sub-type, all are assigned to a single squadron at the recently-constructed Al Kharj air base.

The RSAF's attack capability is also dependent on a mixture of US and British supplied equipment. Most potent is the Tornado IDS, 48 having been contracted for under phase one of "*Al Yamamah*", and most have now been delivered. The aircraft are active with at least one squadron (at Dhahran) and may well also be stationed at Khamis Mushayt. Once again, follow-on procurement (of 12 aircraft) was projected for "*Al Yamamah 2*", but as with the ADV model the status of this in unconfirmed.

A further attack capability rests with the Northrop F-5E Tiger II, about 60 aircraft currently being in service with four squadrons. Roughly half of the fleet equips two units at Taif, one of which has F-5B two-seaters and which probably functions as an operational conversion unit (OCU). About 20 two-seat F-5F Tiger IIs are also in service, distributed amongst the other three squadrons. These include one at Khams Mushayt and one at Tabuk, the latter also controlling the 10 RF-5E Tigereyes that constitute the RSAF's sole tactical reconnaissance capability.

Second-line elements are engaged in tasks such as airlift, communications/liaison and pilot training. Transport resources rely heavily on close to 40 examples of the ubiquitous Lockheed C-130 Hercules. One squadron operates pure transport aircraft from Jeddah alongside about 18 Kawasaki-Vertol KV-107-II helicopters used mostly for search-and-rescue (SAR) tasks. Another squadron resides at Riyadh and is equipped with pure transports and tanker-configured KC-130Hs, eight of the latter having been delivered although only seven remain in use today.

The final unit — appropriately designated No. 1 Squadron — is fundamentally a Royal Flight that operates an unusual assortment of VIP-configured aircraft and helicopters. As well as these VIP machines, a number of civil and pseudo-civil aircraft are available for use by the Saudi Royal Family, including about a dozen assorted Hercules (at least five of which are configured as flying hospitals) plus some Boeing jets.

Pilot training has been concentrated at Riyadh, although the King Faisal Air Academy is expected to move to the new base at Al Kharj. Students begin with grading and assessment on the Cessna 172, thereafter progressing to the Pilatus PC-9 which is in the process of replacing the Strikemaster, although some of the latter may be retained for specialized weapons instruction. A total of 30 PC-9s has been delivered and these are now well established in service, as is the BAe Hawk Mk. 65. Used for advanced instruction, 30 Hawks are active with two squadrons at Dhahran and Al Kharj, the former unit also having a pair of Jetstream 31s which are used to train Tornado navigators.

Above: It may bear US Air Force titles, but this is actually the first of the RSAF's E-3A Sentry AWACS platforms. They were to play a vital role tracking Iraqi aircraft during the Gulf War.

Below: Resplendent in the House of Saud's colours of green trim on a white background, this newly-acquired CN.235M forms part of the RSAF's VIP transport fleet.

EQUIPMENT

Interception:
McDonnell Douglas F-15C Eagle
Panavia Tornado ADV
Attack:
Panavia Tornado IDS
Northrop F-5E Tiger II
Reconnaissance:
Northrop RF-5E Tigereye
AEW:
Boeing E-3A Sentry
Tanking:
Boeing KE-3A Sentry
Lockheed KC-130H Hercules
Elint-Gathering:
Boeing KE-3A Sentry
Transport:
Lockheed C-130E/H Hercules
Airtech CN.235
VIP Transport:
BAe 146 Statesman
Lockheed Jetstar 8
Grumman Gulfstream III
BAe 125-800
LearJet 35A
Lockheed VC-130H Hercules
Airtech CN.235
Agusta-Bell AS.61A-4
Agusta-Bell AB.212
SAR:
Kawasaki-Vertol KV-107-II
Training:
Cessna 172
Pilatus PC-9
BAe Strikemaster Mk.80
BAe Hawk Mk.65
Northrop F-5B Freedom Fighter
Northrop F-5F Tiger II
McDonnell Douglas F-15D Eagle
Navigation Training:
BAe Jetstream 31
Miscellaneous Duties:
Agusta-Bell AB.205A-1
Agusta-Bell AB.206B JetRanger
Agusta-Bell AB.212
Kawasaki-Vertol KV-107-II

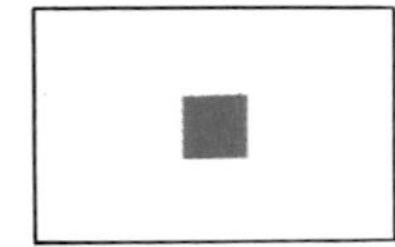

SHARJAH

ALTHOUGH actively involved in the joint defence organization that is collectively known as the United Arab Emirates (which see), Sharjah elected to maintain a measure of independence through the creation of the Amiri Guard Air Wing shortly before the end of 1984. Initially equipped with an Agusta-Bell 206B JetRanger, the Air Wing subsequently acquired two more as well as single examples of the Shorts Skyvan 3M and Shorts 330UT. Both of the latter machines were delivered in 1986, but they have apparently been disposed of fairly recently, with the cash resulting from the deal being used to buy a couple more helicopters.

Main operating base is Sharjah International Airport and the Air Wing presently operates the trio of JetRangers plus two MBB/Kawasaki BK 117s on communications, liaison and internal security tasks.

EQUIPMENT

Miscellaneous duties:
Agusta-Bell AB.206B JetRanger
MBB/Kawasai BK 117.

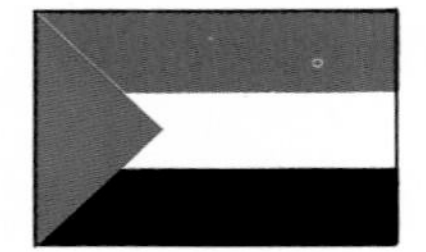

SUDAN

POLITICAL instability and financial difficulties encountered in the last decade have conspired to leave the Sudanese Air Force with a somewhat mixed bag of combat hardware of British, US, Soviet and Chinese manufacture.

In terms of capability, the MiG-23 "Flogger" fighter-bomber is arguably the most potent single type in the inventory. Approximately a dozen are operated (possibly by Libya on behalf of Sudan), other warplanes consisting of a solitary F-5E Tiger II which survives from two delivered in 1984 (eight others were cancelled due to a funding crisis), about 10 MiG-21PFM "Fishbeds" and some Xian F-7B interceptors, plus nine Shenyang F-6s and twice as many Shenyang F-5s in ground-attack missions. Finally, three Strikemaster Mk.90s and three Jet Provost T.55s continue to function in the counter-insurgency (COIN) role.

An almost equally disparate selection of aircraft and helicopters fulfil a variety of transport-related tasks, these including a handful of C-130H Hercules, four Boeing Canada Buffaloes, four C.212 Aviocars, one F-27 Friendship, 15 Romanian-built Pumas and about 10 examples each of the Agusta-Bell AB.212 and Mil Mi-8 "Hip". Two other specially-configured Aviocars are assigned to maritime surveillance missions and general purpose utility functions.

Basic training is almost certainly accomplished outside Sudan, the SAF having barely a dozen dedicated jet trainers, made up of 10 Shenyang FT-5s and two F-5Fs.

EQUIPMENT

Interception:
Mikoyan-Gurevich MiG-21PFM "Fishbed-F"
Xian F-7B
Northrop F-5E Tiger II
Attack:
Mikoyan-Gurevich MiG-23 "Flogger"
Mikoyan-Gurevich MiG-21PFM "Fishbed-F"
Shenyang F-6
Shenyang F-5
COIN:
BAe Strikemaster Mk.90
BAe Jet Provost T.55
Maritime Patrol:
CASA C.212 Aviocar
Transport:
Lockheed C-130H Hercules
Boeing Canada Buffalo
Fokker F-27 Friendship
CASA C.212 Aviocar
Mil Mi-8 "Hip"
IAR-330 Puma
Agusta-Bell AB.212
Communications/Liaison:
Aerospatiale Alouette III
MBB BO 105
Training:
Shenyang FT-5
Northrop F-5F Tiger II

SYRIA

AN IMPLACABLE enemy of Israel, vehemently opposed to almost all that the Jewish state stands for, Syria has traditionally been dependent upon the USSR for arms, obtaining some of its hardware in return for making facilities available to Soviet military forces and purchasing considerably more. Frequent altercations with the Israeli Defence Force/Air Force have generally resulted in Syria retiring from the fray to lick its wounds and seek replacements; but the days of easy availability of new hardware may be at an end, for there is evidence that the USSR is taking a more pragmatic and hard-nosed attitude to the supply of armaments and, in particular, to the matter of payment for those arms.

By and large, the Syrian military establishment appears to be modelled on Soviet lines, with the Air Defence Command being a separate entity to the Syrian Air Force (SAF) and being responsible only for surface-to-air missile and anti-aircraft artillery units. Interceptor forces are therefore under direct SAF control and are organized into Regiments, each of which has three squadrons. As far as equipment is concerned, the long-serving MiG-21 "Fishbed" is still the dominant type and Syria currently has over 200 in service, supported by around 80 MiG-23MF "Floggers" and somewhere in the region of 50 MiG-25 "Foxbats". A more recent and much more capable acquisition is the MiG-29 "Fulcrum" — deliveries evidently began in the summer of 1987 and are continuing — with the SAF expecting to receive no fewer than 80, but requests for the MiG-31 "Foxhound" have yet to be satisfied.

Attack assets are less numerous but the SAF does nevertheless possess a significant potential for offensive operations, having received about 60 MiG-23BN "Floggers" and a similar quantity of Su-22BRL "Fitters" over the past decade or so. These are supported by some MiG-17F "Frescos" which probably double as tactics trainers and which would almost certainly have a hard time of it if committed to combat, especially against Israel. Some Su-7BM "Fitter-Bs" may also still be in service.

Other equipment with a combat role to perform includes a small number of MiG-25R "Foxbat-Bs" which fulfil strategic reconnaissance requirements, and a reasonably large fleet of armed helicopters, including about three-dozen Mi-25 "Hinds" and approximately 50 SA.342L Gazelles, the latter type having apparently been configured to carry and fire

Left: An interesting mix of hardware from East and West characterizes the Sudanese Air Force. Illustrated is one of the four Boeing Canada Buffalo medium-lift transports, wearing a very appropriate desert camouflage scheme.

Left: Syria's regular clashes with Israeli forces have proved to be costly. This SAF Gazelle helicopter was captured by Israeli forces, and now wears dual military insignia.

the AT-3 "Sagger" anti-tank missile in addition to the more normal Euromissile HOT. Assault helicopter operations are mainly dependent on the Mi-8/17 "Hip", roughly 100 being on charge.

Airlift potential is minimal, being confined to six An-12 "Cubs", five An-26 "Curls" and one An-24 "Coke", the latter two types operating in civil markings, as do some seven Yak-40 "Codlings" and a brace of Falcon 20Fs that are employed for VIP duties. This limited fleet can be, and often is, augmented by aircraft of the national airline, Syrianair, whose large Il-76 "Candids" transports must prove particularly useful. Rotary-winged transport tasks are largely the domain of the "Hip", but about 10 Mi-6 "Hooks" are also available, other helicopters with specialist duties to perform including about five Ka-25 "Hormones" and 20 Mi-14 "Hazes" for anti-submarine warfare (ASW) plus 29 or so examples of each of the Mi-2 "Hoplite" and Mi-4 "Hound" for utility/liaison duties.

Pilot training needs are met internally, with initial training being accomplished on the SIAT Flamingo and Yak-11/18. Students then progress via the Aero L-29 Delfin and L-39 Albatros to the MiG-15UTI "Midget" before operational conversion on a two-seat model of the combat type to be flown in front-line service.

EQUIPMENT

Interception:
Mikoyan-Gurevich MiG-25 "Foxbat-A/E"
Mikoyan-Gurevich MiG-29 "Fulcrum"
Mikoyan-Gurevich MiG-23 "Flogger-E/G"
Mikoyan-Gurevich MiG-21PF/PFM/bis "Fishbed-D/J/L"
Attack:
Mikoyan-Gurevich MiG-23BN "Flogger-F"
Sukhoi Su-22BRL "Fitter-J"
Sukhoi Su-7 "Fitter-B"
Anti-Armour:
Mil Mi-25 "Hind"
Aerospatiale SA.342L Gazelle
Reconnaissance:
Mikoyan-Gurevich MiG-25R "Foxbat-B"
Transport:
Antonov An-12 "Cub"
Antonov An-26 "Curl"
Antonov An-24 "Coke"
Mil Mi-6 "Hook"
VIP Transport:
Yakovlev Yak-40 "Codling"
Dassault-Breguet Falcon 20F
Assault Transport:
Mil Mi-8/17 "Hip"
ASW:
Mil Mi-14 "Haze-A"
Kamov Ka-25 "Hormone"
Aerial Survey:
Piper PA-31-350 Navajo
Utility Tasks:
Mil Mi-4 "Hound"
Mil Mi-2 "Hoplite"
Training:
SIAT Flamingo
Yakovlev Yak-11 "Mosse"
Yakovlev Yak-18 "Max"
Aero L-29 Delfin
Aero L-39 Albatros
Mikoyan-Gurevich MiG-15UTI "Midget"
Mikoyan-Gurevich MiG-17F "Fresco"
Mikoyan-Gurevich MiG-21U "Mongol"
Mikoyan-Gurevich MiG-25U "Foxbat-C"
Sukhoi Su-7U "Moujik"

TUNISIA

FINANCIAL constraints prevented the implementation of a succession of attempts to obtain more capable equipment for service with the Republic of Tunisia Air Force (RoTAF), and it is only in the wake of Libyan-backed guerilla activity that some modernization has at last occurred, thanks in no small part to the US Military Assistance Program. This has seen the widely-used Northrop F-5E Tiger II take its place as the RoTAF's principal combat aircraft; an initial batch of a dozen machines delivered in 1984-85 have recently been augmented by seven ex-USAF specimens. Four F-5F two-seaters were also supplied for training duties as part of the original batch. Missions performed by the Tiger IIs include interception and close air support (CAS).

Attack and counter-insurgency (COIN) tasks are undertaken by seven Aermacchi MB.326KTs, and the RoTAF also operates about a dozen two-seat MB.326B/LTs which are principally concerned with training, although they too can be configured for COIN duties. Another trainer aircraft with a measure of combat capability is the SIAI-Marchetti SF.260CT/WT, roughly 21 examples currently being in use.

Airlift potential is limited to just two Lockheed C-130H Hercules tactical transports, supported by 18 Agusta-Bell AB.205A-1s and six Bell UH-1N Iroquois helicopters. These fulfil a variety of tasks, including aerial assault.

EQUIPMENT

Interception:
Northrop F-5E Tiger II
Attack:
Aerimacchi MB.326KT
COIN:
Aermacchi MB.326B/LT
SIAI-Marchetti SF.260CT/WT
Training:
SIAI-Marchetti SF.260CT/WT
Aermacchi MB.326B/LT
Northrop F-5F Tiger II
Communications/Liaison:
SIAI-Marchetti S.208A
Aerospatiale SA.316 Alouette III
Aerospatiale SE-3130 Alouette II
Aerospatiale AS.350B Ecureuil
Transport:
Lockheed C-130H Hercules
Bell UH-1N Iroquois
Agusta-Bell AB.205A-1

Left: A highly unusual dark grey scheme is worn by the two RoTAF C-130H Hercules. They were supplied by the US as military aid.

UNITED ARAB EMIRATES

WITH A GOAL of operating as an integrated structure, the United Arab Emirates Air Force (UAEAF) is funded by the seven Gulf states which constitute the United Arab Emirates, namely Abu Dhabi, Ajman, Dubai, Fujairah, Ras al-Khaimah, Sharjah and Umm al-Qaiwain. In practice, however, the two main elements — the Abu Dhabi Air Force (ADAF) and the Dubai Air Wing (DAW) — do appear to retain a considerable degree of autonomy, especially with regard to the procurement of equipment, and there is little commonality. Be that as it may, the UAEAF established its own distinct chain of command in 1986. Under this, the ADAF is known as the Western Air Command (WAC), while the DAW is the Central Air Command (CAC). For the purposes of this survey UAEAF nomenclature is employed.

WAC combat capability has recently been given a tremendous boost through the delivery of three-dozen Mirage 2000s in late-1989 and early-1990. Ordered as long ago as 1983 to replace existing Mirage 5s, difficulties in integrating US equipment significantly delayed entry into service from the original target date of autumn 1986, and this interlude also witnessed a slight change in the order. In the end, 22 Mirage 2000EAD attack-interceptors constituted the bulk of the aircraft that were ferried to Abu Dhabi, with the balance comprising eight 2000RADs for tactical reconnaissance and six 2000DAD two-seat trainers, although one 2000DAD was destroyed when it crashed on take-off from Bordeaux at the start of its delivery flight.

On attaining operational status, these fighters will presumably supplant the Mirage 5s, but the future of the latter aircraft is by no means certain and they may well be retained, especially in view of recent upheavals in the Gulf region.

Until recently, the Mirage 5s — which consisted of a dozen 5ADs and 14 5EADs plus two 5RADs for reconnaissance and three 5DAD trainers — were assigned to I *Shaheen* Squadron at Sharjah and II *Shaheen* Squadron at Al Dhafra (Maqatra). The latter base is also home for the flying training school equipped with two dozen Pilatus PC-7 Turbo-Trainers and 16 Hawk Mk.63s, and it is worth noting that extra combat potential will accrue from the delivery in the not too distant future of a dozen Hawk Mk.102 armed trainers that were ordered in 1989. One more unit resides at Al Dhafra, this being the *Al Ghezelle* Squadron which has 11 SA.342L Gazelles for anti-armour attack duties.

Other WAC equipment is mainly concerned with second-line tasks and is concentrated at Batin where no fewer than six squadrons are grouped together within a transport wing. These consist of the C-130 Squadron with four C-130H Hercules; the CASA Squadron with four Aviocars; the Buffalo Squadron with five Boeing Canada Buffaloes (all of which are evidently for sale); the Puma Squadron with nine SA.330s and half-a-dozen Alouette IIIs; the Super Puma Squadron with 10 AS.332s (including four for VIP duties); and, finally, the Spray Unit with a pair of Piper PA-36 Pawnee Braves. A pair of Pilatus PC-6B Turbo-Porters have also been added fairly recently, but the parentage of these has still to be ascertained.

A slightly smaller organization, CAC operates its entire inventory from the relatively new air base at Mindhat, to the south of Dubai City. Operational elements are confined to a single fighter squadron (possibly known as III *Shaheen* Squadron) with eight Hawk Mk.61 armed trainers, all of which are being upgraded to Mk.61A standard, and the Transport Squadron which has a somewhat motley assortment of equipment including two Hercules, one Aeritalia G.222, one BN-2T Turbo Islander, plus numerous types of helicopter for utility, search-and-rescue (SAR) and VIP transport tasks. Finally, there is the Flying Training Academy with half-a-dozen SIAI-Marchetti SF.260s, four Aermacchi MB.326KDs, two MB.326LDs and five MB.339As, all of which are able to operate with light armament in the counter-insurgency (COIN) role should the need arise.

Above: Continuing the UAEAF's tradition of buying French fighters is the Mirage 2000, three of which (led by a 2000DAD trainer) are seen here during their delivery flight. Note the variation in camouflage colours.

EQUIPMENT

Abu Dhabi Air Force Western Air Command

Interception:
Dassault-Breguet Mirage 2000EAD
Dassault-Breguet Mirage 5AD/EAD
Attack:
Dassault-Breguet Mirage 2000EAD
Dassault-Breguet Mirage 5AD/EAD
Anti-Armour Attack:
Aerospatiale SA.342L Gazelle
Reconnaissance:
Dassault-Breguet Mirage 2000RAD
Dassault-Breguet Mirage 5RAD
Transport:
Lockheed C-130H Hercules
Boeing Canada Buffalo
CASA C.212 Aviocar
Aerospatiale SA.330 Puma
Aerospatiale AS.332B Super Puma
VIP Transport:
Aerospatiale AS.332M/M1 Super Puma
Communications/Liaison:
Pilatus PC-6B Turbo-Porter
Aerospatiale Alouette III
Aerospatiale AS.350B Ecureuil
Bell 206B JetRanger
Aerial Spraying:
Piper PA-36-285 Pawnee Brave
Training:
Pilatus PC-7 Turbo-Trainer
BAeHawk Mk.63
Dassault-Breguet Mirage 4DAD
Dassault-Breguet Mirage 2000DAD

Dubai Air Wing Central Air Command

Attack:
Aermacchi MB.326KD
Transport:
Lockheed L-100-30 Hercules
Lockheed C-130H-30 Super Hercules
Aeritalia G.222
VIP Transport:
Sikorsky S-76A Spirit
SAR:
MBB BO 105
Communications/Liaison:
Bell 206L LongRanger
Utility:
Pilatus Britten-Norman BN-2T Turbo-Islander
Agusta-Bell 412 Grifon
Bell 214B
Bell 205A
Training:
SIAI-Marchetti SF.260TP
SIAI-Marchetti SF.260W Warrior
Aermacchi MB.326LD
Aermacchi MB.339A

YEMEN

UNDOUBTEDLY one of the world's more obscure air powers is that of Yemen, the inventory of which is an amalgamation of what constituted the air forces of Northern Yemen (Yemen Arab Republic Air Force) and Southern Yemen (Air Force of the People's Democratic Republic of Yemen) prior to the political and military reunification of these two nations, beginning in May 1990.

With the latter having been firmly in the Communist camp, and the former taking steps to break away and renew links with the West, the result is an air force which operates aircraft obtained from both East and West, some rather elderly, side-by-side on a daily basis. Just how this mix compromises the operational effectiveness of the unified air force is difficult to gauge, but there can be little doubt that it certainly has the potential to make Yemen a power to be reckoned with in this volatile part of the world.

Front-line hardware responsible for air defence and attack is dominated by the products of the MiG bureau, spearheaded by the highly-capable MiG-23. Some 50 of these fighter-bombers are believed to be in service, with back-up provided by 60-odd MiG-21s which also perform dual interception and attack duties. Further strength is provided by a small number of F-7M Airguards, this being a Chinese-built version of the dependable MiG-21.

It would appear that Southern Yemen's modest force of Ilyushin Il-28 "Beagle" twin-jet light bombers has not found a home in the new, unified air force, thus increasing dependence on the two Sukhoi designs to fulfil ground attack duties. Likewise, the MiG-17 "Fresco" has passed into the realms of aviation history.

The Soviet link has been taken a stage further in recent years, with confirmed sightings of several MiG-25R "Foxbat-B" reconnaissance fighters. Whether these are actually in the Yemeni inventory is open to speculation; a more realistic explanation of their presence is based on the belief that they are flown by a detachment of Soviet aircrew, the Soviet Union making use of "goodwill" access to Yemeni airfields as part of its attempts to keep a close watch on events within the Middle East region.

Western representation in the front-line fighting force is confined to the Northrop F-5E Tiger II, at least ten of which were obtained by Northern Yemen from Saudi Arabia. These aircraft were initially piloted by Taiwanese aircrew, and although this has now ceased, Yemen continues to receive technical back-up from Taiwan to enable the F-5Es and a quartet of F-5B two-seater trainers to carry on flying.

Transport types currently in use are almost equally diverse in their origins, being spearheaded by a pair of Lockheed C-130H Hercules. With the exception of the two F-27s and two Skyvans, this is the extent of Western participation in what is otherwise a fleet of fixed-wing "twins" of Soviet origin.

Likewise, the two-dozen Mil Mi-8s on transport duty originate in the East; but the rotary-winged fleet tasked with providing an effective liaison force is almost a mirror image of the fixed-wing transport fleet, with US designs built in Italy to the fore. Of the six AB.212s in service, one has been reconfigured internally to meet VIP transport needs. Whether some of the more aged members of the transport fleet will give way to any of the West's new generation of medium-lift "twins" remains to be seen, but it is obviously one area in which a modest investment could result in a significant upgrade in operational effectiveness.

The same can be said of Yemen's small pilot training fleet. Like so many other Third World air forces, Yemen relies to an extent on foreign assistance in this field. However, it does operate some 15 examples of the Yak-11 "Moose" as first-stage trainers, as well two-seat trainer derivatives of the MiG-15, MiG-21 and the Northrop F-5, all three types being utilized in the operational conversion phase of pilot tuition.

EQUIPMENT

Interception:
Mikoyan-Gurevich MiG--23MS "Flogger-E"
Mikoyan-Gurevich MiG-21F "Fishbed-C"
Chengdu F-7M Airguard
Northrop F-5E Tiger II
Attack:
Mikoyan-Gurevich MiG-23B "Flogger-F"
Sukhoi Su-22 "Fitter-J"
Sukhoi Su-20 "Fitter-C"
Northrop F-5E Tiger II
Anti-Armour Attack:
Mil Mi-24 "Hind"
ASW:
Kamov Ka-26 "Hoodlum"
SAR:
Kamov Ka-26 "Hoodlum"
Transport:
Lockheed C-130H Hercules
Antonov An-12 "Cub"
Antonov An-26 "Curl"
Antonov An-24 "Coke"
Ilyushin Il-14 "Crate"
Fokker F-27 Friendship
Shorts Skyvan 3M
Mil Mi-8 "Hip"
Agusta-Bell AB.212
VIP Transport:
Agusta-Bell AB.212
Communications/Liaison:
Mil Mi-4 "Hound"
Agusta-Bell AB.204B
Agusta-Bell AB.205
Aerospatiale Alouette III
Agusta-Bell AB.206B JetRanger
Training:
Yakovlev Yak-11 "Moose"
Mikoyan-Gurevich MiG-15UTI "Midget"
Northrop F-5B Freedom Fighter
Mikoyan-Gurevich MiG-21U "Mongol"

Below: With titles on the forward fuselage proclaiming the new, unified Yemeni Air Force, this C-130H is one of two such four-engined Western transports on charge.

SUB-SAHARAN AFRICA

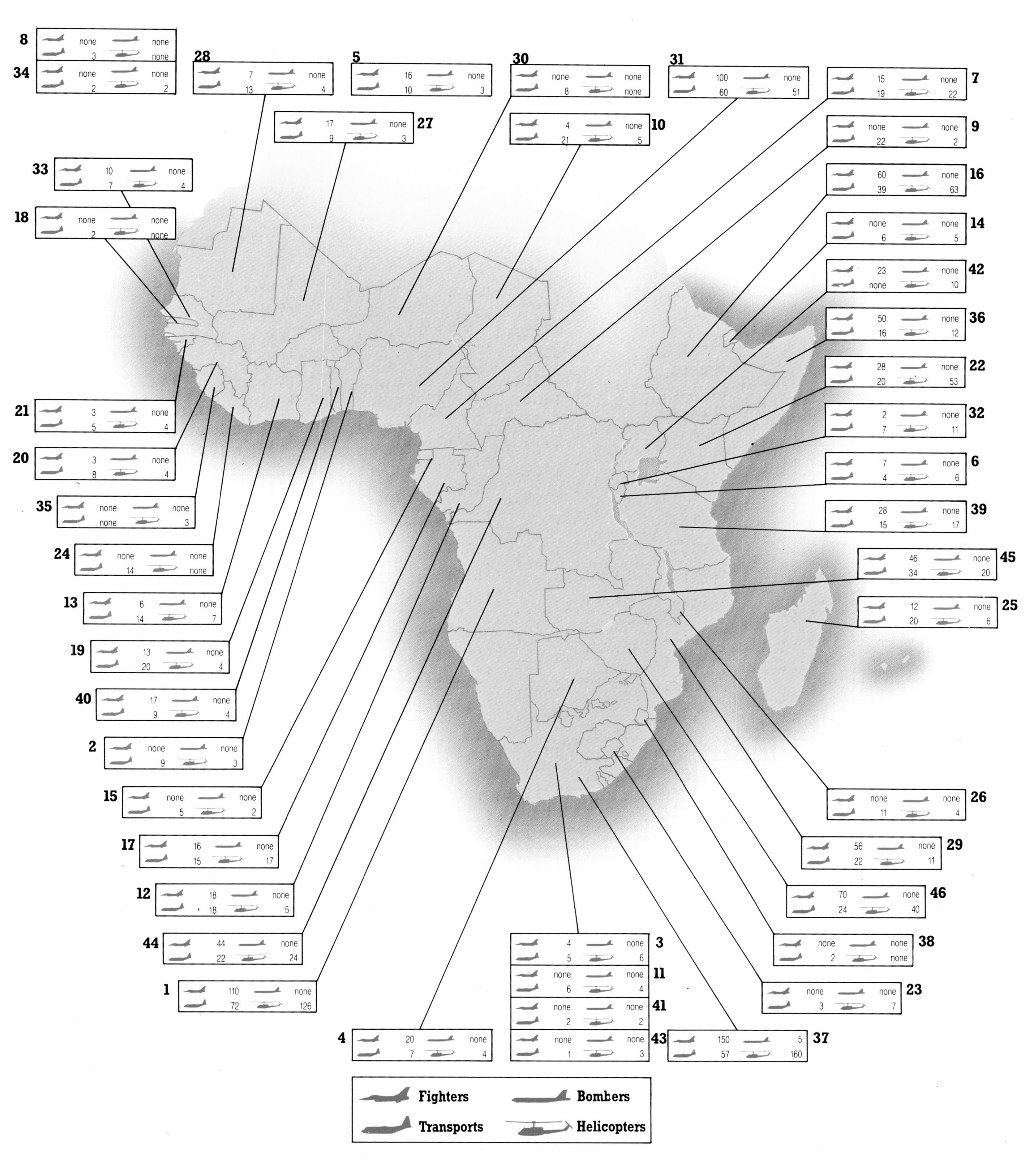
8 none none 3 none
34 none none 2 2
28 7 none 13 4
5 16 none 10 3
30 none none 8 none
31 100 none 60 51
7 15 none 19 22
27 17 none 9 3
10 4 none 21 5
9 none none 22 2
33 10 none 7 4
16 60 none 39 63
18 none none 2 none
14 none none 6 5
42 23 none none 10
36 50 none 16 12
22 28 none 20 53
21 3 none 5 4
32 2 none 7 11
20 3 none 8 4
6 7 none 4 6
35 none none none 3
39 28 none 15 17
24 none none 14 none
45 46 none 34 20
13 6 none 14 7
25 12 none 20 6
19 13 none 20 4
40 17 none 9 4
2 none none 9 3
15 none none 5 2
26 none none 11 4
17 16 none 15 17
29 56 none 22 11
12 18 none 18 5
46 70 none 24 40
44 44 none 22 24
3 4 none 5 6
38 none none 2 none
11 none none 6 4
1 110 none 72 126
23 none none 3 7
41 none none 2 2
4 20 none 7 4
43 none none 1 3
37 150 5 57 160
Fighters
Bombers
Transports
Helicopters

ANGOLA

AFTER A lengthy period of hostilities between Angola and South African-backed UNITA guerilla forces, as well as with South Africa itself, the prospect of peace returning to this war-ravaged former Portuguese colony looks much more realistic. Air power has played its part in the recent fighting and the *Force Aérea Populaire de Angola* (FAPA: Popular Air Force of Angola) has suffered substantial losses both in the air and on the ground, with guerilla forces claiming to have accounted for the destruction of close to 150 aircraft and helicopters between 1985 and 1989.

Although Cuba maintained a considerable number of troops (close to 60,000 at the height of the fighting) in Angola, the primary source of military hardware has been the USSR which has supplied numerous examples of the MiG-17F "Fresco", MiG-21MF "Fishbed-J", MiG-23 "Flogger-G" and Su-22 "Fitter-F" to equip interceptor and attack echelons of the FAPA. This has enabled the inventory to be held at a fairly constant level and the FAPA presently has around 100-120 combat-ready fighters, with the MiG-21MF and Su-22 making up the lion's share of this force.

Counter-insurgency (COIN) has been a key area of activity and the FAPA has considerable expertise in applying aerial firepower to this kind of conflict, other Soviet-supplied resources used for such operations including Mi-8/17 "Hip" and Mil Mi-25/35 "Hind" helicopters.

Some equipment of Western origin is also operated, but this is far less numerous and is generally employed on non-combat tasks like transport (CASA C.212 Aviocar and BN-2A Islander), although some SA.365M Dauphin 2 and SA.342M Gazelle helicopters do fulfil attack and anti-armour missions.

Operations are conducted from numerous airfields and landing strips, many of which are a legacy of the Portuguese occupation. At least 30 bases exist, with jet fighters located at Luanda, Luena, Kuito, Menongue, Mocamedes and Xangongo.

Pilot training appears to be conducted indigenously, on a motley assortment of aircraft obtained from East and West and comprising examples of the Cessna 172, Pilatus PC-7 Turbo-Trainer, Pilatus PC-9, MiG-15UTI "Midget" and MiG-21U "Mongol". Other equipment satisfies a variety of roles, such as maritime reconnaissance, VIP transport, liaison and search and-rescue (SAR).

EQUIPMENT

Interception:
Mikoyan-Gurevich MiG-23MF "Flogger-G"
Mikoyan-Gurevich MiG-21MF "Fishbed-J"
Attack COIN:
Sukhoi Su-22 "Fitter-F"
Mikoyan-Gurevich MiG-23MF "Flogger-G"
Mikoyan-Gurevich MiG-17F "Fresco"
Pilatus PC-7 Turbo-Trainer
Mil Mi-25/35 "Hind"
Mil Mi-8/17 "Hip"
Aerospatiale SA.365M Dauphin 2
Aerospatiale Alouette III
Anti-Armour:
Aerospatiale SA.342M Gazelle
Maritime Patrol:
Embraer EMB-111A Bandeirante
Transport:
Antonov An-12 "Cub"
Antonov An-26 "Curl"
CASA C.212 Aviocar
Pilatus Britten-Norman BN-2A Islander
Antonov An-2 "Colt"
Pilatus PC-6 Turbo-Porter
Mil Mi-8/17 "Hip"
VIP Transport:
Tupolev Tu-134A "Crusty"
Yakovlev Yak-40 "Codling"
Grumman Gulfstream III
Rockwell Commander 690A
SAR:
Aerospatiale SA.315B Lama
Communications/Liaison:
Dornier Do 27
Aerospatiale Alouette III
Aerospatiale SA.365F Dauphin 2
Training:
Cessna 172
Yakovlev Yak-11 "Moose"
Pilatus PC-7 Turbo-Trainer
Pilatus PC-9
Mikoyan-Gurevich MiG-15UTI "Midget"
Mikoyan-Gurevich MiG-21U/UM "Mongol"
Mikoyan-Gurevich MiG-23U "Flogger-C"
Sukhoi Su-22 "Fitter-E"

Left: FAPA hardware has been acquired from a variety of sources in the East and West, and includes a small number of Spanish CASA C.212 Aviocars for transport.

BENIN

ORIGINALLY known as Dahomey, military aviation in Benin was launched with French assistance at around the time that independence was gained in 1960. Since then, the *Force Armées Populaires du Benin* (Popular Armed Forces of Benin) has grown slightly in size, but it still has barely 200 personnel and no more than a dozen or so aircraft. All of the resources currently on charge with the air arm are essentially concerned with transport duties, including the operation of a Presidential Flight.

EQUIPMENT

Transport:
Antonov An-26 "Curl"
Douglas C-47 Dakota
Boeing Canada Twin Otter
Dornier Do 128-2
VIP Transport:
Boeing 707-320
Rockwell Commander 500B
Liaison:
Aerospatiale AS.350/355 Ecureuil
Aerospatiale Alouette II

BOPHUTHATSWANA

FUNCTIONS undertaken by the relatively new Bophuthatswana Defence Force Air Wing are, for the most part, of a non-combatant nature although it has recently acquired some Pilatus PC-7 Turbo-Trainers which have the capability to carry armament and could be employed for counter-insurgency (COIN) work. Operational activities include involvement in the "war" against poachers, and the Air Wing regularly utilizes some of its small fleet of aircraft to monitor the game reserves which make a significant contribution to the national income through tourism. Headquarters of the Defence Force Air Wing are located at Mafeking, and other responsibilities are predominantly transport-related, usually in co-operation with ground elements of the Defence Force.

Right: An air arm very much in its infancy, the Bophuthatswana Defence Force Air Wing has a motley selection of aircraft, including several Alouette IIIs.

EQUIPMENT

COIN:
Pilatus PC-7 Turbo-Trainer
Observation:
Partenavia P.68 Observer
Transport:
CASA C.212 Aviocar
Pilatus PC-6 Turbo-Porter
Liaison:
MBB/Kawasaki BK 117
Aerospatiale AS.355 Ecureuil
Aerospatiale Alouette III
Training:
Pilatus PC-7 Turbo-Trainer

BOTSWANA

PART OF AN integrated defence establishment, the Botswana Defence Force Air Wing came into existence in 1977 as part of the Army and consequently much of its day-to-day activity is conducted in support of ground forces. Organization has stayed fairly constant, with three subordinate elements in existence, each being nominally tasked with a specific mission. Thus, the unit known as Z1 is the combat formation, while Z2 is responsible for communications and training and Z3 conducts tactical transport operations.

Combat capability has been boosted recently through the acquisition of a batch of nine BAe Strikemasters in 1988 (from Kuwait via the manufacturer), these being tasked with counter-insurgency (COIN), a mission in which they are complemented by BN-2A Defenders and seven recently delivered Pilatus PC-7s.

Airlift forces have also been improved through the purchase of a brace of Airtech CN.235s in 1988. Other transport types comprise two BN-2A-III Trislanders, two Skyvan 3Ms and three Bell 412 helicopters, while a BAe 125-800 was also ordered in 1988 for VIP duties although this has spent much of the time under repair after being struck by an air-to-air-missile launched from an Angolan fighter. Consequently, a second example has been acquired.

Above: Long associated with the twin-engined BN-2A Islander, the BDFAW also operates the military variant known as the Defender.

EQUIPMENT

COIN:
BAe Strikemaster Mk.83
Pilatus PC-7 Turbo-Trainer
COIN/Surveillance:
Pilatus Britten-Norman BN-2A Defender
Transport:
Airtech CN.235
Shorts Skyvan 3M
Pilatus Britten-Norman BN-2A-III Trislander
Bell 412
VIP Transport:
BAe 125-800
Communications:
Aerospatiale AS.350 Ecureuil
Training:
Cessna 152
BAe Bulldog 120
Pilatus PC-7 Turbo-Trainer

BURKINA FASO

ANOTHER state that once lay within France's realm of influence, Burkina Faso was formerly known as Upper Volta and retains some links with its colonial past in both titular and hardware terms, for the *Force Aerienne de Burkina Faso* (Burkina Faso Air Force) continues to operate a handful of aircraft that were obtained from France at the time of independence. More recently, a state of uneasy peace has existed with neighbouring Mali in the wake of an inconclusive six-day war that flared up over a border dispute in December 1985.

The Air Force is not, however, an autonomous agency, since it forms part of an integrated defence organization under Army control. Nor is it large, for its inventory of aircraft and helicopters does not exceed a total of 30 machines.

Combat elements are limited to a few MiG-21 "Fishbed" fighters which mainly serve in close air support/attack roles. They are backed up by SF.260s, including some that were obtained from the Philippines via Belgium, these being used for counter-insurgency (COIN) tasks. Other equipment, much of which is old and obsolescent, is engaged on transport and liaison tasks, and includes such veterans as the MH.1521M Broussard and the C-47 Dakota.

EQUIPMENT

Fighter-Attack:
Mikoyan-Gurevich MiG-21 "Fishbed"
COIN:
SIAI-Marchetti SF.260W/WP Warrior
Transport:
BAe 748 Srs.2A
Nord 262C Fregate
Douglas C-47 Dakota
VIP Transport:
Boeing 727-100
Liaison:
Reims-Cessna FRA.172
Reims-Cessna FRA.337
Max-Holste MH.1521M Broussard
Rockwell Aero Commander 500B
Aerospatiale Alouette III
Aerospatiale SA.365N Dauphin 2
Training:
Mikoyan-Gurevich MiG-21U "Mongol"

BURUNDI

BURUNDI'S modest military aviation force of less than 20 aircraft and helicopters is actually controlled by the *Armée Nationale du Burundi* (National Army of Burundi) and is able to deploy only a token combat element equipped with SF.260 Warriors and SA.342L Gazelles that can be configured to carry armaments for counter-insurgency (COIN) applications. Other equipment lacks even this potential and is limited to a few Reims-Cessna FRA.150Ls and Alouette IIIs operating alongside a solitary Do 27 in training, communications and liaison roles.

EQUIPMENT

COIN:
SIAI-Marchetti SF.260W Warrior
Aerospatiale SA.342L Gazelle
Communications/Liaison:
Dornier Do 27
Aerospatiale SA.342L Gazelle
Aerospatiale Alouette III
Training:
SIAI-Marchetti SF.260TP Warrior
Reims-Cessna FRA.150L

CAMEROUN

DESPITE attempts to purchase more potent equipment such as the IAI Kfir and Dassault Breguet Mirage F.1, the *Armee de l'Air du Cameroun* (Cameroun Air Force) has been repeatedly hampered by lack of funds and continues to rely on the Alpha Jet as its primary combat type. Five of the six that were originally delivered in 1983-84 remain active and these are supported by a small number of CM.170 Magister armed trainers which can be used for counter-insurgency (COIN) operations should the need arise, as indeed can a quartet of SA.342L missile-equipped Gazelle helicopters.

Other than that, the Cameroun Air Force is primarily concerned with transport duties and these can be conveniently classified as tactical, VIP and communications/liaison in nature. Types employed in the first category include examples of the C-130 Hercules, Boeing Canada Caribou and Buffalo, C-47 Dakota and IAI Arava, while the VIP fleet is headed by a Boeing 727 and also features several different types of helicopter, all being of French origin. Finally, there is liaison and communications, aircraft employed on such duties including a few veteran Max Holste MH.1521M Broussards obtained second-hand from France as long ago as the early-1960s, when Cameroun was finally granted its independence.

EQUIPMENT

Attack:
Dassault-Breguet Alpha Jet NGEA
COIN:
Dassault-Breguet Alpha Jet NGEA
Aerospatiale CM.170 Magister
Aerospatiale SA.342L Gazelle
Maritime Patrol:
Dornier Do 128-6
Transport:
Lockheed C-130H/H-30 Hercules
Boeing Canada Buffalo
Boeing Canada Caribou
Douglas C-47 Dakota
IAI Arava
VIP Transport:
Boeing 727-200
Grumman Gulfstream III
Dornier Do 128-2
Aerospatiale AS.332L Super Puma
Aerospatiale SA.330C Puma
Aerospataile SA.365N Dauphin 2
Aerospatiale Alouette III
Communications/Liaison:
Max-Holste MH.1521M Broussard
Dornier Do 28B-1
Piper PA-23 Aztec
Aerospatiale Alouette II/III
Aerospatiale SA.315 Lama
Bell 206L-3 LongRanger
Training:
Aerospataile CM.170 Magister

Above: Fitted with a laser rangefinder in a reconfigured nose, the modified close-support variant of the Alpha Jet was procured by Cameroun for ground support operations.

CAPE VERDE

THIS FORMER Portuguese colony has been independent since 1975, but plans are in hand for unification with Guinea-Bissau. In the meantime, the small *Força Aérea Caboverdaine* (Cape Verde Air Force) operates solely as a transport organization, operating three examples of the Antonov An-26 "Curl" from Amilcar Cabral on Sal Island.

EQUIPMENT

Transport:
Antonov An-26 "Curl"

CENTRAL AFRICAN REPUBLIC

LACK OF FUNDS has prevented the small *Escardrille Centrafricaine* of this former French colony from acquiring a combat capability. In view of that, it continues to perform routine transport tasks with a mixture of equipment that has, for the most part, been obtained from French sources.

EQUIPMENT

Transport:
Douglas C-54 Skymaster
Douglas C-47 Dakota
VIP Transport:
Aerospatiale SE.210 Caravelle III
Dassault-Breguet Falcon 20C
Aerospatiale AS.350 Ecureuil
Communications/Liaison:
Max-Holste MH.1521M Broussard
Aermacchi AL.60
SOCATA 235
Aerospatiale Alouette II
Aerospatiale AS.350 Ecureuil

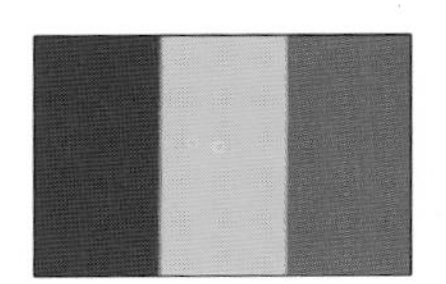

CHAD

A FORMAL resolution of the border dispute with Libya has brought an end to the state of hostility that existed between these two nations, but not before Chad succeeded in capturing a substantial amount of Libyan hardware, including at least two Tu-22 "Blinder" bombers, 11 L-39 Albatross light ground-attack aircraft, three Mi-24 "Hind" gunship helicopters and a couple of SF.260W Warrior armed trainers. Apart from the SF.260s, all of this war booty has been disposed of.

Combat capability of the *Force Aerienne Tchadienne* (Chad Air Force) is extremely limited, a counter-insurgency (COIN) element consisting of the two captured SF.260Ws and an identical number of Pilatus PC-7 Turbo-Trainers. However, it should be noted that a number of rather more potent warplanes are usually to be found in Chad, but these are from the French Air Force which routinely deploys Jaguars and Mirage F.1s to the region.

Other Chadienne resources operate purely in transport roles. Spearheaded by a few C-130 Hercules, the collection also includes a couple of CASA C.212 Aviocars.

EQUIPMENT

COIN:
SIAI-Marchetti SF.260W Warrior
Pilatus PC-7 Turbo-Trainer
Transport:
Lockheed C-130B/H Hercules
Douglas DC-4
Douglas C-47 Dakota
CASA C.212 Aviocar
VIP Transport:
Aerospatiale SE.210 Caravelle VIR
Communications:
Max-Holste MH.1521M Broussard
Pilatus PC-6B Turbo-Porter
Cessna FTB.337

CISKEI

LIKE MANY Third-World states, the Ciskei Defence Force is fundamentally a transport and communications agency operating in support of ground echelons, with a fleet of aircraft and helicopters that barely exceeds 10.

EQUIPMENT

Transport:
Shorts Skyvan 3M
Pilatus Britten-Norman BN-2A Islander
Communications:
Cessna 152
MBB BO 105
MBB/Kawasaki BK 117

COMORES

VIP AND communications duties are undertaken by the two aircraft that presently serve with the tiny Comores Military Aviation Command. Some SF.260 Warriors were also purchased in the late-1970s, but these were soon passed on to Rhodesia, the Comores allegedly acting as a "front" organization.

EQUIPMENT

VIP Transport/Communications:
Cessna 402B
Aerospatiale AS.350B Ecureuil

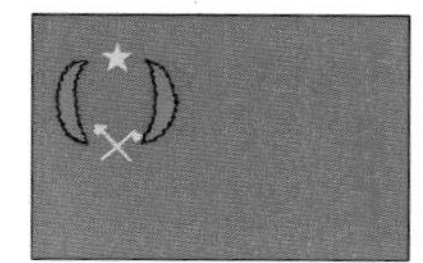

CONGO

SOVIET AND Cuban aid has been the most important source of hardware used by the *Force Aérienne Conglaoise* (FAC: Congo Air Force) for many years now, and this situation appears unlikely to change radically in the immediate future given the political situation that currently prevails.

Combat capability is vested in an unknown number of MiG-21 "Fishbed" fighters, while some MiG-17 "Frescos" may also be in use for ground-attack and close air support, as well as about half-a-dozen L-39 Albatross armed jet trainers. At least one MiG-15UTI "Midget" trainer is believed to be operated.

Apart from that, the FAC possesses about 20 transport aircraft, with the An-24 "Coke" being numerically the most significant single type; other airlift assets include examples of the An-26 "Curl", Nord N.2501 Noratlas, C-47 Dakota and Il-14 "Crate". At least one Nord 262A has also been operated, but this was destroyed when it crashed in early-1990. There is also a VIP element equipped with an SN.601 Corvette and an SA.365C Dauphin, other helicopters comprising pairs of the Alouette II and Alouette III which perform communications and liaison duties.

EQUIPMENT

Interception:
Mikoyan-Gurevich MiG-21 "Fishbed"
Ground Attack:
Mikoyan-Gurevich MiG-17 "Fresco"
Aero L-39ZO Albatros
Transport:
Nord N.2501F Noratlas
Antonov An-24 "Coke"
Antonov An-26 "Curl"
Douglas C-47 Dakota
Ilyushin Il-14 "Crate"
VIP Transport:
Aerospatiale SN.601 Corvette
Aerospatiale SA.365C Dauphin 2
Communications/Liaison:
Aerospatiale Alouette II/III
Training:
Mikoyan-Gurevich MiG-15UTI "Midget"
Aero L-39ZO Albatros

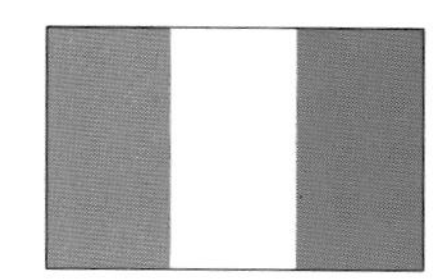

COTE d'IVOIRE

AS FAR AS the age of its equipment is concerned, the *Force Aerienne de Cote d'Ivoire* (Cote d'Ivoire Air Force) has one of the more modern air arms in the region, and close links are retained with its former colonial master, France, which has provided financial aid and military advisers since granting independence in 1960.

A modest combat element is equipped with six Dassault-Breguet Alpha Jets.

EQUIPMENT

Attack:
Dassault-Breguet Alpha Jet
Transport:
Aerospatiale SA.330H Puma
VIP Transport:
Fokker 100
Fokker F-28 Fellowship
Grumman Gulfstream IV
Aerospatiale SA.330C Puma
Aerospatiale SA.365C Dauphin 2
Communications/Liaison:
Beech Super King Air 200
Cessna 421
Cessna F.337E
Aerospatiale SA.365C Dauphin 2
Aerospatiale SA.342 Gazelle
Aerospatiale Alouette III
Training:
Beech F33C Bonanza
Cessna F.150H
Dassault-Breguet Alpha Jet

DJIBOUTI

RESPONSIBILITY for the defence of this strategically-important former French colony is largely entrusted to France, which maintains a sizeable garrison in the country in response to a request from Djibouti's government. Air power elements deployed as part of that package include a number of French Air Force Mirage F.1C interceptors as well as Puma and Gazelle helicopters of the French Army.

Some military assistance is also provided to the small *Force Aérienne Djiboutienne* (Djibouti Air Force), an organization which is principally engaged in transport tasks.

EQUIPMENT

Transport:
Nord N.2501F Noratlas
CASA C.212 Aviocar 200
VIP Transport:
Dassault-Breguet Falcon 50
Dassault-Breguet Falcon 20
Communications/Liaison:
Cessna U206G
SOCATA 235
Aerospatiale AS.355F Ecureuil II
Aerospatiale Alouette II

Above: Evidence of the co-operation between Djibouti's Air Force and French defensive forces, with one of the former's AS.355F Ecureuil IIs hovering over an AMX-30 tank.

EQUATORIAL GUINEA

EQUIPMENT flown by the National Guard of Equatorial Guinea numbers less than 10 aircraft and helicopters. All of these are engaged in transport missions and they include single examples of the Yak-40 "Codling" and Cessna 337, as well as a couple of Alouette III helicopters. In addition, Equatorial Guinea is also reported to have received three CASA C.212 Aviocars as part of an aid package provided by Spain, but there is reason to believe that these are actually Spanish-owned aircraft which are actually maintained and flown by Moroccan personnel.

EQUIPMENT

Transport:
CASA C.212 Aviocar
VIP Transport:
Yakovlev Yak-40 "Codling"
Communications/Liaison:
Cessna 337
Aerospatiale Alouette III

ETHIOPIA

THE SCENE of bitter fighting between government forces and Eritrean guerillas for many years now, Ethiopia has one of the largest air arms in this part of the world and is very heavily dependent upon the USSR for the supply of military hardware. It also receives assistance from Cuba in the form of military advisers. Equipment dating back to the era when Ethiopia looked to the West as an arms supplier is almost certainly no longer in use, with the USA being one of several nations that has placed an embargo on the supply of such hardware. This action was responsible for Ethiopia offering some 20 F-5A/B/Es for sale in the mid-1980s, and these are believed to have ended up in Iran. Other less warlike types such as the T-33A, Saab Safir, Agusta Bell AB.204 and de Havilland Dove are all understood to be in store, effectively grounded by the non-availability of spares.

In consequence, Ethiopian Air Force front-line, combat-ready elements are universally equipped with fighters of Soviet origin. The MiG-21PF "Fishbed-D" is the most numerous single type although reasonable quantities of both the MiG-23BN "Flogger-F" and MiG-17F "Fresco" are also flown, as well as some Shenyang F-6s (Chinese-built MiG-19 "Farmer"). Attrition has taken its toll over the years, most spectacularly in May 1984 when 28 aircraft were destroyed in a guerilla attack on Asmara, but it seems likely that replacements have been made freely available by the USSR — a position that may change as the superpower seeks to establish warmer relationships with the West.

Second-line tasks include transport and liaison, performed by a fleet of mainly Soviet-supplied machines such as the Antonov An-12 "Cub" and Mil Mi-6 "Hook", but some Alouette IIIs and Chetaks (Alouettes built under licence in India) are in service and there is also a VIP-configured Puma helicopter. In addition, Ethiopian Airlines has a pair of Lockheed L-100-30 Hercules freighters and which can be employed for military operations, such as the air-dropping of paratroops.

EQUIPMENT

Interception:
Mikoyan-Gurevich MiG-23BN "Flogger-F"
Mikoyan-Gurevich MiG-21PF "Fishbed-D"
Attack:
Mikoyan-Gurevich MiG-23BN "Flogger-F"
Mikoyan-Gurevich MiG-21PF "Fishbed-D"
Shenyang F-6
Mikoyan-Gurevich MiG-17F "Fresco"
Mil Mi-25 "Hind-D"
Assault:
Mil Mi-8 "Hip"
Maritime Patrol/ASW:
Mil Mi-14 "Haze"
Transport:
Antonov An-12 "Cub"
Antonov An-26 "curl"
Ilyushin Il-14 "Crate"
Mil Mi-6 "Hook"
VIP Transport:
Yakovlev Yak-40 "Codling"
Aerospatiale AS.330 Puma
Communications/Liaison:
SIAI-Marchetti S.205
SIAI-Marchetti S.208
Aerospatiale Alouette III/Chetak
Training:
SIAI-Marchetti SF.260TP
Aero L-39ZO Albatros
Mikoyan-Gurevich MiG-21U "Mongol"

GABON

COMBAT capability of the *Force Aérienne Gabonaises* (Gabon Air Force) rests with the survivors of two batches of Mirage 5s that were delivered in 1978 and 1984. Some 11 aircraft were involved in total and nine are believed to still exist, these being used in dual interceptor and attack roles. However, serviceability is understood to be poor and their value must therefore be considered questionable.

Other combat missions that can be undertaken by this small air arm comprise anti-armour attack with five SA.342L Gazelles, three of which are compatible with the Euromissile HOT anti-tank weapon and unguided rockets, plus counter-insurgency (COIN) for which a couple of AS.350B Ecureuils are employed.

Gabon's military line-up also includes an organization known as *La Guard Presidentielle* (Presidential Guard). Manned almost entirely by mercenaries, it is directly responsible to President Bongo and has an odd mix of equipment which includes VIP-configured examples of the EMB-110 Bandeirante, Falcon 900 and Gulfstream III, as well as a few armed Fouga CM.170 Magisters and T-34C Turbo-Mentors which fulfil COIN and training tasks.

EQUIPMENT

Interception/Attack:
Dassault-Breguet Mirage 5G/5G-II
COIN:
Aerospatiale AS.350B Ecureuil
Anti-Armour:
Aerospatiale SA.342L Gazelle
Maritime Patrol:
Embraer EMB-111A Bandeirante
Transport:
Lockheed C-130H Hercules
Lockheed L-100-20/-30 Hercules
Fokker F-28 Fellowship 1000C
Embraer EMB-110P Bandeirante
Aerospatiale SA.330C/H Puma
Communications/Liaison:
Reims-Cessna FRA.152
Cessna F.337
Aerospatiale Alouette III
Training:
Dassault-Breguet Mirage 5DG

Below: A stylized paint scheme made up of the three colours within Gabon's national flag adorns this pristine F-28 Fellowship. The aircraft is used in the VIP transport role.

PRESIDENTIAL GUARD

COIN:
Aerospatiale CM.170 Magister
Beech T-34C Turbo-Mentor
Transport:
ATR-42F
VIP Transport:
Dassault-Breguet Falcon 900
Grumman Gulfstream III
Embraer EMB-110P Bandeirante
Training:
Beech T-34C Turbo-Mentor
Aerospatiale CM.170 Magister

GAMBIA

WITH A personnel roster that totals no more than 25, the Gambian Air Wing is undoubtedly one of the smallest of the world's "air forces". At present, it has just two aircraft on charge, both being employed purely on transport tasks, mainly in support of this nation's extremely small ground force.

EQUIPMENT

Transport:
Shorts Skyvan 3M
Pilatus Britten-Norman BN-2A Defender

GHANA

HEADQUARTERS of the small Ghana Air Force are located at Burma Camp in the capital city of Accra, and it is from here that operations of the three major subordinate elements — Tactical Command, Logistic Command and Training Command — are directed.

With responsibility for combat units, Tactical Command is clearly the senior element; but when it comes to combat assets, Ghana's Air Force has only a limited capability, being equipped with a small number of single-seat MB-326KBs and MB-339As which are employed on counter-insurgency (COIN) tasks as well as conventional training operations. Other jet-powered equipment consists of a few MB-326F two-seat trainers although it is likely that these have been retired, following the delivery of several ex-Nigerian Air Force Aero L-29 Delfins.

Jet operations are concentrated at Tamale, while other airfields include the main training base at Takoradi, where about 10 Bulldogs are used for primary tuition, student pilots then moving on to the MB-326/L-29. Elements of the transport fleet fly from Accra-Kotka and Takoradi, other types like the BN-2A Islander and Alouette III undertaking routine liaison and communications functions within the company.

Above: Several types now serving with the Ghana Air Force are primarily two-seater trainers, the Bulldog 122s shown here being a perfect example. In all, 13 such aircraft were acquired for use as primary trainers.

EQUIPMENT

COIN:
Aermacchi MB.339A
Aermacchi MB.326KG
Transport:
Fokker F-27 Friendship 400M/600
Shorts Skyvan 3M
CASA C.212 Aviocar
VIP Transport:
Fokker F-28 Fellowship 3000
Bell 212
Communications/Liaison:
Pilatus Britten-Norman BN-2A Islander
Aerospatiale Alouette III
Training:
BAe Bulldog 122
Aero L-29 Delfin
Aermacchi MB.326F
Aermacchi MB.339A

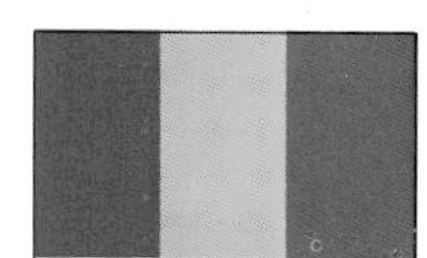

GUINEA

ONE OF A number of African states which have received assistance in return for granting landing rights to Soviet military aircraft, the *Force Aérienne du Guineé* (Guinea Air Force) has a combat echelon equipped with the MiG-21PFM "Fishbed-J", and may still be using a few survivors from a batch of about 10 MiG-17F "Fresco" fighters that were supplied a number of years ago.

Soviet influence is also evident in the transport force which evidently includes a couple of Ilyushin Il-18 "Coots", two Antonov An-12 "Cubs" and a quartet of An-14 "Clods", although Air Guinee's fleet of civil airliners is sometimes called upon to support military operations. Light transport, communications and liaison duties are satisfied by helicopters such as the Puma, Gazelle, Ecureuil and Alouette III.

Pilot training is apparently accomplished in-country, students receiving primary instruction on the elderly Yakovlev Yak-18 "Max" before moving on to the jet-powered L-29 Delfin and MiG-15UTI "Midget".

EQUIPMENT

Interception:
Mikoyan-Gurevich MiG-21PFM "Fishbed-J"
Attack:
Mikoyan-Gurevich MiG-21PFM "Fishbed-J"
Mikoyan-Gurevich MiG-17F "Fresco"
Transport:
Ilyushin Il-18V "Coot"
Antonov An-12 "Cub"
Antonov An-14 "Clod"
Aerospatiale SA.330 Puma
Communications/Liaison:
Aerospatiale SA.342 Gazelle
Aerospatiale AS.350 Ecureuil
Aerospatiale SA.316B Alouette III
Mil Mi-4 "Hound"
Training:
Yakovlev Yak-18 "Max"
Mikoyan-Gurevich MiG-15UTI "Midget"
Aero L-29 Delfin

GUINEA-BISSAU

EVIDENCE of colonial links with Portugal still linger in the *Forca Aerea Guine-Bissau* (Guinea-Bissau Air Force), which inherited a motley assortment of former Portuguese Air Force hardware when this small state was granted independence in 1974, some of which is still in use. Some of this equipment — notably half-a-dozen C-47 Dakotas — now operates in civil markings under a pool arrangement with the national airline, but the principal source of assistance and aircraft is now the USSR, which has supplied at least five MiG-17F "Fresco" fighters, although only three of these are thought to remain active with the sole fighter unit. That unit also has a single MiG-15UTI "Midget" for pilot training and is located adjacent to Air Force headquarters at Bissau-Bissalanca.

EQUIPMENT

Attack:
Mikoyan-Gurevich MiG-17F "Fresco"
Coastal Patrol:
Reims-Cessna FTB.337
Transport:
Douglas C-47 Dakota
Communications/Liaison:
Dornier Do 27A
Aerospatiale Alouette II/III
Training:
Mikoyan-Gurevich MiG-15UTI "Midget"

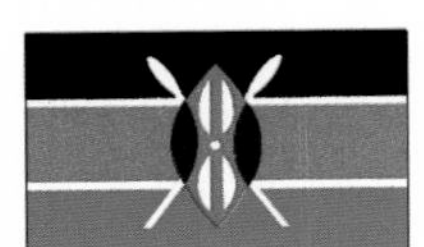

KENYA

ONE OF the more modern and better-organized African air arms, the Kenyan Air Force suffered the indignity of being disbanded in August 1982 following a failed *coup d'etat* by minor ranks. The re-establishment of military flying in Kenya was under Army supervision and it is now officially known as the '82 Air Force, remaining very firmly under Army authority.

Equipment has been obtained almost entirely from Western sources and the main base of operations is at Nanyuki, which is home to a fighter squadron flying the F-5E/F Tiger II. Air-to-air and air-to-ground capability exists, with AIM-9 Sidewinder missiles being used for the former and AGM-65A Mavericks for the latter. Nanyuki also houses training/attack units operating British-built Hawk Mk.82s and Strikemaster Mk.87s, although the latter is now being replaced by the Shorts Tucano Mk.51, a dozen of which were ordered in 1988. Like the Strikemaster, these will have a light ground attack capability. Combat potential may eventually be further enhanced through the purchase of a dedicated light strike aircraft, and Kenya has shown keen interest in the Hawk 200 to fulfil this role, although no order has yet been placed.

Transport forces continue to rely on Canadian-built aircraft, with eight DHC-5 Buffalos due to be augmented by a quartet of Boeing Canada Dash-8s.

Combat-capable elements are rounded out by some 40 MD 500 helicopters, including 15 500MD Defenders for anti-armour attack and 15 500M Scouts, the latter being armed with Chain Guns.

Initial pilot training is undertaken on a dozen or so BAe Bulldogs, with basic and advanced tuition following on the Strikemaster and Hawk, but the delivery of Tucanos should result in the now rather elderly Strikemaster being retired after two decades of sterling service.

EQUIPMENT

Interception:
Northrop F-5E Tiger II
Attack:
Northrop F-5E Tiger II
BAe Hawk Mk.52
BAe Strikemaster Mk.87
COIN:
McDonnell Douglas 500
Anti-Armour:
McDonnell Douglas 500MD TOW Defender
Observation:
McDonnell Douglas 500M Scout
Transport:
Boeing Canada Dash 8
Boeing Canada Buffalo
Dornier Do 28D Skyservant
Aerospatiale SA.330/IAR-330 Puma
VIP Transport:
Piper PA-31P Navajo
Training:
BAe Bulldog 103/127
Shorts Tucano Mk.51
BAe Strikemaster Mk.87
BAe Hawk Mk.52
Northrop F-5F Tiger II

LESOTHO

OPERATING as part of the integrated Royal Lesotho Defence Force, the Air Squadron is fundamentally a transport-orientated echelon that is active in support of government agencies such as the Police (it was formerly known as the Police Mobile Unit Air Wing). It presently has no more than 10 aircraft and helicopters, all of which are based at Maseru, conveniently close to the headquarters element in the Ministry of Defence and Internal Security. Equipment includes a couple of CASA C.212 Aviocar twin-engined light transports which are able to operate safely into most of the 30-odd landing strips that exist within Lesotho. Fixed-wing resources are completed by a Cessna 182Q which may actually be operated under the terms of a leasing arrangement. Helicopters used for transport, liaison and VIP tasks consist of three Bell 412s, two MBB BO105Cs and a turbine-powered Soloy-Westland-Bell 47G.

EQUIPMENT

Transport:
CASA C.212 Aviocar
Bell 412/412SP
Communications/Liaison:
Cessna 182Q
MBB BO 105C
Soloy-Westland-Bell 47G

LIBERIA

THE present status of the Liberian Army's Air Reconnaissance Unit is in doubt following the recent civil war which resulted in the administration of President Doe being overthrown in September 1990. Prior to that, a small number of single-engined Cessnas were flown on liaison and transport duties, although at least three of these served with the paramilitary Justice Air Wing. Some reports indicate that a single Caribou transport may also be operated.

EQUIPMENT

Transport:
Boeing Canada Caribou
Cessna 208 Caravan I
Communications/Liaison:
Cessna 150K
Cessna 172
Cessna 180E
Cessna 206

MADAGASCAR

NORTH KOREA and the USSR are the principal sources of aid and assistance for the *Armée de l'Air Malgache* (Madagascar Air Force), which relies for its combat potential on a single fighter squadron equipped with both the MiG-21FL "Fishbed" and the MiG-17F "Fresco". Employed in dual interception and attack roles, they are supported by a modestly sized transport echelon equipped

Left: Among the duties assigned to Kenya's MD 500 fleet is the patrol of the outback to protect elephants from armed poachers.

with a motley selection of fixed-wing aircraft and helicopters obtained from sources in both the East and West. The most numerous transport type is the Antonov An-26 "Curl", with from four to six aircraft being operated alongside a few Mil Mi-8 "Hip" helicopters. Until recently, there were also a couple of real veterans in the shape of the C-47 Dakota, although the latter have recently been withdrawn from service.

Other resources include a few Piper and Cessna light twins used for communications tasks, and a quartet of Cessna 172s which are employed to assess candidates for pilot training, successful applicants receiving the bulk of their subsequent instruction in the USSR.

EQUIPMENT

Interception:
Mikoyan-Gurevich MiG-21FL "Fishbed-D"
Attack:
Mikoyan-Gurevich MiG-21FL "Fishbed-D"
Mikoyan-Gurevich MiG-17F "Fresco"
Transport:
Yakovlev Yak-40 "Codling"
Antonov An-26 "Curl"
Douglas C-47 Dakota
Pilatus Britten-Norman BN-2A Defender
Mil Mi-8 "Hip"
Communications/Liaison:
Reims-Cessna FRA.337
Piper PA-23 Aztec D
Cessna 310R
Training:
Cessna 172

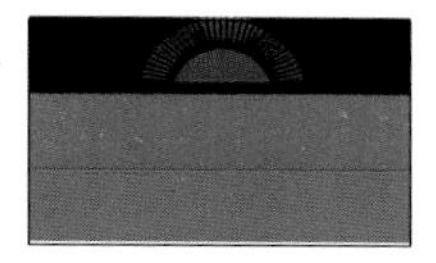

MALAWI

CONTROL OF the dozen or so aircraft which are utilized for military missions by this small African state rests with the Army, which has established an Air Wing with its headquarters and main base at Blantyre-Chileka. Operations are purely transport-related, with a VIP element flying a single BAe 125-800 alongside an SA.365 Dauphin. Tactical transport tasks are met by a quartet of Do 228s, six Do 128 Skyservants and a brace of SA.330 Pumas, while an Alouette III undertakes liaison work.

EQUIPMENT

Transport:
Douglas C-47 Dakota
Dornier Do 228
Dornier Do 128D Skyservant
Aerospatiale SA.330J Puma
VIP Transport:
BAe 125-800
Aerospatiale SA.365N Dauphin 2
Communications/Liaison:
Aerospatiale SA.316B Alouette III

Above: As with many other small air arms around the world, the Islamic Air Force of Mauritania appreciates the ruggedness of the small but effective Short Skyvan 3M.

MALI

ALTHOUGH some assistance was provided by France following the granting of independence to Mali (formerly French Sudan) in 1960, the USSR has been the principal source of technical aid and hardware ever since then and this is readily apparent in the inventory of the *Force Aérienne de la Republique du Mali* (Republic of Mali Air Force) today.

Initial combat jet equipment consisted of five MiG-17 "Frescos" delivered in the latter half of the 1960s, and these were still operational from the main base at Bamako/Senou at the time of the altercation with Burkina-Faso in December 1985 when one was claimed to have been shot down. Recent reports indicate that the "Frescos" have at last been withdrawn, following the supply of MiG-19 "Farmer" and MiG-21 "Fishbed" fighters, quantities mentioned being eight and 14 respectively.

Airlift capability is limited to no more than a dozen aircraft and helicopters, all of which are of Soviet origin, including types like the An-26 "Curl" and the Mi-8 "Hip". There is also a small pilot training establishment with a mixed fleet that includes the Yak-11 "Moose", Yak-18 "Max", Aero L-29 Delfin and MiG-15UTI "Midget".

EQUIPMENT

Interception:
Mikoyan-Gurevich MiG-21 "Fishbed"
Attack:
Mikoyan-Gurevich MiG-21 "Fishbed"
Mikoyan-Gurevich MiG-19 "Farmer"
Transport:
Antonov An-26 "Curl"
Antonov An-24 "Coke"
Antonov An-2 "Colt"
MiL Mi-8 "Hip"
MiL Mi-4 "Hound"
Training:
Yakovlev Yak-11 "Moose"
Yakovlev Yak-18 "Max"
Mikoyan-Gurevich MiG-15UTI "Midget"
Aero L-29 Delfin

MAURITANIA

ONE OF A number of French colonies which gained independence in 1960, the *Force Aérienne Islamique de Mauritanie* (Islamic Air Force of Mauritania) was initially equipped with the usual selection of French "hand-me-downs", but none of the Broussards and C-47s that were handed over remain in service today.

Combat capability of the FAIM consists of five machine-gun and rocket-armed BN-2A Defenders and a pair of Reims-Cessna FTB337s, both types having seen quite a bit of action against Algerian-backed *Polisario* guerilla forces in what was formerly the Spanish Sahara during the late-1970s, with at least one Defender being shot down by ground fire. A successful military coup in 1978 resulted in the termination of combat operations against *Polisario* elements, but armed neutrality patrols are still flown.

Transport forces are confined to a pair of Buffalos and a single Skyvan 3M, the short take-off and landing capabilities of both types allowing them to make good use of the many desert strips. Other tasks include coastal surveillance with a couple of PA-31T Cheyenne IIs.

EQUIPMENT

COIN
Pilatus Britten-Norman BN-2A Defender
Reims-Cessna FTB.337
Coastal Patrol:
Piper PA-31T Cheyenne II
Transport:
Boeing Canada Buffalo
Shorts Skyvan 3M
Communications/Liaison:
Aermacchi AL-60B
Reims-Cessna FRA.337F
McDonnell Douglas 500C

MOZAMBIQUE

THE continuing battle against right-wing *Renamo* guerilla forces dominates the activities of the *Força Popular Aérea de Libertacao de Moçambique* (Popular Air Force for the Liberation of Mozambique), but a substantial proportion of the available air power is believed to be provided by friendly nations. Such assistance includes Cuban-piloted MiG-21 "Fishbeds" although there is considerable doubt as to their ownership: one MiG-21 that was shot-down by *Renamo* forces in 1985 was identified as originating from Ethiopia, even though it was actually flown by a Cuban pilot.

As far as Mozambique's own air force is concerned, this is largely equipped with Soviet-supplied hardware, spearheaded by some 30 MiG-17F "Frescos" which are used in the fighter-bomber role. Other combat-capable equipment consists of a small number of Mil Mi-24/25 "Hind" attack helicopters and about ten Mil Mi-8 "Hip" assault helicopters.

EQUIPMENT

Interception:
Mikoyan-Gurevich MiG-21MF "Fishbed-J"
Attack:
Mikoyan-Gurevich MiG-21MF "Fishbed-J"
Mikoyan-Gurevich MiG-17F "Fresco"
Mil Mi-24/25 "Hind"
Assault:
Mil Mi-8 "Hip"
Transport:
Antonov An-26 "Curl"
Communications/Liaison:
Cessna 152/172/182
Piper Aztec/Apache/Vagabond/Cherokee/Tri-Pacer
Aerospatiale Alouette III
Training:
Piper PA-32 Cherokee Six
Zlin 326
Mikoyan-Gurevich MiG-15UTI "Midget"

NIGER

FRENCH assistance was provided in the wake of independence in 1960, but the *Escardrille Nationale du Niger* (National Flight of Niger) has only ever operated transport and liaison aircraft during its three decades of existence and that philosophy seems unlikely to change, especially since a defence treaty exists linking Niger with France, Benin and the Cote d'Ivoire.

Contemporary equipment numbers less than 10 aircraft, with two C-130H Hercules constituting the "heavy-lift" capability alongside three Nord Noratlas which were obtained from France and West Germany. Of even older vintage is a solitary C-54B Skymaster, while light transport duties are performed by two Dornier Do 228s.

EQUIPMENT

Transport:
Lockheed C-130H Hercules
Douglas C-54B Skymaster
Nord N.2501D/F Noratlas
Dornier Do 228

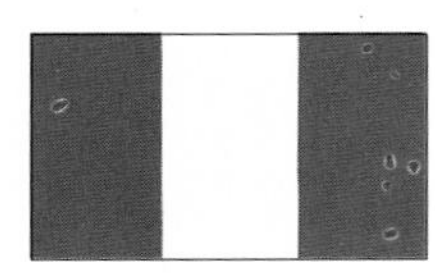

NIGERIA

ONE OF THE largest and best-equipped air arms on the African continent, the Federal Nigerian Air Force has its headquarters in Lagos, from where the activities of four distinct sub-Commands — Strike, Tactical, Training and Logistics — are directed. Force expansion was implemented at the start of the last decade and has continued at a slower rate following the installation of a military government in December 1983.

Combat-capable elements are equipped with hardware obtained from both East and West. Offensive capability is primarily vested in the SEPECAT Jaguar International, 13 single-seat fighter-bombers and five two-seat trainers being delivered by British Aerospace (BAe) in the mid-1980s, and most of these survive although plans to purchase a further 18 failed to come to fruition.

Air defence is the domain of the MiG-21MF "Fishbed-J", of which at least two dozen examples have been received along with a handful of two-seat MiG-21U "Mongols" for pilot training. Light attack tasks are undertaken by the Alpha Jet, two dozen of which have been delivered to Nigeria in two equal-sized batches. The first group, handed over in 1981-82, are dual-role in that they also perform training tasks, while the second group have been assigned to a dedicated light attack squadron. In addition, Nigeria's air force has also taken delivery of 12 Aermacchi MB.339ANs and 24 Aero L-39MS Albatros jet trainers, both of which can be fitted with light armament and used for attack missions.

A measure of combat potential is also possessed by about 20 MBB BO 105Ds that were assembled locally from German-manufactured components. Four of these augmented four BO 105Cs on search-and-rescue (SAR) duties, but the remainder are configured to carry Oerlikon rocket pods and most have since been further modified with roof-mounted sighting devices. Thus far, they apparently lack air-to-surface anti-armour missile launch capability.

EQUIPMENT

Interception:
Mikoyan-Gurevich MiG-21MF "Fishbed-J"
Attack:
SEPECAT Jaguar International
Dassault-Breguet Alpha Jet E
Aero L-39MS Albatros
Aermacchi MB.339A
COIN:
MBB BO 105D
Maritime Patrol:
Fokker F-27MPA Friendship
Transport:
Lockheed C-130H Hercules
Aeritalia G.222
Aerospatiale AS.332M Super Puma
VIP Transport:
Dornier Do 228
SAR:
MBB BO 105CB/D
Utility/Liaison:
Dornier Do 128-2/-6 Skyservant
Training:
BAe Bulldog 123
Aermacchi MB.339
Aero L-39MS Albatros
Dassault-Breguet Alpha Jet E
Mikoyan-Gurevich MiG-21U "Mongol"
SEPECAT Jaguar International
McDonnell Douglas 300C

Left: Though plans to procure a second batch have failed to come to fruition, survivors of the first 18 SEPECAT Jaguar International fighters continue to provide good service.

RWANDA

BELGIAN assistance continues to be provided to the *Force Aerienne Rwandaise* (Rwandan Air Force) which has long wanted to acquire a measure of combat capability, previous attempts to obtain Aermacchi MB.326s and CM.170 Magisters having foundered on the rock of financial restraint. In consequence, current combat potential is confined to a pair of SOCATA Rallye 235 Guerriers which can theoretically fulfil counter-insurgency (COIN) missions. Transport-related tasks are undertaken by obsolescent aircraft such as the Nord Noratlas, backed up by a couple of BN-2A Islanders and a few SA.342L Gazelle and SA.316B Alouette III helicopters. The Air Force also looking after the civil-registered Caravelle III, which is used for VIP transport duties.

EQUIPMENT

COIN:
SOCATA 235 Guerrier
Transport:
Nord N.2501F Noratlas
Pilatus Britten-Norman BN-2A Islander
VIP Transport:
Aerospatiale SE.210 Caravelle III
Communications/Liaison:
Aerospatiale SA.342L Gazelle
Aerospatiale SA.316B Alouette III

Left: Armed with a pair of F2 rocket packs and a quartet of bombs, the SOCATA 235G Guerrier is used by the Rwandan Air Force in the COIN role. To date, only two have been bought.

EQUIPMENT

Communications/Liaison:
MBB BO 105
Aerospatiale AS.355F Ecureuil

SENEGAL

THE confederation between Senegal and the Gambia in 1981 had little noticeable effect on the Senegal Air Force, other than prompting a change of name. It relies on a handful of CM.170 Magisters and SOCATA 235G Guerriers for its modest combat capability.

EQUIPMENT

COIN:
Aerospatiale CM.170 Magister
SOCATA 235G Guerrier
Transport:
Fokker F-27 Friendship 400M
Aerospatiale SA.330F Puma
Communications/Liaison:
Aerospatiale SA.341H Gazelle
Aerospatiale SA.318C Alouette II
Training:
SOCATA 160ST
Socata Rallye 235A
Aerospatiale CM.170 Magister

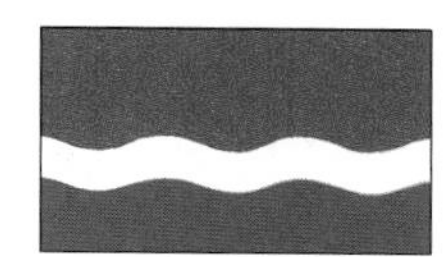

SEYCHELLES

IT SHOULD come as no surprise to learn that the Air Wing of the Defence Force of this former British colony is principally concerned with maritime missions, since the Seychelles consists of now fewer than 92 islands scattered around the Indian Ocean off the east coast of Africa. Most of the handful of aircraft and helicopters that are operated have been received as gifts and equipment presently on charge consists of one Swearingen Merlin IIIB, one BN-2A Maritime Defender, one SOCATA 235E and a brace of Chetak helicopters (Indian licence-built Alouette IIIs). Surveillance is undertaken by the Merlin and Maritime Defender.

EQUIPMENT

Maritime Patrol:
Pilatus Britten-Norman BN-2A Maritime Defender
Swearingen Merlin IIIB
Communications/Liaison:
HAL Chetak
Training:
SOCATA 235E

SIERRA LEONE

THE AIR arm of the Sierra Leone Defence Force has all but ceased to exist, following the transfer of its sole MBB BO 105 and two AS.355F Ecureuils to the civil register. However, these helicopters are still government-owned (in the charge of the Ministry of Defence), being employed for routine communications tasks and as VIP transports.

SOMALIA

DEPENDENCE on foreign assistance has resulted in Somalia turning to a number of diverse sources for military aid and it has at different times been allied with nations in both East and West, most notably the USA as a *quid pro quo* for use of harbour facilities at Berbera and the airfield at Mogadishu.

US assistance has not extended to the supply of warplanes and the Dayuuradaha Xoogga Dalka Somaliyeed (Somali Aeronautical Corps) continues to operate Soviet and Chinese hardware alongside a few Hunters handed on by Abu Dhabi, although there are doubts about the serviceability of much of this equipment.

Interceptor forces consist of less than 10 MiG-21MF "Fishbed-Js", possibly backed up by a number of Xian F-7Bs, this being the Chinese-built copy of the classic MiG-21. Another combat type of Chinese origin is the Shenyang F-6 (MiG-19), close to 30 having been delivered in the early-1980s.

EQUIPMENT

Interception:
Mikoyan-Gurevich MiG-21MF "Fishbed-J"
Xian F-7B
Attack:
Shenyang F-6
BAe Hunter FGA.76
Mikoyan-Gurevich MiG-17F "Fresco"
COIN:
SIAI-Marchetti SF.260WS Warrior
Reconnaissance:
BAe Hunter FR.76A
Transport:
Aeritalia G.222
Antonov An-26 "Curl"
Antonov An-24V "Coke"
Antonov An-2 "Colt"
Agusta-Bell AB.204B
Agusta-Bell AB.212
Communications/Liaison:
Pilatus Britten-Norman BN-2A Islander
Helio H-291 Courier
Training:
Reims-Cessna FRA.150L
Yakovlev Yak-11 "Moose"
Mikoyan-Gurevich MiG-15UTI "Midget"
Mikoyan-Gurevich MiG-21U "Mongol"
BAe Hunter T.76

SOUTH AFRICA

DESPITE the United Nations' (UN) embargo on the supply of military equipment to South Africa, the *Suid Afrikaanse Lugmag* (SAAF: South African Air Force) remains an effective and well-organized agency that has combined covert acquisition of equipment with procurement from an increasingly capable indigenous arms industry, as well as from a number of nations that were prepared to circumvent the UN resolution. Now, at long last, significant political changes are occurring, but the philosophy with regard to the black population has not yet moved sufficiently far to warrant lifting the UN embargo although South Africa's rehabilitation does appear to be coming closer as it slowly sets about the process of dismantling apartheid.

Current SAAF organization centres around two major command establishments created along geographical lines, plus half-a-dozen subsidiary commands which undertake specific duties. Looking first at the former, these comprise Southern Air Command, with responsibility for that portion of the country which lies to the south of the Orange River, and Western Air Command, which covers the remainder.

Each Command operates its own headquarters agency (Southern at Silvermijn, and Western at Windhoek) to control the activities of attached squadrons which are mainly employed on transport, liaison, counter-insurgency (COIN), observation, close air support and reconnaissance duties. An interesting, if somewhat motley assortment of equipment is operated by elements assigned to these Commands, ranging from light helicopters like the Alouette III to tactical transports such as the Lockheed Hercules.

Southern Air Command is the smaller of the two and has just four squadrons that work closely with the South African Navy. In view of this, it should come as no surprise to learn that these units are predominantly concerned with missions of a maritime nature. Two squadrons have Douglas C-47 Dakotas for surveillance, transport and miscellaneous duties, including target-towing for naval gunfire practice, while another uses close to 20 radar-equipped Piaggio P.166S Albatross light twins for maritime reconnaissance and search-and-rescue (SAR) operations. Finally, one squadron has a fleet of Alouette IIIs which satisfy inshore SAR requirements as well as occasionally being deployed aboard Navy frigates and survey vessels.

Western Air Command is a significantly larger establishment, with about a dozen squadrons, including some that are partly staffed by members of the Active Citizen Force (ACF), the latter being a reserve component which also has a few squadrons that are entirely manned by its personnel. Alouette IIIs constitute the sole equipment of two squadrons and are also used by another in conjunction with the medium-sized Puma which forms the main mission equipment of at least three squadrons. Between them, these may be used for communications, transport and more offensive activities, including assault, while some Alouettes have been employed as "gunships" with 0.8in (20mm) cannon.

Fixed-wing elements of Western Air Command include three light observation squadrons. One is solely equipped with Cessna 185s, while the other two use the AM-3CM Bosbok/C4M Kudu and the AM-3CM/Cessna 185. Additional observation assets consist of at least a dozen HB-23/2400 Scanliner motor-gliders obtained from Austria for local assembly, but no operating details are known.

Transport resources also come under Western Air Command management and comprise four squadrons with varied equipment. Tactical airlift is undertaken by one squadron which is equipped with seven long-serving C-130B Hercules and nine C.160Z Transalls and further airlift capability is provided by the commercial operator Safair Freighters, which has up to a dozen L-100-30 Super Hercules on charge, and these can be utilized in support of military operational requirements should it be deemed necessary.

Another airlift unit has aircraft of a rather older vintage, operating about 10 C-47 Dakotas alongside six C-54/DC-4 Skymasters and a single Viscount 781D, the latter actually displaying civilian markings. A few other SAAF aircraft also carry civil identities as standard, these consisting of a quartet of BAe 125-400B "Mercurius" light jet twins plus a few Beech Super King Air 200s and Cessna Citations which undertake VIP airlift tasks with yet another unit. Finally, four Boeing 707s are used for dual tanker/transport and electronic intelligence (Elint) missions by the final Western Command outfit, all four of these aircraft having been obtained from Israel during the summer of 1986.

Heavier firepower is furnished by fighters such as the Mirage and attack aircraft like the Impala and Buccaneer which are grouped together within Airspace Control Command, these aircraft being detached as and when necessary to satisfy the requirements of the geographically-based Commands.

Airspace Control Command also has a headquarters element (at Waterkloof, Pretoria) and manages air traffic control and air defence-dedicated radar networks, as well as anti-aircraft missile forces and the previously-mentioned fighter/attack

Above: That a country as important as South Africa has to rely so heavily on the likes of the Dakota (foreground) and the Skymaster is a direct result of the arms embargo.

Below: A contrast in colours in the skies above South Africa, as a locally-built Atlas Impala I two-seater trainer formates on a Mirage IIICZ and a two-seater IIIBZ.

elements. The latter are predominantly equipped with variations on the Mirage theme, with six squadrons (including two which function as combat flying schools) utilizing IIIEZs and F.1AZs for attacks, IIICZs and F.1CZs as interceptors and IIIRZs for reconnaissance tasks.

In addition, there is the Cheetah, a locally-designed modification of the Mirage III which embodies new avionics and canard foreplanes, and it seems likely that most of the 40-plus Mirage III survivors will be brought up to Cheetah configuration. The Cheetah is presently operational with a training unit and an ACF squadron. Looking further ahead, South Africa is now developing a twin-engined fighter, and this concept, code-named "*Cava*", may well enter service in the mid-1990s.

Remaining Airspace Control Command resources comprise two light bomber outfits. One has no more than a handful of Buccaneers, all that survive from the 16 aircraft delivered in the 1960s, while the other is little better off when it comes to quantity, it being equipped with barely half-a-dozen Canberras, including some T.4s used for training. Finally, there is the locally-produced Atlas Impala 2 (a licence-built Aermacchi MB-326K) — about 80 are flown, mostly by three ACF squadrons, but some serve alongside Mirage IIIs as part of a pilot training unit.

Other functional commands are predominantly concerned with support tasks and include Tactical Support Command, Air Logistics Command, Training Command and Airbases Command. In most instances, missions do not involve flying activity, Tactical Support Command, for instance, being concerned primarily with the construction of temporary landing strips. When it comes to the matter of supply and support, this is the responsibility of Air Logistics Command, an agency which is also intimately involved in formulating future procurement plans. In consequence, it works closely with South Africa's extremely capable and sizeable defence industry.

Training Command is, however, very much in the business of operating aircraft and is tasked with satisfying pilot training requirements which are currently running at a rate of about 120 per year. Instruction begins with the Central Flying School (CFS) at Dunnottar, which is primarily equipped with the veteran T-6 Texan/Harvard, a type that looks like surviving for some time to come, despite its age. The CFS also operates a number of Impala 1s, a type that is used by No.83 Jet Flying School (JFS) at Langebaanweg for intermediate tuition and as an aerobatic display aircraft by the "*Silver Falcons*" team made up of No.83 JFS instructors. Pilots who are earmarked to join combat-ready units thereafter move to a Combat Flying School for operational training on the type that they will eventually fly with a front-line unit.

Further specialized tuition is provided by a few other units which operate examples of most types to be found in the inventory. For instance, No.84 Light Flying School has Bosboks, Kudus and Cessna 185s for observation-related tasks, while the Multi-Engined Flying School is equipped with a few C-47 Dakotas. Additional Schools are active in maritime tasks, using Piaggio P.166s assigned on a "loan" basis from an operational unit, as well as rotary-wing tuition with the Alouette III.

EQUIPMENT

Interception:
Dassault-Breguet Mirage F.1CZ
Dassault-Breguet Mirage IIICZ

Attack:
Dassault-Breguet Mirage F.1AZ
Atlas Cheetah E2
Dassault-Breguet Mirage IIIEZ
BAe Buccaneer S.50
BAe Canberra B(I).12
Atlas Impala 2

Reconnaissance:
Dassault-Breguet Mirage IIIRZ/R2Z

Maritime Patrol:
Douglas C-47 Dakota
Piaggio P.166S Albatross

Observation:
Cessna 185
Atlas AM-3CM Bosbok/C4M Kudu
HB-23/2400 Scanliner

Tanking/Elint-Gathering:
Boeing 707-320

Transport:
Lockheed C-130B Hercules
Douglas DC-4/C-54 Skymaster
Transall C.160Z
Douglas C-47 Dakota
Aerospatiale SA.330C/L Puma

VIP Transport:
Vickers Viscount 781D
Cessna Citation
BAe 125-400B "Mercurius"
Beech Super King Air 200

Communications/Liaison:
Cessna 208 Caravan I
Cessna 185
Atlas AM-3CM Bosbok
Atlas C4M Kudu
Aerospatiale Alouette III

SAR:
Piaggio P.166S Albatross
Aerospatiale Alouette III

Training:
North American T-6 Harvard/Texan
Atlas Impala I
Dassault-Breguet Mirage IIIBZ/DZ
Atlas Cheetah D2Z
BAe Canberra T.4
Aerospatiale Alouette III

Right: While the arms embargo instigated by the UN has hindered the SAAF's abilities to maintain a modern fighting inventory, French hardware, such as the Puma helicopter, is conspicuous by its very presence.

SWAZILAND

TWO examples of the IAI Arava constitute the sole strength of the Umbutfo Swaziland Defence Force Air Wing, these being utilized primarily as transports although they can also be fitted with gun pods. They also feature hardpoints for rocket pods. These latter features enable them to undertake some counter-insurgency (COIN) and border patrol operations from the main base at Matsapa.

Intent to expand the size of the Air Wing apparently exists, but limited finance has thus far prevented the acquisition of any additional aircraft.

EQUIPMENT

COIN/Transport:
IAI Arava

TANZANIA

ACTIVE AS part of an integrated defence establishment, the Air Wing of the Tanzanian People's Defence Force was created with West German assistance during 1964; but that aid was short-lived and Canada stepped in to play an important role during the all-important formative years, supplying military hardware as well as technical and training aid. More recently, China has been a major contributor, and the Air Wing now operates a small combat component equipped entirely with fighter aircraft of Chinese origin.

Most potent is the Xian F-7 interceptor, while a fighter-bomber element operates Shenyang F-6. Some older Shenyang F-5s are also apparently still active.

Transport equipment reflects the one-time close association with Canada and consists of just five DHC-5D Buffaloes and a solitary Pinkiang C-5 (Chinese licence-built An-2 "Colt"), but interest has been shown in obtaining Soviet-built Antonov transports although no firm order has yet materialized. Other types used on light transport duties, such as communications and liaison, consist of about 10 Cessna light twins as well as four Agusta-Bell AB.205s and a couple of Agusta-Bell AB.206B JetRangers.

Training resources are equally limited, initial instruction being given on a handful of Piper PA-28 Cherokee 140s, students thereafter receiving tuition in China. In-country operational training is accomplished with a pair of Shenyang FTG-2s (licence-built MiG-15UTI "Midget").

EQUIPMENT

Interception:
Xian F-7
Attack:
Shenyang F-6
Shenyang F-5
Transport:
Boeing Canada Buffalo
BAe 748
Pinkiang C-5
Communications/Liaison:
Cessna 310Q
Cessna 404 Titan
Agusta-Bell AB.205A
Agusta-Bell AB.206A JetRanger
Training:
Piper PA-28 Cherokee 140
Shenyang FTG-2

TOGO

ALTHOUGH it achieved independence from France in 1960, French assistance for this small African state was instrumental in the establishment of the *Force Aérienne Togolaise* (FAT: Togo Air Force) at the beginning of 1964. Initially active in only a transport capacity, Togo's air force has steadily expanded its capability and now features a combat echelon equipped with a mix of five Alpha Jets and six Embraer EMB-326GC Xavantes which can undertake light attack and counter-insurgency (COIN) missions. Other COIN resources consist of a trio of recently-acquired Aerospatiale TB.30B Epsilons and a few somewhat elderly CM.170 Magisters, although these are mostly utilized for pilot training tasks.

Airlift aircraft of the Transport Flight are less numerous, with perhaps the most useful type being the DHC-5D Buffalo. Two specimens of this rugged performer are operated alongside the VIP-configured F.28 Fellowship and Dassault Falcon 10, which are used for Presidential flights. In addition, a few light planes fulfil communications duties, while the modest number of helicopters that are employed on a variety of transport missions have all been obtained from Aerospatiale.

EQUIPMENT

Attack/COIN:
Dassault-Breguet Alpha Jet
Embraer EMB-326GC Xavante
Aerospatiale CM.170 Magister
Aerospatiale TB.30B Epsilon
Transport:
Boeing Canada Buffalo
Aerospatiale SA.330G Puma
Aerospatiale AS.332L Super Puma
VIP Transport:
Fokker F-28 Fellowship 3000
Dassault-Breguet Falcon 10
Communications/Liaison:
Beech B58 Baron
Cessna 337D
Reims-Cessna FRA.337E
Aerospatiale SA.313B Alouette II
Aerospatiale SA.315B Lama
Training:
Aerospatiale TB.30B Epsilon
Aerospatiale CM.170 Magister

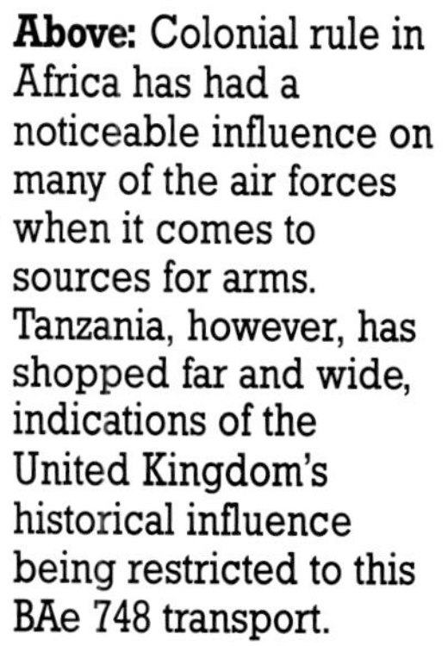
Above: Colonial rule in Africa has had a noticeable influence on many of the air forces when it comes to sources for arms. Tanzania, however, has shopped far and wide, indications of the United Kingdom's historical influence being restricted to this BAe 748 transport.

Below: As with the nearby "homeland" of Transkei, Venda has acquired a brace of MBB/Kawasaki BK 117 multi-purpose helicopters for use by the Venda Defence Force. Up to 10 passengers can be carried, making it an ideal transport asset for the small VDF.

TRANSKEI

ONE OF the tribal homelands that have been established within South Africa, Transkei's small Defence Force activated an air element at Umtata in late 1986 with a pair of CASA C.212 Aviocar transport aircraft. Soon after that, two MBB/Kawasaki BK 117 helicopters were handed over to perform VIP duties at the behest of the Department of the Prime Minister. Pilot training needs are modest and are satisfied in South Africa.

EQUIPMENT

Transport:
CASA C.212 Aviocar
VIP Transport:
MBB/Kawasaki BK 117

UGANDA

THE CURRENT operational status of the Uganda Army Air Force is parlous in the wake of internal and external troubles, as well as the celebrated Israeli raid on Entebbe Airport in 1976 when a substantial proportion of the front-line combat equipment was destroyed. Prior to that it had been reasonably well-equipped, flying a mix of MiG-17F "Frescos" and MiG-21 "Fishbeds" obtained from the Soviet Union via Czechoslovakia. Respective quantities supplied were of the order of 20 and 12, and some are still nominally on the Army Air Force inventory even though they haven't flown for years.

Other equipment that has spent most of the past decade in storage includes the bulk of the former training fleet which consisted of about five Piaggio P.149Ds, five Aero L-29 Delfins and a couple of MiG-15UTI "Midgets". As with the fighters, there seems little likelihood that these aircraft will return to operational flying duties.

Nevertheless, efforts are being made to rebuild, Uganda having contracted with Italy for four SIAI S.211 armed jet trainers and six SF.260s, which are operated alongside a couple of SF.260W Warriors obtained as a gift from Libya in 1987. In addition, a few helicopters are also now operational, fulfilling light transport and communications tasks.

EQUIPMENT

COIN:
SIAI-Marchetti S.211
SIAI-Marchetti SF.260W Warrior
Transport:
Mil Mi-8 "Hip"
Agusta-Bell AB.412 Grifon
Agusta-Bell AB.205
Agusta-Bell AB.206A JetRanger
Training:
SIAI-Marchetti SF.260W Warrior
SIAI-Marchetti S.211
Stored Types:
Aero L-29 Delfin
Mikoyan-Gurevich MiG-15UTI "Midget"
Mikoyan-Gurevich MiG-17F "Fresco"
Mikoyan-Gurevich MiG-21 "Fishbed"
Piaggio P.149D

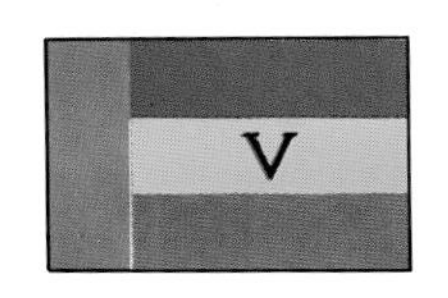

VENDA

ANOTHER OF the black "homelands" created by the South African government, Venda is situated close to the border with Mozambique and is nominally an independent state with its own air arm. Established during the course of 1983, the aviation element of Venda's small Defence Force is principally concerned with transport and communications missions, for which is operates a solitary CASA C.212 Aviocar as well as one Alouette III and a couple of MBB/Kawasaki BK 117s.

EQUIPMENT

Transport:
CASA C.212 Aviocar
Communications/Liaison:
MBB/Kawasaki BK 117
Aerospatiale SA.316B alouette III

ZAIRE

ALTHOUGH by no means large, the *Force Aérienne Zairoise* (Zaire Air Force) is reasonably well equipped and well organized but, like so many African nations, its defence forces do suffer from inadequate funding. In Zaire's case, the lack of finance has almost certainly had some impact on operational readiness rates, and it is believed that most of the surviving Mirage 5s are probably unserviceable due to a lack of adequate spares.

As far as organization is concerned, the Air Force has two major subordinate elements. These consist of the 1st Air Group, which directs the activities of training and support units, and the 2nd Tactical Air Group, which looks after attack and tactical support assets.

The latter is located at Kamina and controls two Wing organizations, with fighter and attack units being consolidated under the 21st Fighter-Attack Wing. Forces at its disposal comprise the few remaining Mirage 5M interceptors (probably no more than five single-seater aircraft plus one 5DM trainer) of No.211 Squadron and the MB.326K light attack aircraft of No.212 Squadron. In addition, there is the 22nd Tactical Transport Wing, with one squadron (No.221) operating two Buffalo transports out of the three that were originally delivered to the FAZ in 1976.

Kinshasa is home for the 1st Air Group which is nominally larger, having three component Wing organizations tasked with logistics support, liaison/communications and training respectively. The 19th Logistic Support Wing has two squadrons under its command, specifically No.191 with five examples of the C-130H Hercules and, possibly, the sole Boeing 707, and No.192 with about half-a-dozen C-47 Dakotas. No.12 Liaison Wing is smaller, with just a single squadron (No.121) to operate most of Zaire's small fleet of helicopters plus three Mitsubishi MU-2Js and some of the 15 or so Cessna 310Rs that have been received. Finally, there is No.13 Training Wing — again, this has two squadrons, No.131 being responsible for elementary and intermediate instruction on the Cessna 150 Aerobat and SIAI-Marchetti SF.260MZ while No.132 provides advanced tuition on the MB.326GB. Until recently, No.132 also flew the T-6G Texan in the training role, but this World War II veteran has now been retired and it is conceivable that Zaire could purchase either the PC-7 or the PC-9 from Switzerland in due course.

EQUIPMENT

Interception:
Dassault-Breguet Mirage 5M
Attack:
Aermacchi MB.326K
Transport:
Boeing 707-320B
Lockheed C-130H Hercules
Boeing Canada Buffalo
Douglas C-47 Dakota
Aerospatiale SA.330C Puma
Aerospatiale AS.332L Super Puma
Communications/Liaison:
Pilatus Britten-Norman BN-2A Islander
Mitsubishi MU-2J
Cessna 310R
Aerospatiale SA.316B Alouette III
Training:
Cessna A.150 Aerobat
SIAI-Marchetti SF.260MZ
Aermacchi MB.326GB
Dassault-Breguet Mirage 5DM
Cessna 310R
Bell 47G

Above: The Zambian Air Force is yet another example of a modest air arm that has come to appreciate fully the virtues of the SF.260, seen here in its training role (unarmed).

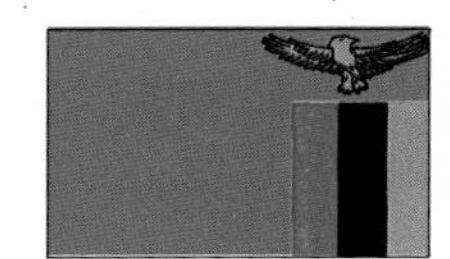

ZAMBIA

NOW firmly within the Soviet sphere of influence, fighter elements of the Zambian Air Force and Air Defence Command are now predominantly equipped with hardware of Eastern origin, with the MiG-21MF "Fishbed-J" serving as the principal interceptor. Just over a dozen are on charge, other combat equipment comprising a similar number of Chinese-built Shenyang F-6 fighter-bombers, about 10 Yugoslavian-supplied SOKO Jastrebs for light attack, and small quantities of the Aermacchi MB.326, SAAB MFI-17 Supporter, SOKO Galeb and SIAI-Marchetti SF.260 armed trainers which could be used in combat should the need arise. ZAF Tactical reconnaissance requirements are met by two RJ-1E Jastrebs although there is considerable doubt as to the operational status of the Jastrebs and Galebs, and they may no longer be serviceable.

Transport capability is dependent on an odd assortment of aircraft and helicopters obtained from both East and West. Vintage varies remarkably, but tactically most useful are the five Buffaloes and four Antonov An-26 "Curls". Other equipment active in airlift-related duties consists of four C-47 Dakotas, a couple of Douglas DC-6Bs, half-a-dozen Dornier Do 28D Skyservants, one BAe 748 (VIP-configured) and three Yakovlev Yak-40 "Codlings" (also VIP-configured). Helicopters comprise six Mil

Left: Only a handful of Dassault-Breguet Mirage 5s remain in service with No.211 Squadron, Zaire Air Force, with the Mirage 5DM shown here being the sole surviving two-seater.

Above: Seven out of nine BAe Hawk T.60s delivered remain in service with the Zimbabwean Air Force, fulfilling fast jet tuition and ground attack responsibilities.

Mi-8 "Hips", a trio of Agusta-Bell 205As and two Agusta-Bell 212s for VIP work.

Initial pilot training is accomplished on the Nanchang CJ-6, with those who successfully complete this phase of instruction progressing to the armed trainers alluded to earlier if they are destined for fixed-wing combat types, or to the Bell 47G if they are going to pilot helicopters. A couple of MiG-21U "Mongols" are also on charge for advanced fighter tuition.

EQUIPMENT

Interception:
Mikoyan-Gurevich MiG-21MF "Fishbed-J"
Attack:
Shenyang F-6
SOKO J-1 Jastreb
Aermacchi MB.326GB
COIN:
SAAB MFI-17 Supporter
SIAI-Marchetti SF.260MZ
Reconnaissance:
SOKO RJ-1E Jastreb
Transport:
Douglas DC-6
Boeing Canada Buffalo
Antonov An-26 "Curl"
Douglas C-47 Dakota
Mil Mi-8 "Hip"
Agusta-Bell AB.205
VIP Transport:
Yakovlev Yak-40 "Codling"
BAe 748
Agusta-Bell AB.212
Communications/Liaison:
Dornier Do 28D Skyservant
Agusta-Bell 47G
Training:
SAAB MFI-17 Supporter
SIAI-Marchetti SF.260MZ
Nanchang CJ-6
Aermacchi MB.326GB
SOKO Galeb
Mikoyan-Gurevich MiG-21U "Mongol"
Agusta-Bell AB.47G

ZIMBABWE

FORMERLY known as Rhodesia, the Air Force of Zimbabwe operates an odd mixture of equipment, flying 1950s-vintage Hunters alongside Chinese-built copies of the MiG-21 received as part of an aid package from China. Persistent reports of the impending supply of 14 MiG-29 "Fulcrum" fighters (including a pair of two-seat trainers) have still to be confirmed, but it is known that Pakistan has given some assistance although this appears to centre around provision of pilot instructors rather than hardware.

Operations are currently conducted from two principal air bases — at Gwelo (formerly known as Thornhill) and New Sarum, near the capital city of Harare — but some Zimbabwean aircraft and personnel are understood to be assisting Mozambique in the fight against *Renamo* guerilla forces active there in the latter country.

Combat elements are for the most part concentrated at Gwelo and centre around a dozen or so Hunter FGA.9 fighter-bombers and a similar number of Chengdu F-7M interceptors, both of which are assigned to No.1 Squadron. Also at Gwelo is No. 2 Squadron with seven BAe Hawk T.60s and 12 SIAI-Marchetti SF.260TP armed trainers, while the broadly similar SF.260C equips No. 6 Squadron at the same base, these also being able to carry light armament for counter-insurgency (COIN) missions. SF.260s have been given the local name of "Genet".

Units located at New Sarum include at least one Squadron which has seen its share of combat action, No. 4 operating some 16 Reims-Cessna FTB.337Gs. Armed with machine guns and SNEB rocket pods, these French-built aircraft are well suited for COIN tasks, and are known as the "Lynx" in Zimbabwean service.

Other residents consist of Nos. 3 and 7 Squadrons which are primarily involved in transport duties, respectively using fixed-wing aircraft and helicopters. Of the fixed-wing equipment, the CASA C.212 Aviocar is now the most numerous type, one of the 11 on hand being configured for VIP tasks, while the others perform a variety of tactical missions. Despite its age, the C-47 Dakota still figures in the inventory, with seven examples operating alongside six examples of the BN-2A Islander.

Rotary-winged equipment with No.7 Squadron is spearheaded by about 20 Alouette IIIs, a type that has also compiled an impressive combat record in COIN operations. Other helicopters presently on hand consist of a dozen Agusta-Bell 412s, five Agusta-Bell 205A Iroquois (known locally as the "Cheetah") and, possibly, a few examples of the Mil Mi-8 "Hip" which reportedly entered service during 1989.

Pilot training has for the past few years been accomplished in the People's Republic of China, students returning to Zimbabwe for further on-type tuition.

EQUIPMENT

Interception:
Chengdu F-7M
Attack:
BAe Hunter FGA.9
BAe Hawk T.60
COIN:
Reims-Cessna FTB.337G "Lynx"
SIAI-Marchetti SF.260C/TP "Genet"
Aerospatiale Alouette III
Transport:
Douglas C-47 Dakota
CASA C.212 Aviocar
Pilatus Britten-Norman BN-2A Islander
Mil Mi-8 "Hip"
Aerospatiale Alouette III
Agusta-Bell AB.412
Agusta-Bell AB.205A "Cheetah"
VIP Transport:
CASA C.212 Aviocar
Agusta-Bell AB.412
Training:
SIAI-Marchetti SF.260C/TP "Genet"
Reims-Cessna FTB.337G "Lynx"
BAe Hawk T.60
BAe Hunter T.80

Index

Illustrations are indexed in italics.

Acknowledgements

The publishers would like to thank all the embassies, defence attaches, manufacturers and individuals who contributed information and photographic material for this book, and Mike Keep for the preparation of all flag artworks included.

Photo Credits

Jacket: (front) Randy Jolly, (back, all four) US DoD, **Endpapers:** US DoD, **Page 1:** US DoD, **2/3:** General Dynamics **4/5:** Lindsay Peacock, **6/7:** Patrick Bunce, **8:** US DoD, **10:** McDonnell Douglas, **11:** (top) Lockheed, (middle) Boeing Helicopters, (bottom) Lockheed, **12:** US DoD, **13:** (top) Boeing, (bottom left) Boeing, (bottom right) US DoD, **14:** (top) Bob Munro, (middle) US DoD, (bottom) Associated Press, **15:** (both) McDonnell Douglas, **16:** (top) Lockheed, (bottom) US DoD, **17:** (both) US DoD, **18:** (top) Boeing, (middle) US DoD, (bottom) Sikorsky, **19:** (top) US DoD, (bottom) General Dynamics, **20:** (top) General Dynamics, (bottom) Bob Munro, **21:** (top) General Dynamics, (bottom) US DoD, **22:** (top) Bob Munro, (bottom) US DoD, **23:** US DoD, **24:** Cessna, **26:** (top) Peter Steinemann, (bottom) Fokker, **27:** (top) Boeing Helicopters, (bottom) Peter Steinemann, **28:** Jon Lake, **30:** (top) Embraer, (bottom) AMD BA, **31:** (top) Embraer, (middle) BAe, **32:** (both) Peter Steinemann, **33:** (both) Peter Steinemann, **34:** (both) Peter Steinemann, **35:** (both) Peter Steinemann, **36:** Peter Steinemann, **37:** Peter Steinemann, **39:** (top) Cessna, (bottom) Shorts, **40:** Beechcraft, **42:** (top) US DoD, (bottom) Embraer, **43:** Bell, **44/45:** Peter Steinemann, **46:** (top) Embraer, (bottom) General Dynamics, **47:** (top) Bell, (bottom) Rockwell, **48:** RAAF, **50:** (top) McDonnell Douglas, (bottom) General Dynamics, **51:** (top) RAAF, (bottom) Pilatus, **52:** (top) McDonnell Douglas, (bottom) BAe, **53:** (top) Robbie Shaw, (bottom) GAF, **54:** BAe, **56:** SAAB-Scania, **57:** (top) Patrick Bunce, (bottom) FAB, **59:** (both) Dave Donald, **60:** (top left) SAAB-Scania, (top right) RDAF, (bottom left) RDAF, **61:** (top) Valmet, (bottom) SAAB-Scania, **62:** (top right) AMD BA, (bottom left) AMD BA, (bottom right) AdA, **63:** AMD BA, **64:** (top right) Richard Gennis, (bottom left) Aerospatiale, (bottom right) SOCATA, **65:** AMD BA, **66:** (top right) Dornier, (bottom) Panavia, **67:** (top right) Bob Munro, (bottom left) Lindsay Peacock, **69:** (top right) AMD BA, (bottom left) Peter Steinemann, **69:** (middle right) Boeing Helicopters, (bottom) Peter Steinemann, **71:** (top) Patrick Walshe, (bottom) Peter Steinemann, **72/73:** (all) AMI, **74:** Boeing, **75:** (top) KLu, (middle) Bob Munro, **76:** (top) KNL, (bottom) General Dynamics, **77:** (bottom) PWL, **78:** Peter Steinemann, **79:** (middle) Lindsay Peacock, **80:** McDonnell Douglas, **81:** (top) Robbie Shaw, (middle) Beechcraft, **82:** (both) SAAB-Scania, **83:** (middle) Swedish Air Force, (bottom) SAAB-Scania, **84:** (both) Peter Steinemann, **85:** Swiss Air Force, **86:** (top) Robbie Shaw, (bottom) Peter Steinemann, **87:** Richard Gennis, **88:** McDonnell Douglas, **89:** (top) KNL, (bottom) Salamander Books, **90:** (both) Salamander Books, **91:** Bob Munro, **92:** (top) Bob Munro, (bottom) Sqn Ldr Tony Paxton, **93:** (top right) Bob Munro, (bottom) BAe, **94:** (top) BAe, (middle) Boeing, **95:** (top) Bob Munro, (bottom) BAe, **96:** (top) Peter Steinemann, (bottom) SOKO, **97:** (top) Peter Steinemann, (bottom) SOKO, **98:** General Dynamics, **100:** (bottom) Peter Steinemann, **101:** Peter Steinemann, **102:** (top) XAC, (bottom) NAMC, **103:** US DoD, **104:** (both) HAL, **105:** (top) HAL, **106:** HAL **107:** (top) Robbie Shaw, (bottom) General Dynamics, **108/109:** (all) US DoD, **110:** General Dynamics, **111:** (top) Northrop, (middle left) Robbie Shaw, **112:** (top) McDonnell Douglas, (bottom) Peter Steinemann, **113:** Peter Steinemann, **114:** Peter Steinemann, **115:** (top left) Robbie Shaw, (bottom right) Lindsay Peacock, **116:** (top left) Robbie Shaw, (bottom) SIAI-Marchetti **117:** (top) SIAI-Marchetti, (bottom) Peter Steinemann, **118/119:** (all) Peter Steinemann, **120:** (top) General Dynamics, (bottom) US DoD, **121:** US DoD, **122:** Peter Steinemann, **125:** (top) Boeing Helicopters, (bottom) McDonnell Douglas, **126:** Bell, **127:** Rex Features, **128:** (middle) General Dynamics, (bottom) US DoD **129:** (top right) IAI, (middle left) IAI, **130:** US DoD, **131:** US DoD, **132:** (top right) AMD BA, (middle right) Beechcraft, **113:** BAe, **134:** (top right) US DoD, (bottom right) US DoD, **135:** (top right) Boeing, (bottom left) Airtech, **138:** AMD BA, **140:** Aerospatiale, **142:** CASA, **143:** (top) Pilatus Britten-Norman, (bottom) Richard Gennis, **144:** AMD BA, **145:** Aerospatiale, **146:** Fokker, **147:** BAe, **148:** McDonnell Douglas, **149:** Shorts, **150:** Bob Munro, **151:** SOCATA, **152:** (top) Richard Gennis, (bottom) Atlas Aircraft, **153:** Aerospatiale, **155:** MBB, **156:** (bottom) AMD BA, **157:** BAe, **Endpapers:** US DoD